Rob Amos makes an important and timely intervention on the impacts of agriculture on biodiversity at a time of planetary crisis. His creative approach and justification for international law's facilitation of agroecology recognises the importance of reconceptualising how humans, and law, interact with the environment.

**Dr Emily Webster**, *University of Cambridge (UK)*

This is a much-needed work on a hugely important topic. Through carefully selected case studies, *Advancing Agroecology in International Law* provides a thought-provoking and detailed analysis of the ability of international legal frameworks to support a transition to agroecology. It is essential reading for anyone interested in creating food systems that feed us while also sustaining the planet.

**Dr Helena Howe**, *University of Sussex (UK)*

Rob Amos has produced a work of rigorous and measured scholarship on a topic that implicates us all: the deeply-rooted interconnections between global agriculture, the global environment, and international law. His case study on the climate crisis's impacts on Kiribati is both a cautionary tale and a convincing argument that the agroecology framework can help map a way forward.

**Prof. Mehmet Konar-Steenberg**, *Mitchell Hamline School of Law (Minnesota, USA)*

# Advancing Agroecology in International Law

Producing enough food is a basic human priority and a critical challenge in the face of a growing population and the deteriorating ecological health of the planet. Modern agricultural practices promise to maximise the productive efficiency of available land but are one of the main drivers of agro- and biodiversity loss. Agroecology, which places ecological sustainability and diversity at the heart of agriculture, is one response to these challenges. It presents agriculture not only as the process through which food is produced but as a dynamic socioecological phenomenon that exists through networks comprising natural and human stakeholders at global, national and subnational levels. Drawing on a combination of agroecological and legal literature, this book explores where there is space in international law to pursue agroecology. Using a range of case studies, it demonstrates how concepts, mechanisms and regulatory approaches in the law advance, and can be reformed to further advance, an agroecological legal framework that allows humanity to meet its agricultural needs in a way that protects the natural and cultural diversity that is fundamental to the ecological integrity of the planet.

**Rob Amos** is a Lecturer in Law at Greenwich University, UK.

## Routledge Research in International Environmental Law

**Climate Change, Forests and REDD**
Lessons for Institutional Design
*Edited by Joyeeta Gupta, Nicolien van der Grijp and Onno Kuik*

**International Environmental Law and the Conservation of Coral Reefs**
*Edward J. Goodwin*

**International Environmental Law and the International Court of Justice**
*Aleksandra Cavoski*

**Enforcement of International Environmental Law**
Challenges and Responses at the International Level
*Martin Hedemann-Robinson*

**Marine Pollution, Shipping Waste and International Law**
*Gabriela Argüello*

**Compensation for Environmental Damage Under International Law**
*Jason Rudall*

**International Environmental Law Compliance in Context**
Mechanisms and Case Studies
*Belen Olmos Giupponi*

**Sustainable Fisheries Management and International Law**
Marine Fisheries in Bangladesh and the Bay of Bengal
*Abdullah Al Arif*

**Marine Conservation and International Law**
Legal Instruments for Biodiversity Beyond National Jurisdiction
*Sarah Louise Lothian*

**Nature Law and Policy in Europe**
*Edited by Andrew L.R. Jackson*

**Environmental Liability and the Interplay between EU Law and International Law**
*Dr Emanuela Orlando*

https://www.routledge.com/Routledge-Research-in-International-Environmental-Law/book-series/INTENVLAW

# Advancing Agroecology in International Law

Rob Amos

Routledge
Taylor & Francis Group
LONDON AND NEW YORK

First published 2024
by Routledge
4 Park Square, Milton Park, Abingdon, Oxon OX14 4RN

and by Routledge
605 Third Avenue, New York, NY 10158

*Routledge is an imprint of the Taylor & Francis Group, an informa business*



*British Library Cataloguing-in-Publication Data*
A catalogue record for this book is available from the British Library

ISBN: 978-1-032-56368-8 (hbk)
ISBN: 978-1-032-59566-5 (pbk)
ISBN: 978-1-003-43517-4 (ebk)

DOI: 10.4324/9781003435174

Typeset in Times New Roman
by Deanta Global Publishing Services, Chennai, India

**To Grandma and Gramps, for teaching me the joy of curiosity**

# Contents

*Foreword* *xii*
*Preface and Acknowledgements* *xiv*
*Table of International Treaties and Agreements* *xv*

**PART 1**
**Protecting Diversity** **1**

**Introduction: Agroecology and the Law** **3**

*Defining Agroecology 5*
*Locating Agroecology in the Law 8*
*The Structure of This Book 12*

1 **Conservation of Agrobiodiversity** **14**

*International Conservation Law and Agriculture 14*
*The Convention on Biological Diversity 16*
*The UN Food and Agriculture Organisation 29*
*Conclusions 33*

2 **Monocultures and Genetic Diversity** **34**

*The Rise of the Monoculture 34*
*Invasive/Alien Species and Disease 35*
*Intellectual Property Rights and Crop Genetic Diversity 39*
*Protecting Traditional Agricultural Knowledge 50*
*Conclusions 55*

3 **Genetically Modified Organisms and Organic Agriculture** **56**

*GMOs in Socioecological Networks 56*
*Organic Agriculture and GMOs in the Context of Agroecology 57*
*Responding to the Risks of GMOs 61*

*Creating Space for GM Crops in Agroecological Networks* 74
*Conclusions* 76

4 **Landscapes** 78

*Defining 'Landscape'* 78
*A Right to Landscape?* 80
*International Programmes for Landscape Protection* 83
*Conclusions* 90

**PART 2**
**Supporting Socioecological Relationships** 91

5 **Ecosystem Services** 93

*Ecosystem Services and Agroecology* 93
*Ecosystem Services and International Conservation Law* 95
*Incorporating Ecosystem Services into International Law* 99
*Conclusions* 110

6 **Soil Conservation and Land Degradation** 112

*Soil and Sustainability* 112
*Soil Conservation in International Law* 113
*A Soil Treaty?* 117
*Land Degradation and Desertification* 122
*Conclusions* 129

7 **Water Conservation** 131

*Our Changing Perceptions of Water* 131
*Natural Water Infrastructure* 132
*Protecting Freshwater Ecosystems in International Law* 135
*Aquaculture* 143
*Conclusions* 148

8 **Climate Change** 150

*Agriculture and Climate Change* 150
*The UN Framework Convention on Climate Change* 152
*Climate Change Adaptation in Kiribati* 154
*Conclusions* 163

**PART 3**
**Agroecology in a Globalised World** **165**

**9 Environmental Assessment** **167**

*The Origins of Environmental Assessment 167*
*Defining Environmental Assessment 168*
*Environmental Assessment in International Law 177*
*(Re)Introducing Ecology to Environmental Assessment 184*
*Conclusions 188*

**10 Transboundary Pollution** **189**

*Agriculture and Pollution 189*
*Transboundary Air Pollution 191*
*Persistent Organic Pollutants 199*
*Unified Approaches to Hazardous Substances and Pollutants 203*
*Conclusions 207*

**11 International Trade** **209**

*Neoliberalism and Agroecology 209*
*Agroecology, Trade and the Environment in the WTO 211*
*The WTO's Rules on Agricultural Trade 215*
*Regulating the Drivers of Zoonotic Disease 221*
*Conclusions 230*

**PART 4**
**Agroecology in Society** **231**

**12 Tracing a Path from Food Security to Food Justice** **233**

*Food (In)Security and International Law 233*
*Food Security 235*
*The Right to Food 239*
*Food Sovereignty 242*
*Food Justice 246*
*Conclusions 251*

**Conclusion: Finding Space for Agroecology** **253**

*Index* *263*

# Foreword

The interrelationship between people, society and nature has puzzled scholars since the dawn of time. Our understanding of this relationship (or lack of it) is reflected in the way in which we use land and the resources that it provides. And it is reflected in how we use land to provide the food that we need to sustain a growing world population. How can we develop modes of land-use that promote efficient agricultural production while at the same time preserving and promoting biodiversity? In other words, how can we ensure food security (producing sufficient food for a growing world population) without damaging the natural environment and its constituent natural processes? Perhaps more importantly, how can we develop the farming systems needed to feed a growing population while *improving and enhancing* the natural environment? 'Agroecology' attempts to answer these questions by applying the principles of ecology to agriculture, i.e. by recognising and respecting the interrelationships within and between natural elements and their physical environment.

This book throws interesting and important new light on these issues. The analysis is premised on the recognition that each farm is an integral element of a socioecological system – a farm is not simply a production unit but is in fact part of a global and local system comprising both natural and human actors. And diversity in what is grown and *how it is grown* is key to ensuring the long-term resilience and sustainability of the natural and social/economic systems on which farms depend. The specific focus of this book is on the role that international law can play in facilitating new approaches to agriculture that recognise this interdependence. To what extent can it be said to reflect the principles and practices of agroecology, and in doing so to maintain this diversity and support the different relationships within these socioecological networks to the benefit of both nature and humans? In doing so it seeks to highlight issues, concepts and mechanisms in international law that create space for agroecology to be pursued.

These themes have important implications for the development of public policy and innovations in farming and its relationships with the natural environment. The promotion of agroecology has, for example, been adopted as a core theme by the UN Food and Agriculture Organisation. At the same time, the promotion of an ecosystem-level approach to managing the natural environment has been promoted under the aegis of the UN Biodiversity Convention. Both the ecosystem approach to managing the natural environment and the application of agroecology require us to consider all aspects of how a farm operates, and recognise and capture its interrelationships with other actors (both human and non-human) in the socioecological network, rather than treat individual issues in isolation. These themes are explored in some detail in the case studies set out in the book, e.g. on the legal responses to water pollution, environmental impact assessment and the regulation of new agricultural technologies.

The analysis developed in the book uses three distinguishing features of agroecology as benchmarks to assess the potential role of international law in promoting agroecology: ecological sustainability; socioecological networks; and systems-level analysis. The arguments developed here cover a wide range of issues of great importance for the future development of farming. They are insightful and important and will be of great value to a diverse range of readers with an interest in environmental law, sustainable agriculture and the international law applicable to farming and land-use. More than that, it will be of great interest to anyone with a focus on improving the sustainability and future development of agriculture and its contribution to securing food security.

Professor Christopher Rodgers
*Emeritus Professor of Law*
Newcastle University, UK

# Preface and Acknowledgements

This book began life as a single chapter for my PhD; one whose length meant that it could not be included in either the final thesis or the resulting monograph – *International Conservation Law: The Protection of Plants in Theory and Practice* (Routledge, 2020). In the eight years since that chapter was conceived, the ecological, legal and social landscape has changed considerably. We are reminded almost daily of the climate and ecological emergency, the impacts of which are manifesting more severely and more rapidly than previously anticipated. New international agreements continue to be adopted in the field of international environmental law, but whether these can deliver meaningful change remains to be seen.

What the consequences will be of our comprehensive destabilisation of the natural world was made plain by the recent pandemic. For all its human costs, however, COVID-19 showed that society can change its behaviours and reduce its ecological impacts in the face of crisis. That this lesson appears not to have been learnt as the world looks to recover may prove to be the greatest tragedy of the pandemic. Fundamental reform is desperately needed.

Agroecology provides a template for this reform. While predominately an agricultural philosophy, its emphasis on respecting the diversity of ecological and social systems, and the connections in and between these, illustrate how society might evolve along a more sustainable track.

Whether space exists to advance agroecology through international law is a huge subject. There are consequently some issues that might legitimately be expected to have been included in this book that have either been omitted or addressed only briefly. Most notably, I focus on crops more so than livestock. This reflects my interest in how the law addresses the challenges of plant conservation but is also because crops tell a story of communities' relationships with land, with nature and with each other that provides a route map to a more sustainable future. The material referenced is generally up-to-date as of 31 March 2023.

I am grateful to the friends and colleagues who have helped me develop the ideas in this book, especially my former supervisors, Helena Howe, Stuart Harrop and Donald McGillivray, as well as Jane Holder, Anicée Defrance, Edward Goodwin, Sonam Gordhan, Bill Howarth, Maria Lee, Emily Lydgate and Jo Smallwood. My family remain a constant source of support and, at times, light relief. I am also indebted to Silvia Cesa-Bianchi for her invaluable research assistance and infectious enthusiasm.

*Rob Amos*
*20 April 2023*

# Table of International Treaties and Agreements

1933 Convention on the Rights and Duties of States (Montevideo) 26 December 1933, in force 26 December 1934, 165 LNTS 19

1946 International Convention for the Regulation of Whaling (Washington) 2 December 1946, in force 10 November 1948, 161 UNTS 72 (as amended 19 November 1956, 338 UNTS 336)

1947 General Agreement on Tariffs and Trade (Geneva) 30 October 1947, 55 UNTS 194, in force provisionally since 1 January 1948 under the 1947 Protocol of Application, 55 UNTS 308

1950 European Convention for the Protection of Human Rights and Fundamental Freedoms (Rome) 4 November 1950, in force 3 September 1953, 213 UNTS 221

1951 Convention Relating to the Status of Refugees (Geneva) 28 July 1951, in force 22 April 1954, 189 UNTS 137

1960 Indus Waters Treaty Between the Government of India, the Government of Pakistan and the International Bank for Reconstruction and Development, 19 September 1960, in force 12 January 1961, 419 UNTS 216

1961 International Convention for the Protection of New Varieties of Plants (Brussels) 2 December 1961, in force 10 August 1968, 15 UNTS 89

1966 International Covenant on Economic, Social and Cultural Rights, 16 December 1966, in force 3 January 1976, 6 ILM 360 (1967)

1968 African Convention on the Conservation of Nature and Natural Resources, Algiers, 15 September 1968, in force 9 October 1969, 1001 UNTS 3

1971 Convention of Wetlands of International Importance, Especially as Waterfowl Habitat (Ramsar) 2 February 1971, in force 21 December 1975, 996 UNTS 245

1972 Convention for the Protection of the World Cultural and Natural Heritage (Paris) 16 November 1972, in force 17 December 1975, 27 UST 37, ILM 1358 (1972)

1973 Convention on International Trade in Endangered Species of Fauna and Flora (Washington) 3 March 1973, in force 1 July 1975, 993 UNTS 243

1976 Convention on Conservation of Nature in the South Pacific (Apia) 12 June 1976, in force 28 June 1990, suspended 2006, IELMT 976:45

1979 Convention on Long-Range Transboundary Air Pollution (Geneva) 13 November 1979, in force 16 March 1983, 18 ILM 1442 (1979)

1979 Convention on the Conservation of Migratory Species of Wild Animals (Bonn) 23 June 1979, in force 1 November 1983, 19 ILM 15 (1980)

1982 Convention on the Conservation of European Wildlife and Natural Habitats (Berne) 19 September 1979, in force 1 June 1982, UKTS 56 (1982)

1982 UN Convention on the Law of the Sea (Montego Bay) 10 December 1982, in force 16 November 1994, 21 ILM 1261 (1982)

1984 Protocol on Long-Term Financing of the Cooperative Programme for Monitoring and Evaluating the Long-Range Transmission of Air Pollutants in Europe (Geneva) 28 September 1984, in force 28 January 1988, 2 SMTE 285

1985 Association of South East Asian Nations Agreement on the Conservation of Nature and Natural Resources (Kuala Lumpur) 9 July 1985, 15 EPL 64 (1985) (not in force)

1985 Protocol to the 1979 Convention on Long-Range Transboundary Air Pollution on the Reduction of Sulphur Emissions or Their Transboundary Fluxes by at Least 30 Per Cent (Helsinki) 8 July 1985, in force 2 September 1987, 2 ILM 1077 (1987)

1989 Convention on the Control of Transboundary Movement of Hazardous Wastes and Their Disposal (Basel) 22 March 1989, in force 5 May 1992, 28 ILM 657 (1989)

1989 ILO Convention 169 Concerning Indigenous and Tribal Peoples, www.ilo.org/dyn/normlex/en/f?p=NORMLEXPUB:12100:0::NO::P12100_ILO_CODE:C169

1991 Convention on Environmental Impact Assessment in a Transboundary Context (Espoo) 25 February 1991, in force 10 September 1997, 30 ILM 802 (1991)

1992 Convention on Biological Diversity (Rio de Janeiro) 5 June 1992, in force 29 December 1993, 31 ILM 822 (1992)

1992 Convention on the Protection and Use of Transboundary Watercourses and International Lakes (Helsinki) 17 March 1992, in force 6 October 1996, 31 ILM 1312 (1992)

1992 UN Framework Convention on Climate Change (New York) 9 May 1992, in force 24 March 1994, 1771 UNTS 107

1994 Agreement Establishing the World Trade Organisation (Marrakesh) 15 April 1994, in force 1 January 1995, 33 ILM 1125 (1994)

1994 Agreement on Trade-Related Aspects of Intellectual Property Rights (Marrakesh) 15 April 1994, in force 1 January 1995, 33 ILM 81 (1994)

1994 Convention to Combat Desertification in Those Countries Experiencing Serious Drought and/or Desertification, Particularly in Africa (Paris) 17 June 1994, in force 26 December 1996, 33 ILM 1328 (1994)

1995 Agreement for the Implementation of the Provisions of the UN Convention on the Law of the Sea Relating to the Conservation and Management of Straddling Fish Stocks and Highly Migratory Fish Stocks (New York) 4 December 1995, in force 11 December 2001, 34 ILM 1542 (1995)

1997 Convention on the Law of Non-Navigational Uses of International Water Courses (New York) 21 May 1997, in force 17 August 2014, 36 ILM 700 (1997)

1997 FAO International Plant Protection Convention, in force 2 October 2005, amending the 1951 Convention (Rome, 6 December 1951, in force 3 April 1952, 150 UNTS 67

1998 Convention on Access to Information, Public Participation in Decision-Making and Access to Justice (Aarhus) 25 June 1998, in force 30 October 2001, 38 ILM 517 (1999)

1998 Convention on the Prior Informed Consent Procedure for Certain Hazardous Chemicals and Pesticides in International Trade (Rotterdam) 11 September 1998, in force 24 February 2004, 38 ILM 1 (1999)

1999 Protocol on Water and Health to the Convention on the Protection and Use of Transboundary Watercourses and International Lakes (London) 17 June 1999, in force 4 August 2005, 38 ILM 1708 (1999)

1999 Protocol to the 1979 Convention on Long-Range Transboundary Air Pollution to Abate Acidification, Eutrophication and Ground-Level Ozone (Gothenburg) 30 November 1999, in force 17 May 2005, UN Doc. EB.AIR/1999

2000 Cartagena Protocol on Biosafety to the Convention on Biological Diversity (Montreal) 29 January 2000, in force 11 September 2003, 39 ILM 1027

2000 European Landscape Convention (Florence) 20 October 2000, in force 1 March 2004, ETS 176

2001 Convention on Persistent Organic Pollutants (Stockholm) 22 May 2001, in force 17 May 2004, 40 ILM 532 (2001)

2001 International Treaty on Plant Genetic Resources for Food and Agriculture (Rome) 3 November 2001, in force 29 June 2004, www.fao.org/plant-treaty/overview/texts-treaty/en/

2002 Association of South East Asian Nations Agreement on Transboundary Haze Pollution (Kuala Lumpur) 10 June 2002, in force 25 November 2003, asean.org/wp-content/uploads/2021/01/ASEANAgreementonTransboundaryHazePollution-1.pdf

2003 Convention for the Safeguarding of Intangible Cultural Heritage (Paris) 17 October 2003, in force 20 April 2006, 2368 UNTS 3

2007 Protocol to the UN Convention on Climate Change (Kyoto) 11 December 1997, in force 16 February 2005, 37 ILM 22 (1998)

2003 Revised African Convention on the Conservation of Nature and Natural Resources (Maputo) 11 July 2003, in force 23/07/2016, au.int/en/treaties/african-convention-conservation-nature-and-natural-resources-revised-version

2009 Convention for the Protection and Assistance of Internally Displaced Persons in Africa (Kampala) 23 October 2009, in force 6 December 2012, 3014 UNTS 3

2010 Protocol on Access to Genetic Resources and the Fair and Equitable Sharing of Benefits Arising from Their Utilisation to the Convention on Biological Diversity (Nagoya) 29 October 2010, in force 12 October 2014, C.N.782.2010.TREATIES-1

2010 Nagoya-Kuala Lumpur Supplementary Protocol on Liability and Redress to the Cartagena Protocol on Biosafety (Nagoya) 15 October 2010, in force 5 March 2018, 3240 UNTS 1

2013 Minamata Convention on Mercury (Kumamoto) 10 October 2013, in force 16 August 2017, C.N.244.2015.TREATIES-XXVII.17

2015 Paris Agreement (Paris) 22 April 2016, in force 4 November 2016, C.N.92.2016.TREATIES-XXVII.7.d

2015 Protocol for the Protection of New Plant Varieties under the Framework of the African Regional Intellectual Property Organisation (Arusha) 6 July 2015, www.aripo.org/wp-content/uploads/2018/12/Arusha-Protocol_20181.pdf (not in force)

2016 Protocol Amending the European Landscape Convention (Strasbourg) 1 August 2016, CETS 219

2023 Agreement under the UN Convention on the Law of the Sea on the Conservation of and Sustainable Use of Marine Biological Diversity of Areas Beyond National Jurisdiction (New York) 4 March 2023, https://www.un.org/bbnj/

# Part 1
# Protecting Diversity

# Introduction
# Agroecology and the Law

The story of humanity is the story of agriculture. Our continuing cultural evolution, from when our ancestors began cultivating crops to modern-day usage of genetically modified organisms, is defined not only by what we grow but how we grow it. These decisions influence annual calendars, religious festivals, local identities and a host of other aspects of daily life.[1] Agriculture also defines our relationships with nature.[2] Our manipulation of the landscape across thousands of years has allowed a distinct subset of biodiversity, what may be termed agrobiodiversity, to develop symbiotic links with agricultural habitats and species.[3] As farming practices change with advances in science and technology, those links come under pressure. The turtle dove (*Streptopelia turtur*), for example, was once a common sight in British farmland but now faces extinction, in part because the wild grassland areas and hedgerows that bordered farmlands and provided the birds food during their breeding season have been given over to more profitable uses. Led by the Royal Society for the Protection of Birds, conservation work is underway to support farmers in managing their activities in a way that still leaves space for species such as the turtle dove.[4]

Modern agricultural practices have a significant adverse impact on agrobiodiversity and the wider natural world. A report by the UN Food and Agriculture Organisation (FAO) warns that the natural resource base for agriculture is being continually degraded globally and locally, with biodiversity decreasing, pressures on ecosystems increasing and nature's consequent capacity to deliver ecosystem

1 R. Amos, 'Reassessing the Role of Plants in Society' (2017) 13 *International Journal of Law in Context* 295, 311.

2 'Agriculture' is difficult to define, but for the purposes of this book may be read as including any process through which humans exert control over and otherwise manipulate species and landscapes to produce commodities for subsistence or trade. This is not a perfect definition, however, and raises questions. Should a retiree who maintains a small allotment as a hobby and sells surplus produce at a local gardening club be subject to the same agricultural regulations as a commercial farmer? Definitions of 'agriculture' in legal instruments can be similarly obscure. Raising gamebirds for sport was found to fall outside the meaning of 'agriculture' in section 1(1) of the UK's Rent (Agriculture) Act 1976 despite this involving essentially the same processes as raising gamebirds for food – *Glendyne (Lord) v Rapley* [1978] 1 WLR 601.

3 J. Santilli, *Agrobiodiversity and the Law* (Earthscan, 2012) 1.

4 https://www.operationturtledove.org/ (last accessed 20/04/2023).

DOI: 10.4324/9781003435174-2

services to humanity diminishing.[5] Too often, ecological processes are manipulated to service humanity, rather than human processes adapted to support nature.[6] The Convention on Biological Diversity's[7] Conference of the Parties identifies a host of problems, including the over-utilisation of mechanisation technologies, growing reliance on monocultures, the misuse of chemicals, overgrazing, poor land management, inadequate pest control and the clearing of natural habitats, which have systematically degraded the natural agricultural resource base.[8] The (often illegal) clearing of rainforest in South America for cattle ranching is a useful illustration of this. It highlights agriculture's immediate impacts, in this case biodiversity loss and the release of carbon emissions caused by the destruction of primary forests, and the more diffuse destabilising effects it has on associated ecological processes.[9] These trends are increasing as humanity works to meet one of its most basic priorities – ensuring that everyone has enough to eat – in the face of growing ecological crises.[10]

Agriculture takes many forms, however, some of which are not only ecologically benign but actively support biodiversity.[11] A lot can be learnt from indigenous agricultural practices. While it cannot be assumed that an activity is inherently sustainable just because it is a traditional indigenous practice, it is the case that the nexus between indigenous cultures and their local environments can manifest itself in the careful cultivation of natural resources so that there is a multiplicity of species rather than an absence.[12] Understanding indigenous relationships with the environment is therefore important not just in respect to agriculture but the wider lessons it can teach in promoting resilience in ecological and social systems.[13]

This book explores the role that international law can play in supporting these systems by facilitating agroecological approaches to agriculture and related processes. By examining a series of case studies, set out at the end of this introduction, it highlights issues, concepts and mechanisms in international law where space potentially exists for agroecology to be pursued. In doing so, the book provides

5 J. Bélanger and D. Pilling (eds), *The State of the World's Biodiversity for Food and Agriculture* (FAO Commission on Genetic Resources for Food and Agriculture Assessments, 2019) ch 4.
6 C. Ross and M. Rupe, 'Agricultural Sources of Water Pollution: How Our History Informs Current Debate' (2016) 17 *Vermont Journal of Environmental Law* 811, 842.
7 Rio de Janeiro, 5 June 1992, in force 29 December 1993, 31 ILM 822 (1992).
8 Decision III/11, Conservation and sustainable use of agricultural biodiversity, UNEP/CBD/COP/DEC/III/11, 1996, Annex I, Part A.
9 C. Neill and others, 'Deforestation for Pasture Alters Nitrogen and Phosphorus in Small Amazonian Streams' (2001) 11 *Ecological Applications* 1817.
10 R. Rajão and others, 'The Rotten Apples of Brazil's Agribusiness' (2020) 369 *Science* 246 and J. Marengo and others, 'Changes in Climate and Land Use Over the Amazon Region: Current and Future Variability and Trends' (2018) 6 *Frontiers in Earth Science* doi: 10.3389/feart.2018.00228.
11 A. Soldi and others, 'Sustainability Assessment of Agricultural Systems in Paraguay: A Comparative Study Using FAO's SAFA Framework' (2019) 11 *Sustainability (Switzerland)* 3745.
12 B. Richardson and D. Craig, 'Indigenous Peoples, Law and the Environment', in B. Richardson and S. Wood (eds), *Environmental Law for Sustainability* (Hart Publishing, 2006) 197–203.
13 N. Lincoln, 'Learning from Indigenous Agriculture' (2019) 2 *Nature Sustainability* 167.

a new perspective on wider questions relevant to the law's continuing evolution, particularly in terms of legal definitions of sustainability, and how it shapes relationships in and between nature and society.

## Defining Agroecology

What the examples of the turtle dove and deforestation in South America show is that it is impossible to conceive of 'a farm' as an isolated entity, the activities of which have no impact beyond the farm gate. It is instead part of a system. This system is ecological. Farmers may only control the activities that occur on their property, but those activities affect the wider environment and a farm can similarly be impacted by external environmental events.[14] The system is also socioeconomic. Farms are connected to their customers; to their suppliers; to the local workforce that they employ; to neighbouring landowners; to the societal structures that regulate their processes; to the logistical infrastructure that transports their products within and beyond national borders; and to other farms that may adopt practices that are compatible with their own, or represent a risk to how they operate. A farm is at the same time embedded in its locality and one link in a globalised production chain.

This idea of a farm being part of a socioecological system is at the heart of the theory of agroecology. Simply defined, agroecology is the application of ecology[15] to agriculture.[16] Although the term entered common use in the 1970s, its origins lie in ancient and traditional forms of land management, particularly those of indigenous communities.[17] It is now a core theme of the FAO, which identifies ten aspects of agroecology, including natural diversity, circular economies, human values and good governance.[18] Agroecology views farms as similar to ecosystems, comprising a combination of elements, each of which contributes to their process of self-renewal.[19] When considering how to enhance the sustainability of

14 E.g., agricultural runoff from fertilisers, pesticides and herbicides is known to pollute local waterways, but regulating this has been controversial because there is rarely a direct causal link between dispersed pollution and agricultural activities – Case C-293/97 *R v Secretary of State for the Environment, ex parte Standley* [1997] ECR I-2603.

15 At its simplest, ecology is the study of the relationships within and between natural elements and their physical environment. There is merit, however, to a more pluralistic understanding of the term that views ecology as encompassing, in a holistic manner, the natural, physical and social sciences, particularly in the context of agriculture where the boundaries between the biotic and the abiotic are blurred. There is, in other words, no distinction between the natural and the human. See A. Philippopoulos-Mihalopoulos, 'Looking for the Space Between Law and Ecology', in A. Philippopoulos-Mihalopoulos (ed), *Law and Ecology: New Environmental Foundations* (Routledge, 2011) 2–3.

16 F. Caporali, 'History and Development of Agroecology and Theory of Agroecosystems', in M. Monteduro and others (eds), *Law and Agroecology: A Transdisciplinary Dialogue* (Springer, 2015) 3–6.

17 S. Hecht, 'The Evolution of Agroecological Thought', in M. Altieri, *Agroecology: The Science of Sustainable Agriculture* (2nd edn, Westview Press, 1995) 1.

18 http://www.fao.org/agroecology/home/en/ (accessed 20/04/2023).

19 Caporali (n 16) 5.

agricultural practices, it is therefore necessary to consider all aspects of how a farm operates, and the corresponding relationships with other actors in the socioecological network, through a systems-level approach to analysis, rather than treat individual issues in isolation.[20] Conventional agricultural scientists have been criticised in this regard. Rather than conduct a holistic assessment of a problem, taking into account how potential solutions would impact on other parts of the system, it has been suggested that they typically limit their consideration to the single question of 'how do we solve X?'.[21] Using a pesticide may eradicate an invasive/alien species, but how would it affect the chemical composition of the soil, or the other elements of agrobiodiversity in and beyond the farm?

Agroecology shares principles with resilience thinking, which places a similar emphasis on systems-level analyses of issues,[22] and is an example of how this broader theory can be put into practice. Under a resilience thinking approach, it is necessary to look at the relationships between actors in a network to understand exactly what the consequences of a particular action may be, recognising that certain impacts, changes in behaviour or the introduction of a new actor may have an irreversible effect on the nature of the system.[23] This is key to understanding agroecological systems. To illustrate: picture a simple network centred around two neighbouring farms that grow crops organically. A new actor, an invasive species, enters the network and threatens the crops. One farm introduces strict control measures to reduce the pest's impact so that it can continue to grow food organically. The other decides that it has no choice but to move away from organic farming and control the invasive species with pesticides. This is effective, but due to the two farms' proximity, the pesticide also affects the neighbouring farm and it consequently loses its organic status. An agroecological/resilience thinking approach, one that adopted a systems-level perspective, would have necessitated an assessment of not only how the pesticides would impact the farm that used them, but also other aspects of the network, i.e. the neighbouring farm. The result might have been that the farm that chose to introduce control measures shared its experiences with its neighbour so that they both remained organic or that it opted to forgo its control measures to also use pesticides, perhaps with the farms jointly negotiating with a single supplier to reduce costs.

Resilience thinking is being applied to an increasing number of fields in law and policy and is particularly relevant to discussions of humanity's interactions with the

20 Similarities can be drawn with actor-network theory in sociology, which posits that when analysing human systems, it is necessary to consider the interactions between human and non-human actors. See, inter alia, J. Murdoch, 'Inhuman/Nonhuman/Human: Actor-Network Theory and the Prospects of a Nondualistic and Symmetrical Perspective on Nature and Society' (1997) 15 *Environment and Planning D: Society and Space* 731.

21 Hecht (n 17) 6–7.

22 D. Chandler, *Resilience: The Governance of Complexity* (Routledge, 2014).

23 B. Walker and D. Salt, *Resilience Thinking: Sustaining Ecosystems and People in a Changing World* (Island Press, 2006) ch 3.

natural world.[24] This is due to the emphasis that it places on diversity. Resilience, something's capacity to positively adapt when subject to external stresses, is one of the main advantages of diversity. When discussing the diversity of ecosystems, Brown Weiss argues that where there are multiple species in a system and that system is disturbed, some species may decline but the integrity of the system itself remains intact.[25] This is evidenced by studies showing that the impacts of invasive/alien species are lower in natural systems with high levels of diversity.[26]

The importance of diversity in agroecology is reflected in Caporali's 10 rules for sustainable agroecological systems:

1. to create diversity within the farm;
2. to integrate crop production and livestock husbandry;
3. to adopt soil conservation measures and minimum tillage practices;
4. to adopt crop rotations;
5. to adopt intercropping and cover cropping;
6. to use genotypes resistant to parasitic attack;
7. to treat the soil with manure and composted organic matter;
8. to practice green manuring;
9. to foster biological control of weeds and pests;
10. to plant and protect hedges.[27]

Many of these rules may simply be regarded as good agricultural practices. Crop rotation, for example, facilitates the recycling of nutrients in soil,[28] while hedgerows are both important natural pathways for species and diverse ecosystems in their own right.[29] Alongside this focus on supporting agrobiodiversity, is an emphasis on organic farming. Note, however, that nothing in these rules precludes the use of modern technology, a criticism that has falsely been made of agroecology in the past.[30] Rather, agroecology should be seen as promoting different technologies, as this is another way of increasing the diversity of agricultural systems. Agroecology is as much about the cultures of agriculture as it is about the ecological foundations. The use of technology must therefore be accepted as legitimate because a

24 M. Harm Benson and R. Kundis Craig, *The End of Sustainability: Resilience and the Future of Environmental Governance in the Anthropocene* (Kansas University Press, 2017).

25 E. Brown Weiss, 'Intergenerational Equity: A Legal Framework for Global Environmental Change', in E. Brown Weiss (ed), *Environmental Change and International Law: New Challenges and Dimensions* (UN University Press, 1992) 402.

26 J. Ackerman and others, 'Biotic Resistance in the Tropics: Patterns of Seed Plant Invasions Within an Island' (2017) 19 *Biological Invasions* 315.

27 Caporali (n 16) 15.

28 Altieri (n 17) ch 11.

29 J. Holder, 'Hedgerows, Laws and Cultural Landscape', in J. Holder and D. McGillivray (eds), *Locality and Identity: Environmental Issues in Law and Society* (Ashgate, 1999) 136.

30 D. Kershen, 'The Contested Vision for Agriculture's Future: Sustainable Intensive Agriculture and Agroecology' (2013) 46 *Creighton Law Review* 591, 593.

community's culture is, in part, defined by the technologies that are available to it.[31] The unique combination of traditional methods and new approaches adopted by each farm will be underpinned by their own knowledge base, developed through the generations. Maintaining the diversity of this knowledge base is just as important to the integrity of agroecological systems as supporting natural diversity within individual farms and the wider networks of which they are part.

To summarise, agroecology represents a different way of thinking about how humanity interacts with nature through agriculture. It sees farms not just as production units but as inextricable parts of global and local systems comprising both natural and human actors. The long-term sustainability of these systems depends on ensuring their resilience through diversity, not just in what is grown but how it is grown as well. A key question, one that this book seeks to answer, is whether there is space in international law to reflect the principles and practices of agroecology so that it maintains this diversity and supports the different relationships in these socioecological networks to the benefit of both nature and humans.

## Locating Agroecology in the Law

When thinking about how agroecology can be pursued through the law, it is necessary to distinguish between what may broadly be considered agroecological law and agricultural law. The latter is primarily concerned with the production processes of agricultural outputs and the administration of farms.[32] Agroecological law, in comparison, seeks to create sustainable agricultural systems by positively developing the relationships between different actors in socioecological networks. Again, there are strong links with ecology, the contemporary focus of which is on protecting and enhancing the interrelationships in and between socioecological systems.[33]

Noe and Alrøe identify two challenges in using the law in this manner. First, a regulation may not have the desired effect if it is based on a flawed or incomplete understanding of the rationales behind certain actors' behaviour. Imposing a tax on pesticides may not reduce their use if cost is not the decisive factor behind a farmer's decision to utilise them.[34] An agricultural system will have a unique logic, based on its philosophy (to farm organically), chosen products (meat, cereals, etc.) and methodologies (traditional, mechanical, etc.). It does not necessarily have 'goals' in the same way as other socioeconomic actors, but instead seeks to reinforce and perpetuate this logic, just as an ecosystem seeks to renew itself through the combined natural processes of its constituent elements.[35]

31 Caporali (n 16) 4, drawing on R. Chandrasoma and J. Lee, *Technocultural Epistemes: A Novel Approach to the Manifestation of Knowledge* (Engineering and Technology Digital Library, 2012).

32 C. Rodgers, *Agricultural Law* (4th edn, Bloomsbury Professional, 2016).

33 G. Mace, 'Whose Conservation?' (2014) 345 *Science* 1558.

34 E. Noe and H. Alrøe, 'Regulation of Agroecosystems: A Social Systems Analysis of Agroecology and Law', in Monteduro and others (n 16) 32–33.

35 ibid 39.

Second, regulating one issue can lead to undesirable side effects, warranting further regulatory action that would have its own unintended consequences.[36] For example, the increased use of biofuels as an alternative energy supply is considered essential if the international community is to meet its objective of limiting the global temperature rise to below 2°C and close to 1.5°C.[37] Introducing regulations to encourage farmers to grow biofuels could result in a drop in food production, with the consequent increase in demand pushing up the price of food crops. This could in turn result in areas of primary habitat being cleared for food production, which would negate any emission reductions that had been achieved by the increased availability of biofuels.[38]

Recognising agroecology in the law is therefore not a top-down process of superimposing norms and concepts over what may be considered distinct disciplines of agricultural law, environmental law, property law and so on, each of which is relevant to only part of an agroecological system. Instead, what is required is a so-called trans-law; a bottom-up approach linking regulatory tools from different legal disciplines and applying them in a coherent manner.[39] Monteduro proposes a suite of measures through which this could be achieved: agroecological information collecting and sharing, agroecological zoning, agroecological planning and agroecological impact assessment.[40] These reflect current debates in environmental law and wider questions of agricultural policy. Agroecological zoning, for example, consists of designating rural areas on the basis of ecological (soil composition, climate, etc.) and socioeconomic (demographics, market conditions, etc.) factors and prohibiting land-uses that are incompatible with these. This is similar to the concept of biosphere reserves, which limit land-uses in zones defined in terms of conservation value so as to integrate protected areas into wider landscapes.[41]

The measures suggested by Monteduro have limited relevance in international law. Although accounting for the transboundary impacts of certain activities is a common feature of environmental assessment regimes,[42] states maintain their own systems of land-use planning. The application of a zoning approach to agriculture would therefore be defined by the external and internal borders of states rather than the natural logic of ecology. Even in the EU, where territorial cohesion has

36 ibid 33.

37 Article 2 of the Paris Agreement, 22 April 2016, in force 4 November 2016, C.N.92.2016.TREATIES-XXVII.7.d. O. Edenhofer and others (eds), *Climate Change 2014: Mitigation of Climate Change, Contribution of Working Group III to the Fifth Assessment Report of the Intergovernmental Panel on Climate Change* (IPCC / CUP, 2014) 12.

38 R. Amos, 'Bioenergy Carbon Capture and Storage in Global Climate Policy: Examining the Issues' (2016) *Carbon & Climate Law Review* 187, 188–189.

39 M. Monteduro, 'From Agroecology and Law to Agroecological Law? Exploring Integration Between *Scientia Ruris* and *Scientia Iuris*', in Monteduro and others (n 16) 78.

40 ibid 79–81.

41 J. Brown, 'The Integration of Man and the Biosphere' (2002) 14 *Georgetown International Environmental Law Review* 741.

42 E.g., the Convention on Environmental Impact Assessment in a Transboundary Context, Espoo, 25 February 1991, in force 10 September 1997, 30 ILM 802 (1991), as amended, discussed in ch 9.

been written into the Treaties,[43] differences in the planning systems of individual Member States, coupled with the contested definitions of the social and political ideal of a 'single European territory', have frustrated efforts to devise a coherent European spatial development policy.[44]

A different approach is therefore needed. A useful starting point is the concept of sustainable development.[45] Defined by the 1987 Brundtland Report as 'development that meets the needs of the present without compromising the ability of future generations to meet their own needs',[46] sustainable development has provided a framework for law and policy at national and international levels built around the assertion that its three pillars – environmental protection, economic development and social equity – are mutually reinforcing.[47] It is unsurprising that the simultaneous pursuit of these goals enjoys universal support. Neither is it surprising that this consensus breaks down when stakeholders attempt to devise a more concrete definition of sustainable development in real-world situations.[48]

The most recent expression of sustainable development can be found in the 2015 Sustainable Development Goals (SDGs), the international community's agenda for 'people, planet and prosperity'.[49] They comprise 17 goals, each of which is defined through a series of sub-targets and indicators. A number of the goals have an explicit environmental focus,[50] reflecting the extent to which international environmental law has been successfully integrated into the international community's wider development agenda.[51] Sustainable agriculture is the focus of SDG-2, the headline target of which is, by 2030, to end hunger and guarantee access to sufficient nutrition to all people. To this end, and again by 2030, SDG-2 calls for, inter alia, a doubling in agricultural production from small-scale farms and the implementation of sustainable agricultural practices that support ecosystems and enhance their resilience against the impacts of climate change.

43 Article 3 of the Treaty on European Union.

44 A. Layard and J. Holder, 'Seeking Spatial and Environmental Justice for People and Places within the European Union', in Philippopoulos-Mihalopoulos (n 15) 175–176.

45 The legal status of sustainable development is subject to debate. The concept per se has not crystallised as a rule of customary international law due to the lack of consensus on a sufficiently clear and precise definition. Certain elements of sustainable development can be said to have achieved customary status, however, and, as Lowe argues, it has interstitial normative effect as an interpretative guide for international rules. See A. Boyle and C. Redgwell, *Birnie, Boyle and Redgwell's International Law and the Environment* (4th edn, OUP, 2021) 117–125 and V. Lowe, 'Sustainable Development and Unsustainable Arguments', in A. Boyle and D. Freestone (eds), *International Law and Sustainable Development* (OUP, 1999).

46 World Commission on Environment and Development, *Our Common Future (The Brundtland Report)*, A/42/427, 4 August 1987, 54.

47 UN, *Report of the World Summit on Sustainable Development*, A/CONF.199/20, Annex, para 5.

48 M. Lee, *EU Environmental Law, Governance and Decision-Making* (2nd edn, Hart Publishing, 2014) 59.

49 A/RES/70/1, 21 October 2015.

50 Including Goals 6 (clean water and sanitation); 7 (affordable and clean energy); 13 (climate action); 14 (life below water); and 15 (life on land).

51 P. Sands and J. Peel, *Principles of International Environmental Law* (4th edn, CUP, 2018) 50.

The relevance of agroecology to SDG-2 is clear. However, the SDGs as an agenda are flawed. Conceptually, an important criticism of sustainable development is that by promoting the idea that its three pillars are complementary, so that gains in one automatically lead to gains in the others, it has allowed economic development to be prioritised to the detriment of environmental protection and social equity.[52] These are long-standing concerns, but the SDGs arguably do nothing to address them.[53] In the implementation of SDG-12 (responsible consumption and production), for example, a significant transboundary gap can be identified, with developed states' assessments of national consumption patterns failing to account for the social, environmental and economic costs to the producer developing states.[54] Development will never be sustainable until consumer nations account for all the impacts of products, rather than just those that fall inside their borders.

From a practical perspective, the SDGs are undermined because the ambition reflected in the agenda is not matched by sufficient efforts to implement them. SDG-15.2, for example, was to halt deforestation by 2020, but this target was missed.[55] It is difficult to see how this Goal is ever going to be achieved while the international agreements concerning forests' conservation are underpinned by their narrow economic values to the states in which they are located, rather than the collective interest of all states, and indeed all life on Earth, in their ecological values.[56]

Pursuing agroecology through the law provides an opportunity to address some of the weaknesses of sustainable development. A core element of sustainable development is the integration of environmental, economic and social concerns in the design and implementation of policies.[57] Central to common conceptualisations of sustainable development is, therefore, that these three pillars are distinct.[58] This can be seen in arguments about the nature of sustainable development,[59] and

52 A. Ross-Robertson, 'Is the Environment Being Squeezed Out of Sustainable Development?' (2003) *Public Law* 249 and W. Beckerman, 'Sustainable Development? Is It a Useful Concept?' (1994) 3 *Environmental Values* 191.

53 N. Eisenmenger and others, 'The Sustainable Development Goals Prioritize Economic Growth Over Sustainable Resource Use: A Critical Reflection on the SDGs from a Socio-Ecological Perspective' (2020) 15 *Sustainability Science* 1101, and L. Kotzé and D. French, 'The Anthropocentric Ontology of International Environmental Law and the Sustainable Development Goals: Towards an Ecocentric Rule of Law in the Anthropocene' (2018) 7 *Global Journal of Comparative Law* 5.

54 R. Amos and E. Lydgate. 'Trade, Transboundary Impacts and the Implementation of SDG12' (2020) 15 *Sustainability Science* 1699.

55 UNECE, *Progress Towards the Sustainable Development Goals: Report of the Secretary General*, E/2020/57, 28 April 2020, para 123.

56 R. Amos, *International Conservation Law: The Protection of Plants in Theory and Practice* (Routledge, 2020) 47–52.

57 Sands and Peel (n 51) 227–229.

58 S. Di Benedetto, 'Agriculture and the Environment in International Law: Towards a New Legal Paradigm?', in Monteduro and others (n 16) 122–123, drawing on M. Koskenniemi, 'The Politics of International Law – 20 Years Later' (2009) 20 *European Journal of International Law* 7.

59 Lydgate observes that rather than mutually reinforcing, the three pillars necessitate a process of balancing, whereby trade-offs must be made between competing environmental, economic and social

its practical expression in law and policy.[60] The SDGs do at least recognise that a holistic approach needs to be taken when devising policies but have done little to change policymaking practices so that this is delivered.[61] As Di Benedetto argues, however, because agroecology is concerned with socioecological systems, in which the interactions between human and natural elements are seen as impacting the ecological integrity of these systems, it is impossible to categorise any one issue as environmental, economic or social. Instead, each is considered one part of the same essential question: how would action X impact on the integrity of this system?[62]

Examining the extent to which agroecology is and could be advanced in international law therefore contributes to a necessary paradigm shift, in which sustainable development as the overarching policy framework is replaced with the principle of ecological sustainability. As we shall see, ecological sustainability is not concerned with the pursuit of any single agenda but rather enhancing the critical ecological integrity of the Earth's systems by framing the inevitable trade-offs between environmental protection, economic development and social equity in ecological terms.[63] Both ecological sustainability and agroecology therefore answer the concerns raised above about the priority that sustainable development allows to be given to economic development at the expense of the environment. Under an agroecological/ecological sustainability framework, the pursuit of such development will only be legitimate if the integrity of the overall system is maintained.[64]

## The Structure of This Book

Summarising the above, there are three distinguishing features of agroecology that will be used as benchmarks in our analysis of international law: ecological sustainability; socioecological networks; and systems-level analysis. In terms of specific areas where agroecology may be particularly relevant, either as a framework for discussion or a basis for potential reforms, these features immediately lead us to areas of the law concerned with the protection and conservation of nature, as well as those that seek to facilitate stakeholder engagement in decision-making processes. Following the trans-law approach, it is also possible to identify legal concepts, issues and mechanisms that represent points of contact between equally legitimate but potentially conflicting policy goals, activities taken in pursuit of these, and agriculture. Taking together these aspects of the law's relationship with

---

priorities – E. Lydgate, 'Sustainable Development in the WTO: From Mutual Supportiveness to Balancing' (2012) 11 *World Trade Review* 621.

60 See Article 11 of the Treaty on the Functioning of the European Union, which explicitly calls for the integration of environmental protection requirements into other areas of EU policy.

61 Kotzé and French (n 53).

62 Di Benedetto (n 58).

63 K. Bosselmann, *The Principle of Sustainability: Transforming Law and Governance* (2nd edn, Routledge, 2017) ch 2.

64 Amos (n 56) 228–234.

agroecology, we can identify a series of pertinent case studies that reveal the extent to which agroecology is, and could be, advanced in international law:

1. Conservation of agrobiodiversity
2. Monocultures and genetic diversity
3. Genetically modified organisms and organic agriculture
4. Landscapes
5. Ecosystem services
6. Soil conservation and land degradation
7. Water conservation
8. Climate change
9. Environmental assessment
10. Transboundary pollution
11. International trade
12. Food security, rights, sovereignty and justice

This is not an exhaustive list. Neither should the order in which they are presented be read as inferring any kind of hierarchy. Each corresponds to a legitimate part of agriculture's socioecological networks or is capable of influencing the relationships between different actors within these. Combined, they reveal international law's potential and limitations in managing the complexities of the socioecological networks that underpin the progression of agricultural thought and practice, and therefore the continuing evolution of humanity's relationships with the natural world.

# 1 Conservation of Agrobiodiversity

## International Conservation Law and Agriculture

Human society is dependent on the proper functioning of agricultural networks and associated ecosystems,[1] but our actions are placing agrobiodiversity in an increasingly precarious position.[2] In short, diversity in crops, livestock and associated species is decreasing, land productivity is declining and the threats faced by agrobiodiversity are growing. Notwithstanding indications from the UN Food and Agriculture Organisation (FAO) that sustainable management practices are becoming more widespread, the legal frameworks currently in place, whether these are to increase our knowledge of agrobiodiversity, support stakeholders in ensuring their practices are sustainable or protect endangered species and habitats, are failing to adequately respond to agriculture as a cause of, and sector that is impacted by, biodiversity loss.[3]

To guide international efforts in tackling the drivers behind this loss, in 2010 states party to the Convention on Biological Diversity adopted the Strategic Plan for Biodiversity, centred on the Aichi Biodiversity Targets.[4] Agriculture and associated land management practices were covered in Target 7:

> By 2020, areas under agriculture, aquaculture and forestry are managed sustainably, ensuring conservation of biodiversity.

1 J. Bélanger and D. Pilling (eds), *The State of the World's Biodiversity for Food and Agriculture* (FAO Commission on Genetic Resources for Food and Agriculture Assessments, 2019) ch 2.

2 ibid ch 4.

3 ibid xxxvii–xli.

4 Rio de Janeiro, 5 June 1992, in force 29 December 1993, 31 ILM 822 (1992). Decision X/2, The Strategic Plan for Biodiversity 2011–2020 and the Aichi Biodiversity Targets, UNEP/CBD/COP/DEC/X/2, 29 October 2010, Annex. The 2020 Strategic Plan was the successor to an earlier target 'to achieve by 2010 a significant reduction of the current rate of biodiversity loss' (Decision VI/26, Strategic Plan for the Convention on Biological Diversity, UNEP/CBD/COP/DEC/VI/26, 2002). The Third Global Biodiversity Outlook concluded that not only had this earlier target not been met but that pressures on biodiversity continued to grow – Secretariat of the Convention on Biological Diversity, *Global Biodiversity Outlook 3* (2010).

DOI: 10.4324/9781003435174-3

The mid-term assessment of the Aichi Targets suggested that without increased efforts, Target 7, along with most of the other Targets, would not be achieved.[5] Some progress in addressing agriculture's impacts on biodiversity has been made. The use of chemical pesticides has stabilised, for example, although has not fallen below levels seen in previous decades.[6] Overall, however, the Fifth Global Biodiversity Outlook, the final report on the Aichi Targets, concluded that biodiversity continues to decline in agricultural landscapes and that agricultural practices remain a major driver of biodiversity loss.[7] This raises questions over the efficacy of the long-standing international instruments that address the impacts of agriculture on agrobiodiversity and the wider natural world. This chapter focuses on two: the Biodiversity Convention and the FAO's 2001 International Treaty on Plant Genetic Resources for Food and Agriculture.[8]

There are other legal instruments relevant to the conservation of agrobiodiversity that I do not have space to examine in detail. Of particular note is the EU's Common Agricultural Policy (CAP). Historically, this has been perceived as hugely damaging from an ecological perspective, with subsidies being targeted towards increasing food production and addressing regional economic inequalities rather than supporting agrobiodiversity.[9] Considerable reform has been undertaken to 'green' the CAP, but protecting the environment is arguably still treated, at best, as merely equivalent to providing financial support to farmers.[10] Two reports on the design and implementation of the CAP show that it continues to treat the conservation of agrobiodiversity as a secondary concern to socioeconomic considerations.[11] As we saw in the introduction, human actors and interests are legitimate components of agroecology's socioecological networks. However, agroecology is also based on the premise that advancing agriculture's socioeconomic agenda will only be possible where the ecological integrity of agricultural systems, and the wider ecological systems of which they are part, is maintained. Despite numerous reforms, the CAP has yet to reflect this sufficiently.[12]

5 Secretariat of the Convention on Biological Diversity, *Global Biodiversity Outlook 4* (2014) 13.

6 Secretariat to the Convention on Biological Diversity, *Global Biodiversity Outlook 5* (2020) 64.

7 ibid 64–66.

8 Rome, 3 November 2001, in force 29 June 2004. Text available at: https://www.fao.org/plant-treaty/overview/texts-treaty/en/ (last accessed 20/04/2023).

9 P. Taylor, *Beyond Conservation: A Wildland Strategy* (Earthscan, 2005) 187–190 and J. Scott, *Development Dilemmas in the European Community: Rethinking Regional Development Policy* (Open University Press, 1995) 108–111.

10 I. Doussan and H. Schoukens, 'Biodiversity and Agriculture: Greening the CAP Beyond the Status Quo?', in C. Born and others (eds), *The Habitats Directive in Its EU Environmental Law Context: European Nature's Best Hope?* (Routledge, 2015).

11 European Court of Auditors, *Biodiversity on Farmland: CAP Contribution Has Not Halted Decline* (Special Report 13/2020) and European Commission, *Evaluation of the Impact of the CAP on Habitats, Landscapes and Biodiversity* (November, 2019).

12 G. Pe'er and others, 'A Greener Path for the EU Common Agricultural Policy' (2019) 365 *Science* 449,

How the law provides for the conservation of agrobiodiversity and its associated ecosystems, and the balance that is struck between this and other policy objectives, is therefore an indicator of how much space exists for agroecology in international legal frameworks. It is nevertheless important to recognise that conservation per se may not be a principal goal of farmers. As noted in the introduction, an agricultural system does not necessarily have the same objectives as might be identified for other human entities and social constructs but instead acts to support and reinforce its own unique logic.[13] The extent to which conservation forms part of this logic will depend on the agricultural methods and philosophies that each system employs.

## The Convention on Biological Diversity

As the principal global conservation instrument, applying not only to all species but 'the ecological complexes of which they are part',[14] the Biodiversity Convention is an important instrument through which agroecological approaches to agriculture can be pursued. The Convention has not, however, lived up to its potential,[15] evidenced by numerous studies tracking increasing rates of biodiversity loss,[16] leading commentators to question whether it has instead frustrated conservation efforts.[17] The only substantive obligation that is not qualified by references to national capabilities or discretionary terms is the duty of Contracting Parties to report on measures that have been adopted to implement the Convention.[18] In other words, the Biodiversity Convention only obliges states to record the gradual demise of nature.[19]

I have discussed the merits of the Convention as a conservation instrument elsewhere and so will not address them in detail here.[20] Instead, this chapter will look at the non-binding programmes of work that have evolved out of the Convention's framework, specifically those on agricultural biodiversity and the

13 E. Noe and H. Alrøe, 'Regulation of Agroecosystems: A Social Systems Analysis of Agroecology and Law', in M. Monteduro and others (eds), *Law and Agroecology: A Transdisciplinary Dialogue* (Springer, 2015) 39.

14 Article 2.

15 W. Reid, 'Halting the Loss of Biodiversity: International Institutional Measures', in L. Guruswamy and J. McNeely (eds), *Protection of Global Biodiversity: Converging Strategies* (Duke University Press, 1998) 172–174.

16 Including R. Almond and others (eds), *Living Planet Report 2022 – Building a Nature-Positive Society* (WWF, 2022) and RBG Kew, *The State of the World's Plants Report – 2016* (Royal Botanic Gardens, Kew, 2016).

17 E.g. L. Guruswamy, 'The Convention on Biological Diversity: A Polemic', in Guruswamy and McNeely (n 15).

18 Article 26.

19 S. Harrop, 'Biodiversity and Conservation', in R. Falkner (ed), *The Handbook of Global Climate and Environment Policy* (Wiley Blackwell, 2013) 49.

20 R. Amos, *International Conservation Law: The Protection of Plants in Theory and Practice* (Routledge, 2020) ch 2.

ecosystem approach, and the Global Biodiversity Framework.[21] Consideration will also be given to the desirability of a new protocol to the Biodiversity Convention on sustainable agriculture. It is worth noting, however, that one reason why the provisions of the Convention per se may be lacking in legal force is the negotiating states' desire to prevent international conservation obligations from infringing on national development priorities.[22] That agroecology promotes diversity in all agricultural networks, including at the global level, means that any agroecological legal framework will not be overly proscriptive in terms of agricultural methodologies and will therefore be compatible with the peremptory norm of permanent sovereignty over natural resources.[23] On the other hand, that one of agroecology's central premises is that the resilience of agroecosystems depends on their diversity does mean that such a framework would entail some form of obligation to ensure that diversity is restored, maintained and enhanced. Given the failure of the 'soft' approach of the Biodiversity Convention in halting biodiversity loss,[24] this obligation would arguably need to be framed in much stronger legal terms than typically seen in the Biodiversity Convention and wider international conservation law.

### *The Programme of Work on Agricultural Biodiversity*

The sustainable use of agricultural biodiversity was discussed at the Biodiversity Convention's first Conference of the Parties (COP), with a programme of work being agreed at COP-3[25] and formally endorsed at COP-5.[26] The objectives of this programme are similar to those of the Convention:

(a) To promote the positive effects and mitigate the negative impacts of agricultural systems and practices on biological diversity in agro-ecosystems and their interface with other ecosystems;
(b) To promote the conservation and sustainable use of genetic resources of actual and potential value for food and agriculture;
(c) To promote the fair and equitable sharing of benefits arising out of the use of genetic resources.[27]

21 Decision 15/4, Kunming-Montreal Global Biodiversity Framework, CBD/COP/DEC/15/4, 19 December 2022.

22 J. Smallwood and others, 'Global Biodiversity Governance: What Needs to Be Transformed?', in I. Visseren-Hamakers and M. Kok (eds), *Transforming Biodiversity Governance* (CUP, 2022).

23 This gives states the right to freely exploit natural resources that are within their jurisdiction, although it can now be argued that this rule has evolved to contain an element of sustainable use – N. Schrijver, *Sovereignty Over Natural Resources: Balancing Rights and Duties* (CUP, 1997) Ch 4.

24 S. Harrop and D. Pritchard, 'A Hard Instrument Goes Soft: The Implications of the Convention on Biological Diversity's Current Trajectory' (2011) 21 *Global Environmental Change* 474.

25 Decision III/11, Conservation and sustainable use of agricultural biological diversity, UNEP/CBD/COP/DEC/III/11, 1996.

26 Decision V/5, Agricultural biological diversity: review of phase I of the programme of work and adoption of a multi-year work programme, UNEP/CBD/COP/DEC/V/5. 2000, Annex.

27 ibid para 2. Article 1 of the Convention.

Certain features of these objectives mark the programme of work out as being more progressive than its parent treaty. There is a greater emphasis on ecosystems and the interactions within and between these, for example, reflecting agroecology's approach to systems-level analysis of issues. It is not enough just to consider how an action will impact a specific agroecosystem, but how this action, and its consequences, will affect related systems and the wider socioecological network. Within this ecosystem approach, the programme of work also recognises the importance of respecting indigenous and local knowledge and practices, and of adopting an interdisciplinary perspective of issues, which again reflects agroecology.[28]

The programme of work on agricultural biodiversity comprises four programme elements, each with its own objectives, activities and means of implementation. The most relevant of these to the current discussion is programme element 2 on adaptive management. In the context of conservation, adaptive management is a process through which the ongoing experiences from strategies, programmes and activities are used to inform their continuing operation.[29] Conservation becomes a circular learning process: a particular approach to an activity, such as conserving a species, is adopted; the approach is evaluated in terms of impact, strengths and weaknesses; the results of this evaluation inform changes to the approach; the merits of the new approach are assessed. This can be resource-intensive and risks emphasising producing conservation outputs, i.e. the compilation of reports, over achieving positive conservation outcomes. It does, however, allow for early interventions if an approach is not delivering the desired results or leads to unintended adverse consequences, either on the target entity, other species and habitats, or the wider socioecological network.

Central to programme element 2 is the compilation of case studies, principally by public and civil bodies at the national level but with support, where necessary, from international organisations. The case studies cover specific examples of agricultural systems, the impacts of certain practices and strategies to mitigate the impacts of climate change.[30] Developing these is again a continuous process, with experiences from previous studies informing the design of future ones.[31] Their purpose is to identify ecosystem services provided by agricultural biodiversity, recognise best practices for sustainable agriculture and assess the impacts of agricultural practices on biodiversity.[32] In relation to promoting agroecology in the international conservation legal framework, these case studies serve two functions. First, they provide evidence on the types of practices that support the links in and between agricultural and wider ecosystems. They highlight the benefits that come

28 ibid para 4. See ch 2.

29 M. Wells and T. McShane, 'Integrating Protected Area Management with Local Needs and Aspirations' (2004) 33 *Ambio* 513, 516. See also N. Salafsky and R. Margoluis, 'Threat Reduction Assessment: A Practical and Cost-Effective Approach to Evaluating Conservation and Development Projects' (1999) 13 *Conservation Biology* 830.

30 https://www.cbd.int/programmes/areas/agro/cs.aspx (last accessed 20/04/2023).

31 Decision V/5 (n 26) Programme Element 2, Ways and Means.

32 ibid 2.1.

from recognising and respecting these links, in terms of supporting ecosystem services and the ecological integrity of agriculture's natural resource base. Second, they demonstrate the value of protecting traditional and local farming methods as equally legitimate components of a diverse global agrosystem, while recognising the potential contributions of modern technologies. To illustrate, a case study on eco-farming in China looked at, inter alia, how the recycling of waste products from local and subsistence agriculture can help to address energy poverty in remote rural communities.[33]

Supporting local and indigenous farmers is also central to programme element 3: capacity building. A broad range of activities is envisaged to deliver on this aspect of the programme of work, including establishing partnerships between farmers and professional and academic stakeholders, ensuring farmers and other stakeholders can participate in relevant decision-making processes and, importantly, raising public awareness of the importance of small-scale farming to sustainable agriculture.[34] Each of these can be seen as enhancing the links between human actors in agricultural networks and highlighting their relationships with natural entities.

The other programme elements under the programme of work on agricultural biodiversity are assessments and mainstreaming. The former concerns the identification of trends in the state of agricultural biodiversity and the reasons for these, while the latter encourages states to incorporate sustainable agriculture into other policy areas. They therefore provide the broader framework through which the holistic appraisal and management of agriculture can be pursued in accordance with agroecological principles. However, that agricultural biodiversity continues to decline, in part because of the unsustainability of common agricultural practices, raises questions over whether the framework provided by the programme of work is sufficient.

In 2008, a review of the programme of work was published. However, other than noting that the programme 'continues to provide a relevant framework to achieve the objectives of the Convention',[35] it provides little in the way of evaluation. Instead, it merely calls on states and other stakeholders to renew their efforts to promote agricultural sustainability.[36] Sufficient action to meet Aichi Target 7 was clearly not taken, however, as the Fifth Global Biodiversity Outlook shows.[37] This is a further reflection of the critical flaw of the Biodiversity Convention regime, i.e. that it appears incapable of addressing the causes of biodiversity decline, and indicates that this weakness applies as much to agrobiodiversity as it does to the wider natural world.

33 X. Dayuan, 'China's Eco-Farming – An Effective Approach for Conservation and Sustainable Use of Agricultural Biodiversity' (Nanjng Institute of Environmental Sciences), available from (n 30).

34 Decision V/5, (n 26) Programme Element 3.

35 Decision IX/1, In-depth review of the programme of work on agricultural biodiversity, UNEP/CBD/COP/DEC/IX/1, 9 October 2008, para 3.

36 ibid.

37 Secretariat to the Convention (n 6) 64–66.

**The Ecosystem Approach**

The programme of work on agricultural biodiversity, as with all initiatives pursued under the Biodiversity Convention, is situated within the treaty's ecosystem approach.[38] At its simplest, an ecosystem approach comprises strategies 'for the integrated management of land, water and living resources'.[39] More sophisticated conceptualisations go beyond this and seek to integrate environmental regulation, across multiple levels of governance, with the regulation of socioeconomic processes that directly impact the environment.[40] In this regard, ecosystem approaches reflect agroecology's understanding of the integrated nature of agricultural systems. They also align with sustainable development as a policy framework and, as I discuss below, arguably share the same weakness of failing to give due weight to ecological imperatives.

No single definition of the ecosystem approach enjoys universal support.[41] In international instruments, an ecosystem approach often takes the form of a general obligation to protect the ecosystem of a given biome, supplemented by additional, but also generically phrased, provisions on specific issues. In the 1997 UN Convention on the Law of Non-Navigational Uses of International Watercourses,[42] for example, Article 20 calls on states to 'protect and preserve the ecosystems of international watercourses', with Articles 21 and 22 dealing in broad terms with the prevention, reduction and control of pollution and preventing the introduction of invasive/alien species. Article 23 further strengthens the ecosystem approach by calling on states to take all necessary measures with respect to a watercourse to protect the wider marine environment.[43]

As a conservation regime, the Watercourses Convention can be criticised for qualifying these obligations with arbitrary thresholds, such as 'significant harm', references to other rules of international law, and that their subsequent interpretation has been as obligations of due diligence rather than of result.[44] Regarding the merits of its ecosystem approach, Articles 20–23 must be read in the light of the wider instrument. Article 5, which sets out the Convention's general principles, states that 'an international watercourse shall be used and developed... with a view to attaining optimal and sustainable utilisation thereof and benefits therefrom... consistent with adequate protection of the watercourse'. Guidance on what constitutes 'sustainable utilisation' is provided by Article 6, which lists factors to be taken into account. These include 'Geographic, hydrological, climatic, ecological

38 Decision V/6, Ecosystem approach, UNEP/CBD/COP/DEC/V/6, 22 June 2000.

39 ibid Part A, para 1.

40 V. De Lucia, 'Competing Narratives and Complex Genealogies: The Ecosystem Approach in International Environmental Law' (2015) 27 *Journal of Environmental Law* 91, 92–93.

41 ibid.

42 New York, 21 May 1997, in force 17 August 2014, 36 ILM 700 (1997).

43 See O. McIntyre, 'The Emergence of an "Ecosystem Approach" to the Protection of International Watercourses under International Law' (2004) 13 *Review of European Community and International Environmental Law* 1.

44 Amos (n 20) 113.

and other factors of a natural character' and socioeconomic factors, such as the social and economic needs of affected states, the interests of populations dependent on the watercourse and existing and potential uses of the watercourse. These are all legitimate concerns. The issue is how the relationship between them is defined in Article 6(3):

> The weight to be given to each factor is to be determined by its importance in comparison with that of other relevant factors. In determining what is a reasonable and equitable use, all relevant factors are to be considered together and a conclusion reached on the basis of the whole.

This reflects the fundamental weakness of sustainable development, i.e. that it allows critical ecological priorities to be treated as no more than equivalent to socioeconomic concerns. A true ecosystem approach would implement a principle of ecological sustainability, under which trade-offs between environmental, economic and social interests are framed by the Earth's carrying capacity.[45] The ecosystem approach of the 1997 Convention is further undermined by the obligation to not cause significant harm in Article 7 applying specifically to other watercourse states, not to watercourses per se.

A similar emphasis on anthropocentric concerns can be seen in other ecosystem approaches in international environmental instruments. The ecosystem approach of the UN Convention on the Law of the Sea (LOSC),[46] arguably a consequence of its subsequent interpretation and application rather than the deliberate intent of its negotiators,[47] focuses on commercially valuable marine species.[48] This is carried into the 1995 Implementation Agreement on Fish Stocks, which only calls for the protection of ecosystems and ecosystemic relationships that are important for maintaining commercial fish populations.[49] In contrast, the ecosystem approach is explicitly listed in Article 5 of the 2023 LOSC Agreement on the Conservation and Sustainable Use of Marine Biological Diversity of Areas Beyond National Jurisdiction, but how this will be taken forward remains to be seen.[50]

Notwithstanding that the way the ecosystem approach is typically applied in international law can be criticised for giving undue weight to anthropocentric concerns, that its exact meaning varies according to context is arguably one of the concept's strengths. It allows for the specific characteristics of the relevant biome to be taken into account in the design of regulatory strategies. Conceptually, however,

45 K. Bosselmann, *The Principle of Sustainability: Transforming Law and Governance* (2nd edn, Routledge, 2017) Ch 2.
46 Montego Bay, 10 December 1982, in force 16 November 1994, 21 ILM 1261 (1982), Article 194(5).
47 D. Freestone, 'The Conservation of Marine Ecosystems under International Law', in M. Bowman and C. Redgwell, *International Law and the Conservation of Biodiversity* (Kluwer Law International, 1996) 103.
48 Amos (n 20) 96.
49 ibid. New York, 4 December 1995, in force 11 December 2001, 34 ILM 1542 (1995). E.g., Article 5.
50 Text available at: https://www.un.org/bbnj/ (last accessed 20/04/2023).

De Lucia identifies four basic elements that underpin all ecosystem approaches: integration, integrity, information and iteration.[51] Each of these underscores the relevance of the ecosystem approach to the implementation of agroecology through international law.

Integration, considered to be the central idea behind the ecosystem approach,[52] encompasses not just recognising the integrated nature of the natural world but the concomitant need for the integration of environmental and non-environmental regulatory approaches and of cross-jurisdictional, multilevel governance frameworks.[53] This corresponds to agroecology's focus on socioecological networks, and the recognition that actions targeted at one aspect will impact the entire network. There is also a shared emphasis in agroecology and the ecosystem approach on promoting ecological integrity, i.e. the proper health and functioning of ecosystems. De Lucia suggests that the growing emphasis on this in international environmental law constitutes evidence of a shift towards a more ecocentric regulatory paradigm.[54] Notwithstanding that greater space for ecocentric ideas can potentially be identified in international environmental law,[55] I am not convinced by this suggestion. There is an important distinction between recognising nature's ecological value (the roles played by different natural elements in supporting an ecosystem) and an ecocentric understanding of nature's intrinsic value (natural entities are worthy of consideration regardless of their value to humans and nature).[56] It is the case that the law is increasingly recognising the importance of supporting the ecological values of natural entities, evident in implementation guidance of international instruments and decisions of international courts and tribunals,[57] but this is arguably to facilitate nature's provision of ecosystem services for the benefit of humans, rather than for nature's own sake. Furthermore, any suggestion of a paradigm shift in international environmental law must be viewed in the context of sustainable development, which, as has been illustrated both normatively and empirically, remains deeply anthropocentric.[58]

51 V. De Lucia, 'A Critical Interrogation of the Relation between the Ecosystem Approach and Ecosystem Services' (2018) 27 *Review of European, Comparative & International Environmental Law* 104, 105.

52 Expert Meeting on the Ecosystem Approach, Review of the Principles of the Ecosystem Approach and Suggestions for Refinement: A Framework for Discussion, UNEP/CBD/EM-EA/1/3, 3 July 2003, para 8.

53 De Lucia (n 51) 105.

54 ibid. See also De Lucia (n 40) 104–106.

55 Amos (n 20) ch 10.

56 The question of how nature is, could and should be valued is more complex than this, but beyond the scope of this work. See instead ibid ch 1.

57 E.g. J. Perry and C. Falzon, *Climate Change Adaptation for Natural World Heritage Sites: A Practical Guide* (UNESCO, 2014) 29–32 and *Indus Waters Kishenganga Arbitration (Pakistan v India)*, Final Award of the Court of Arbitration, 20th December 2013, para 99.

58 N. Eisenmenger and others, 'The Sustainable Development Goals Prioritize Economic Growth Over Sustainable Resource Use: A Critical Reflection on the SDGs from a Socio-Ecological Perspective' (2020) 15 *Sustainability Science* 1101, and L. Kotzé and D. French, 'The Anthropocentric Ontology

The information and iteration aspects of the ecosystem approach reflect the adaptive management approaches inherent to agroecological practices. The effective implementation of the ecosystem approach depends on the availability, and sufficient understanding, of information relating to complex, integrated natural processes operating across multiple ecological levels. Due to the uncertainties inherent to this information, it is necessary for regulatory approaches to be able to adapt to new information as it becomes available.[59]

The Biodiversity Convention has developed arguably the most sophisticated framework for implementing an ecosystem approach, defined through a series of principles.[60] These reflect the complex, overlapping prisms through which an ecosystem can be perceived,[61] but also provide space for an agroecological approach to the conservation of agrobiodiversity. Together, Principles 1, 2, 11 and 12 constitute a framework that recognises nature and society as combining a series of socio-ecological networks, in which it is impossible to separate one from the other. They emphasise the importance of not only recognising the validity of local and indigenous understandings of the environment (Principles 1 and 11) but of ensuring that these communities are provided sufficient opportunities to engage in the design and implementation of governance strategies as well (Principle 2). They also call for interdisciplinary approaches to ecosystem management, recognising that actions towards one policy goal may undermine efforts to achieve another (Principle 12). This is also reflected in Principle 3, which calls on stakeholders to consider both the direct effects of their actions and their potential impacts on other connected systems. Also related to this is Principle 9 and its incorporation of adaptive management into the Convention's ecosystem approach. This Principle notes that 'change is inevitable', not just through natural evolution but as a result of humanity's short- and long-term impacts on the environment. Anticipating, where possible, and accounting for this change must therefore be central to governance strategies and the diversity that comes from applying agroecology to agricultural practices would facilitate this.

Principles 4 and 5 frame ecosystem approaches in an economic context. They do not, however, merely reaffirm the flawed mainstream application of sustainable development, but instead offer the more nuanced appreciation, inherent to ideas of agroecology, that economic prosperity is contingent on ecological health. Principle 4 notes that market distortions that 'undervalue natural systems and populations' lead to the destruction of nature being seen as more profitable than its conservation. It calls for these perverse incentives to be addressed so that all stakeholders, from multinational corporations to subsistence farmers, recognise the value of maintaining functioning ecosystems.[62] This more ecologically-aware economic approach is

of International Environmental Law and the Sustainable Development Goals: Towards an Ecocentric Rule of Law in the Anthropocene' (2018) 7 *Global Journal of Comparative Law* 5.

59 De Lucia (n 51) 105.

60 Decision V/6 (n 38) Part B.

61 De Lucia (n 40) 111–112.

62 See also Target 18 of the Global Biodiversity Framework (n 21).

supported by Principles 7 and 8, which call for ecosystem management strategies to be devised on appropriate timescales, thereby challenging the short-term outlooks that typically define governance strategies.[63]

Lastly, Principle 10 calls for a fundamental change in conservation law and policy through a departure from the dichotomy between protected and unprotected species. This is arguably the most important of the 12 principles, as it reflects a core principle of environmental law, namely prevention,[64] and would be a better representation of contemporary thinking in conservation practice.[65] Distinguishing between protected and unprotected species can be resource-intensive, as it requires detailed assessments of species to determine their conservation status, and the administrative and cost burden of these can mean that lists are not updated regularly.[66] It can again also lead to an inappropriate emphasis on conservation outputs at the expense of positive conservation action.[67] The difficulty is that there are limited resources available for conservation and so priorities have to be established and trade-offs made.[68] Would it be better to devote resources to saving an extremely rare species facing imminent extinction, or instead support other species that are declining but not yet on the edge? This is not a hypothetical question. In 2019, the last *Achatinella apexfulva*, a tree snail endemic to the Hawaiian island of Oahu, died. Named George, after Lonesome George, the sole Pinta Island tortoise (*Chelonoidis abingdonii*) who died in 2012, scientists provided this snail with specialist care while they searched Hawai'i for a mate for over a decade.[69] From an economic perspective, it could be argued that the resources that were devoted to George would have been better spent on other species with a greater chance of survival. This is not a purely economic issue, however. *Achatinella apexfulva* would have played a distinct role in its ecosystem and that role, however small, has now been lost. It is also a moral issue. Do we have the right to condemn another species to extinction when it is our actions that have caused its demise? That environmental instruments and literature on the constituent elements of sustainable development refer to the

63 B. Richardson, *Time and Environmental Law: Telling Nature's Time* (CUP, 2017) ch 1.

64 The prevention of environmental harms is 'better' (however that is defined) than their remediation. This would also answer Harrop's concerns regarding the legal protection of commonplace biodiversity – S. Harrop, 'Conservation Regulation: A Backward Step for Biodiversity?' (1999) 8 *Biodiversity and Conservation* 679.

65 G. Mace, 'Whose Conservation?' (2014) 345 *Science* 1558.

66 R. Amos, 'Assessing the Impact of the Habitats Directive: A Case Study of Europe's Plants' (2021) 33 *Journal of Environmental Law* 365, 387.

67 The Biodiversity Convention has been criticised in this regard – Harrop and Pritchard (n 24).

68 K. Wilson and others, 'Prioritizing Trade-Offs in Conservation', in N. Leader-Williams and others (eds), *Trade-offs in Conservation: Deciding What to Save* (Wiley-Blackwell / ZSL, 2010).

69 https://www.nationalgeographic.com/animals/2019/01/george-the-lonely-snail-dies-in-hawaii-extinction/ (last accessed 20/04/2023). *Achatinella apexfulva* were hermaphrodites, so any other snail could have been a mate for George.

importance of preserving the natural world for future generations means that this question is not devoid of legal content.[70]

To aid states in applying the Biodiversity Convention's principles on the ecosystem approach, five points of operational guidance have been developed. States should endeavour to focus on the relationships and processes within ecosystems; enhance benefit-sharing; use adaptive management practices; carry out management actions at the scale appropriate for the issue being addressed, with decentralisation to the lowest appropriate level; and ensure intersectoral cooperation.[71] On the one hand, the overlap between this guidance and core tenets of agroecology is clear. Each focuses on maintaining and enhancing relationships in socioecological networks, calls for adaptive management processes in biodiversity governance and recognises the essential role of different communities and stakeholders in devising and implementing strategies. On the other hand, the guidance does not provide any substantive measures that can be implemented at the national or sub-national level and often only affirms the general aspirations expressed in the ecosystem approach principles. It can also be criticised for locating the Convention's ecosystem approach firmly within anthropocentric perceptions of the value of nature. Under point 2 on benefit-sharing, for example, it is noted that 'Benefits that flow from the array of functions provided by biological diversity at the ecosystem level provide the basis of human environmental security and sustainability. The ecosystem approach seeks that the benefits derived from these functions are maintained and restored'. Nothing in the operational guidance suggests that an activity might be inherently unsustainable and so should not be undertaken on any scale. Further, while the operational guidance recognises that 'many components of biodiversity control the stores and flows of energy, water and nutrients within ecosystems', this is a rather cursory assessment of the critical role biodiversity plays in maintaining the Earth's life-supporting systems and nothing in the guidance encourages states to undertake conservation work just for the benefit of nature itself.

On one level, the ecosystem approach devised under the Biodiversity Convention comprises a sound framework and provides clear space through which agroecology can be applied to the conservation of agro- and biodiversity. It goes further than the approaches set out in other regimes in recognising human and natural entities as forming coherent, interconnected socioecological networks and the consequent need to maintain, restore and enhance the relationships within and between these. The Convention's ecosystem approach also adopts a more nuanced perspective on the economic rationales behind conservation; it is not the exploitation of nature that leads to long-term prosperity, but its conservation. However, that the operational guidance is overtly anthropocentric, establishing the ecosystem approach primarily

70 E.g., Article 4 of the Convention for the Protection of the World Cultural and Natural Heritage (Paris) 16 November 1972, in force 17 December 1975, 27 UST 37, ILM 1358 (1972) and E. Brown Weiss, 'Implementing Intergenerational Equity', in M. Fitzmaurice and others (eds), *Research Handbook on International Environmental Law* (Edward Elgar, 2010).

71 Decision V/6 (n 38) Part C.

as a means of perpetuating sustainable use without acknowledging that certain uses will never be sustainable, or that it is also legitimate to undertake conservation just for conservation's sake, limits how far this broadly conceived, non-binding framework can transform the Convention into a more ecologically informed body of law that positively advances agroecology.

### *Agriculture and the Global Biodiversity Framework*

The publication of the Fifth Global Biodiversity Outlook marked the end of the 2020 Strategic Plan for Biodiversity. In its place, the parties to the Biodiversity Convention have adopted the Kunming Global Biodiversity Framework, centred around the vision that 'by 2050, biodiversity is valued, conserved, restored and wisely used, maintaining ecosystem services, sustaining a healthy planet and delivering benefits essential for all people'.[72] Complementing this is the 2030 mission:

> To take urgent action to halt and reverse biodiversity loss to put nature on a path to recovery for the benefit of people and planet by conserving and sustainably using biodiversity and by ensuring the fair and equitable sharing of benefits from the use of genetic resources…[73]

There is some merit to the new Framework. It goes further in recognising different perceptions of the value of nature[74] and highlights the importance of conserving biodiversity to the wider sustainable development agenda.[75] However, the Global Biodiversity Framework adopts the same flawed approach of setting non-binding global targets to which national action will contribute. Four broad 2050 Goals are established, the key one being Goal A, which relates to ecosystem integrity, extinction and genetic diversity.[76] Alongside these, 23 Action Targets have been adopted for 2030.[77] As I have argued elsewhere, this 'global target, national action' approach in international environmental law may be a necessary reflection of states' differing ecological conditions and need to determine their own priorities in conservation and environmental policy, but without binding national targets, the law simply lacks the ability to compel states to deliver international agenda.[78]

Agriculture is specifically addressed in Action Target 10:

> Ensure that areas under agriculture, aquaculture, fisheries and forestry are managed sustainably, in particular through the sustainable use of biodiversity,

72 (n 21) para 10.
73 ibid para 11.
74 ibid para 7(b).
75 ibid para 8.
76 ibid para 12. Goal B concerns sustainable use of biodiversity; Goal C relates to access and benefit-sharing; and Goal D covers implementation support.
77 ibid para 13.
78 Amos (n 20) 38 and R. Amos and E. Lydgate 'Trade, Transboundary Impacts and the Implementation of SDG 12' (2020) 15 *Sustainability Science* 1699, 1701–1702.

> including through a substantial increase of the application of biodiversity friendly practices, such as sustainable intensification, agroecological and other innovative approaches, contributing to the resilience and long-term efficiency and productivity of these production systems...

The explicit reference to agroecology in the Global Biodiversity Framework is welcome, particularly given the emphasis placed on this in the Fifth Global Biodiversity Outlook.[79] It is debatable, however, whether this will instigate the action needed to either address the continuing decline in agrobiodiversity loss or mitigate agriculture's impacts on the natural world. As noted, the 'global target, national action' approach of the Convention's strategies lacks sufficient legal force, as does the Convention itself due to the qualified nature of its obligations and its non-binding programmes of work. The same criticism does not apply, at least to the same extent, to the two protocols that have been adopted to address the specific issues of the transboundary movement of living modified organisms[80] and the access and sharing of benefits of genetic resources.[81] Notwithstanding states' evident desire to prevent international conservation obligations from impinging on sovereign rights to development, it is therefore legitimate to question the potential utility of a protocol on sustainable agriculture.

It is beyond the scope of this work to provide a detailed consideration of what constitutes an 'effective' conservation treaty.[82] For the current discussion, it is sufficient to note that a key criterion is that the instrument includes clear, legally binding obligations.[83] The content of a sustainable agriculture protocol's obligations can be drawn from agroecological principles highlighted in the introduction to this work. In relation to diversity, for example, states should accept binding national targets to not only prevent further loss but increase the diversity of agrosystems. Such targets should include diversity of species and, reflecting agroecology's wider systems-level perspective of agriculture, diversity of farming methods in accordance with national ecologies and cultures. Indicative lists of practices, such as encouraging crop rotations, using vegetation to help manage water retention and strictly controlling the use of chemicals, could be provided as guidance on how to design sustainable agricultural systems.[84]

A sustainable agriculture protocol would also be a suitable instrument through which the agricultural zoning approach proposed by Monteduro, discussed in the

79 Secretariat to the Convention (n 6) 160–162.

80 Montreal, 29 January 2000, in force 11 September 2003, 39 ILM 1027.

81 Nagoya, 29 October 2010, in force 12 October 2014, C.N.782.2010.TREATIES-1.

82 See instead Amos (n 20) 57–62.

83 G. Shaffer and M. Pollack, 'Hard vs. Soft Law: Alternatives, Complements, and Antagonists in International Governance' (2010) 94 *Minnesota Law Review* 706; and T. Treves and others (eds), *Non-Compliance Procedures and Mechanisms and the Effectiveness of International Environmental Agreements* (CUP, 2009).

84 M. Altieri, *Agroecology: The Science of Sustainable Agriculture* (2nd edn, Westview Press, 1995) ch 5.

introduction, could be implemented.[85] This could be in the form of an ambitious obligation on states to map their entire territory in terms of permissible agricultural practices or take a more limited approach of requiring states to designate protected agricultural areas in which certain practices are prohibited to preserve the characteristics and local knowledge bases of the area. Such an approach could be complemented by obligations of transboundary cooperation so that states avoid permitting conflicting land uses across borders.

This links to what would be another important category of obligations: clear participatory rights for all stakeholders. The rationales behind this are similar to those for providing for stakeholder participation in other areas of environmental decision-making. Different stakeholders will provide distinct types of information to decision-makers, which should lead to better, or at least more informed, decisions.[86] A local subsistence farmer that utilises knowledge built up over generations will provide a very different, but equally legitimate, perspective of how something will impact an agrosystem to a Western-trained scientist who has only been observing the system for a short time. This would also help to deliver environmental justice for such communities, a core element of which is ensuring that those stakeholders who will be affected by a decision are given early, effective and ongoing opportunities to participate in the decision-making process.[87]

Devising a protocol that is theoretically sound is relatively easy. Designing one that is practically capable of achieving its objectives is more difficult. In the case of a sustainable agriculture protocol, an immediate problem, and one that is not limited to this context, would be establishing baselines against which progress could be measured. Sufficient data on the status of agrobiodiversity may simply not exist in some states. Tracking progress will also be resource-intensive, with many developing states relying on technical and financial support. The lack of capacity in these areas is an ongoing concern, due to the importance of accurate national reporting in monitoring national and global trends in biodiversity, and resulted in the Global Environment Facility providing considerable financial support to developing states.[88] The application of the protocol would also still be defined by states' borders, which would limit the effectiveness of measures such as Monteduro's zoning proposals. Obligations of international cooperation may prevent one state from establishing an area for genetically-modified crop production next to an organic farming zone of its neighbour but could not mandate the adoption of joint spatial planning policies to take account of ecological and geophysical features of

85 M. Monteduro, 'From Agroecology and Law to Agroecological Law? Exploring Integration Between *Scientia Ruris* and *Scientia Iuris*', Monteduro and others (n 13) 79–81.

86 J. Steele, Participation and Deliberation in Environmental Law: Exploring a Problem-Solving Approach' (2001) 21 *Oxford Journal of Legal Studies* 415.

87 D. Schlosberg, *Defining Environmental Justice: Theories, Movements, and Nature* (OUP, 2007) ch 2.

88 P. Herkenrath, 'The Implementation of the Convention on Biological Diversity – A Non-Government Perspective Ten Years On' (2002) 11 *Review of European Community and International Environmental Law* 29, 30–31.

the landscape. Another basic issue would be whether a legally binding protocol that sought to partially direct national development policies would attract sufficient support to enter into force.

There is also a more fundamental risk in adopting a sustainable agriculture protocol. Such an agreement would arguably require a stricter level of protection of species and habitats than Article 8 of the Biodiversity Convention, which calls on states to adopt a range of conservation measures but only 'as far as possible and as appropriate'. In principle, developing stronger conservation obligations through an agriculture instrument would be a positive step. However, this could legitimise the conditioning of the conservation of nature on its contribution to a human endeavour, in this case agriculture. International conservation law has already been undermined by the prioritisation of nature's anthropocentric values over its ecological values.[89] These anthropocentric values are of greater relevance in agriculture but cannot be accepted as a prerequisite of conservation. Nevertheless, a stronger legal framework for sustainable agriculture, and other issues relevant to conservation, should still be seen as preferable to continuing with the same non-binding approach that has clearly failed to halt biodiversity loss.

### The UN Food and Agriculture Organisation

The FAO oversees a number of instruments that regulate different aspects of the conservation of agrobiodiversity. These vary in legal status and agroecological merit. Phytosanitary issues, for example, are addressed through the 1997 International Plant Protection Convention (IPPC).[90] This aims to prevent and control the spread of harmful entities by requiring the export of 'plants, plant products and other regulated articles or consignments thereof' to be accompanied by a phytosanitary certificate.[91] As I discuss in the next chapter, the IPPC can be criticised for defining 'plant pest' in terms of economic, rather than ecological, harm.[92] It is consequently of limited use in protecting those aspects of agrobiodiversity that are of negligible economic value but significant ecological value. In contrast, the FAO's Sustainability Assessment of Food and Agriculture (SAFA) is potentially an important mechanism that encourages the application of principles of agroecology at all stages of agricultural production.[93]

Arguably, the most significant conservation instrument overseen by the FAO is the International Treaty on Plant Genetic Resources for Food and Agriculture (PGRT). The FAO's rules on protecting and ensuring access to plant genetic resources for food and agriculture were initially contained in the non-binding

89 Amos (n 20) ch 1.

90 In force 2 October 2005, amending the 1951 Convention (Rome, 6 December 1951, in force 3 April 1952, 150 UNTS 67, as revised by the FAO Conference in 1979). Text available at: https://www.ippc.int/en/core-activities/governance/convention-text/ (last accessed 20/04/2023).

91 Article V.

92 Articles VII and II. See also Amos (n 20) 175–179.

93 FAO, *SAFA Guidelines Version 3.0* (2014) 2–5. See ch 9 for discussion.

1983 International Undertaking on Plant Genetic Resources.[94] Following the adoption of the Biodiversity Convention, which also addresses the utilisation of natural genetic resources,[95] the Undertaking was revised into a legally binding treaty intended to work alongside the 1992 Convention.[96] The focus on genetic resources rather than species reflects an important point in the conservation of biodiversity, namely that is not enough just to conserve the diversity *of* species. It is also necessary to conserve diversity *within* species.[97]

Noting the PGRT preamble's reference to their 'special nature', Santilli suggests that plant genetic resources for food and agriculture warrant specific regulation in international law because they are the result of hundreds of years of domestication and selection by humans, to the extent that they are no longer capable of surviving in the wild.[98] I would expand on this and argue that what differentiates agrobiodiversity, including its genetic diversity, from other natural entities is that it is the only context in which the coupling of 'conservation and sustainable use', which is a typical construction in both the PGRT and the Biodiversity Convention and, in the case of the latter, can be read as implying that conservation is only a means to the end of sustainable use,[99] is ecologically coherent. Whereas other categories of biodiversity can be conserved without being exploited, agrobiodiversity depends on the continuation of certain agricultural practices.

The PGRT's objectives are, in conjunction with the Biodiversity Convention, the conservation and sustainable use of plant genetic resources for food and agriculture and ensuring the equitable sharing of benefits resulting from their utilisation.[100] The treaty may be defined as a living instrument, as the definition of 'plant genetic resources for food and agriculture' includes 'any genetic material of plant origin of actual *or potential* value' (emphasis added).[101] The number of species that fall within its scope will therefore continue to grow as scientific research discovers new plants and new agricultural uses for plants. This flexibility is a key strength of the PGRT and marks it out from other conservation instruments that limit their remit to lists of species contained in what are often outdated, inaccurate and insufficient annexes and appendices.[102] The exception in the PGRT regime is the Multilateral System for access and benefit-sharing, the application of which

94 FAO Resolution 8/83, 23 November 1983. Elaborated through Resolutions 4/89, Agreed Interpretation of the International Undertaking, 29 November 1989 and Resolution 5/89, Farmers' Rights, 29 November 1989.

95 Articles 8(j) 15. These provisions were expanded by the 2010 Nagoya Protocol. Although a more robust regime than the Biodiversity Convention, the Nagoya Protocol can be criticised for failing to distinguish between different types of user of genetic resources. See further Amos (n 20) 221–223.

96 P. Sands and J. Peel, *Principles of International Environmental Law* (4th edn, CUP, 2018) 425.

97 See ch 2.

98 J. Santilli, *Agrobiodiversity and the Law* (Earthscan, 2012) 119.

99 Amos (n 20) 25.

100 Article 1.

101 Article 2.

102 Amos (n 20) 66–76.

is limited to those species in Annex I.[103] Frison is critical of this, arguing that the Annex is too restricted,[104] but in my view it is a pragmatic approach. It ensures that there is clarity over the species to which states are legally obliged to ensure fair access. Additionally, the criticism that outdated lists means that conservation action is not targeted at the species most in need of protection does not apply to Annex I of the PGRT, as this is not a list of endangered species.

The PGRT is structured in seven parts. The focus of our discussion in this chapter will be on Part II (General Provisions), as this is most relevant to conservation and where we can identify the greatest space in which different aspects of the agroecology agenda can be pursued.[105] Conservation is primarily addressed in Article 5. Like other instruments, the PGRT distinguishes between in situ and ex situ conservation, although there is some debate over how on-farm conservation fits into this. It has been argued that on-farm conservation qualifies as in situ conservation because it occurs in a (semi) natural setting, but this is not necessarily compatible with the typical understanding that in situ conservation refers to conservation in the wild.[106] Although in practice this may just be a question of semantics, how on-farm conservation is defined could carry implications. There is a suggested hierarchy in conservation action in the Biodiversity Convention, with ex situ conservation labelled as only 'complementing' in situ action.[107] This is despite growing recognition that in situ and ex situ activities are equally important components of successful conservation projects.[108] De Boef does not even apply the label of 'conservation' to on-farm activities, preferring instead to use 'management' as a better reflection of the human and ecological processes that underpin agriculture.[109]

Article 5 lists the conservation activities that states are encouraged to take. States are called on to develop an inventory of plant genetic resources for food and agriculture, including species of potential use, taking into account the status of and variation in existing populations. Understanding the identity of target species and their current status is an important first step in any conservation strategy, made more difficult in the case of plants due to the relatively common practice, at least compared to animals, of reclassifying species and subspecies following new genetic research, but note must again be made of the potential risk in prioritising

103 PGRT, Part IV. See ch 2.

104 C. Frison, *Redesigning the Global Seed Commons: Law and Policy for Agrobiodiversity and Food Security* (Routledge, 2018) 196–197.

105 The other parts of the PGRT are: I (Introduction); III (Farmers' Rights); IV (The Multilateral System of Access and Benefit-Sharing); V (Supporting Components); VI (Financial Provisions); and VII (Institutional Provisions). Dispute settlement is covered by Annex II. See Santilli (n 98) 118–148 and H. Cooper, 'The International Treaty on Plant Genetic Resources for Food and Agriculture' (2002) 11 *Review of European Community and International Environmental Law* 1.

106 Santilli (n 98) 127.

107 Article 9.

108 Amos (n 20) 205–206.

109 W. de Boef, *Tales of the Unpredictable: Learning about Institutional Frameworks that Support Farmer Management of Agrobiodiversity* (Wageningen University, 2000) cited in Santilli (n 98) 127.

the surveying of species over their actual conservation. Article 5.1(a) can also be criticised for only asking states to assess the threats to plant genetic resource for food and agriculture where this is 'feasible'. Similarly, Article 5.2 requires states to, 'as appropriate', eliminate or otherwise minimise threats to plant genetic resources for food and agriculture, but nothing in the PGRT identifies what these threats might be or the type of responses that might be appropriate.[110]

Articles 5.1(b), (e) and (f) provide a framework for ex situ conservation. (b) asks states to promote the collection of plant genetic resources for food and agriculture and information relevant to those that are under threat or of potential use. Article 5.1(d) calls on them to cooperate in the development of an 'efficient and sustainable' system of ex situ conservation, including the development and sharing of technologies that would improve the sustainable use of plant genetic resources, and (f) requires states to monitor the 'viability, degree of variation, and the genetic integrity' of ex situ collections. This last point is particularly important, as it answers concerns raised in relation to other ex situ collections that the material being stored is no longer viable for reintroduction purposes.[111] The proper management of ex situ collections should be considered an important element of an agroecological legal framework. It can help to ensure the diversity of systems by allowing for the reintroduction of species that are lost. Ex situ collections also support socio-ecological networks. They constitute a recognition of how humanity's impacts are undermining the integrity of agriculture's natural resource base and are one insurance policy against this.

In comparison, the measures that directly address on-farm and in situ conservation are vague and brief but still serve to support socioecological networks. Article 5.1(c) encourages states to 'promote or support', again 'as appropriate', the on-farm conservation efforts of farmers and local communities. Similarly, subparagraph (d) requires states to 'promote' in situ conservation of 'wild crop relatives and wild plants for food production' by supporting indigenous and local communities. These measures are reinforced by Part III of the PGRT, which addresses farmers' rights. According to Article 9, these rights include the protection of relevant traditional knowledge and the right to participate in decisions relating to the conservation and sustainable use of plant genetic resources for food and agriculture.[112]

Turning to sustainable use, Article 6.1 states that the Contracting Parties 'shall develop and maintain appropriate policy and legal measures that promote the sustainable use of plant genetic resources for food and agriculture'. This is followed by a non-exhaustive list of measures, including promoting diversity in farming systems and improving the genetic diversity of plant varieties used in agriculture. Particularly relevant in terms of agroecology is Article 6.2(c), which calls on states

110 Although see Bélanger and Pilling (n 1) ch 3.

111 N. Krigas and others, 'Analysis of the *Ex Situ* Conservation of the Greek Endemic Flora at National, European and Global Scales and of Its Effectiveness in Meeting GSPC Target 8' (2016) 150 *Plant Biosystems* 573.

112 See ch 2.

to promote the breeding of plant varieties that are 'adapted to social, economic and ecological conditions'. The social element of this is an important reflection of the cultural diversity of human actors in socioecological networks and, as I explore in chapter 12, relevant to discussions of food justice.

These provisions are complemented by Part II of the PGRT. This addresses international cooperation and technical assistance, particularly for developing states and states with economies in transition, in ensuring the conservation and sustainable use of plant genetic resources for food and agriculture. These measures are not just about maximising agricultural productivity, but doing so sustainably, and so, as with certain elements of the Biodiversity Convention's programme of work on agricultural biodiversity, provide a wider policy and institutional framework through which agroecology can be delivered at the international level.

To summarise, the PGRT contains clear space in which agroecological approaches can be pursued at the international level. Of particular note is the importance attached to supporting ex situ conservation measures. However, the treaty still falls short of providing a sufficiently robust framework for conservation. Like the Biodiversity Convention, its provisions are qualified by discretionary terms and references to national legislation and so the PGRT is incapable of compelling states to take actions necessary to prevent the continuing decline in agrobiodiversity loss.

## Conclusions

The conservation of agrobiodiversity is a prerequisite to the successful implementation of agroecological approaches to the regulation and practice of sustainable agriculture. As numerous reports show, states' efforts to protect this diversity have failed. The reasons why are evident when we analyse two important conservation regimes: the Biodiversity Convention and the PGRT.

With regard to the Biodiversity Convention, it is well-established that it lacks sufficiently strong obligations. Consequently, although the programme of work on agricultural biodiversity reflects core elements of agroecology, including the importance of recognising and respecting local and indigenous agricultural practices, it has not delivered the necessary actions at the national level to halt and reverse declines in agrobiodiversity. Adopting a sustainable agriculture protocol could go some way in addressing this concern, notwithstanding the practical difficulties associated with this and the risks in explicitly linking conservation obligations to whether a species contributes to human endeavours. It is concerning, therefore, that the Global Biodiversity Framework broadly adopts the same approach of setting non-binding global targets that have consistently failed to protect biodiversity.

The PRGT, one of the most important conservation instruments overseen by the FAO, again reflects key aspects of agroecology but also lacks legally binding obligations so that these aspects can be delivered in practice. Unless and until the international community fundamentally alters its approach, agrobiodiversity will continue to decline and the potential of agroecology to deliver sustainable agriculture will be limited.

# 2 Monocultures and Genetic Diversity

## The Rise of the Monoculture

The previous chapter was concerned with measures in international law to protect agrobiodiversity primarily at the species and ecosystem levels. This is not enough, however, to support the ecological integrity of agricultural systems or the wider natural world. It is also necessary to maintain sufficient genetic diversity *within* species to enable their continuing evolution, as well as to ensure the health and integrity of wider ecological systems.

Traditionally, the genetic diversity of crops has been maintained by farmers carefully selecting varieties of plants that have shown characteristics that lend themselves to the ecological conditions of the region. It is believed that 6,000 species have been cultivated for agricultural purposes, but today only 200 are widely produced at the global level, with just nine accounting for two-thirds of all crop production.[1] By itself, this would be concerning, but research suggests that diversity within these species has also fallen dramatically.[2] A 1996 report by the Food and Agriculture Organisation (FAO) noted that in the United States, 91% of field maize varieties had been lost during the course of the 20th century, along with 86% of apple varieties, 95% of cabbage varieties, 94% of peas and 81% of tomatoes. Similar losses in genetic material are predicted to have occurred in other countries.[3] In a second report, published in 2010, there was insufficient data to reach any firm conclusions on how on-farm diversity has changed since the first report,[4] but crop and crop genetic diversity were estimated to have further declined.[5]

Principal causes of the fall in crop and crop genetic diversity can be traced to the post-war period of the mid-20th century. To provide enough food to rapidly growing

1 FAO, *The State of the World's Biodiversity for Food and Agriculture* (FAO Commission on Genetic Resources for Food and Agriculture, 2019) 114.

2 There are similar issues with diversity in livestock breeds. In 2019, it was estimated that around 40 species provide most of the world's meat, milk and eggs. Of 7,745 locally reported livestock breeds, 594 were considered extinct and just under 1,900 as at risk of extinction – ibid.

3 FAO, *Report on the State of the World's Plant Genetic Resources for Food and Agriculture* (FAO, 1996) 14.

4 FAO, *The Second Report on the State of the World's Plant Genetic Resources for Food and Agriculture* (FAO Commission on Genetic Resources for Food and Agriculture Assessments, 2010) 4.

5 ibid.

DOI: 10.4324/9781003435174-4

populations, deliberate efforts were made to encourage farmers to grow genetically uniform monocultures of a small number of high-yielding crop varieties, in place of their locally grown and genetically diverse varieties. The success of these endeavours was labelled as 'the Green Revolution'.[6] This coincided with calls by European commercial plant breeders for intellectual property rights (IPRs) to be granted over plant varieties, as they recognised the economic potential of these more efficient crops.[7]

Alongside the collapse in the number of cultivated crops has been a reduction in the number of commercial plant breeders. The lack of competition between the world's seed producers raises prices for farmers, and consequently the end-users of farming products, reduces the choice of farmers when selecting what seeds to grow and, contrary to the views expressed by proponents of the mergers between these companies,[8] disincentivises innovation.[9] In addition to disadvantaging consumers, the reduction in innovation due to the absence of competitive pressure also carries implications for the genetic diversity of the world's crops. The IPRs that a few global corporations hold over the majority of seed varieties restrict the free use and exchange of seed that has underpinned the natural evolution of crop species and enabled farmers to maintain the genetic health of their crops and the wider agro-ecosystems.

I begin this chapter by considering the risks that monocultures pose to agri- and ecological systems through an analysis of how international law responds to invasive/alien species (IAS) and disease. As with many areas of the law, the agroecological merit of regimes designed to address these threats is mixed and so important reforms can be identified. Attention then turns to rules concerning IPRs over crop varieties. We will trace the development of the law in this area in relation to the respective rights of commercial plant breeders and farmers to utilise seed and the implications of this for the advancement of agroecology in international law. Finally, the protection of local and traditional agricultural knowledge is discussed. An important premise of this work is that enhancing the sustainability of agricultural systems, through the application of agroecology, is as dependent on diversity of culture as it is on diversity of nature. Protecting the knowledge base that underpins different agricultural practices and 'ways of doing' is therefore essential.

## Invasive/Alien Species and Disease

There is sufficient evidence to conclude that the Green Revolution delivered on its aims of improving productivity and food security in the short term.[10] The dramatic

6 C. Frison, *Redesigning the Global Seed Commons: Law and Policy for Agrobiodiversity and Food Security* (Routledge, 2018) 8.

7 J. Santilli, *Agrobiodiversity and the Law: Regulating Genetic Resources, Food Security and Cultural Diversity* (Routledge, 2012) 77.

8 Cited in S. Mahoney, 'Owning the World's Seed Supply: How Seed Industry Mergers Threaten Global Food Security' (2019) 31 *Georgetown Environmental Law Review* 564, 564.

9 A. Douglas, 'Agribusiness and Antitrust: The Bayer–Monsanto Merger, Its Legality, and Its Effect on the United States and European Union' (2018) 7 *Global Business Law Review* 156.

10 R. Evenson and D. Gollin, 'Assessing the Impact of the Green Revolution, 1960 to 2000' (2003) 300 *Science* 758, 761.

rise in monoculture plantations, however, has come at a severe and increasing ecological cost.

One of the most concerning issues relating to monocultures is their vulnerability to IAS and disease. Resilience is one of the key benefits of diversity, with diverse systems better able to cope with and recover from disturbances, such as the introduction of an IAS, than less-diverse systems.[11] The risks of over-reliance on monocultures are evident when we examine the 19th century Irish potato famine. In the mid-1800s, around 90% of Ireland's population was dependent on genetically uniform potato plantations. When the pathogen, *Phytophthora infestans*, was introduced, it was able to quickly spread throughout the plantations, ruining most of the crops over several years.[12] The resulting famine is estimated to have led to the deaths of approximately a quarter of Ireland's population and forced many others to emigrate.[13] This is a useful illustration of the connections between the ecological and social aspects of the networks that underpin agriculture. In this case, the absence of diversity not only destroyed the livelihoods of Irish farmers but had catastrophic impacts on the health and economy of wider society as well.

The growing prevalence of monocultures means that global food networks are becoming more vulnerable to threats such as *Phytophthora infestans*. Due to the transnational nature of food supply chains, international law has an important role to play in responding to those threats. I have examined international law's approach to IAS and plant diseases extensively elsewhere and so provide only a summary here.[14]

IAS are addressed by multiple international bodies, the principal ones in terms of agriculture being the FAO and the Convention on Biological Diversity.[15] The FAO administers the 1997 International Plant Protection Convention (IPPC),[16] a phytosanitary agreement that aims to secure 'common and effective action to prevent the spread and introduction of pests of plants and plant products and to promote appropriate measures for their control'.[17] 'Plants' are defined by the IPPC as 'living plants and parts thereof, including seeds and germplasm', while 'plant

11 E. Brown Weiss, 'Intergenerational Equity: A Legal Framework for Global Environmental Change', in E. Brown Weiss (ed), *Environmental Change and International Law: New Challenges and Dimensions* (UN University Press, 1992) 402. See also M. Harm Benson and R. Kundis Craig, *The End of Sustainability: Resilience and the Future of Environmental Governance in the Anthropocene* (University of Kansas Press, 2017) Ch 3.

12 The origins of the pathogen are unclear, but research suggests that it originated in Mexico – E. Goss and others, 'The Irish Potato Famine Pathogen *Phytophthora infestans* Originated in Central Mexico Rather than the Andes' (2014) 111 *Proceedings of the National Academy of Sciences* 8791.

13 Santilli (n 7) 15–16.

14 R. Amos, *International Conservation Law: The Protection of Plants in Theory and Practice* (Routledge, 2020) ch 8.

15 Rio de Janeiro, 5 June 1992, in force 29 December 1993, 31 ILM 822 (1992).

16 In force 2 October 2005, amending the 1951 Convention (Rome, 6 December 1951, in force 3 April 1952, 150 UNTS 67, as revised by the FAO Conference in 1979). Text available at: https://www.ippc.int/en/core-activities/governance/convention-text/ (last accessed 20/04/2023).

17 IPPC, Article I(1).

products' are 'unmanufactured material of plant origin (including grain) and those manufactured products that, by their nature or that of their processing, may create a risk for the introduction and spread of pests'.[18] These are suitably wide definitions covering both crops and crop products. 'Pest' is similarly broadly defined as 'any species, strain or biotype of plants, animal or pathogenic agent injurious to plants or plant products'.

The flaw in the IPPC from an ecological perspective is the type of pests against which states may impose phytosanitary measures. States may only require phytosanitary measures for quarantine and regulated non-quarantine pests,[19] not for all pests, and how the IPPC defines these is problematic. A quarantine pest is 'a pest of *potential economic importance* to the area endangered thereby and not yet present there, or present but not widely distributed and being officially controlled', and a regulated non-quarantine pest is 'a non-quarantine pest whose presence in plants for planting affects the intended use of those plants with an *economically unacceptable impact* and which is therefore regulated within the territory of the importing contracting party' (emphasis added). In other words, only pests that present a risk of economic damage may be subject to phytosanitary measures under the IPPC.

It might be argued that despite this restriction, the IPPC is a useful instrument when it comes to controlling agricultural pests. Any pest that is a threat to agriculture clearly poses a risk of economic harm and so would be a legitimate target under the IPPC for phytosanitary measures. This does not reflect the idea of the farm as only one element in a socioecological network, however. It is possible that a pest, although not a danger to a farm's crops, is a threat to the wildflowers that the farmer leaves growing along the boundaries of their fields. The direct economic impact of this pest may be questionable. However, the devastation of the wildflowers following the introduction of the pest would go on to impact other elements in the socioecological network, including (agro)biodiversity and then the farmer. The populations of insects that the farmer relies on to pollinate their crops could collapse with the disappearance of the wildflowers, for example.

Turning to the Biodiversity Convention, IAS have been an area of concern since the treaty's adoption in 1992, with Article 8(h) calling on states, 'as far as possible and as appropriate', to 'Prevent the introduction of, control or eradicate those alien species which threaten ecosystem, habitats or species'.[20] Immediately, it is clear that the Biodiversity Convention goes beyond the purely economic focus of the IPPC. Article 8(h) has since been elaborated by the Convention's Subsidiary Body on Scientific, Technical and Technological Advice, which, in 2002, adopted the

18 IPPC, Article II.

19 IPPC, Article VI.

20 See also Decision IV/1, Report and recommendations of the third meeting of the Subsidiary Body on Scientific, Technical and Technological Advice and Instructions by the Conservation of the Party to the Subsidiary Body on Scientific, Technical and Technological Advice, UNEP/CBD/COP/DEC/IV/1, 1998.

Guiding Principles for the Prevention, Introduction and Mitigation of Impacts of Alien Species that Threaten Ecosystems, Habitats or Species.[21]

The Guiding Principles, central to which are the precautionary and ecosystem approaches (Guiding Principles 1 and 5), first call on states to prevent the introduction and spread of IAS through border controls and quarantine measures (Guiding Principle 7). Where preventative measures fail, the first response that should be considered under the Guiding Principles is eradication (Guiding Principle 13). If this is not feasible, for example because detecting and simultaneously destroying all of the IAS populations is impossible,[22] then states should contain the outbreak (Guiding Principle 14), or otherwise control the spread and impact of the IAS (Guiding Principle 15). That intentional introductions are permitted under the Guiding Principles, subject to appropriate authorisation and a risk assessment (Guiding Principle 10), is concerning; primarily because the impacts of IAS on the health of affected ecosystems can be extreme, but also because the inevitable unpredictability in introducing an alien species into an ecosystem means that the intended result may never be achieved.[23]

From an agroecological perspective, the Guiding Principles are generally sound. Permitting the intentional introduction of species is concerning, given the potential risks, but subjecting this to authorisation and risk assessment is a pragmatic approach. Any risk assessment should reflect a systems-level approach so that the full extent of the likely impacts of the alien species can be understood. There are also wider concerns over the efficacy of the Biodiversity Convention's approach to IAS, confirmed by the Fifth Global Biodiversity Outlook's conclusion that despite localised successes in eradicating IAS, rates of new outbreaks remain unchanged.[24] As such, an argument can be made for IAS to be the subject of a new protocol to the Convention that imposes stronger obligations regarding the detection and control of IAS, intentional introductions and capacity-building for developing states.[25] This would also respond to the criticism that the Biodiversity Convention lacks binding rules on the key drivers of biodiversity loss.[26]

In contrast to the extensive work on IAS, little has been done under the Biodiversity Convention on legal responses to the spread of disease.[27] This may be because disease, although a contributory factor in specific cases, is not considered to be a leading driver of extinction.[28] An important step would be establishing a

21 Decision VI/23, Alien species that threaten ecosystems, habitats or species, UNEP/CBD/COP/DEC/VI/23, 2002, Annex.

22 E.g., J. Beggs and others, 'The Difficulty of Reducing Introduced Wasps (*Vespula vulgaris*) Populations for Conservation Gains' (1998) 22 *New Zealand Journal of Ecology* 55.

23 S. Riley, 'Heads I Win, Tails You Lose: Uncertainty and the Protection of Biodiversity from Invasive Alien Species' (2011) 14 *Asia Pacific Journal of Environmental Law* 139.

24 Secretariat to the Convention on Biological Diversity, *Global Biodiversity Outlook 5* (2020) 74–77.

25 Amos (n 14) 173–174.

26 ibid 171.

27 ibid 188.

28 K. Smith and others, 'Evidence for the Role of Infectious Disease in Species Extinction and Endangerment' (2006) 20 *Conservation Biology* 1349.

programme of work to examine the nature and extent of the threat that disease currently poses to biodiversity, both generally and agricultural crops specifically, with a view to determining whether this is a suitable subject for a new protocol to the Convention, or is more appropriately addressed through pre-existing mechanisms that target other causes of biodiversity loss.[29]

## Intellectual Property Rights and Crop Genetic Diversity

Given the weaknesses in international legal response mechanisms to IAS and disease, it is essential that ecological safeguards are developed so that agricultural systems, and their natural and human components, can withstand a biological invasion. The difficulty is that the law has developed in such a way as to frustrate farmers in continuing their central role in building these safeguards, through the expansion of IPRs to varieties of crop plants.

The purpose of IPRs is to incentivise innovation by permitting inventors to temporarily enjoy a monopoly over new and novel products. The same theory applies in agriculture: the granting of exclusive rights to produce and sell new seeds incentivises plant breeders to continually produce varieties, thereby increasing crop diversity. This, however, ignores the critical role farmers have played in this regard since the first humans began cultivating crops, irrespective of any economic incentive.[30] In other words, the application of IPRs to crop varieties illustrates the law's failure to understand that farms pursue activities for purposes of self-renewal and the reinforcement of their distinct logics and philosophies.[31]

### *The Convention for the Protection of New Varieties of Plants*

The demands of European plant breeders for IPRs over plant varieties resulted in the 1961 Convention for the Protection of New Varieties of Plants (UPOV Convention),[32] which is overseen by the International Union for the Protection of New Varieties of Plants, established in the same year. The UPOV Convention has undergone several revisions to reflect advances in plant breeding technology, the most recent being the 1991 Act of the Convention.[33]

Prior to the adoption of the UPOV Convention, the principal instrument for protecting intellectual property in plant varieties was the United States' Patent Act 1930. European plant breeders wanted to establish a *sui generis*, i.e. unique,

29 Amos (n 14) 188–189.

30 Santilli (n 7) 77–78.

31 E. Noe and H. Alrøe, 'Regulation of Agroecosystems: A Social Systems Analysis of Agroecology and Law', in M. Monteduro and others (eds), *Law and Agroecology: A Transdisciplinary Dialogue* (Springer, 2015) 39.

32 Brussels, 2 December 1961, in force 10 August 1968, 15 UNTS 89.

33 Unless otherwise stated, all references to the UPOV Convention in this chapter are to the 1991 Act. Note that a small number of states are still bound by the 1978 Act – https://www.upov.int/edocs/pubdocs/en/upov_pub_423.pdf (last accessed 20/04/2023).

system, however, due to the limitations of such patent laws. Under patent law, any new plant variety that incorporates a patented variety requires the original breeder's consent to produce and market that new variety. In contrast, under an IPR mechanism, if Breeder A utilises genetic material that is the intellectual property of Breeder B to create a new plant variety and that variety is clearly distinguishable from Breeder B's variety, Breeder A does not need Breeder B's consent to produce and distribute their new variety. In other words, a *sui generis* IPR system protects the incentive for innovators by maintaining their exclusivity over their specific invention but still maximises the accessibility of genetic material for other plant breeders so that they can make their own contributions to genetic diversity.[34]

To be eligible for protection under the UPOV Convention, a plant variety must be new, distinct, uniform and stable.[35] The definitions of these are contained in Articles 6 to 9 of the Convention, and although they appear straightforward, their application has proven controversial. Seed produced by farmers that is adapted to local conditions struggles to meet the UPOV criteria. They rarely demonstrate sufficient uniformity across generations, for example. Most seed available on the market is therefore that which is produced by commercial plant breeders. Not only does this reduce genetic diversity, as commercially produced seed is genetically uniform, it can undermine the food security of communities that rely on seed that is adapted to grow in the unique ecological conditions of their region.[36]

The scope of the plant breeder's right in the UPOV Convention is set out in Article 14 and affords significant protection to plant breeders. Article 14(1)(a) subjects, inter alia, the propagation and sale of protected breeds to the authorisation of the breeder. The same applies to harvested material of the variety and any product made from such harvested material.[37] Note that this is not an exhaustive list and states are free to add to it when implementing the Convention.[38]

Exceptions to the plant breeder's rights are contained in Article 15. There are two parts to Article 15, the first of which deals with mandatory exceptions for which the contracting parties must provide:

(1) The breeder's right shall not extend to
 (i) acts done privately and for non-commercial purposes,
 (ii) acts done for experimental purposes and
 (iii) acts done for the purpose of breeding other varieties, and, except where the provisions of Article 14(5) apply, acts referred to in Article 14(1) to (4) in respect of such other varieties.

34 Santilli (n 7) 79.

35 UPOV Convention, Article 5. 'Variety' is defined in botanical terms by Article 1 of the Convention. See also UPOV Council, *Explanatory Notes on the Definition of Variety under the 1991 Act of the UPOV Convention*, UPOV/EXN/VAR/1, 21 October 2010.

36 Mahoney (n 8) 575–576.

37 UPOV Convention, Articles 14(2) and (3).

38 UPOV Convention, Article 14(4).

On first reading, this appears to maintain the freedom of plant breeders to utilise varieties produced by other breeders when creating their own varieties. However, the scope of the freedom enjoyed by plant breeders is curtailed by Article 14(5), which states that the plant breeder's right, as defined in Article 14(1)(a), also applies to varieties that are 'essentially derived from the protected variety'. 'Essentially derived' is defined by Article 15(b) as:

(i) [the new variety] is predominately derived from the initial variety, or from a variety that is itself predominately derived from the initial variety, while retaining the expression of the essential characteristics that result from the genotype or combination of genotypes of the initial variety,
(ii) it is clearly distinguishable from the initial variety and
(iii) except for the differences which result from the act of deviation, it conforms to the initial variety in the expression of the essential characteristics that result from the genotype or combination of genotypes of the initial variety.

The purposes of Article 14(5) were to ensure that the UPOV system rewarded substantial plant breeding efforts and to prevent breeders from effecting the most minimal of changes to a variety by inserting a single new gene and then securing commercial rights over what is essentially the same as a variety that has been produced by another breeder.[39] Initially, there was confusion over the level of genetic differentiation that was needed before a new variety could be said to fall outside the meaning of 'essentially derived'.[40] In response, additional guidance was published in 2017, which states that a variety should be considered to be essentially derived from another variety 'when it retains virtually the whole genotype of the other variety'.[41] The guidance goes on to note that 'A derived variety could not, in practice, retain the expression of the essential characteristics of the variety from which it is derived unless it is almost entirely derived from the initial variety', with 'essential characteristics' being broadly defined in relation to the genetic, biological and ecological traits of varieties, as well as traits that make them economically valuable to the initial breeder.[42] This indicates that a variety must be virtually identical in all its important features to be considered 'essentially derived' from another variety.

The second part of the Article 15 exceptions to plant breeders' rights is optional, i.e. states may choose to provide for it but are under no obligation to do so:

39 Santilli (n 7) 92–93.

40 J. Cubero, 'The Point of View of a Plant Breeder on the International Treaty on Plant Genetic Resources for Food and Agriculture', in C. Frison and others (eds), *Plant Genetic Resources and Food Security: Stakeholder Perspectives on the International Treaty on Plant Genetic Resources for Food and Agriculture* (Routledge, 2011) 199.

41 UPOV Council, *Explanatory Notes on Essentially Derived Varieties under the 1991 Act of the UPOV Convention*, UPOV/EXN/EDV/2, 6 April 2017, 5.

42 ibid 5–6.

(2) Notwithstanding Article 14, each Contracting Party may, within reasonable limits and subject to the safeguarding of the legitimate interests of the breeder, restrict the breeder's right in relation to any variety in order to permit farmers to use for propagating purposes, on their own holdings, the product of the harvest which they have obtained by planting, on their own holdings, the protected variety covered by Article 14(5)(a)(i) or (ii).

This reflects the so-called farmer's exception, or farmer's right, to IPRs over plant varieties. It has long been accepted that farmers routinely save seed from harvests to resow in subsequent years, as well as exchange seeds with other farmers to promote genetic diversity within the overall crop species, thereby improving the health and resilience of their own plantings.[43] This practice was implicitly accounted for in earlier versions of the UPOV Convention, which restricted plant breeders' rights to the commercial utilisation of protected varieties. Non-commercial use of a protected variety, as indicated in Article 15(1)(i), is not subject to the breeder's authorisation and farmers saving and exchanging seed to use on their own land was widely considered to qualify as non-commercial. The inclusion of the farmer's right in the 1991 Act might be considered a welcome development in that it creates a clear legal basis for this. However, Article 15(2) expressly limits farmers to saving seed and replanting it on their own land. Exchanges between farmers are not permissible. The UPOV Convention consequently shatters the socioecological connections between farmers, undermines crop diversity and limits the space in which agroecology can be pursued at the international level. Cubero argues that it is not in farmers' interests to continually save and reuse seed from the same variety because varietal degeneration means that the overall health of the crop will gradually deteriorate. They should instead regularly acquire new seeds from 'official' seed producers.[44] In the narrow context of Article 15(2), this argument is valid but also serves to demonstrate the extent to which agricultural plant breeding has been captured by commercial entities. The problem is not farmers making excessive use of their exception to IPR rules, but rather the unnecessarily restrictive interpretation of this exception in the UPOV Convention. Reaffirming farmers' right to exchange seed on a non-commercial basis would allow for a level of genetic diversity to be developed within crops that would reduce the risk of varietal degeneration.

Permitting the non-commercial exchange of seed between farmers should be considered an essential step in facilitating the creation of greater genetic diversity in crops and a prerequisite to advancing agroecology in this area of the law. A model for this reform can be found in India's Protection of Plant Varieties and Farmers' Rights Act 2001, section 39(iv) of which states, 'a farmer shall be deemed to be entitled to save, use, sow, resow, exchange, share or sell his farm produce

43 J. Posada, 'Intellectual Property Rights: New Approach Supporting Farmers' Rights' (2016) 9 *International In-house Counsel Journal* 1, 2–3.

44 Cubero (n 40) 199.

*including seed of a variety protected under this Act...*' (emphasis added).[45] The 2001 Act is considered to strike the right balance between the interests of farmers (and agrobiodiversity) and plant breeders and is clearly more compatible with principles of agroecology than the UPOV Convention.[46]

### *The Agreement on Trade-Related Aspects of Intellectual Property Rights*

Initially, membership of the UPOV Conventions mostly comprised developed states. The situation changed with the adoption of the 1994 Agreement on Trade-Related Aspects of Intellectual Property Rights[47] (the TRIPS Agreement) as a principal instrument of the World Trade Organisation (WTO).[48] Many developing states opposed the inclusion of IPRs in the WTO's remit during the Uruguay round of negotiations, instead preferring to leave the World Intellectual Property Organisation (WIPO), the activities of which are discussed below, as the leading international IPR body.[49] The reasons for this were twofold. First, innovation is rarely central to developing states' economies. It is therefore a legitimate policy choice for them to promote the social and economic welfare of their citizens by having more relaxed IPR rules that facilitate the production of cheaper domestic copies of innovations developed elsewhere.[50] Second, that multiple trading issues are addressed simultaneously during the WTO negotiating process meant that block-voting, which is the norm for developing states in WIPO, is less feasible. Their overall negotiating position on international IPR rules is consequently weaker than it would be if they had remained outside the purview of the WTO.[51] Through concessions and the threat of sanctions, however, developing states acquiesced to IPRs forming part of the WTO's remit.[52]

Under Article 27(1) of the TRIPS Agreement, states must provide for patents 'for any invention, whether products or processes, in all fields of technology, provided that they are new, involve an inventive step and are capable of industrial application'. This dramatically increased the scope of international rules on

45 There are limitations on farmers' right to sell seed of protected varieties, but these are nowhere near as restrictive on farmers as the UPOV Convention and are less controversial because this is more likely to be for a commercial purpose.

46 Posada (n 43) 6.

47 Marrakesh, 15 April 1994, in force 1 January 1995, 33 ILM 81 (1994).

48 Santilli (n 7) 81–82.

49 P. Roffe, 'Bringing Minimum Global Intellectual Property Standards into Agriculture: The Agreement on Trade-Related Aspects of Intellectual Property Rights (TRIPS)', in G. Tansey and T. Rajotte (eds), *The Future Control of Food: A Guide to International Negotiations and Rules on Intellectual Property, Biodiversity and Food Security* (Routledge, 2008) 50.

50 M. Trebilcock and others, *The Regulation of International Trade* (4th edn, Routledge, 2013) 516–517.

51 Santilli (n 7) 81–82.

52 R. Andersen, *Governing Agrobiodiversity: Plant Genetics and Developing Countries* (Ashgate, 2008) 150.

patents, which previously allowed states to exclude certain sectors.[53] There are certain exceptions to this general obligation, however, including Article 27(3):

> Members may also exclude from patentability:
>
> (b) plants and animals other than micro-organisms, and essentially biological processes for the production of plants and animals other than non-biological and microbiological processes. However, Members shall provide for the protection of plant varieties either by patents or by an effective *sui generis* system or by any combination thereof…[54]

Although the TRIPS Agreement does not describe what would constitute an 'effective *sui generis*' system, the UPOV Convention is widely held to be the model *sui generis* system.[55] It is not compulsory to implement the UPOV Convention, however. As noted above, India has devised its own *sui generis* system that provides for a more generous, and agroecologically appropriate, farmers' right to use and exchange the seed of protected varieties. Additionally, states party to the African Regional Intellectual Property Organisation have adopted the Arusha Protocol for the Protection of New Plant Varieties under the Framework of the African Regional Intellectual Property Organisation.[56] In terms of the farmer's right, however, this closely follows the UPOV Convention in that it restricts farmers to saving and reusing seed on their own land,[57] leading Kabau and Cheruiyot to conclude that the Protocol is insufficient to protect some of the world's poorest farmers.[58]

### ***Reasserting Farmers' Rights in International Law***

Over the past few decades, there has been growing recognition of the need to protect what remains of agriculture's genetic resource base and to reinforce farmers' role in this endeavour.[59] As we saw in chapter 1, the International Treaty on Plant Genetic Resources for Food and Agriculture (PGRT)[60] contains reasonably comprehensive, if qualified, provisions concerning the conservation and sustainable

53 Santilli (n 7) 82.

54 See also Article 27(2), which allows patents to be refused on '*ordre public* and morality' grounds, including for environmental purposes.

55 Andersen (n 52) 146.

56 Adopted 6 July 2015 (not in force). Text available at: https://www.aripo.org/wp-content/uploads/2018/12/Arusha-Protocol_20181.pdf (last accessed 20/04/2023).

57 Arusha Protocol, Article 22(2).

58 T. Kabau and F. Cheruiyot, 'The Arusha Protocol on Plant Varieties Protection: Balancing Breeders' and Farmers' Rights for Food Security in Africa' (2019) 9 *Queen Mary Journal of Intellectual Property* 303. See also P. Munyi and others, 'Opportunities and Threats to Harmonisation of Plant Breeders' Rights in Africa: ARIPO and SADC' (2016) 24 *African Journal of International and Comparative Law* 86.

59 FAO (n 4) Ch 1.

60 Rome, 3 November 2001, in force 29 June 2004. Text available at: https://www.fao.org/plant-treaty/overview/texts-treaty/en/ (last accessed 20/04/2023).

use of plant genetic resources. The emphasis of Article 6 is protecting and supporting farmers in their role as creators and users of crop genetic diversity. Article 6.2(b) recommends that states strengthen research that seeks to maximise intra- and inter-species variation 'for the benefit of farmers, especially those who generate and use their own varieties', while Article 6.2(d) requires states to promote 'the expanded use of local and locally adapted crops, varieties and underutilised species'. Similarly, Article 6.2(f) suggests that states:

> [support], as appropriate, the wider use of diversity of varieties and species in on-farm management, conservation and sustainable use of crops and [create] strong links to plant breeding and agricultural development in order to reduce crop vulnerability and genetic erosion…

This could be read as a tacit acknowledgement that the role of farmers in creating crop diversity has become too restricted by commercial enterprises' domination of the plant breeding industry; an interpretation that is supported by Article 6.2(g), which proposes that states review and, 'as appropriate', adjust laws concerning variety release and seed distribution. It is regrettable that when negotiating the PGRT, states did not go one step further and include a specific recommendation, if not an obligation, to recognise farmers' right to save and exchange seed, including of protected varieties.

Farmers' rights are specifically addressed in Article 9. Although only a single provision of the PGRT, and one that is heavily qualified even for a conservation instrument, this is nevertheless significant. Article 9.1 recognises 'the enormous contribution that the local indigenous communities and farmers of all regions of the world… have made and will continue to make for the conservation and development of plant genetic resources…'. This reads more as a preambular statement, however, and contains nothing by way of obligation or recommended course of action for states.

The only substantive provision in Article 9 is paragraph 2, which begins by stating that 'The Contracting Parties agree that the responsibility for realising Farmers' Rights, as they relate to plant genetic resources for food and agriculture, rests with national governments'. This is in marked contrast to developed states' efforts, beginning with the UPOV Convention and carried through into the negotiation of the TRIPS Agreement, to ensure that plant breeders' rights were protected at the international level. It goes on to list the types of measures that states may take to protect farmers' rights, including the protection of traditional agricultural knowledge, the right to participate in the sharing of benefits resulting from the utilisation of plant genetic resources and the right to participate in decisions concerning the conservation and sustainable use of plant genetic resources. These touch on an issue that has yet to be addressed in this work: the protection of agriculture's knowledge base. As I argue below, in addition to ensuring a high level of genetic diversity exists within crops, it is also necessary to ensure that local and traditional understandings of agricultural practices, including those relating to plant breeding, are protected.

Although important, particularly from a justice perspective,[61] the rights to participate in benefit-sharing and decision-making have only an indirect bearing on farmers' ability to freely exchange seed to promote crop diversity. This is instead covered in Article 9.3, which states that 'Nothing in this Article shall be interpreted to limit any rights that farmers have to save, use, exchange and sell farm-saved seed/propagating material, subject to national law and as appropriate'. This is important to the extent that it is an explicit recognition in international law that it is legitimate for farmers to exchange seed. Like Article 6.2(g), however, this still falls short of obliging states to expressly permit this activity in the case of protected varieties.

### *The Multilateral System of Access and Benefit-Sharing*

Promoting access to plant genetic resources for food and agriculture is the principal rationale behind the PGRT's Multilateral System of Access and Benefit-Sharing.[62] This is a framework through which the genetic material of certain crop species is made available to interested parties, who share the benefits resulting from their access to these resources through the PGRT mechanism. It is primarily aimed at farmers in developing countries, but any legal or natural entity may request access to the material provided that it is for purposes relating to the conservation and sustainable use of plant genetic resources for food and agriculture.[63] Contracting Parties are required to take the necessary legal and administrative measures to ensure this, as well as to enable natural and legal persons in their jurisdiction to access material held in other Contracting Parties,[64] in accordance with any guidelines published by the PGRT's Governing Body.[65] This recognises the global interdependence of all actors in agricultural socioecological networks, including state and non-state actors, in relation to crop genetic diversity and is consequently an important means through which agroecology can be advanced through the PGRT framework.[66] The genetic resources available in the Multilateral System include

61 P. Cullet, 'Environmental Justice in the Use, Knowledge and Exploitation of Genetic Resources', in J. Ebbesson and P. Okowa (eds), *Environmental Law and Justice in Context* (CUP, 2009).

62 PGRT, Part IV – https://www.fao.org/plant-treaty/areas-of-work/the-multilateral-system/landingmls/en/ (last accessed 20/04/2023).

63 Although Article 12.2 suggests that only persons located in the contracting states can access the Multilateral System, agreements between the PGRT's Governing Body and the International Agricultural Research Centres of the Consultative Group on International Agricultural Research, an FAO stakeholder partnership, make it clear that material can also be made available to parties based in non-contracting states. See G. Moore and E. Frisson, 'International Research Centres: The Consultative Group on International Agricultural Research and the International Treaty on Plant Genetic Resources for Food and Agriculture', in Frison and others (n 40) 158.

64 PGRT, Article 12.2.

65 PGRT, Article 19.3(a) – http://www.fao.org/plant-treaty/areas-of-work/the-multilateral-system/policy-guidance/en/ (last accessed 20/04/2023).

66 World Intellectual Property Organisation, *A Guide to Intellectual Property Issues in Access and Benefit-sharing Agreements* (Geneva: WIPO, 2018) 74–75.

those held in ex situ collections of the International Agricultural Research Centres of the Consultative Group on International Agricultural Research (CGIARs),[67] as well as other relevant international institutions.[68]

The genera and species of crops and other agricultural plants that are covered by the Multilateral System are listed in Annex I of the PGRT. A total of 64 crops are included, accounting for 80% of the world's consumption.[69] This is significant, but there are notable exceptions, including soybean, groundnut and a number of tropical species.[70] The list of crops included in the Annex changed repeatedly during the PGRT's negotiation, at one point being limited to just 12,[71] and it remains open to the Contracting Parties to amend the list by following the procedures set out in Articles 23 and 24 of the PGRT.

Note, also, that only genetic material of varieties that are 'under the management and control of the Contracting Parties and in the public domain' are included in the scope of the Multilateral System.[72] Genetic resources that are in the private sphere, i.e. plant varieties that are subject to IPRs, are not automatically included, although states are committed to encouraging private entities that hold rights over protected varieties to make these available through the Multilateral System.[73]

Conditions for accessing plant genetic resources through the Multilateral System are set out in Article 12.3. As noted above, this may only be granted for the purpose of 'utilisation and conservation for research, breeding and training for food and agricultural, provided that such purpose does not include chemical, pharmaceutical and other non-food/feed industrial uses'.[74] Access shall be expeditious and at minimal cost, if not free.[75] To facilitate this, the PGRT's Governing Body has devised a standard material transfer agreement (SMTA), in accordance with Article 12.4, which is the mandatory form of contract that parties wishing to participate in the Multilateral System must use.[76] The use of a model contract not only harmonises conditions of access and benefit-sharing for all parties seeking to make use of the Multilateral System but also serves to protect those parties, including developing states and local farmers, that may lack the expertise or financial resources to engage in complex legal negotiations with multinational corporations over conditions of access.

67 Moore and Frison (n 63).

68 PGRT, Article 11.5.

69 (n 62).

70 M. Halewood, 'Governing the Management and Use of Pooled Microbial Genetic Resources: Lessons from the Global Crop Commons' (2010) 4 *International Journal of the Commons* 404, 408.

71 E. Lim and M. Halewood, 'Appendix 3: A Short History of the Annex I List', in Tansey and Rajotte, n 57.

72 PGRT, Article 11.2.

73 PGRT, Article 11.3.

74 PGRT, Article 12.3(a). If a crop has multiple food and non-food uses, its inclusion in the Multilateral System will be determined by its importance to food security.

75 PGRT, Article 12.3(b).

76 (n 62).

The parties to an SMTA will be the provider and recipient of the genetic material in question, not the states in which those parties are located. In other words, the SMTA is a contract between non-state legal persons under which the provider agrees to deliver the requested material and the recipient commits to sharing the benefits resulting from their use of that material through the mechanisms of the PGRT. It is therefore a means of connecting different stakeholders in broader socioecological networks. The PGRT Governing Body will designate a representative to act as the third-party beneficiary to any agreement, which responds to the potential problem of the provider of the material having no interest in enforcing the recipient's obligations under an SMTA because they are not a direct beneficiary of the agreement.[77]

Article 13.2 establishes four mechanisms for the sharing of benefits resulting from access to plant genetic resources through the Multilateral System. These benefits should primarily go to or otherwise assist farmers, particularly in developing states.[78] First, the exchange of non-confidential information relating to, inter alia, 'catalogues and inventories, information on technologies, results of technical, scientific and socioeconomic research, including characterisation, evaluation and utilisation, regarding those plants genetic resources…' is facilitated through the Global Information System on Plant Genetic Resources for Food and Agriculture, established under Article 17 of the PGRT. The Global Information System is designed to be a single point of entry for information relating to the conservation and sustainable use of plant genetic resources for food and agriculture. It has developed partnerships with other relevant bodies, including the World Information and Early Warning System on Plant Genetic Resources for Food and Agriculture, an FAO body that plays a leading role in assessing the status of agricultural genetic resources,[79] and the CGIARs.[80]

Second, the Contracting Parties have undertaken to provide access to and ensure the transfer of technology that is created using genetic material accessed through the Multilateral System, particularly to developing states, least developed states and states with economies in transition. This is to be achieved through the relevant thematic groups established under the PGRT, as well as other research partnerships and joint ventures. Related to this is the third benefit-sharing mechanism, capacity-building. The Contracting Parties have agreed to prioritise the establishment of research and education facilities and programmes in developing and least developed states and states with economies in transition and, as far as possible, locating research activities in these states.

77 G. Moore, 'Protecting the Interests of the Multilateral System under the Standard Material Transfer Agreement', in M. Halewood and others (eds), *Crop Genetic Resources as a Global Commons: Challenges in International Law and Governance* (Routledge, 2013).

78 PGRT, Article 13.3.

79 http://www.fao.org/wiews/en/ (last accessed 20/04/2023).

80 See FAO/PGRT, Resolution 3/2015: The Vision and the Programme of Work on the Global Information System, IT/GB-6/15/Res 3.

Finally, monetary and other benefits gained through the commercialisation of products that are plant genetic resources for food and agriculture and incorporate material accessed through the Multilateral System should be paid into the PGRT's Benefit-sharing Fund.[81] The purpose of this is to support projects, especially in developing countries, that relate to the conservation and sustainable use of plant genetic resources. Applications for funding may be made by any governmental or non-governmental organisation that is based in a developing country and, in addition to generally complying with the PGRT's objectives, relate to at least one of the three priority areas identified by the Governing Body:

1. Information exchange, technology transfer and capacity-building;
2. Managing and conserving plant genetic resources on farms; and
3. Sustainable use of plant genetic resources.[82]

In its most recent call for proposals, particular attention was paid to promoting agricultural systems', including agrobiodiversity's, resilience and ability to adapt to climate change.[83] A diverse range of 20 projects, each in a different country, was funded during the fourth project cycle.[84] All these projects advanced multiple aspects of the agroecology agenda. A project in Ethiopia, for example, focused on strengthening the connections between nearly 30 community seedbanks by creating a national platform, allowing for the sharing of best practice between seedbanks in different agroecological zones and improving farmers' access to the seedbanks to diversify local agricultural systems.[85] The fourth project cycle was completed in 2018, but, at the time of writing, a fifth project cycle has yet to be announced. This is unfortunate given the scheme's potential in terms of promoting agroecology in agricultural practice at a time when the challenges posed to farmers in developing countries, particularly in relation to climate change, are increasing.

That the benefits resulting from access to plant genetic resources via the Multilateral System accrue to farmers and the wider international community means that these resources essentially constitute a global commons. This is a radical departure from international law's typical approach to natural resources which, notwithstanding certain developments relating to obligations of sustainable use,

81 Established in accordance with PGRT Article 19.3(f) and administered by the Treaty's Governing Body. See FAO/PGRT, Commentary on Structural Elements for the Development of a Subscription Model/System, IT/OWG-EFMLS-4/15/4, 2 October 2015.

82 FAO/PGRT, The Benefit-Sharing Fund: Crop diversity for food security, ITPGFRA-A16, 1. Available at: http://www.fao.org/plant-treaty/areas-of-work/benefit-sharing-fund/overview/en/ (last accessed 20/04/2023).

83 FAO/PGRT, *Fourth Call for Proposals of the Benefit-sharing Fund* (2017), 2. Available at ibid.

84 http://www.fao.org/plant-treaty/areas-of-work/benefit-sharing-fund/projects-funded/bsf-fourth-cycle/en/ (last accessed 20/04/2023).

85 http://www.fao.org/plant-treaty/areas-of-work/benefit-sharing-fund/projects-funded/bsf-details/en/c/1198833/?iso3=ETH (last accessed 20/04/2023).

remains rooted in the peremptory norm of the permanent sovereignty of states.[86] In terms of advancing agroecology, the commons approach is potentially a more appropriate framework to reflect the interconnections inherent to agriculture's socioecological networks and to deliver agroecology's priority of diversity in agricultural systems.[87] There are certain limitations in the design and operation of both the Multilateral System and its parent treaty that must be overcome to fully realise their potential in this regard, however. Farmers' right to freely save and exchange all plant varieties, regardless of any IPR protection, must be explicitly recognised in the PGRT, as well as the other international agreements discussed in this chapter. The scope of the Multilateral System should also be expanded. While Frison's proposal that the Multilateral System should mirror the PGRT, i.e. cover all plant genetic resources that are of actual or potential value to agriculture,[88] is problematic for practical and political reasons,[89] there are species that are undeniably important to some of the world's poorest and most vulnerable farmers and communities that could be included.

## Protecting Traditional Agricultural Knowledge

Communities around the world have not only developed crops that are attuned to local growing conditions, but unique bodies of local knowledge, grounded in traditional agricultural practices. Protecting this knowledge is as important, due to the emphasis placed by agroecology on the cultural dimensions of agriculture,[90] as protecting the agrobiodiversity that has evolved through its application. To express this another way, agrobiodiversity must be seen as being socially constructed as it represents the continuous culmination of the application of bodies of knowledge that inform and are informed by community practices and experiences.[91]

Alongside this diversity aspect of protecting traditional agricultural knowledge, there is a justice element.[92] The pursuit of justice for indigenous communities is an important objective for international law in its own right but should also be considered an essential element of an agroecological legal framework. The knowledge and practices of these communities contribute to the overall diversity of agriculture's local and global socioecological networks and in that respect are as central

86 Amos (n 14) 11–13.
87 See ch 12.
88 Frison (n 6) 196–197.
89 As noted above, the scope of the Multilateral System was a contentious issue in the negotiation of the PGRT – Lim and Halewood (n 71).
90 F. Caporali, 'History and Development of Agroecology and Theory of Agroecosystems', in Monteduro and others (n 31).
91 P. Street, 'Spaces of Diversity in Diverse Spaces', in J. Holder and C. Harris (eds), *Law and Geography* (OUP, 2003) 330. I do not have space to consider the application of Convention for the Safeguarding of Intangible Cultural Heritage (Paris) 17 October 2003, in force 20 April 2006, 2368 UNTS 3, but this is being increasingly used by states to protect traditional knowledge and practices associated with agriculture – Santilli (n 7) ch 11.
92 I use 'justice' here in a general sense, without applying any specific theory or meaning.

to the sustainability of agriculture and wider human society as ensuring sufficient diversity within and between species and ecosystems.[93]

The respect and protection of indigenous cultures had long been a matter for discussion in international fora, but in 2000 attention turned to the issue of biopiracy, i.e. commercial enterprises securing exclusive legal rights, through IPRs, over practices that are embedded in and lifted from indigenous and local communities' cultures.[94] Following a meeting in 2000, WIPO established its Intergovernmental Committee on Intellectual Property and Genetic Resources, Traditional Knowledge and Folklore (the IGC) to act as a forum for discussion and negotiation on new international instruments on these subjects.[95] Progress under the IGC could only be described as slow, however, as after more than 20 years there is still little consensus not only on what the objectives of these treaties and means of achieving these should be but on the definitions of key terms. Taking the latest Draft Articles on the Protection of Traditional Knowledge as an example, there are currently four proposed definitions for 'misappropriation'. A review of Alternative 2 reveals the divergence of views in the negotiators and the types of issues that are proving contentious.

> Alt 2: The use of [protected] traditional knowledge of another where the [subject] matter]/[traditional knowledge] has been acquired by the user from the holder through improper means or a breach of confidence and which results in a violation of national law in the provider country, recognising that acquisition of traditional knowledge through lawful means such as [independent discovery or creation], reading books, receiving from sources outside of intact traditional communities, reverse engineering, and inadvertent disclosure resulting from the holders' failure to take reasonable protection measures is not [misappropriation/misuse/unauthorised use/unfair and inequitable uses].[96]

From a justice perspective, Alternative 2's requirement that the use of traditional knowledge to be a breach of a state's national law is problematic, as an indigenous community's customary law may not be adequately reflected by this.[97] Similarly,

93 B. Richardson and D. Craig, 'Indigenous Peoples, Law and the Environment', in B. Richardson and S. Wood (eds), *Environmental Law for Sustainability* (Hart Publishing, 2006) 195–197. See Ch 4 for further discussion of indigenous rights.

94 B. Ong, 'Biotechnology Innovations, Genetic Resources and Traditional Knowledge: Current Developments at the World Intellectual Property Organization', in M. Jeffery and others (eds), *Biodiversity Conservation, Law + Livelihoods Bridging the North-South Divide* (CUP, 2008) 554–555.

95 WIPO General Assembly, *Matters Concerning Intellectual Property and Genetic Resources, Traditional Knowledge and Folklore*, WO/GA/26/6, 25 August 2000.

96 The Protection of Traditional Knowledge: Draft Articles. Facilitators' Rev., June 19, 2019, Article 1. Available at: https://www.wipo.int/meetings/en/doc_details.jsp?doc_id=439178 (last accessed 20/04/2023). The square brackets in Alternative 2 indicate that even agreement on the terms of potential options has proven elusive.

97 Richardson and Craig (n 93) 210–225.

means of discovery such as drawing on sources from outside the community in question or inadvertent disclosure by a member of that community would still be unethical without an obligation of due diligence on the potential user to ensure that their utilisation of the knowledge they have gained would not violate the rights of, or otherwise offend, the relevant community. In contrast, the exception of 'independent discovery or creation', where any similarity to the traditional practices of a local or indigenous community can be shown to be genuinely coincidental, is arguably a legitimate defence for innovators.

There are other concerns, beyond the practicalities of specific provisions in legal instruments, in attempting to define the traditional knowledge of local and indigenous communities in ways that are compatible with mainstream and internationalised legal constructs such as IPRs. Antons suggests that this leads to communities having to define their culture in terms that meet the expectations of remote policymakers,[98] which merely serves as another form of colonisation,[99] only this time dressed up as a means of recognising the legitimacy of those cultures. Drahos goes further and argues that traditional knowledge, which is grounded in the interdependence and indivisibility of the natural world, is fundamentally incompatible with legal frameworks designed to provide specific protection over a strictly defined and isolated aspect of the environment.[100]

Despite WIPO's failure to negotiate an instrument to protect traditional knowledge, local and indigenous communities' knowledge of and interest in their local genetic resources is not completely unprotected in international law. Article 8(j) of the Biodiversity Convention calls on states, 'as far as possible and as appropriate', to:

> Subject to its national legislation, respect, preserve and maintain knowledge, innovations and practices of indigenous and local communities embodying traditional lifestyles relevant for the conservation and sustainable use of biological diversity and promote their wider application with the approval and involvement of the holders of such knowledge, innovations and practices and encourage the equitable sharing of the benefits arising from the utilisation of such knowledge, innovations and practices;[101]

Work to elaborate on this provision began in 2000, when the Biodiversity Convention COP established the Ad Hoc Working Group on Access to Genetic

98 C. Antons, 'Traditional Cultural Expressions and Their Significance for Development in a Digital Environment: Examples from Australia and Southeast Asia', in C. Graber and M. Burri-Nenova (eds), *Intellectual Property and Traditional Cultural Expressions in a Digital Environment* (Edward Elgar, 2008) 295.

99 S. Smallacombe, 'On Display for Its Aesthetic Beauty: How Western Institutions Fabricate Knowledge about Aboriginal Cultural Heritage', in D. Ivison and others (eds), *Political Theory and the Rights of Indigenous Peoples* (CUP, 2000).

100 P. Drahos, *Intellectual Property, Indigenous People and Their Knowledge* (CUP, 2014) 202–203.

101 See also Article 15.

Resources and Benefit Sharing.[102] Following agreement at the 2002 World Summit on Sustainable Development that a new instrument should be negotiated under the Biodiversity Convention to address access and benefit-sharing issues,[103] the Working Group was requested to begin developing a protocol to implement the access and benefit-sharing provisions of the Convention, with a formal invitation made to WIPO to provide technical assistance.[104] This work culminated in the adoption of the 2010 Nagoya Protocol on Access and Benefit-sharing.[105]

The objectives of the Nagoya Protocol are similar to those of the PGRT's Multilateral System, i.e. to ensure that any benefits resulting from the utilisation of genetic resources are shared equitably.[106] There are important differences between the two mechanisms, however.[107] First, the scope of the Protocol is significantly broader, as it covers all natural genetic resources under the jurisdiction of a state, not just plants that are of actual or potential value to agriculture.[108] Whereas the genetic resources covered by the Multilateral System are considered a common resource, access to which is conditioned only by the purposes for which applicants seek to use the requested material, the natural genetic resources covered by the Nagoya Protocol are considered to fall under the jurisdiction of the state of origin.[109] Access to genetic resources under the Protocol is therefore subject to the prior informed consent of the state of origin and, if that state's national law allows, the consent of the community of origin as well,[110] on the basis of mutually agreed terms.[111] This is more restrictive, potentially making it harder for commercial plant breeders to gain access to genetic material and make their own contributions to crop diversity.

A second key difference, and a consequence of the Protocol's emphasis on state sovereignty over natural resources, is that any benefits resulting from access must be shared only with the state (and potentially community) of origin, rather than the wider communities that are, through the mechanisms established under the PGRT,

102 Decision V/26, Access to genetic resources (2000).

103 UN, *Plan of Implementation of the World Summit on Sustainable Development* (September 2002) para 44(o). Available at: https://www.un.org/esa/sustdev/documents/WSSD_POI_PD/English/WSSD_PlanImpl.pdf (last accessed 20/04/2023).

104 Decision VII/19, Access and benefit-sharing as related to genetic resources (Article 15), UNEP/CBD/COP/DEC/VII/19, 13 April 2004.

105 Nagoya, 29 October 2010, in force 12 October 2014, C.N.782.2010.TREATIES-1.

106 Nagoya Protocol, Article 1.

107 Despite these, the flexibility inherent to both the PGRT and the Nagoya Protocol mean that the regimes are generally compatible – C. Chiarolla and others, 'An Analysis of the Relationship between the Nagoya Protocol and Instruments related to Genetic Resources for Food and Agriculture and Farmers' Rights', in E. Morgera and others (eds), *The 2010 Nagoya Protocol on Access and Benefit-Sharing in Perspective: Implications for International Law and Implementation Challenges* (Brill, 2012).

108 Nagoya Protocol, Article 3.

109 Nagoya Protocol, Article 6(1).

110 Nagoya Protocol, Article 6(2).

111 See further E. Morgera and others, *Unravelling the Nagoya Protocol: A Commentary on the Nagoya Protocol on Access and Benefit-Sharing to the Convention on Biological Diversity* (Brill, 2015).

the beneficiaries of the utilisation of materials accessed through the Multilateral System. There is therefore no equivalent to the PGRT's SMTA under the Protocol. Instead, Contracting Parties are required to provide information to the Access and Benefit-sharing Clearing House, established by Article 14 of the Nagoya Protocol, on, inter alia, domestic legal and administrative arrangements for access and benefit-sharing and, if they exist, model contractual clauses will apply in agreements with potential users. The Nagoya Protocol does not, therefore, serve global agroecological networks in the same way as the PGRT's Multilateral System.

Notwithstanding these issues, the Nagoya Protocol is potentially a powerful means through which the traditional knowledge of local and indigenous communities can be protected. Article 7 requires the Contracting Parties, as appropriate and in accordance with national law, to ensure that traditional knowledge is only accessed with the prior informed consent of the community concerned and on the basis of mutually agreed terms. Also relevant is Article 12, which calls on states to not only consider the customary laws and practices of indigenous and local communities when implementing the Protocol but also to support these communities in developing culturally acceptable procedures and conditions for access to their traditional knowledge. Importantly Article 12(4) requires states, 'as far as possible, not [to] restrict the customary use and exchange of genetic resources and associated traditional knowledge within and amongst indigenous and local communities…'. The exchange of knowledge and material for the purposes of supporting and enhancing agrobiodiversity is therefore implicitly recognised as a legitimate pursuit by the Protocol.

There is therefore a distinction in the Protocol between natural genetic resources, which remain under the jurisdiction of states, and traditional knowledge, which is recognised as the belonging to the community in question. Note, however, that only traditional knowledge 'associated with genetic resources' is covered by the Protocol; knowledge relating to other aspects of indigenous and local cultures is excluded. In this respect, the Protocol's understanding of traditional knowledge is significantly narrower than the Biodiversity Convention's, which includes knowledge of ecosystems,[112] and WIPO's.[113] This may be why negotiations on the Protocol found agreement on this issue, while the WIPO negotiators continue to struggle.

The contribution that the Nagoya Protocol makes to the development of agroecology in international law is therefore mixed. That the rights of communities of origin are conditioned by national law limits the protection the Protocol affords to these communities in relation to their traditional knowledge. On the other hand, it goes further than other instruments in recognising the legitimacy of the exchanging of local material and knowledge between communities. This is arguably where the real agroecological value of the Nagoya Protocol lies. While the frequent references

112 Article 8(j) of the Biodiversity Convention refers to traditional knowledge relating to biological diversity, which is defined in Article 2 as encompassing species and ecosystems.

113 Morgera and others (n 111) 30.

to national law are regrettable, the Nagoya Protocol establishes an important baseline to protect the integrity of the traditional knowledge that underpins the farming practices of local and indigenous communities around the world.

## Conclusions

That farmers' right to save, use and exchange seed on a non-commercial basis to promote genetic diversity in crop varieties has received renewed attention in international law is welcome. The strict IPRs that commercial entities enjoy over an increasing proportion of the world's crop seeds have fractured the connections between different members of agriculture's socioecological networks and severely reduced the diversity of and within crops. Recognition of farmers' right to freely exchange seed to promote diversity is growing, but to date has yet to be codified in sufficiently robust legal language.

In contrast, states have arguably succeeded in promoting access to and the fair sharing of benefits resulting from the use of genetic resources and associated knowledge. The PGRT's Multilateral System is an innovative regime, with its treatment of crop genetic resources as a global commons being an important reflection of the interdependent and integrated nature of the socioecological networks that agroecology sees as being synonymous with agriculture. Its primary weakness is its limited scope, with crops that are essential in terms of health, economics and culture to some of the world's poorest communities currently not included in Annex I of the Convention.

In contrast, the Nagoya Protocol has a much wider application, covering all natural genetic resources. Its state-centric focus, however, coupled with its narrow approach to traditional knowledge, qualifies its compatibility with agroecology. The Protocol's ability to enable the free development of crop diversity at the same time as protecting the rights and cultures of local and indigenous communities depends on the willingness of states to progressively implement its provisions.

The development of the law in this area can therefore be seen as tracking the same trajectory as the legal concept of sustainable development. Increasing priority was given to economic concerns, starting with the 1961 UPOV Convention, its revisions through to the 1991 Act that imposed unnecessary and ecologically and culturally ignorant restrictions on farmers' right to use and exchange seed, and culminating in the TRIPS Agreement, which firmly established the IPRs of plant varieties in a forum that suited the economic interests represented by developed states. Now, through the PGRT and Nagoya Protocol, the international community has indicated its acceptance that the status quo is not only unsustainable but dangerous for economic and social prosperity, but has been unwilling to take sufficiently robust action so that those powerful, narrow, economic interests are forced to give way to universal ecological imperatives. Until this happens, with a necessary first step being a new revision of the UPOV Convention that incorporates a farmers' right that is more in line with India's Protection of Plant Varieties and Farmers' Rights Act, there will be a limit to how far agroecology can be advanced in international law.

# 3 Genetically Modified Organisms and Organic Agriculture

## GMOs in Socioecological Networks

The preceding chapter looked at some of the measures in international law intended to preserve and promote genetic diversity in crops. Such steps may, in part, be characterised as a response to the rapid globalisation and industrialisation of agriculture, one consequence of which is the replacement of local crop diversity with monocultures comprising single strains of genetically modified crops.[1] It should now be clear that the over-reliance on monocultures is contrary to agroecology, which promotes diversity.[2] This emphasis on diversity, however, should not be seen as limited to within individual farms. It is just as important, in terms of local, regional and global food security, to ensure the diversity of wider agricultural networks.[3] A farm that utilises genetically modified organisms (GMOs), while lacking internal crop diversity, will nevertheless contribute to the diversity of an agricultural system if other farms in that system cultivate a wider range of crops. For certain communities, crops that are more resilient may also provide greater food security in the face of deteriorating environmental conditions, thereby also enhancing the social elements of agroecology's socioecological networks. GMOs are therefore useful in highlighting the inherent links between natural and human elements of these networks and the connections between the natural and human dimensions of 'environmental' problems.[4]

Their use is nevertheless contentious, due not only to their potential environmental impacts but also the risk they pose to the traditions and livelihoods of communities that rely on farming methods that reject non-natural inputs.[5] Criticisms

1 I use 'genetically modified' to mean an organism that is modified so that it has a genetic composition that would never naturally occur because it incorporates genetic materials of multiple species. This should be distinguished from 'genetically engineered' organisms, which have not had foreign genes inserted into them but rather have been bred so that a genetic composition that could naturally occur is achieved immediately, rather than through a lengthy process of natural selection.

2 M. Liebman, 'Polyculture Cropping Systems', in M. Altieri, *Agroecology: The Science of Sustainable Agriculture* (2nd edn, Westview Press, 1995).

3 See ch 12.

4 J. Holder, 'New Age: Rediscovering Natural Law' (2000) 53 *Current Legal Problems* 151, 155.

5 The use of GMOs in the rearing of livestock has proven just as controversial due to their perceived risks to environmental and human health. See further, A. van Eenennaam, 'GMOs in Animal Agriculture: Time to Consider Both Costs and Benefits in Regulatory Evaluations' (2013) 4 *Journal of Animal Science and Biotechnology* 37.

DOI: 10.4324/9781003435174-5

of GMOs also extend beyond the practical into the ethical, with those who engage in the manipulation of genomes being accused of 'playing God',[6] and risking ecological catastrophe as a result.[7] Proponents of organic farming, in particular, have condemned the use of GMOs in agriculture.

GMOs being the saviour/end of humanity are two extreme positions in a complex debate, neither of which accurately represents the true nature of the opportunities and risks for society that come with their cultivation.[8] This chapter explores how the positions of GM and organic farming advocates might be reconciled and each agricultural philosophy considered a legitimate element of diverse agricultural systems. It begins by considering how organic agriculture and GMOs fit into agroecology. Emphasis is placed on the social element of the organic movement, which has arguably been lost in how organic agriculture is typically defined in debates over its merits, as well as the opportunities for greater crop and societal resilience that are actually offered by GMOs, rather than merely presumed by their proponents. Attention then turns to how the risks of GMOs are addressed through regulation, using the EU's legislation and the Convention on Biodiversity's Protocol on Biosafety[9] as case studies. There are two issues to consider here – adequately addressing the environmental risk of GMOs and reconciling scientific assertations that this risk is minimal with public concerns that cannot easily be accounted for in technical assessments – and each has implications for how agroecology can be pursued through the law. Finally, we will look more closely at how the differences between the pro- and anti-GM lobbies might be resolved in an agroecology framework.

## Organic Agriculture and GMOs in the Context of Agroecology

Organic farming as a movement has been traced to the 18th century, although some of its core principles can be identified as early as the 16th century.[10] The term did not enter common usage until the 1960s, when it was presented as a response to the dramatic growth of chemical use and industrialisation in agriculture.[11] This has since been translated into a certification procedure of products and processes that rejects non-natural inputs in farming.[12] As is illustrated by the International Federation of Organic Agriculture Movement's (IFOAM) definition, though,

6 R. Stewart and M. Martinez, 'International Aspects of Biotechnology: Implications for Environmental Law and Policy' (1989) 1 *Journal of Environmental Law* 157, 158, cited in Holder (n 4) 154.

7 Holder (n 4).

8 F. Wickson and others, 'Should Organic Agriculture Maintain Its Opposition to GM? New Techniques Writing the Same Old Story' (2016) 8 *Sustainability* 1105, 2.

9 Rio de Janeiro, 5 June 1992, in force 29 December 1993, 31 ILM 822; Protocol on Biosafety, Montreal, 29 January 2000, in force 11 September 2003, 39 ILM 1027.

10 D. Treadwell and others, 'From Philosophy to Science: A Brief History of Organic Horticulture in the United States' (2003) 38 *HortScience* 1009, 1009–1011.

11 ibid.

12 Wickson and others (n 8) 3.

organic agriculture's agenda goes beyond opposition to chemical usage and is as much a social movement as it is an environmental one:

> Organic Agriculture is a production system that sustains the health of soils, ecosystems, and people. It relies on ecological processes, biodiversity and cycles adapted to local conditions, rather than the use of inputs with adverse effects. Organic Agriculture combines tradition, innovation and science to benefit the shared environment and promote fair relationships and good quality of life for all involved.[13]

There are similarities between this and the definition of agroecology established in the introduction to this work. Each emphasises the importance of maintaining the socioecological networks that underpin agricultural systems. Organic agriculture is a collaborative partnership between nature and people that rests on the maintenance of ecological processes. In terms of its more overtly social aspects, no one would consider the promotion of fair relationships between people controversial. Care must nevertheless be taken when considering how the social elements of organic agriculture may be implemented in practice. Organic agriculture has been connected to promoting localism in food systems as a response to the globalised industrialisation of agriculture, for example,[14] but there is nothing inherently sustainable or just about local food movements. Kenyan farmers that export to the United Kingdom typically enjoy better health and welfare than farmers who deliver to only domestic markets, due to the higher workplace standards demanded by Western supermarket chains. To cut these farmers out of British markets in the name of localism would be to undermine their livelihoods.[15] This is not to say that there are no advantages of localism in food systems, an important one being transparency of food supply. Rather, it highlights the need to adopt global, systems-level perspectives on what may appear to be only local issues.[16]

The correlations between organic farming and agroecology do not mean that GM farming is inevitably incompatible with agroecology. Both should be considered legitimate elements of diverse agricultural systems. It has been argued that rather than operating in isolation, GM and organic farming represent the two extremes of a single spectrum of agricultural methodologies,[17] and the full expanse of this spectrum could be considered one definition of what agroecology means in

13 https://www.ifoam.bio/why-organic/organic-landmarks/definition-organic (last accessed 20/04/2023).

14 P. McMichael. 'A Food Regime Genealogy' (2009) 36 *Journal of Peasant Studies* 139, 142.

15 J. Agyeman, *Introducing Just Sustainabilities: Policy, Planning, and Practice* (Zed Books, 2013) 66, drawing on P. Cross and others, 'Does Farm Worker Health Vary Between Localised and Globalised Food Supply Systems?' (2009) 35 *Environment International* 1004.

16 R. Amos and others, *Living Sustainability in Higher Education: Connecting Communities, Learning and Justice* (2025, forthcoming) ch 6.

17 R. Sonnino and T. Marsden, 'Beyond the Divide: Rethinking Relationships Between Alternative and Conventional Food Networks in Europe' (2006) 6 *Journal of Economic Geography* 181.

practice. The difference is that while few would contest that organic agriculture belongs in agroecological systems, the place of GM crops is not as self-evident. This is not simply because of the potential risks that have been identified in the use of GM crops. Rather, it is because if these risks were to manifest and neighbouring systems that employ different farming methods were contaminated, or (agro) biodiversity was reduced as a result of a GMO's release, the ecological and social diversity on which agroecology is founded would be undermined.

A range of GMOs have been engineered to respond to contemporary challenges in agriculture.[18] These can be broadly grouped into five categories. Pest-resistant crops are presented as a response to Rachel Carson's condemnation of chemical pesticides in *Silent Spring*.[19] Extracting genes from the bacteria *Bacillus thuringiensis* and inserting these into crops give these plants an inbuilt insecticide, thereby reducing the need for chemical sprays. Similar techniques have been used to develop disease-resistant crops, with a main benefit again being that this reduces the need for chemical fungicides.[20]

Reducing pollution resulting from the excess run-off of agricultural chemicals aligns with organic and agroecological approaches to agriculture.[21] Pest- and disease-resistant crops still carry risks for agroecological networks, however. It is possible for cross-fertilisation to occur between GM crops and related wild species, resulting in an unintended transferral of the inherent resistance into the wild. At first, this may seem to be a good thing; wild plants that are resistant to pests and diseases will thrive, thereby increasing plant diversity. Again, though, it is necessary to adopt a systems-level perspective. Research has been conducted into a laboratory-created gene that allows crops to produce a pheromone that aphids release when threatened, alerting nearby aphids to potential danger.[22] The idea is that this would reduce aphid damage because they would avoid crops that release this pheromone.[23] However, if wheat that contained this gene went on to hybridise with natural grass species, releasing the gene into the wild, aphid populations could collapse due to the lack of food. This would in turn impact those species that prey

18 For an overview of how GMOs are created, and the regulatory implications of evolving production methods, see S. Khan and others, 'Role of Recombinant DNA Technology to Improve Life' (2016) *International Journal of Genomics* 2405954, and J. Kuzma and A. Kokotovich, 'Renegotiating GM Crop Regulation' (2011) 12 *EMBO Rep* 883.

19 R. Carson, *Silent Sprint* (Hamilton, 1963); K. Gerasimova, 'Debates on Genetically Modified Crops in the Context of Sustainable Development' (2016) 22 *Science and Engineering Ethics* 525, 537.

20 N. Fedoroff and D. Kershen, 'Agricultural Biotechnology – An Opportunity to Feed a World of Ten Billion' (2014) 118 *Penn State Law Review* 859, 867.

21 Altieri (n 2) chs 13 and 14.

22 E. Schwartzberg and others, 'Alarm Pheromone Emission by Pea Aphid, *Acyrthosiphon pisum*, Clones Under Predation by Lacewing Larvae' (2008) 128 *Entomologia Experimentalis et Applicata* 403.

23 L. Cui and others, 'The Functional Significance of E-β-Farnsene: Does It Influence the Populations of Aphid Natural Enemies in the Field?' (2012) 60 *Biological Control* 108.

on aphids and other agricultural pests, leaving the crops vulnerable to future pest outbreaks.[24]

Herbicide-resistant crops have also been developed. Bacteria in soil breaks down harmful agents used in chemical herbicides and scientists can insert the relevant genes from these bacteria into crops, enabling them to do this themselves.[25] Rather than reduce chemical usage, however, these GMOs facilitate it, as crops that are resistant to herbicides can be treated more liberally. This may reduce the competition crops face from weed species, thereby potentially increasing yields, but the environmental implications of greater chemical usage are obvious.[26]

A fourth category of GM crops are those that are more nutritious or productive than non-GM crops. Golden Rice is often cited as an example of these.[27] The agroecological benefits of these and herbicide-resistant crops primarily lie in how they support the social elements of agriculture's socioecological networks. GM crops that produce greater yields not only increase a farmer's income but also enhance the food security of associated communities. Greater food security, which depends as much on the availability of nutritious food as it does on the availability of sufficient quantities of foods, is also provided by crops that address nutritional deficits in communities.[28] At the same time, however, communities' long-term food security will be undermined if the widespread cultivation of GM crops results in a loss of local crop diversity and associated traditional farming knowledge.[29]

The final category of GM crops is climate-resistant crops, which will attract more attention as local, regional and global climate patterns radically alter. The advantage offered by these crops is not that they outperform non-GM crops in all circumstances. Rather, it is that their yields are less affected when growing conditions deteriorate.[30] As with GM crops that provide increased or more nutritious yields, the primary benefits of climate-resistant crops are their enhancement of food security for communities. Here, however, these benefits take the form of allowing communities to remain in what may be a degraded local environment while still producing enough food to sustain themselves. As I explore in chapter 8, environmental degradation and the consequent inability to produce sufficient food is a key driver behind environmental migration, which not only impacts communities that are forced to migrate but also those that are then required to provide support. Predicting future ecological conditions, given the uncertainty surrounding

24 T. Walker, *Plant Conservation: Why It Matters and How It Works* (Timber Press, 2013) 195–196.

25 Fedoroff and Kershen (n 20) 866–867.

26 See Ch 10.

27 E. Hodson De Jaramillo, 'Ecological Aspects of Biosafety', in K. Chowdhury and others (eds), *Biosafety of Genetically Modified Organisms: Basic Concepts, Methods and Issues* (FAO, 2009) 85.

28 H. Lee and S. Krimsky, 'The Arrested Development of Golden Rice: The Scientific and Social Challenges of a Transgenic Biofortified Crop' (2016) 4 *International Journal of Social Science Studies* 51.

29 See ch 2.

30 Fedoroff and Kershen (n 20) 871.

the impacts of climate change, is challenging, however, and there is a risk that the crops that are engineered today will be of little use to future generations.[31]

If fully realised, the potential of these different GM crops is nothing short of ending global hunger. This ignores, however, that principal sources of global food insecurity relate less to there being insufficient quantities of food and more to broader social barriers certain communities face in accessing food.[32] There are also two assumptions behind GM proponents' ambitions that are not supported by the evidence. First, while GM crops *may* be a solution to a range of problems, to date the majority of GM crops that are being cultivated are those that have innate pesticide or herbicide resistance, with the latter comprising around half of GM agricultural use.[33] GM crops that offer other advantages, including climate-resistance, are being developed but are yet to be deployed on a scale that would constitute a viable response to the impacts of climate change.[34]

Second, GM crops do not respond to the issue of low yields in organic agriculture because there is a lack of evidence to suggest that organic agriculture inevitably or consistently has lower yields than other types of farming.[35] Further, for advocates of GM crops to claim that lower yields are a problem for organic farmers is to misunderstand the basic philosophy that underpins organic agriculture.[36] As was highlighted in the book's introduction, while all farmers seek to make a living, maximising profits through increased yields is not necessarily the principal factor behind their decisions. An organic farmer may be more concerned about enhancing crops and related agrobiodiversity to ensure the long-term sustainability of their endeavours than marginally increasing their yields by relying on a GM monoculture.

## Responding to the Risks of GMOs

### *Risk Regulation*

Concerns over GMO cultivation essentially relate to the risk this poses to the ecological and cultural foundations of agriculture's socioecological networks. The concept of risk is critically important in environmental law.[37] While defining environmental law can be problematic, one narrow definition we may consider, aligning

31 L. Guruswamy, 'Sustainable Agriculture: Do GMOs Imperil Biosafety?' (2002) 9 *Indiana Journal of Global Legal Studies* 461, 475–476.

32 See ch 12.

33 Wickson and others (n 8) 4.

34 G. Graff and others, 'The Research, Development, Commercialization, and Adoption of Drought and Stress-Tolerant Crops', in N. Tuteja and S. Gill, *Crop Improvement under Adverse Conditions* (Springer, 2013).

35 V. Seufert and others, 'Comparing the Yields of Organic and Conventional Agriculture' (2012) 485 *Nature* 229.

36 Wickson and others (n 8) 6–7.

37 M. Stallworthy, *Understanding Environmental Law* (Sweet & Maxwell, 2008) ch 6.

with purposive understandings of the law,[38] is that environmental law is society's attempt, through regulation, to avert or mitigate identified but unquantified risks of environmental harm. Risk may be seen as connecting the apparently abstract technicalities of environmental law with broader social values that are also fundamental to its purpose and operation.[39] In regulatory practice, however, there is frequently a tension between what are presented or perceived as 'facts' produced by experts and the immeasurable, socially rooted values of individuals and communities that do not easily translate into the technical frameworks of scientific assessments.[40] GMOs are a prime example of this and reveal some of the challenges in building diversity in agricultural systems.

The choice to regulate an activity in terms of risk leads to regulatory structures focused on the production and evaluation of information.[41] The basis of decisions switches from the information that is available to the difficulties arising from the absence of information. There are numerous examples in environmental law where, although some scientific uncertainty may persist, policymakers have sufficient information on which to base their decisions.[42] In other cases, however, there is a significant degree of uncertainty over the existence, scale and likelihood of a particular risk that is associated with an otherwise desirable activity.[43] In these circumstances, a balance must be struck between allowing society to advance through technological innovation and industrial application, on the one hand, and the need to avoid certain types and levels of harm on the other.

How this balance is struck in law and policy is through the application of the precautionary principle. Originating in German domestic law as the *Vorsorgeprinzip*, the precautionary principle is now a common feature of international and national environmental regimes,[44] as well as a core environmental principle of the EU.[45] Most regimes adopt the construction set out in Principle 15 of the Rio Declaration on the Environment and Development,[46] or a close variation thereof:

38 E. Fisher and others, *Environmental Law: Text, Cases and Materials* (2nd edn, OUP, 2019) 10–12.

39 R. Attfield, *Environmental Ethics* (Policy Press, 2003) chs 1 and 2.

40 M. Lee, 'Beyond Safety? The Broadening Scope of Risk Regulation' (2009) 62 *Current Legal Problems* 242.

41 S. Kingston and others, *European Environmental Law* (CUP, 2017) 460–461.

42 E.g., when authorising the release of common pollutants through industrial permitting. See further C. Abbot, *Enforcing Pollution Control Regulation: Strengthening Sanctions and Improving Deterrence* (Hart Publishing, 2009).

43 Examples include nanotechnology – R. Falkner and N. Jaspers, 'Regulating Nanotechnologies: Risk, Uncertainty and the Global Governance Gap' (2012) 12 *Global Environmental Politics* 30; and the use of assisted colonisation as a conservation technique for endangered species – J. Lopez, 'Biodiversity on the Brink: The Role of "Assisted Migration" in Managing Endangered Species Threatened with Rising Seas' (2015) 39 *Harvard Environmental Law Review* 157.

44 P. Sands and J. Peel, *Principles of International Environmental Law* (4th edn, CUP, 2018) 229–240.

45 Treaty on the Functioning of the European Union, Article 191.

46 A/CONF.151/26, 12 August 1992.

> Where there are threats of serious or irreversible damage, lack of full scientific certainty shall not be used as a reason for postponing cost-effective measures to prevent environmental degradation.[47]

This represents a weak interpretation of the precautionary principle: mitigatory measures should not be avoided simply because there is some doubt over an identified risk. It has been criticised for merely reflecting good practice rather than introducing an extra dimension to decision-making, but at the very least the proper application of this version of the principle creates space for public debate over decisions regarding certain activities.[48] A strong interpretation of the precautionary principle, in contrast, mandates that no action be taken unless it can be shown to entail no risk. This is of course impossible and so the strong precautionary principle has been criticised for having the effect of freezing all socioeconomic activity,[49] or for resulting in equivalent or even greater harm than the proposed activity.[50]

In the EU, the precautionary principle has been adapted to best serve the environmental objective being pursued in a given situation, reflecting its nature as more of a guide for decision-makers that must be read in the legislative context in question, rather than a precise uniform standard.[51] In relation to conservation, for example, the Court of Justice of the European Union (CJEU) held that the obligation to conduct an appropriate assessment of an activity that will affect a site protected under the Habitats Directive[52] arose out of the 'mere probability' that the activity may negatively impact on the site's conservation objectives and that, in light of the precautionary principle, 'such a risk exists if it cannot be excluded on the basis of objective information'.[53] In contrast, regarding a Commission ban on the use of certain antibiotics in animal feed, the European Court of First Instance (now General Court) held that precautionary measures 'may be taken only if the

47 In some environmental agreements, reference is made to the precautionary approach, reflecting the United States' resistance to formally recognising the precautionary principle as a formal principle of international law – J. Wiener, 'Precaution', in Bodansky and others (eds) *The Oxford Handbook of International Environmental Law* (Oxford: OUP, 2007) 601. On the legal status of the precautionary principle, see J. Peel, 'Precaution', in *The Oxford Handbook of International Environmental Law* (2nd edn, OUP, 2021).

48 M. Lee, *EU Environmental Law, Governance and Decision-Making* (2nd edn, Hart Publishing, 2014) 5–6.

49 C. Sunstein, 'Beyond the Precautionary Principle' (2003) 151 *University of Pennsylvania Law Review* 1003, 1020. Other interpretations of the precautionary principle have been developed around the idea of avoiding certain types of harm – C. Sunstein, 'Irreversible and Catastrophic' (2006) 91 *Cornell Law Review* 841.

50 R. Amos, *International Conservation Law: The Protection of Plants in Theory and Practice* (Routledge, 2020) 75.

51 E. Scotford, *Environmental Principles and the Evolution of Environmental Law* (Bloomsbury, 2019) 89–90.

52 Directive 92/43/EEC on the conservation of natural habitats and of wild fauna and flora [1992] OJ L206/7, Article 6(3).

53 Case C-127/02 *Landelijke Vereniging tot Behoud van de Waddenzee v Staatssecretaris van Landbouw, Natuurbeheer en Visserij (Waddenzee)* [2004] ECR I-7405, paras 41 and 44.

risk, although the reality and extent thereof have not been "fully" demonstrated by conclusive scientific evidence, appears nevertheless to be adequately backed up by the scientific data available at the time when the measure was taken'.[54] 'Adequately backed up' is arguably a higher standard for precautionary action than a 'mere probability', with one explanation for the different approaches being that the proper operation of the Habitats Directive relies on the obligation to conduct an appropriate assessment of potentially harmful activities being interpreted broadly.[55]

Precaution is often incorporated into legal frameworks through risk assessment provisions. A risk assessment may be defined as a scientific process through which the nature, scale and likelihood of risks associated with a particular activity are, as far as possible, quantified.[56] It is important to remember that even after a risk assessment has been conducted, scientific uncertainty persists. Subsequent experience may provide a conclusive answer to what was a central point of concern under a previous risk assessment, but other unknowns will remain, or new unknowns will be created as that answer gives rise to its own questions. While this is the foundation of scientific research, it poses a challenge for regulatory processes which, for the sake of legitimacy and efficiency, require firm and accurate scientific conclusions so that appropriate responses to environmental harms can be adopted.[57]

Risk assessment should be seen as only one part of risk-based regulatory process. Equally important is risk management. That scientists are intimately involved in risk assessment means that there is often a conflation of scientific knowledge with fact. Risk assessments do not produce facts, however, only predictions informed by the available evidence.[58] How to respond to these predictions is ultimately a political decision, informed both by the risk assessment and, importantly, public consultations. There will be a number of ways to manage an identified risk, ranging from avoiding the risky activity completely, through different mitigatory measures that offer varying degrees of safeguard, to simply accepting the risk and carrying on regardless.

Underpinning risk management is risk acceptability, i.e. the question of 'how safe is safe enough?'[59] This is a purely political determination, which will be informed by the specific cultures and concerns of those that are making it, underscoring that different people will reach conflicting but equally legitimate decisions based on the same scientific assessments. GMOs are themselves an example of

54 Case T-13/99 *Pfizer Animal Health SA v Council of the European Union* [2002] ECR II-3405, para 144. The Court found that the Commission's decision was adequately backed up by the available scientific data.

55 See Advocate General Kokott's Opinion to *Waddenzee* (n 53) paras 69–74.

56 Note that the precise meaning of 'risk assessment' will vary according to disciplinary, regulatory and jurisdictional context – Fisher and others (n 38) 39.

57 J. Applegate, 'Bridging the Data Gap: Balancing the Supply and Demand for Chemical Information' (2008) 86 *Texas Law Review* 1365, 1395.

58 Kingston and others (n 41) 465.

59 Lee (n 40) 243–247.

this, with very different public attitudes to GM crops being the source of major tensions between the United States and EU in the World Trade Organisation (WTO).[60]

Risk management highlights the false dichotomy between expertise and democratic expressions of public will, revealing instead how public administration is informed by both.[61] It also illustrates the difficulties decision-makers face in balancing expert assurances that a risk is minimal, or can be contained, with persistent public doubts grounded in either (perhaps irrational) scepticism of the science or in values that cannot adequately be accounted for in risk assessment processes. The implications of this for the regulation of controversial technologies become clear when we consider the EU's experiences in GMO authorisation.

### *GMO Authorisation in the EU*

There are internal contradictions in what the EU says about GMOs and its approach to their regulation. GMOs, along with biotechnology more generally, are primarily presented as an economic issue, with their successful deployment seen as a way of enhancing the economic development of the EU, in the context of the internal market but also in terms of global economic competition.[62] The Commission highlights, for example, the importance of biotechnology to the 'modernisation of the European industry' and the consequent need to 'identify and remedy obstacles to the biotechnology industry'.[63] In contrast, a rigorous, to the point of unnecessarily onerous for some commentators,[64] authorisation procedure has been developed to ensure that risks posed by GMOs to the environment and human health are properly addressed. The role of the authorisation process goes beyond simply responding to risks, however, and is also seen as a way for the EU to legitimise itself in the eyes of sceptical European citizens because it shows the EU to be actively responding to public concerns.[65]

The two core pieces of EU legislation on GMO authorisation are the Deliberate Release Directive (DRD)[66] and the Food and Feed Regulation (FFR).[67] The former

60 See *European Communities – Biotech (Measures Affecting the Approach and Marketing of Biotech Products)* WT/DS291/AB/R; WT/DS292/AB/R; WT/DS293/AB/R 29 September 2006 and *EC – Hormones (Measures Concerning Meat and Meat Products)* WT/DS26/AB/R, WT/DS48/AB/R, 16 January 1998.

61 E. Fisher, *Risk Regulation and Administrative Constitutionalism* (Hart Publishing, 2007) 6–17.

62 M. Lee, *EU Regulation of GMOs: Law and Decision Making for a New Technology* (Edward Elgar, 2008) 61.

63 https://ec.europa.eu/growth/sectors/biotechnology_en (last accessed 20/04/2023).

64 S. Dickhut, 'Genetically Modified Organisms in the United Kingdom: A Proposal for Moderate GMO Regulations Post-Brexit and an Opportunity in Genetically Modified Wheat' (2017) 22 *Drake Journal of Agricultural Law* 293, 304–307.

65 Lee (n 62) 62.

66 Directive 2001/18/EC on the deliberate release into the environment of genetically modified organisms [2001] OJ L 106.

67 Regulation 1829/2003 on genetically modified food and food [2003] OJ L 268.

covers the deliberate release of GMOs into the environment or their placement on the European market, with 'deliberate release' defined as:

> Any intentional introduction into the environment of a GMO or a combination of GMOs for which no specific containment measures are used to limit their contact with and to produce a high level of safety for the general population and the environment.[68]

The FFR covers 'GMOs for food use', 'food containing or consisting of GMOs' and 'food produced from or containing ingredients produced from GMOs',[69] as well as 'GMOs for feed use', 'feed containing or consisting of GMOs' and 'feed produced from GMOs'.[70] There is some overlap between the two regimes, as a GM-food product that is placed on the market will fall within the remit of both the FFR and the DRD. In these circumstances, applicants may apply for a single authorisation under the FFR subject to an environmental risk assessment under the DRD, or make two separate applications.[71]

There is not space to examine the DRD and FFR authorisation procedures in detail here, but they are broadly similar.[72] In essence the European Food and Safety Authority (EFSA) produces a risk assessment on an application to cultivate GMOs, although due to their lack of financial and technical resources, EFSA will often merely review the risk assessment submitted by the applicant.[73] This is problematic in a number of respects. First, there is an obvious issue of bias, and while a patently flawed assessment might be identified through EFSA's review, more nuanced downplaying of certain risks or emphasising of mitigatory factors may not be challenged.[74] Second, as I go on to discuss, the EFSA opinion is highly influential, almost to the point of being determinative, in the authorisation process and so that it is essentially lifted from information presented by applicants raises obvious legitimacy issues. Further legitimacy issues relate to the fact that even just

68 Directive 2001/18/EC, Article 2(3).

69 Regulation 1829/2003, Article 3. The FFR uses the same definition of 'food' as that set out in Article 2 of Regulation 178/2002 laying down the general principles and requirements of food law, establishing the European Food Safety Authority and laying down procedures in matters of food safety [2002] OJ L 31.

70 Regulation 1829/2003, Article 15. For the definition of 'feed' see Article 3(4) of Regulation 178/2002.

71 Regulation 1829/2003, Recital 33.

72 Lee (n 62) 64–71.

73 M. van Asselt and others, 'Science, Knowledge and Uncertainty in EU Risk Regulation', in E. Vos and M. Everson (eds), *Uncertain Risks Regulated* (Routledge-Cavendish, 2008).

74 This issue is not limited to GMOs. Under Article 5 of Directive 2011/92/EU on the assessment of the effects of certain public and private projects on the environment [2012] OJ L 26 (as amended by Directive 2014/52/EU [2014] OJ L 124), responsibility for producing the environmental impact assessment report rests on the developer, and this is often the only detailed information on the proposal that will be available to decision-makers. See J. Holder, *Environmental Assessment: The Regulation of Decision Making* (OUP, 2004) 97–99.

reviewing a technical assessment of the risks posed by a specific, specialised and potentially brand-new GMO may be beyond the means of the regulator. As such, the role of the applicant becomes less about persuading the regulator of the merits of their application and more about simply providing the information on which the decision will be based.[75]

Once compiled, EFSA's opinion is circulated to all Member States and the Commission, as well as made publicly available. The final authorisation decision is made by the Commission and Member States through comitology, i.e. the system of committees through which Member States supervise the Commission's implementation of EU law,[76] on the basis of a draft opinion prepared by the Commission for the Standing Committee on Plants, Animals, Food and Feed.[77] Article 7(1) of the FFR states that 'Where the draft decision is not in accordance with the opinion of [EFSA], the Commission shall provide an explanation for the differences'. This suggests that the Commission may depart from EFSA's opinion, although in practice there is limited scope to do so. Through a series of case law, the CJEU has made clear that any decisions responding to risk must be based on the best available scientific evidence, which EFSA's opinion purports to represent, and so to act in a manner inconsistent with this would leave the Commission open to judicial challenge.[78]

That GMO authorisations are subject to comitology's examination procedure, and therefore require a qualified majority to accept *or* reject the Commission's draft decision,[79] is the reason why the EU's authorisation regime remains dysfunctional. The balance between pro- and anti-GMO Member States is such that no qualified majority can be reached either way. When this happens, the decision is first referred to the Council, which is similarly unable to reach a qualified majority as the political composition of the Member States is the same as that of the comitology committee, and so the decision falls finally to the Commission to make on its own.[80] The Commission typically adopts its draft decision, for the reasons relating to the CJEU's approach to risk-based decision-making highlighted above, meaning

75 Kingston and others (n 41) 464–465.

76 Regulation 182/2011 laying down the rules and general principles concerning mechanisms for control by Member States of the Commission's exercise of implementing powers [2011] OJ L 55. Under Article 2 of this Regulation, decisions relating to GMOs, as well as, inter alia, other matters relating to the environment, are subject to the examination procedure, the alternative being the advisory procedure. The key differences between these procedures is that while opinions can be adopted by a simple majority under the advisory procedure (Regulation 182/2011, Article 4), opinions under the examination procedure require a qualified majority, as defined in Article 16(4) of the Treaty on European Union (Regulation 182/2011, Article 5). See P. Craig, 'Delegated Acts, Implementing Acts and the New Comitology Regulation' (2011) 36 *European Law Review* 671.

77 https://ec.europa.eu/food/horizontal-topics/committees/paff-committees_en (last accessed 20/04/2023).

78 Kingston and others (n 41) 462. E.g., Case T-74/00 *Artegodan v Commission* [2002] ECR II-4945, paras 197 et seq.

79 (n 76).

80 Kingston and others (n 41) 475.

that EFSA's opinion, primarily informed as it is by the applicant's submissions, has a larger role in the authorisation process than the language of the legislation might suggest.[81] As such, rather than being a model example of how the EU institutions can respond to public concerns, in the context of GMO authorisation EFSA merely reinforces the notion of a faceless Brussels bureaucracy that overrides the national interests of Member States.

From an agroecological perspective, the EU's approach to authorisation presents a mixed picture. On the one hand, the absence of GM crops means that this is one less pressure on already depleted crop- and related agrobiodiversity. There has not, for instance, been the same proliferation of monocultures in Europe that has been seen in the United States and other countries.[82] On the other hand, the development of the diversity of agricultural systems in the EU and its Member States is being frustrated by the EU's inability to authorise GMOs that are considered scientifically safe but politically unacceptable to a sufficiently large blocking minority of Member States. As noted above, GM farming is not necessarily better than other types of agriculture, but it is different and therefore makes its own contribution to the integrity and resilience of agriculture's socioecological networks.

### *Coexistence in the EU*

Opposition to GMOs based on their socio-cultural impacts, rather than a specific environmental risk, is at the heart of the coexistence question, i.e. how can GM crops be cultivated alongside other forms of agriculture? In the EU, the difficulty in accounting for concerns over how GM cultivation would impact on local traditions and cultures through a decision-making process that prioritises scientific evidence has been exacerbated by the Commission's previous characterisation of coexistence as a purely economic issue. Provided that the cultivation of GMOs did not impact on the internal market, then no coexistence issues were considered to arise.[83] The implications of this position for Member States under domestic political pressure to protect specific agricultural traditions is evident in the *Land Oberösterreich* case, in which Austria's attempt to prohibit GMO cultivation in a region with a strong organic agricultural industry was rejected on the grounds that they had failed to meet the requirements of what is now Article 114(5) TFEU.[84]

81 ibid 462.

82 https://www.ers.usda.gov/data-products/adoption-of-genetically-engineered-crops-in-the-us/recent-trends-in-ge-adoption/ (last accessed 20/04/2023).

83 M. Lee, 'The Governance of Coexistence Between GMOs and Other Forms of Agriculture: A Purely Economic Issue?' (2008) 20 *Journal of Environmental Law* 193, 199.

84 Joined Cases C-439/05 and C-454/05 *Land Oberösterreich and Austria v Commission* [2007] ECR I-7141 (appealing T-366/03 and T-235/04). Article 114(5) TFEU sets out the conditions on which a Member State may derogate from an EU harmonisation measure. On the difficulties Member States face in justifying a restriction on GMO cultivation under Article 114(5), see L. Krämer, 'Regional Ban on GMO – Admissibility Under Article 95(5)?' (2008) 5 *Journal for European Environmental and Planning Law* 117.

In response to the dual problems of a non-functioning authorisation process and the limited grounds on which Member States could raise non-economic coexistence concerns, in 2015 a new Article 26b was introduced to the DRD.[85] This adds two dimensions to the GMO authorisation process. During the procedure itself, a Member State may issue a demand that the geographic scope of the authorisation be amended to exclude some or all its territory. The applicant then has a period of 30 days in which they can either adjust their application or confirm the original intended geographic scope.[86] The expectation is that applicants will revise where they intend to release the GMO rather than continue pushing to release into a territory where there is significant public objection.[87]

If no demand is made, or the applicant confirms the originally intended scope, Member States may, under Article 26b(3), adopt domestic measures that prohibit or restrict the cultivation of GMOs covered by the DRD and FFR. In addition to being reasoned, proportional, non-discriminatory and otherwise in accordance with EU law, measures that limit GMO cultivation must be based on 'compelling grounds', such as:

(a) environmental policy objectives;
(b) town and country planning;
(c) land use;
(d) socioeconomic impacts;
(e) avoidance of GMO presence in other products without prejudice to Article 26(a);
(f) agricultural policy objectives;
(g) public policy.

This list is representative of the diverse range of qualitative issues with which Member States may be faced as part of local political opposition when seeking to implement an EU-level GMO authorisation.[88] The references to environmental and agricultural policy objectives are particularly relevant in the context of agroecology, as they provide a basis for restricting GMO cultivation to ensure the wider diversity of the agricultural system in question. Dobbs suggests, for example, that Article 26(b) could be used to justify a policy that restricts GMO cultivation to promote crop genetic diversity and the sustainability of a state's agricultural systems, thereby responding to some of the issues raised in the previous chapter.[89]

85 Directive 2015/412/EU amending Directive 2001/18/EC as regards the possibility for the Member States to restrict of prohibit the cultivation of genetically modified organisms (GMOs) in their territory [2015] OJ L 68/1. See Recitals (6) and (7) of the Directive's preamble.

86 Article 26b(2).

87 Kingston and others (n 41) 481.

88 G. Winter, 'Cultivation Restrictions for Genetically Modified Plants' (2016) 7 *European Journal of Risk Regulation* 120, 125–132.

89 M. Dobbs, 'Genetically Modified Crops, Agricultural Sustainability and National Opt-Outs: Enclosure as the Loophole?' (2017) 54 *Common Market Law Review* 1093.

The rationale behind Article 26b is twofold. First, it creates grounds on which Member States opposed to the cultivation of GM crops can limit their cultivation while still complying with EU law. It also provides a means through which those Member States that are open to GM cultivation can develop the internal market for GM crops. Article 26b can be criticised as constituting a process of deharmonisation, i.e. the rolling back of the internal market and the reintroduction of national discretion to condition free trade. However, this deharmonisation was arguably necessary, not only for recognising that GMO authorisations are more appropriately addressed at the national level because of the impacts on local agricultural systems and cultures but because the failure of the centralised approach to authorisation challenged the functioning of the internal market.[90]

Further, and without wishing to downplay its significance, the EU is more than the internal market, and Article 26b reflects this.[91] Article 3 of the Treaty on European Union states that the EU 'shall respect its cultural and linguistic diversity, and shall ensure that Europe's cultural heritage is safeguarded and enhanced'. Agricultural diversity must be considered to form part of this heritage. Article 26b formally recognises the cultural roots of national economies and that Member States legitimately, and necessarily, pursue policy objectives that extend beyond the economic.[92] This clearly accords with the theory of agroecology, in which economic considerations do not override the critical cultural aspects of agriculture and the diversity in and of agricultural systems that this supports.

Evidence from the case law as to whether the agroecological potential of Article 26b will be met is mixed. On the one hand is the *Fidenato* case, which concerned an attempt by Italy to ban the cultivation of a GM crop under the emergency measures set out in Article 34 of the FFR.[93] The CJEU held that the prohibition was unlawful for reasons similar to why Austria's ban on GMO cultivation in *Land Oberösterreich* was struck down, i.e. Italy had failed to provide new scientific evidence of a serious risk to human health or the environment. While Article 26b was not in direct contention in this case, it was open to the CJEU to take it into account in its ruling. Rather than reflect the EU's new approach to GMO authorisation, however, the CJEU confirmed its earlier rulings on scientific evidence in cases where Member States raise environmental risk as grounds for derogating from a harmonised EU standard.[94] On the other hand is the *Regione Autonoma Friuli Venezia Giulia* case, which was a Preliminary Reference regarding the application of Article 26a of the DRD.[95] Here, the CJEU confirmed that Member States may

90 M. Lee, 'GMOS in the Internal Market: New Legislation on National Flexibility' (2016) 79 *Modern Law Review* 317, 332.

91 ibid 324.

92 Kingston and others (n 41) 481.

93 Case C-111/16 *Fidenato and Others* ECLI:EU:C:2017:676.

94 A. Guida, 'The 2017 *Fidenato* Case and the 2015 Directive: The Curious Case of GMOs in Europe' (2020) 29 *Review of European, Comparative and International Environmental Law* 291, 298.

95 Case C-24/21 *PH v Regione Autonoma Friuli Venezia Giulia and Direzione centrale risorse agroalimentari, forestali e ittiche* ECLI:EU:C:2022:526.

adopt bans on GMO cultivation as part of the measures they are required to take to prevent cross-border contamination by GMOs, showing greater deference to national discretion in the regulation of GM cultivation.

It is important to note that neither of these cases deal directly with Article 26b. They indicate, however, that Dobbs may be correct in arguing that states wishing to ban GMO cultivation on the basis of Article 26b may have more success if they seek to justify any prohibition on the grounds of promoting agricultural sustainability rather than on narrower environmental protection grounds, where there is long standing jurisprudence on the requisite standard of scientific evidence from which the CJEU appears reluctant to depart.[96]

***The Biosafety Protocol***

We see a similar tension between scientific assessments of risk and non-technical public values in the 2000 Protocol on Biosafety's approach to the transboundary movement of living modified organisms (LMOs).[97] In brief, the state of export shall notify the competent national authority of the state of import prior to the movement of an LMO that is to be intentionally introduced into the state of import's environment.[98] This notification must include, inter alia, taxonomic information, information regarding how and through what processes the LMO was modified and the regulatory status of the LMO in the state of export.[99] On receipt of the notification, the procedure set out in Article 10 will ordinarily apply.[100] Decisions made under Article 10 are based on a risk assessment, details of which are set out in Article 15 and Annex III of the Protocol. This risk assessment is intended to be a comprehensive process, with key stages including the identification of 'any novel genotypic and phenotypic characteristics associated with the [LMO] that may have adverse effects on biological diversity in the likely potential receiving environment', an evaluation of how likely it is that these effects will materialise, the potential consequences should they be realised and, interestingly, 'A recommendation as to whether or not the risks are acceptable or manageable…'.[101]

96 Dobbs (n 89). See also Lee (n 90) 327–328.

97 That the Biosafety Protocol only applies to *living* modified organisms, not all GMOs, is a key point of difference between the Protocol and other GMO instruments. The reason for the more limited scope was the United States' insistence that it is organisms per se that potentially pose an environmental risk, not the process through which they are created. See H. Marquard, 'Scope', in C. Bail and others (eds), *The Cartagena Protocol on Biosafety: Reconciling Trade in Biotechnology with Environment & Development?* (Earthscan, 2002).

98 Biosafety Protocol, Article 8. The state of export may delegate this duty to the actual exporter. 'Intentional introduction into the environment' excludes LMOs that will only be used as food or feed, or processed, which are covered by a separate, less rigorous regime set out in Article 11.

99 Biosafety Protocol, Annex I.

100 Under Article 9(2)(c), the state of import must inform the notifier whether the procedure Article 10 will apply or the state of import's own regulatory framework. The domestic regulatory framework must still be compatible with the Protocol, however – Article 9(3).

101 Biosafety Protocol, Annex III, para 8.

This last point raises a number of issues. Primary responsibility for conducting the risk assessment rests with the party of import, but this can be delegated to the exporter, i.e. the legal person wishing to export the LMO.[102] Doing so, however, gives the exporter an even greater role in the decision-making process than that typically enjoyed by applicants in the EU's authorisation process due to the explicit inclusion of risk management and acceptability in the scope of the risk assessment. Whether or not a risk is manageable is, in part, a technical issue: do technologies exist that reduce the likelihood or severity of the risk in question? This is reflected in Article 16 of the Protocol, which requires states to 'establish and maintain appropriate mechanisms, measures and strategies to regulate, manage and control risks identified in the risk assessment…'. As noted above, however, risk management is also a political determination, with the question of whether a risk is *acceptable* being one that can only be answered through a political process. An applicant is unlikely to suggest that the risks associated with their LMO are unacceptable.

Links between the Biosafety Protocol and agroecology can be found in the importance to each of adopting interdisciplinary approaches at every stage of regulation. As we saw in the introduction, for agroecologists, agricultural systems can only be understood, and problems addressed, if a holistic, systems-level approach is taken, drawing on multiple disciplines.[103] GMOs and their potential to contaminate nearby organic farms are an excellent example of this. The introduction of GMOs should not just be considered in terms of what it means for the applicant, but what it means for the wider socioecological network of which that applicant is one inseparable part. Redgwell makes a similar point, noting that an important step in resolving the conflict in the GMO debate is the sound analysis of information grounded in a range of disciplines, including ecology, biology and socioeconomic studies.[104]

As with the new Article 26b in EU law, how much space currently exists for non-technical considerations in the Biosafety Protocol is debatable.[105] During the Protocol's negotiations, there was a tension between developed states, which preferred what has been described as a 'sound science' approach of basing decisions on the most current scientific data,[106] and developing states, which recognised that the impacts of LMOs cannot be adequately summarised in a purely scientific

102 Biosafety Protocol, Article 15(2).

103 E. Noe and H. Alrøe, 'Regulation of Agroecosystems: A Social Systems Analysis of Agroecology and Law', in M. Monteduro and others (eds), *Law and Agroecology: A Transdisciplinary Dialogue* (Springer, 2015).

104 C. Redgwell, 'Biotechnology, Biodiversity and International Law' (2005) 58 *Current Legal Problems* 543, 544, drawing on IUCN, *Genetically Modified Organisms and Biosafety: A Background Paper for Decision-Makers and Others to Assist Consideration of GMO Issues* (August 2004), 5.

105 O. Tung 'Transboundary Movements of Genetically Modified Organisms and the Cartagena Protocol: Key Issues and Concerns' (2014) 17 *Potchefstroom Electronic Law Journal* 1739, 1758–1759.

106 Redgwell (n 104) 557.

assessment.[107] The position of developing states is more in line with agroecology and is reflected in Article 26 of the Protocol:

1. The Parties, in reaching a decision on import under this Protocol or under its domestic measures implementing the Protocol, may take into account, consistent with their international obligations, socioeconomic considerations arising from the impact of [LMOs] on the conservation and sustainable use of biological diversity, especially with regard to the value of biological diversity to indigenous and local communities.

There are two points to note in this provision. First, and in comparison to the language used in Article 15 on the role of science in risk assessment, Article 26 is phrased in discretionary terms. There is therefore no requirement for states to account for the value of biodiversity to indigenous and local communities, or consider an LMO's potential impacts on the diversity of agricultural systems when deciding whether to authorise its import. Pursuing an ecologically grounded approach to agriculture remains an option rather than an obligation. Second, any such consideration must be 'consistent with [states'] international obligations'. This may primarily be read as meaning their obligations under international trade law,[108] and there have been several disputes brought through the WTO's dispute process in relation to what has been perceived as the overly restrictive regulation of GMO imports.[109] The true extent of the freedom afforded by Article 26 of the Biosafety Protocol therefore remains unclear. However, given the emphasis placed on scientific evidence as the basis of the risk assessment procedure throughout the Protocol, it is unlikely that socioeconomic concerns alone will be enough to lawfully prohibit the importation of an LMO.[110]

Conspicuous by their absence from the Protocol are detailed provisions on what the response should be in the event of an LMO being found to have a considerably worse environmental impact than was predicted in the risk assessment. Article 17 of the Biosafety Protocol simply imposes duties of notification and consultation in the event of an unintentional transboundary movement. A similar observation can be made in relation to the 2010 Nagoya-Kuala Lumpur Supplementary Protocol on Liability and Redress,[111] adopted pursuant to Article 27 of the Biosafety Protocol.[112] Article 5 of the Supplementary Protocol merely calls on states to ensure that any

107 R. Andrén and B. Parish, 'Risk Assessment', in Bail and others (n 97) 333.

108 Redgwell (n 104) 564–568.

109 (n 60).

110 Redgwell (n 104) 558.

111 Nagoya, 15 October 2010, in force 5 March 2018, UNTS 3240 1.

112 For discussion of the liability implications of GMO cultivation, see T. Redick, 'Liability Prevention for Agricultural Biotechnology' (2017) 22 *Drake Journal of Agricultural Law* 31. On the Supplementary Protocol specifically, see L. Shiyi, 'Legal Mechanism for International Damage Caused by Transboundary Transference of Modified Living Organism' (2020) 17 *US-China Law Review* 169.

operators involved in the release of an LMO 'Take appropriate response measures', as determined by the competent national authority concerned.

Measures to respond to the environmental impacts of an LMO are also missing from the Implementation Plan for the Biosafety Protocol, the emphasis of which is on states complying with their obligations under the Protocol and corresponding capacity-building efforts.[113] It would not be appropriate for the Meeting of the Parties to the Biosafety Protocol to be overly prescriptive in the measures to be taken in the event of significant environmental harm being caused by an LMO, as any response will have to be tailored to the specific impacts and ecological, socio-economic and cultural landscape of the state concerned. However, broad guidance, similar to the Guiding Principles for the Prevention, Introduction and Mitigation of Impacts of Alien Species that Threaten Ecosystems, Habitats or Species discussed in the previous chapter,[114] could have been devised to aid states in protecting both agrobiodiversity and the diversity of their agricultural industry.

## Creating Space for GM Crops in Agroecological Networks

Article 26 of the Biosafety Protocol and Article 26b of the DRD respond to a particular political problem that has arisen in the context of GMO authorisation. Proponents of GM crops may have a point when they argue that it is not the environmental or health risks that are preventing GM crops from being authorised for release, but the apparent inability of regulatory systems to find a politically acceptable way to manage these risks.[115] Provisions such as those discussed in this chapter have not resolved the tensions between the pro- and anti-GMO states in formal decision-making processes, but merely provided mechanisms through which public values can be prioritised over expert opinion. This is a legitimate position in terms of public policy – decisions on the type of society we wish to be must be based on more than technical and economic considerations – but in the absence of an unmanageable scientific risk, the complete exclusion of GM crops should be considered just as contrary to agroecology's emphasis on diversity in agriculture as the widescale cultivation of GM monocultures.

That proponents of organic agriculture are hostile to the introduction of GM crops to the environment is well-known.[116] The criticisms of organisations such

113 Decision CP-10/3, Implementation plan for the Cartagena Protocol on Biosafety, CBD/CP/MOP/DEC/10/3, 19 December 2022.

114 Decision VI/23, Alien species that threaten ecosystems, habitats or species, UNEP/CBD/COP/DEC/VI/23, 2002. See ch 2.

115 I. Potrykus, 'Lessons from the "Humanitarian Golden Rice" Project: Regulation Prevents Development of Public Good Genetically Engineered Crop Products' (2010) 27 *New Biotechnology* 466. A related issue is the lack of harmonisation in GM regulations across jurisdictions, meaning that a single crop must go through multiple approval processes – M. Lusser and H. Davies, 'Comparative Regulatory Approaches for Groups of New Plant Breeding Techniques' (2013) 30 *New Biotechnology* 437.

116 See IFOAM, *Genetic Engineering and Genetically Modified Organisms* (Position Paper, November 2016) 5.

as IFOAM are not exclusively founded on the perceived or exaggerated risks of GMOs to organic agriculture or the wider environment, however. Their objections also relate to the obscure and technically focused processes through which GMOs are authorised.[117] In 2016, while restating their opposition to the use of GMOs in agriculture except for purposes of vaccinating livestock or where mandated by law,[118] the IFOAM also set out conditions for their introduction:

> Products such as GMOs must not be introduced, unless they have been subjected to a rigorous, democratic, and transparent assessment of the technology through participatory processes that include decision-makers from every area of society and every group of people who will be impacted by the technology. Any introduction of GMOs should be limited to controllable circumstances.[119]

These touch on a number of critical issues, relating not just to sound environmental regulation but to the fair and just administration of public policy as well. Questions of how to ensure the proper participation of relevant stakeholders in decisions relating to agricultural policy are explored later in this book.[120] At this stage, it is sufficient to note that the IFOAM is effectively calling for the proper implementation of the two-stage risk process established above, i.e. technical risk assessment followed by an inclusive political process of risk management.

As far as the EU's authorisation procedures are concerned, it could be argued that these requirements have been met, at least theoretically. The release of a GMO is conditioned on it being subject to a scientific risk assessment, followed by a process in which the democratically elected governments of the Member States decide whether to approve or reject the application.[121] In practice, of course, problems remain and the extent to which the EU's procedure is 'rigorous, democratic and transparent' is debatable. As noted above, EFSA is not in a position to conduct its own review of the risks associated with a particular GMO and must instead rely on the information provided by the applicant. The democratic merit of the process is also questionable, as the Commission typically reverts to its original decision if comitology fails to produce a majority to approve or reject an application, although the introduction of Article 26b to the DRD goes some way in inserting national concerns over culture and tradition into what were primarily economic and expert determinations. Nevertheless, the EU's approach does provide a template for how the concerns of GM opponents can be addressed and for how GM crops can be incorporated into a diverse agricultural system.

117 Wickson and others (n 8) 10. A similar point is made by Gerasimova in relation to Oxfam's position on GMOs – (n 19) 531–532.

118 IFOAM (n 116) 3.

119 ibid 4.

120 Chs 9 and 12.

121 With regard to the Biosafety Protocol, whether IFOAM's conditions have been satisfied can only be assessed by examining each Contracting Party's national implementing legislation.

*Table 3.1* IFOAM principles of organic agriculture

| | |
|---|---|
| Health | Organic agriculture should sustain and enhance the health of soil, plant, animal, human and planet as one and indivisible. |
| Ecology | Organic agriculture should be based on living ecological systems and cycles, work with them, emulate them and help sustain them. |
| Fairness | Organic agriculture should build on relationships that ensure fairness with regard to the common environment and life opportunities. |
| Care | Organic agriculture should be managed in a precautionary and responsible manner to protect the health and wellbeing of current and future generations and the environment. |

In elaborating their agricultural agenda, the IFOAM has established four principles of organic agriculture (Table 3.1).[122] Notwithstanding the IFOAM's stated opposition to GMOs, I suggest that there is nothing in how these principles are defined that represents an *a priori* prohibition on GM crops. In the right circumstances, GM crops may actually be seen as furthering these principles, just as they may be seen as furthering principles of agroecology when deployed as one part of a diverse agri-system. Climate-resistant GM crops may be crucial in ensuring the health and wellbeing of future generations in regions where ecological conditions have deteriorated, for example.

There is also a definite ecocentric thread running through these principles. Notions of care have been associated with ecofeminism, for example, although this has been used as much as a basis for criticising what is considered to be the mischaracterisation and denigration of women's role in society as it has as a defining feature of women's relationship with the natural world.[123] Similarly, the idea of planet Earth and its constituent elements being an indivisible single entity is reflective of the wild law principle of wholeness,[124] and the basic rationale behind Lovelock's Gaia theory.[125] It is beyond the scope of this work to consider in detail the links between ecocentrism and sustainable agriculture, but there is a shared emphasis on redefining human interactions with land between many ecocentric theories and agroecology.[126]

## Conclusions

The creation of new crops that offer higher yields from lower inputs, or resilience in increasingly harsh growing conditions, could go a long way in meeting the global

122 https://www.ifoam.bio/why-organic/shaping-agriculture/four-principles-organic (last accessed 20/04/2023).

123 K. Warren, 'The Promise and Power of Ecofeminism' (1990) 12 *Environmental Ethics* 125.

124 I. Mason, 'One In All: Principles and Characteristics of Earth Jurisprudence', in P. Burdon (ed), *Exploring Wild Law: The Philosophy of Earth Jurisprudence* (Wakefield Press, 2011) 36–37.

125 J. Lovelock, *Gaia: A New Look at Life on Earth* (reprint edn, OUP, 2009).

126 A. de Nitto, 'On the Humanity of Land', in Monteduro and others (n 103).

community's aspiration of zero hunger by 2030.[127] And yet GMOs remain highly controversial, due not only to their perceived environmental risks but their implications for traditional farming communities as well. This underscores what may be considered a principal weakness of sustainable development, both as a normative framework and as a specific policy agenda. Consensus can easily be reached over a broad range of goals that are considered to constitute sustainable development: ending hunger, eradicating poverty, transitioning to a low-carbon economy and so on. This consensus disappears, however, when attention turns to exactly *how* these objectives are to be achieved.

Agroecology offers a framework through which a consensus can be restored. Its emphasis on diversity means that it is not a question of choosing one approach to farming over another, but facilitating both so that local, regional and global agricultural systems are able to deliver long-term food security in the face of growing ecological challenges. The polarised nature of the GMO debate, however, means that implementing this aspect of the agroecology agenda is problematic. Experience in the EU illustrates how expert assessments of the environmental risk posed by GM crops fail to adequately account for non-technical public concerns over how the introduction of GMOs may undermine their livelihoods, if they rely on an organic agricultural industry, or otherwise impact on local cultures and traditions.

Recent reforms to EU law, and the reference to broader socioeconomic issues in the Biosafety Protocol, mean that such normative concerns are not excluded from authorisation decisions. These mechanisms, however, have not resolved the fundamental tension between proponents and opponents to GMOs. Instead, they have merely legitimised the prohibition of GM crops for political reasons in the absence of any scientific justification. That this reduces the diversity of agricultural systems means that this approach is just as contrary to agroecology as mandating the cultivation of GM crops in all regions provided that it is environmentally safe to do so. A key step towards true reconciliation would be reflecting the calls of bodies such as the IFOAM for more robust, democratic and transparent authorisation procedures, so that those who oppose GMO cultivation can see how their concerns are being taken into account. This is as much a question of ensuring regulators have sufficient technical and financial capacity as it is of the merits of the legal framework.

Nevertheless, notwithstanding the importance of enhancing the diversity of agricultural systems, there will be some areas where GMO cultivation will remain in principle inappropriate, due to the risk of contamination to traditional forms of agriculture. Additional levels of protection should be considered for such landscapes and how international law provides for this will be our focus in the next chapter.

127 A/RES/70/1, 21 October 2015, Goal 2.

# 4 Landscapes

## Defining 'Landscape'

Agricultural systems are integral to landscapes and in some states, such as the United Kingdom, may be considered one of the archetypal landscapes.[1] These landscapes are under increasing pressure from a range of sources, environmental and socioeconomic, which are driving changes in agricultural practices that may themselves hasten the deterioration of agricultural systems.[2] This puts at risk not only the natural entities that form those landscapes but the biodiversity and human cultures that have evolved alongside them. Consideration of landscapes therefore brings together several key issues addressed in the preceding chapters, including the conservation of agrobiodiversity at species and genetic levels, the protection of traditional agricultural knowledge and the centrality of agricultural practices to local identities. How these are addressed through legal measures for landscape protection reveals a lot about the current support in the law for the socioecological networks that underpin agroecological understandings of agriculture.

The term 'landscape' operates on different levels and its precise meaning will vary depending on context.[3] In simple terms, the physical features of an area, natural and artificial, combine to form a landscape and collectively lend themselves to labels such as rural, urban and industrial. A second, deeper, understanding of landscape centres around an individual's perceptions of an area and its constituent features, informed by their background, culture and experiences.[4] As someone who has grown up in Britain, my first reaction to an area of rainforest would be to see it as an untamed jungle, but a member of a native indigenous tribe would be able to distinguish between the true wilderness and those parts of the forest that are care-

1 There is of course significant diversity in these landscapes. The typical farmyard surrounded by fields of crops and grazing in England is very different to the traditional croft-steads of Scotland.

2 FAO, *Globally Important Agricultural Heritage Systems: Combining Agricultural Biodiversity, Resilient Ecosystems, Traditional Farming Practices and Cultural Identity* (2018) 4–5.

3 K. Olwig, 'Historical Aspects of Multifunctionality in Landscapes: Opposing Views of Landscape', in J. Brant and others (eds), *Multifunctional Landscapes: Interdisciplinary Approaches to Landscape Research and Management* (Centre for Landscape Research, 2000).

4 J. Holder, 'Hedgerows, Laws and Cultural Landscape', in J. Holder and D. McGillivray (eds), *Locality and Identity: Environmental Issues in Law and Society* (Ashgate, 1999) 133–134, drawing on S. Schama, *Landscape and Memory* (Fontana, 1996) 7.

DOI: 10.4324/9781003435174-6

fully cultivated in accordance with cultural traditions. Equally, that tribesperson might view the fields of rural England as an entirely humanised landscape, whereas to me, and certainly in contrast to the city in which I work, England's countryside is very much a natural environment. The histories of the people with which an individual identifies will also shape their perceptions of a landscape. If an indigenous tribe was evicted from their ancestral lands to make way for a nature reserve, a descendant of that community would associate the area with a historic injustice.[5] In contrast, an NGO worker lacking this cultural understanding would primarily see the area for its conservation opportunities.

Landscapes are therefore as much a reflection of socio-cultural practices and experiences as they are of our physical interventions in the environment.[6] An example of this can be seen in Bali, where a complex system of irrigation for rice paddies is inextricably linked to the region's water temples. The temples were constructed over natural springs so that the water could be used for ceremonial and other purposes. Once finished with, it is channelled down the mountains to irrigate the rice paddies, which have gradually shaped the mountainsides over centuries.[7] The rate of water flow is controlled by associations of local farmers, called *subaks*, and a single river system can host a large number of these.[8] The potential problems the *subaks* face are common to other shared water systems, such as the downstream users' reliance on upstream users permitting enough water to flow to meet their needs.[9] It is in the interests of the *subaks* to cooperate, however, due to the mutual ecological and economic benefits. Coordinating when the paddies are flooded has been shown to reduce agricultural pests because it deprives them of their habitats throughout the system, for example.[10] It also has a wider effect on the health of the network by regulating its biochemical processes.[11] Attempts to interfere with the *subaks* and modernise agricultural practices in Bali had a significant adverse impact on the ecology of the region and consequently fractured the complex social systems that had evolved out of the water temples.[12] This demonstrates the costs of

5 This was once a common practice to satisfy Western ideas of 'wilderness' and the belief that nature needed 'pristine' areas free from humans to thrive – A. Gomez-Pompa and A. Kaus, 'Taming the Wilderness Myth' (1992) 42 *Bioscience* 271.

6 It is not just humans that can physically alter landscapes. African forest elephants (*Loxodonta cyclotis*) have, over generations, cleared pathways and clearings that are now distinctive features of many forests – C. Rosin and others, 'Assessing the Effects of Elephant Foraging on the Structure and Diversity of an Afrotropical Forest' (2020) 52 *Biotropica* 502.

7 J. Lansing, *Perfect Order: Recognizing Complexity in Bali* (Princeton University Press, 2006) 38–41.

8 172 *subaks* are located within the Oos and Petanu rivers basins – ibid 12.

9 D. Freestone and S. Salman, 'Ocean and Freshwater Resources', in D. Bodansky and others (eds), *The Oxford Handbook of International Environmental Law* (OUP, 2007) 351–360.

10 J. Lansing and T. de Vet, 'The Functional Role of Balinese Water Temples: A Response to Critics' (2012) 40 *Human Ecology* 453, 454–456.

11 J. Lansing, '"Water Temples" and the Management of Irrigation' (1987) 89 *American Anthropologist* 326, 327.

12 Lansing (n 7) 6–10.

failing to adopt an agroecological approach to managing agriculture. While modernisation has its place in any agroecological policy, this must be pursued in a way that recognises the value of locally based knowledge and practices, particularly if they are embedded in a community's culture and history.

## A Right to Landscape?

Deeper understandings of landscape underpin discussions of a right to landscape, itself an expression of an individual's sense of belonging to a particular area.[13] In an international context, although no explicit right to landscape exists, Strecker suggests that one may nevertheless be drawn from pre-existing human rights. First, it is argued that rights of public participation, as expressed in the Aarhus Convention on Access to Information, Public Participation in Decision-Making and Access to Justice,[14] provide a procedural means through which individuals and communities can exert control over the management of their landscape.[15] In terms of Aarhus, it is noted that the right to environmental information includes the right to information about landscape.[16] Further, that 'the public' is broadly defined for purposes of participating in environmental decision-making is considered to recognise the collective interest that a community, as opposed to an affected individual, may have in protecting their landscape.[17] These points are valid, and facilitating public participation in decision-making serves broader purposes than simply protecting the environment,[18] but I question whether such rights are a sound basis for a right to landscape. The difficulties communities face in establishing standing to bring actions against development that will change the character of an area without necessarily causing direct injury to any one person's private interests are well-documented and appear to preclude the development of a right to landscape through Aarhus-type procedural rights, at least without significant reform.[19]

A potentially stronger basis for a right to landscape are rights that reflect cultural relationships between communities and land. As I discuss further below, indigenous rights instruments contain rights relevant to different aspects of indigenous communities' relationships with land, including physical management and spiritual connection. These are clear substantive norms, but that they have no real

13 D. Scott and A. Smith, '"Sacrifice Zones" in the Green Energy Economy: Toward an Environmental Justice Framework' (2017) 62 *McGill Law Journal* 861, 886–890.

14 Aarhus, 25 June 1998, in force 30 October 2001, 38 ILM 517 (1999).

15 A. Strecker, 'The "Right to Landscape" in International Law', in S. Egoz and others (eds), *The Right to Landscape: Contesting Landscape and Human Rights* (Routledge, 2011) 63–64.

16 Articles 2.3(a) and 4.

17 Articles 2.4 and 2.5. Strecker (n 15) 64.

18 J. Steele, 'Participation and Deliberation in Environmental Law: Exploring a Problem-Solving Approach' (2001) 21 *Oxford Journal of Legal Studies* 415.

19 C. Poncelet, 'Access to Justice in Environmental Matters – Does the European Union Comply with Its Obligations?' (2012) 24 *Journal of Environmental Law* 287.

equivalent in broader human rights instruments means that they are of limited use when it comes to establishing a universal right to landscape.[20]

It is not just cultural rights of communities that are absent from general human rights instruments. All the rights that they contain are typically presented as rights of the individual, not of a collective, and these cannot easily be applied to notions of landscape that are centred on community relationships with a particular region.[21] The Council of Europe has expressly stated that the European Convention on Human Rights[22] does not provide a general right to a healthy environment,[23] for example, and the European Court of Human Rights has only engaged with questions of environmental quality where this can be established as a constituent element of one of the specific rights set out in the Convention.[24] The Court has been more open to environmental protection arguments where they are used to justify the infringement of an individual's rights,[25] but this should be seen as the Court recognising environmental protection as a legitimate public interest, not a public right to a clean environment.[26] The oversight bodies of other regional human rights regimes have been more willing to read a collective dimension into individual rights to property and a private life, but typically only when the community concerned belongs to an indigenous people.[27]

However, there are cases where a substantive communal environmental right of potentially universal application has been established in law, albeit in a national context. In England and Wales, local communities may apply to register land as a town or village green (TVG) where they can prove that they have enjoyed, as of right, certain pastimes on the site for a period of at least 20 years.[28] If successful, registration ensures that the landowner cannot undertake any activity that would prevent the community from continuing to engage in those pastimes. The concept

20 Strecker (n 15) 59–60.

21 ibid 57–58.

22 Rome, 4 November 1950, in force 3 September 1953, 213 UNTS 221.

23 Council of Europe, *Manual on Human Rights and the Environment* (2nd edn, Council of Europe Publishing, 2012) 7.

24 E.g., the right to a private and family life in Article 8. In *Lopez Ostra v Spain* (1995) 20 EHRR 357 it was held that sufficiently serious pollution can prevent someone from enjoying their home to the extent that it infringes on their rights, and in *Fadeyeva v Russia* (2007) 45 EHRR the Court stated that although not every incidence of pollution will breach Article 8, that Russia had failed to implement its own policy of moving people who were being impacted by toxic emissions from a steelworks meant that a violation could be established.

25 E.g., the European Commission on Human Rights decision in *Herrick v United Kingdom* (1985), 11185/84.

26 See Article 1 of Protocol 1 to the Convention.

27 E.g., the Inter-American Court of Human Right's judgment in *Mayagma (Sumo) Awas Tingni Community v Nicaragua* (2001) Series C No.79, paras 148–149.

28 Commons Act 2006, s.15. The term 'as of right' has been interpreted as a tripartite test requiring those seeking to register the site that residents of the locality have engaged in pastimes on the land in question without force, stealth or the permission of the landowner (*nec vi, nec clam, nec precario*). See, inter alia, *R (on the application of Lewis) v Redcar and Cleveland Borough Council and another* [2010] UKSC 11, 17–20.

of the TVG has broader significance, beyond the scope of this work, than its land-use implications, but it is worth noting that it shares a similar grounding in ideas of localism and community ownership to landscape that transcend legalistic constructs of private property rights and offers opportunities to consider land in broader socioecological contexts.[29]

I am not proposing that the TVG legislation should be expanded to create a right to landscape. Although land of any character may qualify as a green for the purposes of the Commons Act 2006,[30] the stereotypical green space at the heart of an English village illustrates the scale of an area to which the legislation is intended to apply. It protects clearly defined, relatively small spaces, rather than the expansive, in some ways unconstrained panorama of a landscape. It does, however, legitimise discussions of a universal communal right to landscape in a way that reliance on indigenous and other human rights instruments may not.

With regard to what a right to landscape specifically entails, Olwig applies in parallel individual property rights and customary use rights inherent to common law systems, such as those exercised over TVGs.[31] The assertion of the former, or the compensation of landowners for conditioning or preventing the assertion of these, promotes at the same time continuity of the unique character of a landscape and diversity within that landscape by allowing landowners to contribute to the continuing evolution of the land. A right to landscape in this regard essentially takes the form of a legal presumption, with the acceptability of a proposed activity contingent on whether it is in keeping with the character of an area. Admittedly, this is a vague standard, but could be given meaning through the indicative lists of either prima facie permissible or prohibited activities compiled through consultation with local communities, or through the creation of formal local development strategies that determine the type of development that is appropriate for a locality.[32] Rights of customary use reinforce individual and community connections with landscape, and Olwig includes natural entities in those who should be seen as exercising these.[33] This is reflective of Leopold's land-ethic, which sees humans and

29 D. McGillivray and J. Holder, 'Locality, Environment and Law: The Case of Town and Village Greens' (2007) 3 *International Journal of Law in Context* 1.

30 Although there may be certain legal conditions that prevent a site from being designated as a TVG. In *R (on the application of Lancashire County Council) v Secretary of State for the Environment, Food and Rural Affairs; R (on the application of NHS Property Services Ltd) v Surrey County Council and another* [2019] UKSC 58 the Supreme Court ruled that land that is held by a public body for a statutory purpose may not be registered under the Commons Act if this would conflict with that statutory purpose.

31 K. Olwig, 'The Right Rights to the Right Landscape?', in Egoz and others (n 15).

32 An example of how this might work can be found in s.38A of the Planning and Compulsory Purchase Act 2004 (as amended by the Localism Act 2011), which allows planning authorities in England to create neighbourhood development plans. These are developed through consultations with the local community and, following approval in a local referendum, will create a presumption in favour of planning applications that are compatible with the plan and a presumption against applications that are not.

33 Olwig (n 31) 48.

nature as equal members of one community, and demonstrates a latent but vital ecocentric dimension to ideas and expressions of landscape.[34] While the proposition that nature has legal rights has yet to be widely accepted, at least in Western legal and administrative procedures, increasing space to pursue such ecocentric approaches can be identified at both international and national levels.[35]

In terms of advancing agroecology, a right to landscape similar to that envisaged by Olwig would serve two purposes. First, it would provide a specific avenue through which a community's sense of belonging, founded on local understandings of how agricultural practices have contributed more to an area than the simple provision of food,[36] can be reflected in decision-making. Second, it would strengthen the position of farmers that employ traditional practices in their efforts to challenge the expansion of modern methods that may be fundamentally incompatible with their ways of farming, and thereby enhance the diversity of national and international agrosystems.[37] There is little indication to suggest that such a right will emerge in international law, however. Instead, more traditional legal mechanisms have been developed to safeguard unique, culturally significant and diverse agricultural landscapes.

## International Programmes for Landscape Protection

Conservation theory has undergone a series of paradigm shifts in recent decades so that the previous emphasis on individual species, habitats and threats has given way to a focus on the links between nature and society – a so-called 'people and nature' model of conservation.[38] Although they remain anchored in instruments that predate these advances in conservation practice and so largely retain the outdated siloed approach,[39] conservation law and policy have also evolved to now pivot around more holistic ideas of the ecosystem approach,[40] reflecting the increasingly prominent role that the concept of 'the ecosystem' has in law.[41] As we saw in chapter 1, the Biodiversity Convention's interpretation of the ecosystem approach includes consideration of the interactions between people and the natural world, and given that landscapes shape and are shaped by these relationships, it is therefore curious that the geographical and intellectual idea of 'landscape' has, to date, received comparatively little attention in international law and policy. A number of programmes have been adopted, however, and provide important space

34 A. Leopold, *A Sand County Almanac and Sketches Here and There* (OUP, 1949) 204.

35 R. Amos, *International Conservation Law: The Protection of Plants in Theory and Practice* (Routledge, 2020) 239–247.

36 The Balinese water temples being one example.

37 Such as the implications of cultivating genetically modified organisms in areas that have traditionally used organic methods.

38 G. Mace, 'Whose Conservation?' (2014) 345 *Science* 1558.

39 Amos (n 35) 7–8.

40 See ch 1.

41 R. Brooks and others, *Law and Ecology: The Rise of the Ecosystem Regime* (Ashgate, 2002).

in which agroecology's emphasis on socioecological networks can be developed at the international level.

### *The Satoyama Initiative*

Recognising landscapes as the physical manifestations of socioecological networks is a central rationale of the Satoyama Initiative,[42] a stakeholder partnership established in 2010 by the Japanese Government and the UN University Institute for the Advanced Study of Sustainability.[43] It has been endorsed by the Biodiversity Convention's Conference of the Parties[44] and counts a number of relevant ministries from developed and developing states among its members, alongside local government bodies, academic institutions and NGOs.[45] The Initiative is essentially a platform for information exchange and collaborative work to enhance ecosystem services that have been degraded as a result of negative changes in land-use patterns.[46] In addition to hosting global and regional events to bring together its members and external partners, the Satoyama Initiative facilitates the development of case studies highlighting how the relationships between nature and society can be enhanced in different ecological and socioeconomic contexts.[47]

A key strength of the Initiative is that it recognises that communities not only influence their local landscapes but have an important role in protecting them as well. One case study from Ghana examines how Community Resource Management Areas have empowered local communities in ensuring that common resources are utilised sustainably by allowing them to take ownership of how those resources are managed.[48] A central element to such programmes is training local communities in participatory monitoring techniques so that they can track progress in achieving

42 'Satoyama' refers to what may be classed as landscapes in Japan consisting of small settlements surrounded by woodland, rivers and other natural features that provide ecosystem services and land that has been converted through traditional agricultural practices – K. Takeuchi, 'Rebuilding the Relationship between People and Nature: The Satoyama Initiative' (2010) 25 *Ecological Research* 891, 892. There are similar concepts in other countries, such as 'manuel' in Korea and 'dehesa' in Spain – B. Berglund and others, 'Traditional Farming Landscapes in Scandinavia and Japan: Global Revival through the Satoyama Initiative' (2014) 43 *Ambio* 559, 574.

43 https://satoyama-initiative.org/about/ (last accessed 20/04/2023). See also the Paris Declaration on the Satoyama Initiative (2010).

44 Decision X/32, Sustainable use of biodiversity, UNEP/CBD/COP/DEC/X/32, 29 October 2010.

45 (n 43).

46 K. Takeuchi and others, 'Satoyama Landscape as Socio-Ecological System: Historical Changes and Future Perspective' (2016) 19 *Current Opinion in Environmental Sustainability* 30.

47 https://satoyama-initiative.org/case_study/#start (last accessed 20/04/2023).

48 Y. Osei-Owusu and A. Frimpong, 'Empowering Communities for Natural Resource Management: The Case of Community Resource Management Areas (CREMA) in Western Ghana', in S. Subramanian and others (eds), *Understanding the Multiple Values Associated with Sustainable Use in Socio-Ecological Production Landscapes and Seascapes* (UN University Institute for the Advanced Study of Sustainability, 2019).

communally adopted management plans,[49] where these exist, but also so that they can present what policymakers typically consider to be legitimate evidence (i.e. evidence that is grounded in Western scientific practice) to official decision-making procedures.[50] Providing for community participatory monitoring can also serve wider conservation agenda, such as by aiding in the national implementation of the Biodiversity Convention,[51] which again demonstrates its value in supporting the connections between nature and communities.

Despite its membership including government agencies, the Satoyama Initiative can best be described as a bottom-up approach to landscape protection. By connecting and empowering communities, not only with each other but with their local environment, the Initiative seeks to strengthen socioecological networks and is consequently one way in which an agroecological approach can be incorporated into international law. Its close collaboration with the Biodiversity Convention illustrates how this might be achieved. That the Satoyama Initiative is a bottom-up regime means that there are limits to what it can deliver, however. Evidence from other areas of international environmental law suggests that without institutional oversight, grassroots programmes lack sufficient authority to restrain the unsustainable activities of non-participants that undermine the ecological and sociocultural elements of the networks concerned.[52] This relates to the broader issue of how common resources might be sustainably managed, with Hardin's 'tragedy of the commons' highlighting the challenges in ensuring this.[53] While experience from the Balinese water temples shows that common resources can be effectively managed,[54] an argument can nevertheless be made for a more formal recognition in law of agricultural landscapes that are the consequence of a coevolution of nature and culture.

49 K-C. Lee and S-Y. Yan, 'Participatory Planning and Monitoring of Protected Landscapes: A Case Study of an Indigenous Rice Paddy Cultural Landscape in Taiwan' (2019) 17 *Paddy and Water Environment* 539.

50 S. Sabzwari and D. Scott, 'The Quest for Environmental Justice on a Canadian Aboriginal Reserve', in Y. Le Bouthillier and others, *Poverty Alleviation and Environmental Law* (Edward Elgar, 2012) 92–94.

51 R. Mackenzie, 'Monitoring and Assessment of Biodiversity under the Convention on Biological Diversity and Other International Agreements', in A. Lawrence, *Taking Stock of Nature: Participatory Biodiversity Assessment for Policy, Planning and Practice* (CUP, 2010) 35–43.

52 E.g., A. Tal and J. Cohen, 'Bringing "Top-Down" to "Bottom-Up": A New Role for Environmental Legislation in Combating Desertification' (2007) 31 *Harvard Environmental Law Review* 163.

53 In short, Hardin argues that the exploitation of commons will inevitably be unsustainable because although the benefits of excessive use accrue to the individual pursuing that use, the costs associated with it are divided between everyone who utilises the commons – G. Hardin, 'The Tragedy of the Commons' (1968) 162 *Science* 1243. For a response to Hardin's arguments, see E. Ostrom, *Governing the Commons: The Evolution of Institutions for Collective Action* (CUP, 2015) and B. Weston and D. Bollier, *Green Governance: Ecological Survival, Human Rights, and the Law of the Commons* (CUP, 2013).

54 Lansing (n 7) 8.

***The Globally Important Agricultural Heritage Systems Initiative***

To help safeguard distinct agricultural landscapes, in 2002 the UN Food and Agriculture Organisation (FAO) established the Globally Important Agricultural Heritage Systems (GIAHS) Initiative. GIAHS are defined as 'outstanding landscapes of aesthetic beauty that combine agricultural biodiversity, resilient ecosystems and a valuable cultural heritage'.[55] This definition is ambiguous and can be criticised for applying an unnecessary measure of inherent anthropocentric value, i.e. aesthetics, to systems that are primarily about ecological function.[56] It has, however, been elaborated through a series of objective criteria relating to a system's support of local communities; its agrobiodiversity; the presence of local or traditional knowledge systems; wider cultures and value systems that are embedded in the site; and the overall stability of the land- (or sea-) scape.[57] These demonstrate the relevance of the GIAHS Initiative to agroecology, as they recognise the centrality of culture and knowledge systems to agriculture alongside the integrity of its natural resource base. Further, they reflect Richardson's point that, due to the inherent links between people and landscape, landscapes and their associated ecosystems can only be protected if the related human capital is also maintained.[58]

Proposals for including sites in the GIAHS list are typically made by FAO member states, but can also be submitted by other stakeholders through a relevant government agency. In addition to explaining how a site fulfils the five criteria, a proposal must be accompanied by an action plan detailing how the site and the systems that it supports will be actively conserved and how progress in this regard will be measured.[59] The GIAHS Scientific Advisory Group has a central role in evaluating proposals and, following a site visit by appointed experts, will determine whether a site is designated. At the time of writing, 74 GIAHS sites have been designated in over 20 countries.[60] The majority of these are located in the Asia and Pacific region.[61]

The GIAHS Initiative highlights issues in the management of agroecological systems that require support through international law and policy, including conservation, land tenure and the rights of indigenous communities, intellectual property rights and trade.[62] Conservation, intellectual property rights and trade are

55 http://www.fao.org/giahs/en/ (last accessed 20/04/2023).

56 International conservation law more generally can be criticised in this regard – Amos (n 35) Ch 1.

57 http://www.fao.org/giahs/become-a-giahs/selection-criteria-and-action-plan/en/ (last accessed 20/04/2023).

58 B. Richardson, 'Restoring Layered Geographies: Ecology, Society and Time' (2017) 26 *Griffith Law Review* 154.

59 (n 57).

60 http://www.fao.org/giahs/giahsaroundtheworld/designated-sites/en/ (last accessed 20/04/2023).

61 This can be contrasted with sites designated under the World Heritage Convention (n 72) below, where approximately half of the current 1,157 sites are located in Europe – https://whc.unesco.org/en/list/stat (last accessed 20/04/2023).

62 S. Harrop, 'Globally Important Agricultural Heritage Systems: An Examination of Their Context in Existing Multilateral Instruments Dealing with Conservation and Land Tenure' (2009) 12 *Journal of International Wildlife Law & Policy* 127.

addressed elsewhere in this book and so will not be discussed here.[63] In terms of indigenous rights, the issue of tenure can be complex and contentious, particularly where a state's national law is superimposed over, or does not otherwise recognise, the internal customary laws of an indigenous community.[64] There is, however, a range of hard and soft law international instruments that call on states to recognise and protect indigenous rights to land and the traditional practices that underpin those communities' relationships with their local environments.[65] It is in these that we find measures that promote agroecology's emphasis on protecting the cultures and traditions that frame humanity's interactions with land. An important provision in this regard is Article 7(1) of International Labour Organisation Convention 169 concerning Indigenous and Tribal Peoples (1989):[66]

> The peoples concerned shall have the right to decide their own priorities for the process of development as it affects their lives, beliefs, institutions and spiritual well-being and the lands they occupy or otherwise use, and to exercise control, to the extent possible, over their own economic, social and cultural development. In addition, they shall participate in the formulation, implementation and evaluation of plans and programmes for national and regional development which may affect them directly.

Two aspects of this provision are relevant to the protection of GIAHS and any indigenous cultures that influence and are influenced by their management. First, the right to determine priorities for development must encompass agricultural priorities. This right would be meaningless if an indigenous community was forced to adopt or adapt to an agricultural system that is incompatible with their traditional approaches to land management. Second, the rights to participation must include both the right to participate in the development of national and regional agricultural

63 Ch 1, 2 and 11, respectively.

64 Harrop (n 62) 155–156.

65 The extent to which these are relevant, and the experiences of different indigenous peoples when seeking to exercise their rights, varies according to the legal, political, social and historical contexts of both the communities concerned and the states in which they are located – B. Richardson and D. Craig, 'Indigenous Peoples, Law and the Environment', in B. Richardson and S. Wood (eds), *Environmental Law for Sustainability* (Hart Publishing, 2006).

66 Text available at: www.ilo.org/dyn/normlex/en/f?p=NORMLEXPUB:12100:0::NO::P12100_ILO_CODE:C169 (last accessed 20/04/2023). Also relevant in this context is the UN Declaration on the Right of Indigenous Peoples, A/RES/61/295, 13 September 2007, Article 20(1) of which recognises indigenous peoples' right to 'maintain and develop their political, economic and social systems or institutions, to be secure in the enjoyment of their own means of subsistence and development, and to engage freely in all their traditional and other economic activities'. Although the Declaration lacks the same legal force as the ILO Convention, it has been argued that it represents emerging rules of customary international law. This argument has been strengthened since the four states that voted against the Declaration – Australia, Canada, New Zealand and the United States – reversed their position. See M. Barelli, 'The Role of Soft Law in the International Legal System: The Case of the United Nations Declaration on the Rights of Indigenous Peoples' (2009) 58 *International and Comparative Law Quarterly* 957.

policies and the right to participate in decisions on other policies that may impact those agricultural practices. The importance of this latter point is illustrated by the *Aerial Herbicide Spraying Case*, a discontinued International Court of Justice dispute concerning the aerial spraying of illegal coca plantations by Colombia over its border with Ecuador.[67] The spraying of herbicides, part of the Plan Colombia counter-drugs strategy, had a significant adverse impact on the health and environment of the indigenous Awá population, including the destruction of their crops.[68] Had the Awá been consulted over the design and implementation of Plan Colombia, steps could have been taken to mitigate these impacts.

This case consequently serves as a useful reminder that to be effective, international measures for the protection of the environment and human rights depend on their proper application at the national level.[69] That the GIAHS Initiative is a non-binding programme limits its ability to protect agricultural systems and the different cultures and bodies of knowledge that underpin them. No formal legal obligations result from designation, with states only called on to monitor and report on the implementation of the action plans.[70] If a GIAHS treaty was negotiated, states would likely qualify any obligations with soft language and references to national law.[71] However, the wider institutional arrangements that would support such a treaty could help to promote compliance by facilitating capacity-building efforts and, potentially, applying a sanctioning system. This has been observed in relation to the World Heritage Convention,[72] which adopts a similar approach to identifying and designating sites that are considered to be of global natural and/or cultural significance.[73] There is scope for collaboration between the World Heritage Convention and the GIAHS Initiative, although this is limited by the Convention's focus on sites that are considered to be of outstanding universal

67 *Aerial Herbicide Spraying (Ecuador v Colombia)* (2008). The case was withdrawn following an agreement between the states concerning the future operation of Plan Colombia. https://www.icj-cij.org/en/case/138 (last accessed 20/04/2023).

68 Addendum to the Report of the United Nations Special Rapporteur on the Situation of Human rights and Fundamental Freedoms of Indigenous Peoples, A/HRC/4/32/Add.2, 28 December 2006, paras 26–33. In contrast, the aerial spraying, and Plan Colombia generally, is considered to have been ineffective at destroying the target drug plantations – D. Mejía, *Plan Colombia: An Analysis of Effectiveness and Costs* (Washington DC: Brookings Institution, 2015), 5, and T. Franz, 'Plan Colombia: Illegal Drugs, Economic Development and Counterinsurgency – A Political Economy Analysis of Colombia's Failed War' (2016) 34 *Development Policy Review* 563.

69 A. Xanthaki, *Indigenous Rights and United Nations Standards* (CUP, 2007) ch 6.

70 http://www.fao.org/giahs/become-a-giahs/designation-process/en/ (last accessed 20/04/2023).

71 This is a common issue in international environmental law and international conservation law particularly. See D. Victor and others (eds), *The Implementation and Effectiveness of International Environmental Commitments* (MIT Press, 1998) 662 and Amos (n 35) 35–36.

72 Paris, 16 November 1972, in force 17 December 1975, 27 UST 37, 11 ILM 1358 (1972).

73 E. Goodwin, 'The World Heritage Convention, the Environment, and Compliance' (2009) 20 *Colorado Journal of International Environmental Law & Policy* 157.

value.[74] Agricultural areas are included in the World Heritage List,[75] but being listed as a GIAHS does not necessarily mean that a site would meet the criteria of the World Heritage Convention.[76]

### *The European Landscape Convention*

There is value in the non-binding, bottom-up approaches of the GIAHS and Satoyama Initiatives. The former has provided a framework to aid states in identifying and protecting culturally significant landscapes, while the latter has proven successful in bringing together stakeholders to develop and share best practice. However, in the context of environmental protection, particularly conservation, it can be argued that to be effective, international law must be framed in legally binding instruments that contain specific and mandatory obligations.[77] The 2000 European Landscape Convention, adopted to 'promote landscape protection, management and planning, and to organise European cooperation on landscape issues',[78] goes some way in meeting these criteria, but also falls short in certain respects.

A strength of the Convention, in contrast to the World Heritage Convention, is that it covers 'everyday or degraded landscapes'.[79] This, coupled with it adopting a more holistic and coherent understanding of the concept of 'landscape' than previously seen in a European legal context,[80] makes it a potentially important model through which agroecology can be pursued in international law. The European Landscape Convention reflects agroecology's framing of agriculture as a socioecological system by rejecting the false distinction between the natural and the human. Under the Convention, a landscape is as much about the actions and interactions of people as it is its natural features.

The European Landscape Convention is undermined, however, by a lack of detailed obligations concerning the actual protection of landscapes. In relation to identification and assessment, for example, Article 6(C) merely calls on states to identify landscapes in their territories and to 'analyse their characteristics and the forces and pressures transforming them'.[81] There is no specific duty to mitigate pressures that are having a negative impact. Instead, states 'undertake' to adopt

74 Articles 1 and 2. See also the Convention's Operational Guidelines, WHC.19/01, 10 July 2019, paras 49–53.

75 These include the cultural landscape of the Honghe Hani Rice Terraces in China and Italy's Vineyard Landscape of Piedmont: Langhe-Roero and Monferrato.

76 Harrop (n 62) 149.

77 Amos (n 35) 57–62.

78 Florence, 20 October 2000, in force 1 March 2004, ETS 176, Article 3.

79 European Landscapes Convention, Article 2.

80 M. Roe, 'The European Landscape Convention: A Revolution in Thinking about 'Cultural Landscapes'' (2007) 23 *Journal of Chinese Landscape Architecture* 10. See also M. Déjeant-Pons, 'The European Landscape Convention: From Concepts to Rights', in Egoz and others (n 15) 51–52.

81 'Landscape' is defined in Article 1 as 'an area, as perceived by people, whose character is the result of the action and interaction of natural and/or human factors'.

undefined measures for landscape protection and management.[82] Similarly, Article 6(D) calls on states to establish quality objectives for their different landscapes, but little guidance is provided on the content of these.

Consideration should therefore be given to devising a new instrument for landscape conservation. One option would be to adopt a landscape protocol to the Biodiversity Convention, which would have the advantages of established institutional support and a scope that extends beyond Europe. In terms of detailed obligations, a template for these is provided by the GIAHS Initiative.[83] Landscape quality objectives could be based on the GIAHS designation criteria,[84] with states, as a minimum, required to maintain and enhance those natural and cultural characteristics of a landscape that led to its designation. Requiring landscape action plans to be devised, coupled with stronger monitoring and review measures, would also create a more robust and proactive conservation regime. Additionally, lessons could be learnt from the technical and financial support measures provided by the World Heritage Convention, which have proven successful at promoting compliance with that regime's conservation obligations.[85]

## Conclusions

Through specific instruments, such as the Satoyama and GIAHS Initiatives, the European Landscape Convention and agreements concerning indigenous rights, international law has recognised that a landscape is not only a collection of natural and human features but a cultural space that can only be understood by appreciating that the same area can be perceived differently according to an individual's experiences and history. Space exists, therefore, to protect the holistic relationships between nature and humanity as these are physically, intellectually and emotionally expressed through landscape that agroecology views as the heart of agricultural systems.

The difficulty is that there is no global, legally binding instrument that is sufficiently robust to protect agricultural landscapes and the distinct cultures that have evolved around them. The European Landscape Convention has some merit, its recognition of the value in 'ordinary' landscapes being particularly important, but it falls short in setting meaningful legal obligations regarding the protection of these. Developing a new landscape instrument for this purpose, drawing on the GIAHS Initiative designation criteria and the facilitative approach to compliance of the World Heritage Convention, would be an important step towards protecting the diversity of agricultural systems that is central to agroecology.

82 Article 6(E).

83 Certain reforms have already been adopted through the Protocol amending the European Landscape Convention, Strasbourg, 1 August 2016, CETS 219, which has yet to enter into force. The reforms contained in this Protocol are superficial, however, and do not address the concerns raised here.

84 (n 57).

85 Goodwin (n 73).

# Part 2

# Supporting Socioecological Relationships

# 5 Ecosystem Services

## Ecosystem Services and Agroecology

In Part 1, we explored the frameworks through which key socioecological aspects of agriculture are supported in international law. We considered how the law addresses the conservation of agrobiodiversity, at species and genetic levels; how agricultural cultures, as defined by local and traditional knowledge, are protected; and how concerns over these relate to the perceived environmental and socioeconomic risks that modern farming practices pose to agriculture's socioecological networks. Evident from those discussions is the importance of adopting integrated approaches if an agroecological understanding of sustainable agriculture is to be successfully pursued through international law. Conserving on-farm biodiversity can only be achieved if related elements of agrobiodiversity are also supported; the diversity of agricultural systems can only be maintained if the multitude of traditional farming cultures is protected; and coexistence between traditional and modern farming philosophies will only be possible if regulatory decision-making incorporates societal values alongside technical considerations.

To advance agroecology, it is also critical that an integrated approach is taken to the management of the natural processes that occur in agricultural and related ecosystems.[1] This includes an integrated consideration of environmental media, which has long been a concern in environmental legal literature.[2] While this has been widely addressed at the national level, albeit to varying degrees of effectiveness,[3] and notwithstanding conceptual developments such as the ecosystem approach and wider efforts to coordinate the work of supranational bodies,[4] international law as it applies to environmental media, and the processes that occur within and across these, continues to be characterised by distinct regimes and frameworks.[5]

1 R. Norgaard and T. Sikor, 'The Methodology and Practice of Agroecology', in M. Altieri, *Agroecology: The Science of Sustainable Agriculture* (2nd edn, Westview Press, 1995).

2 R. Macrory, 'The Scope of Environmental Law', in G. Winter (ed), *European Environmental Law* (Dartmouth, 1996).

3 J. Dryzek, *The Politics of the Earth: Environmental Discourses* (4th edn, OUP, 2021) ch 8.

4 B. Chambers, *Interlinkages and the Effectiveness of Multilateral Environmental Agreements* (UNUP, 2008) ch 2.

5 A. Boyle and C. Redgwell, *International Law & the Environment* (4th edn, OUP, 2021) 85–88.

DOI: 10.4324/9781003435174-8

The nature of these frameworks and their potential to advance agroecology are our focus in Part 2, beginning with ecosystem services.

Simply defined, ecosystem services are benefits people enjoy from functioning ecosystems.[6] Compiling a comprehensive list, even just of services specifically related to agriculture, would be impossible, not least because our understanding of ecological processes and how they underpin human societies is far from complete.[7] They include the creation of soil and renewal of soil fertility; crop pollination; natural pest control; climate regulation; and inspiring and enabling cultural practices.[8] The fundamental importance to agroecology of maintaining the natural world's capacity to deliver such ecosystem services should therefore be clear, not just in terms of their relevance to agriculture's ecological integrity but also its core social elements.

That ecosystem services are declining around the world is therefore concerning. The latest Global Assessment published by the Intergovernmental Science-Policy Platform on Biodiversity and Ecosystem Services (IPBES), an independent body that provides scientific advice to guide global biodiversity decision-making, concludes that ecosystem functionality and its concomitant capacity to deliver benefits to society are degrading at unprecedented rates.[9] Of particular relevance to this work is the finding that while agricultural production may have increased substantially since 1970, agricultural ecosystem services, including pollinator diversity and carbon retention in soil, have deteriorated.[10]

The decline of ecosystem services and agricultural ecosystem services in particular should not be surprising. Ecosystem services are a product of healthy, functioning and diverse ecosystems, and we have already seen how agricultural systems are being degraded through habitat loss, species decline and other anthropogenic impacts. It does, however, raise questions over how international law provides for the protection of ecosystem services. The integration of ecosystem services into policies designed to deliver an agroecological definition of sustainable agriculture might be considered relatively straightforward. There is, for example, a significant degree of commonality between the origins and operation of ecosystem services and the ecosystem approach as legal concepts,[11] with the relevance of the latter to agroecology being discussed in chapter 1. Ecosystem services are also one representation of agroecology's socioecological networks because they emphasise the dependence of socioeconomic processes on functioning ecosystems. However,

6 UNEP, *Ecosystems and Human Well-Being: A Framework for Assessment* (Island Press, 2003) 53.

7 Secretariat of the Convention on Biological Diversity, *The Economics of Biodiversity: Statistics and Sound-Bites* (EPRM Unit, 6 June 2018).

8 G. Daily, 'Introduction: What Are Ecosystem Services?', in G. Daily (ed), *Nature's Services: Societal Dependence on Natural Ecosystems* (Island Press, 1997) 3–4.

9 E. Brondizio and others (eds) *Global Assessment Report of the Intergovernmental Science-Policy Platform on Biodiversity and Ecosystem Services* (IPBES, 2019) XIV.

10 ibid XV.

11 V. De Lucia, 'A Critical Interrogation of the Relation between the Ecosystem Approach and Ecosystem Services' (2018) 27 *Review of European, Comparative and International Law* 104.

while in theoretical terms there may be substantial overlap between the protection of ecosystem services and other nature-orientated policy goals, such as biodiversity conservation, in practice trade-offs often need to be made. If resources for conservation are limited, a choice could have to be taken between protecting a site that hosts important ecosystem services but has relatively poor biodiversity, and one with greater biodiversity but provides few ecosystem services, for example.[12] Even under a policy of prioritising ecosystem services, trade-offs are necessary. Howe et al ask whether priority should be given to services that enhance pre-existing benefits for local communities, services that would provide new benefits or services that would generally maximise economic growth so as to reduce poverty.[13] Where both biodiversity conservation and the protection of ecosystem services can be advanced simultaneously, choices may still have to be made between enhancing services that benefit individual species and services that support wider ecosystem functionality.[14]

Critically, adopting agroecological approaches to agriculture has been identified as an important means through which the decline of ecosystem services might be addressed.[15] The purpose of this chapter, therefore, is to explore the ways in which ecosystem services are incorporated into the law. I begin by examining how ecosystem services fit into international conservation law's frameworks and decision-making processes. Consideration is given to the apparent discrepancies between how conservation law and conservation practice approach the question of nature's relationships with society, and the extent to which the design and operation of the IPBES facilitates agroecological approaches to decision-making. In the second half of the chapter, attention turns to how different mechanisms that build ecosystem services into law and policy raise potential obstacles to the pursuit of agroecology.

## Ecosystem Services and International Conservation Law

That nature provides benefits has long factored into societal decision-making, notably in relation to the location and expansion of human settlements.[16] The concept of ecosystem services is a relatively recent invention, however, first emerging in scientific discourse in the 1960s[17] and not comprehensively addressed in international

12 R. Goldman and others, 'Trade-Offs in Making Ecosystem Services and Human Well-Being Conservation Priorities', in N. Leader-Williams and others, *Trade-Offs in Conservation: Deciding What to Save* (Wiley-Blackwell / ZSL, 2010) 58–63.

13 C. Howe and others, 'Distinct Positions Underpin Ecosystem Services for Poverty Alleviation' (2020) 54 *Oryx* 375.

14 ibid.

15 Brondizio and others (n 9) 357.

16 E.g. K. Sikk and others, 'Environment and Settlement Location Choice in Stone Age Estonia' (2020) 24 *Estonian Journal of Archaeology* 89 and P. Nunn, 'Geographical Influences on Settlement-Location Choices by Initial Colonizers: A Case Study of the Fiji Islands' (2009) 47 *Geographical Research* 306.

17 R. King, 'Wildlife and Man' (1966) 20 *New York Conservationist* 8, cited in UNEP (n 6). An early attempt to define ecosystem services in terms of economic value can be seen in W. Westman, 'How Much Are Nature's Services Worth?' (1977) 197 *Science* 960.

environmental policy until the UN's 2005 Millennium Ecosystem Assessment.[18] It has since become a focal point for discussions in global biodiversity policy fora, most notably as a result of the work of the IPBES, discussed below.

One consequence of ecosystem services being a relatively new legal concept is that, compared to habitats and species, there is little international law in the form of binding treaty obligations specifically concerned with their protection. This speaks to the wider issue, relevant to agroecology, that international conservation law, as it is set out in key global and regional conservation agreements, has failed to keep pace with developments in conservation practice.[19] Mace traces the evolution of conservation practice through four stages.[20] Until the 1960s, a 'conservation for itself' paradigm prevailed. This emphasised the importance of preserving areas of pristine 'wilderness', a term that reflects colonial man's (this being a deliberate use of the masculine) perception of nature as jungle in need of mastery.[21] During the 1970s and 1980s, when four major global biodiversity treaties were adopted,[22] alongside three principal regional agreements,[23] conservation practice followed a 'nature despite people' model, which focused on protecting individual species and habitats and responding to threats to these in isolation. A radical shift occurred in the form of 'nature for people' in the 1990s when ecosystems became the target for action in recognition of society's dependence on the natural world. The Biodiversity Convention[24] reflects this to a degree, although that states have found it necessary to adopt species-, habitat- and issue-specific programmes of work indicates that the implementation of a holistic conservation policy is difficult to achieve in practice. Finally, the turn of the millennium has seen a 'people and nature' approach to conservation, which recognises the fundamental importance of having robust societal and cultural structures in place that ensure that humanity's interactions with nature protect and restore, rather than degrade, ecosystem resilience and functionality.[25] In other words, contemporary conservation practice does

18 UNEP (n 6).

19 R. Amos, *International Conservation Law: The Protection of Plants in Theory and Practice* (Routledge, 2020) 7.

20 G. Mace, 'Whose Conservation?' (2014) 345 *Science* 1558.

21 W. Adams, *Against Extinction: The Story of Conservation* (Earthscan, 2004) 102–107.

22 Convention of Wetlands of International Importance, Especially as Waterfowl Habitat (Ramsar) 2 February 1971, in force 21 December 1975, 996 UNTS 245; Convention for the Protection of the World Cultural and Natural Heritage (Paris) 16 November 1972, in force 17 December 1975, 27 UST 37, 11 ILM 1358 (1972); Convention on International Trade in Endangered Species of Fauna and Flora (Washington) 3 March 1973, in force 1 July 1975, 993 UNTS 243; and Convention on the Conservation of Migratory Species of Wild Animals (Bonn) 23 June 1979, in force 1 November 1983, 19 ILM 15 (1980).

23 The Convention on Conservation of Nature in the South Pacific (Apia) 12 June 1976, in force 28 June 1990, suspended 2006, IELMT 976:45; Convention on the Conservation of European Wildlife and Natural Habitats (Berne) 19 September 1979, in force 1 June 1982, UKTS 56 (1982); and Association of South East Asian Nations Agreement on the Conservation of Nature and Natural Resources (Kuala Lumpur) 9 July 1985, 15 EPL 64 (1985) (not in force).

24 Rio de Janeiro, 5 June 1992, in force 29 December 1993, 31 ILM 822 (1992).

25 Mace (n 20).

not focus on protecting ecosystems per se, but the broader framework of interactions within and between nature and people so as to enhance the former's capacity for self-renewal and, as a result of this, the delivery of ecosystem services.

The 'people and nature' model of conservation practice clearly aligns with core tenets of agroecology. It reflects agroecology's concept of socioecological networks in which it is impossible to divide the natural from the human, and that social structures should therefore be designed to facilitate positive interactions between nature and humanity while minimising negative ones.[26] That international conservation law largely remains grounded in treaties that pursue a 'nature despite people' approach therefore limits its compatibility with agroecology, although as was highlighted in earlier chapters, soft law developments in key regimes are a better reflection of 'people and nature'.[27] Nevertheless, taking into account both the apparent mismatch between international conservation law and contemporary thinking in conservation practice and that ecosystem services are not necessarily located in the same areas as high levels of biodiversity,[28] there is a question over whether international environmental law is structurally capable of protecting ecosystem services. The latest Global Assessment by the IPBES suggests that it is not,[29] although that biodiversity in general is continuing to decline indicates that the ineffectiveness of law and policy is not a problem that is limited to ecosystem services.[30]

One response to diminishing ecosystem services was the establishment of the IPBES. In particular, this addressed the specific concern, shared by a range of stakeholders, that a lack of reliable and independent scientific information on the state of biodiversity was a major obstacle to the implementation of the Biodiversity Convention, particularly in developing states.[31] This is curious, as the strongest obligation in the Biodiversity Convention is for states to produce reports on the status of their biodiversity and the measures taken to protect it[32] and significant support has been given to developing states to assist them in meeting this obligation.[33] It is true, though, that prior to the creation of the IPBES there was no equivalent

26 Similarities can also be drawn with the ecocentric theory of wild law, which calls for societal structures to be designed in such a way as to enhance connections within and between nature and humanity. See C. Cullinan, *Wild Law: A Manifesto for Earth Justice* (2nd edn, Green Books, 2011) 30–32.
27 De Lucia (n 11) 109–110. E.g., the discussion of the ecosystem approach in ch 1 and the frameworks for landscape protection in ch 4.
28 Goldman and others (n 12).
29 Brondizio and others (n 9).
30 Amos (n 19) Part 2.
31 A. Vadrot, *The Politics of Knowledge and Global Biodiversity* (Routledge, 2014) ch 3.
32 Article 26 of the Biodiversity Convention states: 'Each Contracting Party shall… present to the Conference of the Parties, reports on measures which it has taken for the implementation of the provisions of this Convention and their effectiveness in meeting the objectives of this Convention'. The mandatory language of this provision contrasts with the qualified nature of other obligations in the Convention. See S. Harrop, 'Biodiversity and Conservation' in R. Falkner (ed), *The Handbook of Global Climate and Environment Policy* (John Wiley & Sons, 2013).
33 M. Bowman and others, *Lyster's International Wildlife Law* (2nd edn, CUP, 2010) 623–624.

body operating in the field of biodiversity conservation to the Intergovernmental Panel on Climate Change, which has a central role in providing scientific information to decision-makers on climate change issues.[34]

The IPBES's rationale is, inter alia, to 'strengthen the science-policy interface for biodiversity and ecosystem services for... sustainable development'.[35] Note, though, that the IPBES mandate also speaks of strengthening 'long-term human well-being',[36] and this contrasts with the language of 'future generations' that has long been associated with sustainable development.[37] The choice of the negotiators to include the term 'human wellbeing' might simply be a consequence of the Millennium Ecosystem Assessment, which also refers to human wellbeing,[38] being the impetus behind the creation of the IPBES.[39] It nevertheless adds an important dimension to policy discussions. The idea of wellbeing speaks to individual human experiences,[40] thereby raising questions of environmental and social justice in a way that has arguably been excluded from the interpretation and application of the concept of 'future generations' in environmental law and policy.[41] In this regard, it is arguably better placed to account for factors such as an individual's connection to particular farming practices and landscapes, discussed in chapters 3 and 4.

The inclusion of human wellbeing in the mandate of the IPBES might therefore suggest that the Platform is open to non-Western worldviews on nature and, in particular, worldviews that prioritise nature's non-anthropocentric values over its anthropocentric ones.[42] However, Brandt and Vadrot argue that inherent to the IPBES are certain epistemological selectivities, i.e. governance structures and mechanisms that favour particular forms and sources of knowledge to the exclusion of others, that are grounded in Western ways-of-doing. They note that Bolivia's concerns that the emphasis on ecosystem services in the new science-policy interface platform excluded their perceptions of the natural world as Pachamama were

34 J. Fitzgerald, 'The Intergovernmental Panel on Climate Change: Taking the First Steps Towards a Global Response' (1990) 14 *Southern Illinois University Law Journal* 231.

35 UNEP/IPBES/3/3, Report of the third ad hoc intergovernmental and multi-stakeholder meeting on an intergovernmental science-policy platform on biodiversity and ecosystem services, 11 June 2020, Annex, para 6.

36 ibid.

37 E. Brown Weiss, 'Intergenerational Equity: A Legal Framework for Global Environmental Change', in E. Brown Weiss (ed), *Environmental Change and International Law: New Challenges and Dimensions* (UN University Press, 1992).

38 UNEP (n 6).

39 L. Duvic-Paoli, 'The Intergovernmental Science-Policy Platform for Biodiversity and Ecosystem Services or the Framing of Scientific Knowledge within the Law of Sustainable Development' (2017) 19 *International Community Law Review* 231, 234–236.

40 ibid 244.

41 E.g., my discussion of what references to future generations mean in the context of the World Heritage Convention – Amos (n 19) 26.

42 U. Pascual and others, 'Valuing Nature's Contributions to People: The IPBES Approach' (2017) 26 *Current Opinion in Environmental Sustainability* 7.

essentially ignored during negotiations to establish the IPBES.[43] Similarly, when Venezuela raised concerns in the Biodiversity Convention's Conference of the Parties (COP) that the IPBES might operate in such a way as to reject non-Western science, the response was that participation through the IPBES gave developing countries an opportunity to develop their capacity to produce 'real' science.[44] On this basis, the IPBES does not support the diverse local and traditional agricultural knowledge base central to agroecology and, as a corollary to this, the communities that hold this knowledge and constitute agriculture's socioecological networks.[45]

While it is possible to question the extent to which the IPBES incorporates non-Western epistemologies and value systems, in the decade since its establishment it has proven an invaluable source of data on the state of the world's biodiversity and how this impacts on nature's ability to deliver ecosystem services. Devising legal mechanisms for the protection of ecosystems on the basis of this information, however, has proven challenging and this is arguably due to the difficulties that ecosystem services present as a subject of law and policy.

## Incorporating Ecosystem Services into International Law

Ecosystem services potentially encompass all interactions in and between ecosystems and so, as a single monolithic concept, do not readily translate into law and policy. Consequently, various approaches to categorising ecosystem services have been devised, based on, inter alia, biological groupings and broad descriptions, such as services from renewable and non-renewable resources.[46] The approach favoured in the Millennium Ecosystem Assessment is to classify ecosystem services by the function that they perform in relation to human society. Four, in some cases overlapping, categories have been identified: provisioning, regulating, supporting and cultural services (Table 5.1). As well as providing the means through which the concept of ecosystem services can be incorporated into decision-making, the functional approach to classifying ecosystem services has the advantage of reflecting different aspects of agroecology's socioecological networks. Provisioning services

43 U. Brandt and A. Vadrot, 'Epistemic Selectivities and the Valorisation of Nature: The Cases of the Nagoya Protocol and the Intergovernmental Science-Policy Platform on Biodiversity and Ecosystem Services (IPBES)' (2013) 9 *Law, Environment and Development Journal* 204, 214. This can be contrasted with the Outcome Report of the 2012 UN Conference on Sustainable Development, *The Future We Want*, A/RES/66/288, 11 September 2012, which explicitly recognises the legitimacy of concepts such as Pachamama (para 39).

44 Brand and Vadrot, ibid 215.

45 This speaks to the wider point that the decolonisation of Western epistemological hegemonies should be considered a prerequisite to the transition towards just and sustainable societies, as defined by the Sustainable Development Goals. See R. Amos and others, *Living Sustainability in Higher Education: Connecting Communities, Learning and Justice* (2025, forthcoming) ch 3.

46 R. de Groot and others, 'A Typology for the Description, Classification and Valuation of Ecosystem Functions, Goods and Services' (2002) 41 *Ecological Economics* 393 and J. Norberg, 'Linking Nature's Services to Ecosystems: Some General Ecological Concepts' (1999) 29 *Ecological Economics* 183, both cited in UNEP (n 6) 56.

*Table 5.1* Ecosystem services classifications

| *Service type* | *Description* | *Agricultural examples* |
|---|---|---|
| Provisioning Services | Tangible assets that can be acquired from functioning ecosystems | Food; biofuels; crop genetic diversity |
| Regulating Services | Natural processes enabled by functioning ecosystems | Pollination; natural pest control |
| Supporting Services | Long-term ecosystemic functioning that underpins other ecosystem services | Nutrient cycling; provision of habitat for agrobiodiversity |
| Cultural Services | Intangible benefits gained from functioning ecosystems | Agricultural knowledge generation; social cohesion and identity |

are physical benefits provided by nature.[47] They include crops, i.e. a product of agricultural systems, but also crop genetic diversity and therefore maintaining such services delivers on other aspects of agroecological agenda. Regulating services essentially relate to natural processes,[48] such as crop pollination, and again can only be properly maintained by ensuring sufficient agrobiodiversity. Related to these are supporting services, which are more long-term processes such as nutrient cycling through environmental media, but are again key to maintaining the proper functioning of agricultural systems.[49] In contrast, cultural services cover the ways in which ecological health and integrity underpin social interactions and processes.[50] These are particularly evident in the context of agriculture, not only as reflective of agroecology's perception of farming systems as part of wider socioecological networks but also in terms of how agriculture's natural timetable has influenced societal calendars.[51]

The functional classification of ecosystem services constitutes a means through which the complex relationships in and between ecosystems, and the benefits these provide to humans, can be expressed in a manner that is amenable to the design of law and policy.[52] Further, ecosystem services as a policy device present nature in a more holistic manner than the species-, habitat- and issues-specific approaches typical of 20th century conservation agreements and are therefore a better reflection of the 'people and nature' framework of contemporary conservation practice.[53] There is, however, a risk that by defining ecosystem services by functionality, or in

47 ibid 56–57.
48 ibid 57–58.
49 ibid 59–60.
50 ibid 58–59.
51 R. Amos, 'Reassessing the Role of Plants in Society' (2017) 13 *International Journal of Law in Context* 295, 311.
52 M. van der Belt and others, 'Scientific Understanding of Ecosystem Services', in UN, *The First Global Integrated Marine Assessment* (CUP, 2016) 6.
53 Mace (n 20).

other reductionist terms, the true complexity of ecosystemic processes is ignored in favour of managing systems for the purpose of maximising specific benefits.[54] It could consequently lead to a failure to adopt the systems-level approach to decision-making required for the implementation of agroecology. Managing a watercourse so that the maximum amount of water possible can be extracted to irrigate crops, for example, may undermine its ability to support connected ecosystems, which would reduce overall (agro)biodiversity. Further, the application of ecosystem services as a concept has proven contentious, as it represents a deliberate choice to frame the value of nature anthropocentrically, potentially to the exclusion of non-anthropocentric considerations.[55] The focus, in other words, is on valuing nature for the direct benefits they provide to humans, i.e. its instrumental value, rather than its intrinsic or ecological value,[56] and this may limit the extent to which the concept of ecosystem services, as it is expressed in international law, may be used to advance agroecology.

The distinction between instrumental value (value based on the direct benefits provided to humans) and ecological value (value based on the role played in an ecosystem) is not always clear. As the concept of ecosystem services itself demonstrates, a natural entity can simultaneously hold both instrumental and ecological value and ecological value has, on occasion, been included within understandings of instrumental value.[57] Pollinators are a useful illustration of this, particularly where the plants they pollinate are crops.[58] In the context of law, however, it is nevertheless important to understand precisely how something is valued because it speaks to the motivations behind a particular regulatory choice, and therefore the scope of protection provided by that regulation.[59] A policy of sustainable agriculture that is primarily founded on nature's instrumental value may exclude certain aspects of agrobiodiversity, for example, as the case of the turtle dove (*Streptopelia turtur*) highlighted in this book's introduction illustrates. The turtle dove has evolved to rely on certain farming practices for its food supply, meaning that it legitimately falls under definitions of agrobiodiversity,[60] but plays little role in providing an

54 J. Ruhl and others, *The Law and Policy of Ecosystem Services* (Island Press, 2007) 32–34.

55 G. Luck and others, 'Ethical Considerations in On-Ground Applications of the Ecosystem Services Concept' (2012) 62 *Bioscience* 1020, 1022.

56 There is an extensive body of literature on the value of nature, comprising various and overlapping interpretations. I have previously set out a framework of five interpretations: instrumental (anthropocentric value consisting of direct exploitation); inherent (anthropocentric value where there is no direct exploitation, such as aesthetics); intrinsic (value the something has in and of itself, regardless of the perceptions of others); ecological value (value based on the role an entity plays in its ecosystem); and negative (how an entity undermines the positive value of something else). I adopt the same definitions for the purposes of this work. See Amos (n 19) 17–24.

57 Bowman and others (n 33) 62.

58 G. Nabhan and S. Buchmann, 'Services Provided by Pollinators', in Daily (n 8).

59 C. Harrison and others, 'Capturing Values for Nature: Ecological, Economic and Cultural Perspectives', in J. Holder and D. McGillivray (eds), *Locality and Identity: Environmental Issues in Law and Society* (Ashgate Publishing, 1999) 86–88.

60 J. Santilli, *Agrobiodiversity and the Law* (Earthscan, 2012) 1.

ecosystem service of direct consequence to the farm. It would consequently not be a priority target for conservation action under a policy framework founded on the instrumental values of nature, and the wider links between the farm and its sociological networks would therefore not be respected.

This reveals a tension between agriculture, as typically understood in the Western world, and agroecology. Agriculture is primarily grounded in nature's instrumental value; its purpose is to produce food and other products for human consumption by utilising plants, animals and ecological processes. Agroecology, on the other hand, places much greater emphasis on nature's ecological value and the natural processes of self-renewal in and beyond any one agricultural system.[61] I have argued elsewhere that it is international law's predominant focus on nature's instrumental values that is a core reason why efforts to address biodiversity loss have failed.[62] This leads to short-term and fragmented decision-making, concerned with maximising the economic values of specific aspects of nature, rather than policies that support the long-term integrity of the natural world as a whole.[63] As we have seen in the preceding chapters, this criticism is equally applicable to those legal instruments concerned with promoting sustainable agriculture.

I am not suggesting that agreements relevant to agricultural practices should not be concerned with promoting nature's instrumental values. These are legitimate ways of perceiving the value of nature and can be a persuasive argument in favour of conservation.[64] Rather, I am arguing that these should be a secondary concern to protecting nature's ecological values, as it is these that underpin nature's capacity to deliver on the instrumental values, manifested through ecosystem services, on which agriculture and other social endeavours depend. It is therefore necessary to reorientate the value-basis of the law so that it is framed by, reflects and seeks to enhance nature's ecological value.[65]

How this might be achieved, in the context of both agroecology and wider nature conservation efforts, is through the adoption of ecological sustainability as the law's overarching framework in place of the flawed model of sustainable development.[66] As noted previously, sustainable development has been criticised for presenting its three pillars of environmental protection, economic development and social equity as mutually reinforcing, thereby failing to recognise the realities that, first, trade-offs between and within the three are inevitable,[67] and second, that

61 F. Caporali, 'History and Development of Agroecology and Theory of Agroecosystems', in M. Monteduro and others, *Law and Agroecology: A Transdisciplinary Dialogue* (Springer, 2015) 3–6.

62 Amos (n 19) ch 1.

63 H. Rolston III, 'Are Values in Nature Subjective or Objective?', in R. Elliot and A. Gare (eds), *Environmental* Philosophy (Open University Press, 1983) 136.

64 A. Wiersama, 'Wildlife', in L. Rajamani and J. Peel (eds), *The Oxford Handbook of International Environmental Law* (2nd edn, OUP, 2021) 555–556.

65 Amos (n 19) 16.

66 ibid 228–234.

67 E. Lydgate, 'Sustainable Development in the WTO: From Mutual Supportiveness to Balancing' (2012) 11 *World Trade Review* 621, 622.

such trade-offs must respect the carrying capacity of the relevant ecosystem(s).[68] An alternative definition of sustainable development, incorporating a notion of ecosystem services, is provided by Pearce and Turner. They suggest that economic development should only be pursued in a manner that maintains nature's capacity to deliver ecosystem services over the long-term, defined in relation to two rules. Renewable resources should only be utilised at a rate equal to or less than their capacity to regenerate, and the use of non-renewable resources should be optimised in accordance with substitutability between resources and technological developments.[69]

From an agroecological perspective, Pearce and Turner's construction of sustainable development has the advantage of placing the ecosystem services on which agricultural systems rely at the centre of policy considerations. In doing so, they also provide guidance on when sustainable development's three pillars actually will be mutually reinforcing: it is when socioeconomic development is pursued in a way that does not undermine nature's capacity to deliver ecosystem services. However, their approach is also problematic. Inherent to their rule on non-renewable resources is an assumption that technology can substitute natural capital, which is a common criticism of weak interpretations of sustainability,[70] and there is no apparent recognition that utilisation of a particular resource may never be sustainable. Similarly, their rule for renewable resources has already been tested in international law and states have proven incapable of restraining their exploitation of species to sustainable levels. Following the failure of the Blue Whale Unit as a mechanism to regulate commercial whaling,[71] in 1974 the parties to the International Convention for the Regulation of Whaling (ICRW) agreed the New Management Procedure (NMP), which took effect in 1976.[72] Whale species covered by the regime were divided into stocks according to geographic location and each stock was assigned to one of three categories depending on how their estimated population level corresponded to each species' maximum sustainable yield, i.e. the rate at which individual animals could be removed from the wild

68 World Commission on Environment and Development, *Our Common Future (The Brundtland Report)*, A/42/427, 4 August 1987, 24.

69 D. Pearce and K. Turner, *Economics of Natural Resources and the Environment* (Harvester Wheatsheaf, 1990) 24.

70 Weak sustainability can be contrasted with strong sustainability, which rejects the substitution of natural capital with artificial/technological alternatives. See D. Pearce and E. Barbier, *Blueprint for a Sustainable Economy* (Earthscan, 2000) 23–24.

71 In short, whale species were assigned a value corresponding to how much oil they provided in contrast to a blue whale (*Balaenoptera musculus*) and quotas were assigned on that basis. E.g., two fin whales (*Balaenoptera physalus*) were equivalent to one blue whale. This approach was flawed in several respects, a key one being that it put greater pressure on the larger species as it was more cost-effective for whalers to meet their quotas by catching a small number of large whales than a large number of smaller whales – J. Scarff, 'The International Management of Whales, Dolphins and Porpoises: An Interdisciplinary Assessment' (1977) 6 *Ecology Law Quarterly* 323, 351–352.

72 Washington, 2 December 1946, in force 10 November 1948, 161 UNTS 72 (as amended 19 November 1956, 338 UNTS 336).

without undermining the species' capacity for self-renewal. This model was abandoned when it became clear that whale populations were continuing to decline at an unsustainable rate and replaced in 1986 by the moratorium on commercial whaling, which remains in place to this day.[73] While in extremely localised conditions management mechanisms based on maximum sustainable yield might be feasible if common rules can be agreed,[74] given that states have so far proven unable to halt rates of biodiversity loss it seems unlikely that any broader sustainable development policy based on ideas of sustainable yield will be effective. This is particularly true in the context of agriculture, where it is not just a question of exploiting separate species or populations, as was the case under the ICRW, but a much wider range of natural entities and processes, the destabilisation of which would have knock-on effects for other elements of the relevant network.[75] This again highlights the significance of applying systems-level analysis to decision-making processes, which is a key component of any agroecological framework.[76]

More desirable from an ecological perspective than Pearce and Turner's proposal is the principle of ecological sustainability.[77] However, the application of this in practice could prove controversial if it would prevent the unsustainable exploitation of an ecosystem service necessary to sustain a basic level of human subsistence. For example, a period of prolonged drought may require a local village to extract an amount of water from the only nearby water source to irrigate their crops, which results in it no longer being capable of sustaining the local ecosystem. A strict application of the principle of ecological sustainability would require the water source to be preserved at the expense of the villagers' crops, regardless of what this would mean for their ability to feed themselves. In such circumstances, the unsustainable course of action would arguably be justified.[78] As I have discussed elsewhere, the true value of the ecological sustainability principle is not that it would always lead to a sustainable approach being taken. Rather, it would shift the nature of the decision-making process by creating a presumption in favour of sustainability, with the onus of having to rebut that presumption being placed

73 Note that the moratorium only applies to commercial whaling. Whaling by indigenous groups for subsistence and cultural reasons is still permissible, which has been controversial. See J. Firestone and J. Lilley, 'Aboriginal Subsistence Whaling and the Right to Practice and Revitalize Cultural Traditions and Customs' (2005) 8 *Journal of International Wildlife Law and Policy* 177.

74 This is the essence of Ostrom's rebuttal to Harden's tragedy of the commons hypothesis – E. Ostrom, *Governing the Commons: The Evolution of Institutions for Collective Action* (CUP, 2015) and G. Hardin, 'The Tragedy of the Commons' (1968) 162 *Science* 1243. See further, Ruhl and others (n 54) 160–164,

75 The unsustainable exploitation of whales also had knock-on effects for marine ecosystems. See J. Roman and others, 'Whales as Marine Ecosystem Engineers' (2014) 12 *Frontiers in Ecology and the Environment* 377.

76 E. Noe and H. Alrøe, 'Regulation of Agroecosystems: A Social Systems Analysis of Agroecology and Law', in Monteduro and others (n 61).

77 See the book's introduction.

78 Although other factors would also have to be considered, such as the availability of other food supplies and the dependence of other communities on the same water source.

on those who would pursue the unsustainable activity.[79] This raises its own challenges in the context of agroecology, however, as it lifts management decisions from individual farms to a sphere of wider societal concern. It may be in a farmer's immediate interests to employ a different practice on their land, but if this decision would reduce the diversity of the wider farming network, or negatively impact on a shared resource, then the challenge would be for the farmer to explain why their private interest should override the public interest in maintaining the integrity of the wider socioecological network. While this may be possible, particularly if the farmer could demonstrate how the revised practices would serve other aspects of agroecological or sustainability agenda, there will in the first place be a conflict with that farmer's property rights and economic freedoms. Alongside recasting sustainable development, therefore, it is also necessary to address the dominant framing of natural resource management by individual property rights.[80] Ecological sustainability, coupled with the core agroecological concept of socioecological networks, offers the alternative narrative that Grecksch and Holzhausen believe is necessary to achieve this.[81]

***Payments for Ecosystem Services***

Related to the concern of how ecosystem services represent a particular interpretation of the values of the natural world is their potential to lead to a commodification of nature.[82] This is not inevitable. James-Bell draws a distinction between the use of ecosystem services as a metaphor for the connections between humanity and nature, which would represent the socioecological networks central to agroecology, and as an instrument through which nature is deconstructed and assigned a monetary value.[83] The reinforcement of nature's instrumental values is arguably more likely, however, if nature is defined in terms of ecosystem services. Hahn et al identify seven degrees of commodification associated with ecosystem

79 Amos (n 19) 232. This presumption will be meaningless unless it is properly enforced. Arguably the closest mechanism that currently exists in law is Article 6 of the EU Habitats Directive 92/43/EEC [1992] OJ L206/7, which states, inter alia, that activities that may have a significant negative impact on sites protected under EU law may only proceed 'imperative reasons of overriding public interest'. Evidence suggests, however, that ordinary socioeconomic interests too frequently override a protected site's conservation objectives – D. McGillivray, 'Compensatory Measures under Article 6(4) of the Habitats Directive: No Net Loss for Natura 2000?' in C. Born and others (eds), *The Habitats Directive in its EU Environmental Law Context: European Nature's Best Hope?* (Routledge, 2015) 109–113.

80 K. Grecksch and J. Holzhausen, 'Property Rights Revisited – Are Narratives the Way Forward?' (2017) 9 *International Journal of Law in the Built Environment* 94.

81 ibid.

82 E. Turnhout and others, 'Rethinking Biodiversity: From Goods and Services to "Living With"' (2013) 6 *Conservation Letters* 154.

83 J. Bell-James, 'Ecosystem Services as a Metaphor in Environmental Law: Balancing Intrinsic and Instrumental Values' (2020) 39 *University of Queensland Law Journal* 525, 534–535.

services.[84] At point zero, the value of nature is defined in purely ecological, even intrinsic terms, and is associated with ecocentric ideas such as rights of nature.[85] Their remaining six points are all grounded in nature's instrumental values, with point one being the prioritisation of nature's instrumental values but without going so far as assigning monetary values, and point six being complete commodification or financialisation, whereby nature is reduced to and sold as a series of financial instruments. Forest bonds, through which forest owners sell bonds to raise finance using the forests themselves as collateral, are given as an example of this.[86]

It is this potential for ecosystem services to be used as a way of commodifying nature that leads De Lucia to suggest that, rather than an organising principle that facilitates the making of policy trade-offs in ecological terms, ecosystem services are instead a means through which ecosystemic relationships are deconstructed so that specific anthropocentric benefits can be individually addressed.[87] This is an important criticism of the practice of payments for ecosystem services (PES), i.e. paying those who manage land to do so in a way that provides an ecosystem service.[88] It is notable that PES are reflected in point four of Hahn et al's six degrees of commodification.[89] Similarly, it has been observed that PES are often only employed to protect ecosystem services where the technological alternative to those services is extremely expensive.[90] In other words, PES are a hollow case of strong sustainability,[91] adopted out of economic necessity rather than recognition of the critical need to maintain natural capital regardless of technological advance.

PES are nevertheless a legitimate response to the fact that because they are public goods, i.e. freely accessible by all, landowners have little economic incentive in maintaining ecosystem services,[92] and there are numerous examples of how PES

84 T. Hahn and others, 'Purposes and Degrees of Commodification: Economic Instruments for Biodiversity and Ecosystem Services Need Not Rely on Markets or Monetary Valuation' (2015) 16 *Ecosystem Services* 74.

85 ibid 75.

86 ibid 78–79, drawing on M. Cranford and others, *Unlocking Forest Bonds: A High-Level Workshop on Innovative Finance for Tropical Forests* (WWF Forest & Climate Initiative, Global Canopy Programme and Climate Bonds Initiative, 2011).

87 De Lucia (n 11) 107.

88 J. Salzman and others, 'Payments for Ecosystem Services: Past, Present and Future' (2018) 6 *Texas A&M Law Review* 199, 204–205.

89 Hahn and others (n 84) 77–78.

90 C. Reid and W. Nsoh, *The Privatisation of Biodiversity: New Approaches to Conservation Law* (Edward Elgar, 2016) 84.

91 (n 70).

92 J. Salzman, 'What Is the Emperor Wearing? The Secret Lives of Ecosystem Services' (2011) 28 *Pace Environmental Law Review* 591, 595. Note that PES are not the only way that ecosystem services might be provided for through legal structures. Alternatives included direct regulation of activities that might impact on ecosystem services and cap-and-trade market mechanisms. See, inter alia, J. Ruhl and J. Salzman, 'Global Assessment of the Law and Policy of Ecosystem Services' (2020) 39 *University of Queensland Law Journal* 503 and B. Pardy, 'The Logic of Ecosystems: Capitalism, Rights and the Law of "Ecosystem Services"' (2014) 5 *Journal of Human Rights and the Environment* 136, 138.

have successfully delivered environmental agenda at both local and global levels.[93] Salzman refers to the example of New York paying communities in local watersheds to maintain the quality of their water supply to avoid the expense of a water treatment plant.[94] Even with economic incentives to preserve ecosystem functionality, however, success is not guaranteed. In 2014, Norway reached an ambitious agreement to pay Liberia $150 million to end illegal deforestation, increase the area of forest designated as a protected area and otherwise support positive forest management, all by 2020, to maintain Liberia's forests as an important carbon sink.[95] Despite this, illegal deforestation remains a problem in Liberia,[96] and annual rates of primary forest loss remain as high as they were when the agreement with Norway was reached.[97]

The difficulties Liberia has faced in ending illegal deforestation illustrate that to be effective, PES must operate within a wider regulatory framework through which any agreement can be properly enforced.[98] On the other hand, evidence also suggests that PES, particularly in relation to water services, carbon storage and habitat preservation, represent a viable conservation strategy in the absence of more robust environmental legal frameworks.[99] They are also a useful mechanism where compulsion would prove politically controversial, as in the case of compelling farmers to manage their land in particular ways.[100]

At the international level, PES form part of the positive economic incentive measures that states are encouraged to adopt through the Biodiversity Convention's work on Economics, Trade and Incentive Measures.[101] Pursuant to Article 11 of the Convention,[102] COP Decision IX/6 called for studies into, inter alia, PES and their implications for key stakeholders,[103] and significant work was done towards Target 3 of the Aichi Biodiversity Targets, discussed in chapter 1.[104] Also relevant here

93 Ruhl and others (n 54) Part III.

94 J. Salzman, 'A Field of Green? The Past and Future of Ecosystem Services' (2006) 21 *Journal of Land Use and Environmental Law* 133, 139–140.

95 https://www.smithsonianmag.com/smart-news/norway-paying-liberia-stop-deforestation-180952824/ (last accessed 20/04/2023).

96 https://news.mongabay.com/2021/11/liberia-loggers-felling-trees-outside-concession-as-government-stands-by/ (last accessed 20/04/2023).

97 https://www.globalforestwatch.org/dashboards/country/LBR (last accessed 20/04/2023).

98 C. Rodgers, 'Towards a "New" Agricultural Law? Securing "Public Goods" from Agriculture' (2019) 24 *Drake Journal of Agricultural Law* 241, 245–247.

99 Salzman and others (n 88).

100 Historically, conservation obligations in the United Kingdom were primarily voluntary in nature, as conservation was not considered sufficiently important to justify interfering with private property rights – C. Reid, *Nature Conservation Law* (3rd edn, Thomas Reuters, 2009) 39.

101 https://www.cbd.int/incentives/positive.shtml (last accessed 20/04/2023).

102 Each Contracting Party shall, as far as possible and as appropriate, adopt economically and socially sound measures that act as incentives for the conservation and sustainable use of components of biological diversity.

103 Decision IX/6, Incentive measures (Article 11), UNEP/CBD/COP/DEC/IX/6, 9 October 2008.

104 Decision X/2, The Strategic Plan for Biodiversity 2011–2020 and the Aichi Biodiversity Targets, UNEP/CBD/COP/DEC/X/2, 29 October 2010, Annex. Target 3 was: 'By 2020… incentives,

is The Economics of Ecosystems and Biodiversity (TEEB) initiative and its programme on agriculture and food.[105] TEEB seeks to highlight the economic value to agriculture of biodiversity and ecosystem functionality and the interconnections between natural ecosystems, agrosystems and wider society. It does so by bringing together stakeholders from a range of disciplines, in a similar fashion to the Satoyama Initiative discussed in chapter 4, to conduct systems-level analyses of agricultural systems, practices and products in an explicit rejection of the 'silo-thinking' approach to the consideration of how agriculture impacts, and is impacted by changes to, society and the natural world.[106] As we examined in the introduction, the adoption of systems-level approaches in decision-making is an important component of any agroecological legal framework, as this is the only way to ensure that the full impacts of decisions, across the complete socioecological network of which agricultural systems are part, can be addressed. This applies just as much in the context of the relationships between agricultural ecosystem services.[107]

While international fora such as TEEB and the other work of the Biodiversity Convention have important roles in guiding and facilitating PES programmes, as with virtually all conservation measures, these ultimately rely on implementation at the national level. Rodgers views PES as an option for the future, post-Brexit, agricultural policy in the United Kingdom. He notes that linking agriculture subsidies to the provisioning of ecosystem services would connect farmers, as the supplier of ecosystem services, with those services' end-users, thereby overcoming the problem that ecosystem services are typically public goods for which landowners receive no direct payment for providing.[108] From an agroecological perspective, the advantages of such an approach are twofold. First, it creates another mechanism through which the ecological integrity of natural ecosystems, within and connected to agricultural systems, is protected. There is evidence from virtually every state in the world suggesting that, overall, biodiversity is continuing to decline at the national level,[109] indicating that traditional legal approaches to conservation, grounded primarily in subjecting endangered habitats and species to different forms of regulation, are ineffective.[110] Returning to our discussion of the values of nature, this may be a consequence of a degree of incompatibility between the rationale behind the conservation measures (to protect nature's intrinsic and ecological values) and the motivations of actors involved in the exploitation of species and

including subsidies, harmful to biodiversity and eliminated, phased out or reformed in order to minimize or avoid negative impacts, and positive incentives for the conservation and sustainable use of biodiversity are developed and applied.' The Fifth Global Biodiversity Outlook concluded that little progress had been made towards this Target – Secretariat to the Convention on Biological Diversity, *Global Biodiversity Outlook 5* (2020) 44.

105 http://teebweb.org/our-work/agrifood/ (last accessed 20/04/2023).

106 K. Fiedler and others, 'Life Cycle Costing and Food Systems: Concepts, Trends, and Challenges of Impact Valuation' (2018) 8 *Michigan Journal of Environmental and Administrative Law* 1, 42–43.

107 Ruhl and others (n 54) 18–20.

108 Rodgers (n 98) 244–245.

109 See the national reports submitted by states party to the Biodiversity Convention under Article 26: https://www.cbd.int/reports/ (last accessed 20/04/2023).

110 Amos (n 19) ch 2.

habitats (nature's instrumental values). By designing conservation measures that reflect how those that utilise nature perceive nature's value, PES have the potential to achieve significant buy-in from key stakeholders, a prerequisite to success for any policy.[111]

Second, PES support relationships between different actors that exist but may not be explicitly recognised in agriculture's socioecological networks, manifesting and formalising these through legal agreements. These agreements, however, will need to be more complex than the binary arrangements that typify the provision of services (i.e. between supplier and user). Rodgers proposes the use of conservation covenants, building on the experiences of, inter alia, Australia and the United States.[112] These would comprise an agreement between all relevant landowners and a so-called 'responsible body', typically a state entity, that would act on behalf of the public to enforce the terms of the covenant, under which the landowners would manage land in such a way as to ensure that it continued to provide ecosystem services.[113] Similar ideas have been explored in the context of applying the public trust doctrine to ensure public access to green spaces and serve to lift nature into a legal sphere in which the collective public interest is reflected in how privately owned land is managed.[114]

The success of such approaches rests on a number of factors.[115] An important one is that it must be sufficiently clear where property rights over those aspects of nature that produce the ecosystem services lie.[116] Two issues may complicate this. The first is where the relevant elements of the natural world are not subject to property rights under the applicable legal system. In the United Kingdom, wild fauna cannot be subject to ownership, which means that a landowner may not charge for any direct ecosystem service, such as pollination or natural pest control, which they provide.[117] Rodgers' response to this is to pursue an input-based approach to PES, i.e. landowners are paid for managing land so that it supports a wide range of species rather than for the benefits provided by the species per se.[118] This overcomes the problem of lack of legal ownership but raises the question of what, if any, payment should be made in the event that the landowner manages the land as agreed but the expected ecosystem services do not materialise. Second, the locus, nature and extent of any property rights, as well as any

111 ibid 219–221.

112 Rodgers (n 98) 251–252.

113 See also work relating to landscape enterprise networks, i.e. groups of stakeholders that manage land so as to produce an ecosystem service of behalf of a demand-side user – C. Rodgers and H. Kendall, 'Implementing Landscape-Scale Environmental Management: Landscape Enterprise Networks' (2023) 35 *Journal of Environmental Law* 87.

114 D. McGillivray and J. Holder, 'Locality, Environment and Law: The Case of Town and Village Greens' (2007) 3 *International Journal of Law in Context* 1, 12–15. See also C. Rodgers and D. Grinlinton, 'Covenanting for Nature: A Comparative Study of the Utility and Potential of Conservation Covenants' (2020) 83 *Modern Law Review* 373.

115 Reid and Nsoh (n 90) ch 5.

116 Ruhl and others (n 54) ch 4.

117 Rodgers (n 98) 246.

118 ibid.

obligations attached to those rights, may not be immediately clear.[119] One contentious issue in global climate policy, for example, is the extent to which indigenous communities can participate in schemes that reward the management of forests as carbon sinks,[120] due to the weak nature of indigenous land rights.[121] As was observed in chapters 2 and 4, respecting indigenous rights delivers on important aspects of the agroecological agenda. Here, they serve to underscore the importance of facilitating wide stakeholder engagement in the design and operation of conservation covenants for the provision of ecosystem services.[122] As Holligan argues, enhanced public participation is essential in ensuring that any conservation covenant reflects the priorities of the wider community rather than just those party to the agreement.[123] It was noted above that when designing policies to maximise ecosystem services, trade-offs, either between protecting ecosystem services and pursuing other conservation objectives or between different forms of ecosystem services, will need to be made. Allowing for participation in the drafting of conservation covenants increases the chances of those trade-offs being considered legitimate by society, particularly by those who will be impacted by those decisions.[124] For advancing agroecology, this should be considered vital as it is a core element of the systems-level approach to problem analysis and decision-making that is essential if agroecology is to be implemented in practice. It is only by including every member of a socioecological network that the full extent of how a decision, such as the adoption of a conservation covenant over a shared natural resource, will impact on all actors can be understood and, if necessary, addressed.[125]

## Conclusions

Ecosystem services are an interesting concept in the context of advancing agroecology in international law, as their potential to do so depends on how this term is utilised in policy and decision-making processes. On the one hand, it speaks to society's dependence on the health and proper functioning of natural ecosystems,

119 S. Lockie, 'Market Instruments, Ecosystem Services, and Property Rights: Assumptions and Conditions for Sustained Social and Ecological Benefits' (2013) 31 *Land Use Policy* 90.

120 E.g., the scheme to reduce deforestation and forest degradation (REDD+) adopted under the UN Framework Convention on Climate Change, New York, 9 May 1992, in force 24 March 1994, 1771 UNTS 107. See G. Cerbu and others, 'Locating REDD: A Global Survey and Analysis of REDD Readiness and Demonstration Activities' (2011) 14 *Environmental Science and Policy* 168.

121 J. Tridgell, 'Seeing REDD: Carbon Forest Programmes and Indigenous Rights' (2016) *Australian Journal of Environmental Law* 86.

122 Broad stakeholder engagement is an important aspect of wider theories of environmental justice. See D. Schlosberg, *Defining Environmental Justice: Theories, Movements, and Nature* (OUP, 2007) 25–29.

123 B. Holligan, 'Narratives of Capital versus Narratives of Community: Conservation Covenants and the Private Regulation of Land Use' (2019) 30 *Journal of Environmental Law* 55, 70–72.

124 J. Steele, 'Participation and Deliberation in Environmental Law: Exploring a Problem-Solving Approach' (2001) 21 *Oxford Journal of Legal Studies* 415, 424–425.

125 V. Kolinjivadi and others, 'Juggling Multiple Dimensions in a Complex Socio-Ecosystem: The Issue of Targeting in Payments for Ecosystem Services' (2015) 58 *Geoforum* 1.

as it is only when these conditions are met that the natural world will be able to deliver services to humans. As such, ecosystem services illustrate the interconnectedness of the agroecological concept of the socioecological network and how positive and negative anthropogenic impacts on the environment will result in positive and negative feedback for society. This in turn reinforces the case for adopting systems-level analyses of decisions relevant to agriculture, notwithstanding the potential conflicts this may cause with individual farmers' property rights.

On the other hand, to frame humanity's relationships with the natural world in the language of ecosystem services constitutes a deliberate choice to prioritise nature's anthropocentric, specifically its instrumental, values. While these can be a powerful incentive to preserve ecosystem functionality, there is also a risk that it leads to a deconstruction of nature and the commodification of its individual aspects. From an agroecological perspective, this is a core criticism of the use of PES as a mechanism through which ecosystem services can be addressed through the law. A further issue is highlighted by the example of the agreement between Norway and Liberia, namely that to be effective, PES must operate under a robust legal framework. Conservation covenants are one way to overcome this in national law that could align with agroecology, as they formalise relationships in socioecological networks that might otherwise go unacknowledged. This would be contingent, however, on there being sufficient stakeholder engagement prior to their adoption so that the potential impacts on all actors in the relevant network can be taken into account.

Two key reforms can be identified at the international level that would mitigate the risk of ecosystem services merely serving as another vehicle through which nature is managed according to its narrow instrumental values. Firstly, sustainable development as the overarching policy framework should be replaced with a principle of ecological sustainability. This would ensure that trade-offs between different policy choices are made in the context of the natural world's capacity to deliver ecosystem services. Second, greater efforts should be made to ensure that non-Western views on humanity's relationships with the natural world are reflected in the work of key institutions, such as the IPBES. That these were explicitly recognised in the Biodiversity Convention's Global Biodiversity Framework is encouraging,[126] although as we observed in chapter 1, there has yet to be a fundamental shift in the primary framings of international conservation law and policy.

126 Decision 15/4, Kunming-Montreal Global Biodiversity Framework, CBD/COP/DEC/15/4, 19 December 2022, Annex, para 7(b).

# 6 Soil Conservation and Land Degradation

## Soil and Sustainability

Soil is fundamentally important to agricultural systems and ecosystems generally. A healthy soil system, i.e. one in which high yields of nutritious crops can be grown with minimal environmental impact,[1] contributes to ecosystem resilience, comprises and supports high levels of biodiversity, and delivers a range of other ecosystem services across the four functional categories of these discussed in the previous chapter.[2] It is estimated that a single gram of healthy soil contains one billion cells of bacteria, hundreds of metres of fungal hyphae, or connecting structures, and a host of different species ranging in evolutionary complexity.[3] The maintenance of soil quantity and quality is consequently critical if agroecology is to be pursued through the law. Additionally, soil conservation has been linked to the achievement of the Sustainable Development Goals (SDGs).[4] Lal and others note that a number of the SDGs, including 2 (zero hunger), 13 (climate action) and 15 (life on land), are directly linked to soil health, while others, such as 5 (gender equality), 10 (reduced inequalities) and 16 (peace, justice and strong institutions), have some correlation to sustainable soil management.[5] In relation to the latter, for example, food security is considered an important means of preventing conflict, and, particularly for rural communities in developing countries, this will be dependent on there being sufficiently healthy soil to allow them to support themselves.[6]

1 F. Magdoff, 'Soil Quality and Management', in Miguel Altieri, *Agroecology: The Science of Sustainable Agriculture* (2nd edn, Westview Press, 1995) 349.

2 L. Brussaard and others, 'Soil Biodiversity for Agricultural Sustainability' (2007) 121 *Agriculture, Ecosystems and Environment* 233; UNEP, *Ecosystems and Human Well-Being: A Framework for Assessment* (Island Press, 2003) 56–60.

3 FAO and others, *State of Knowledge of Soil Biodiversity – Status, Challenges and Potentialities, Report 2020* FAO, 2020) 13.

4 A/RES/70/1, 21 October 2015.

5 R. Lal and others, 'Soils and Sustainable Development Goals of the United Nations: An International Union of Soil Sciences Perspective' (2021) 25 *Geoderma Regional* e00398. See also J. Ladha, 'Achieving the Sustainable Development Goals in Agriculture: The Crucial Role of Nitrogen in Cereal-Based Systems' (2020) 163 *Advances in Agronomy* 39.

6 Lal and others, ibid 9–10.

DOI: 10.4324/9781003435174-9

It is concerning, therefore, that soil is being increasingly eroded and degraded by agricultural practices, undermining a farm's ecological capacity for self-renewal and also causing a range of other adverse environmental impacts.[7] To give two examples highlighted by the Secretariat of the Biodiversity Convention,[8] on-farm soil erosion has been shown to lead to sedimentation and consequent degradation of water systems, undermining their ecological health and capacity to deliver ecosystem services, and it is estimated that 230 million tonnes of nutrients are removed from agricultural soils every year through agricultural practices, leaving them less able to support agricultural production and agrobiodiversity.[9] It is due to such impacts that the failure to properly address soil conservation is considered to be a leading reason why the international community appears on track to miss, inter alia, SDGs 2 and 15.[10]

This chapter explores the different contexts in which soil conservation has been addressed in international law. I begin by considering the work of the UN Food and Agricultural Organisation (FAO) and the Biodiversity Convention. While the instruments that have been adopted under these bodies have some agroecological merit, their impact is limited due to their non-binding legal nature. With this in mind, attention turns to whether a soil treaty should be adopted as a new means for advancing agroecology in international law and what form this might take. The final section of the chapter addresses the global problem of desertification and land degradation, of which the decline in soil quantity and quality is a driving factor. We will examine how the 1994 UN Convention to Combat Desertification (the Desertification Convention)[11] attempts to respond to this problem at the same time as protecting dryland habitats, the maintenance of which is also important for supporting agricultural systems.

## Soil Conservation in International Law

Despite the recognised importance of, and threats to, soil, the international community has not developed a coherent approach to its conservation, notwithstanding individual successes at the national level.[12] The situation has improved, however, since the first half of the 20th century, when little effort was made to deal specifically with soil conservation,[13] and to say that international law has ignored soil, as

7 F. Verheijen and others, 'Tolerable Versus Actual Soil Erosion Rates in Europe' (2009) 94 *Earth-Science Reviews* 23.

8 Rio de Janeiro, 5 June 1992, in force 29 December 1993, 31 ILM 822 (1992).

9 Secretariat of the Convention on Biological Diversity, *Water and Biodiversity – Natural Solutions for Water Security* (2013) 41.

10 Lal and others (n 5) 4 and 9.

11 Paris, 17 June 1994, in force 26 December 1996, 33 ILM 1328 (1994).

12 E.g., N. Li and others, 'The Successful Ecograss Project and the Policy and Legal Issues Met and Solved', in Michael Jeffery and others (eds), *Biodiversity Conservation, Law + Livelihoods: Bridging the North-South Divide* (CUP, 2008).

13 K. Milde, 'Legal Principles and Policies of Soil Conservation' (1951) 20 *Fordham Law Review* 45.

some suggest,[14] is unfair. This is not to say that reforms are not required, particularly to facilitate a more agroecological approach to agricultural issues.

One of the earliest instruments to address soil conservation was the FAO's 1981 World Soil Charter.[15] This was an innovative document, highlighting issues that have only recently been directly addressed at the international level. Among the 1981 Charter's principles, for example, is the recognition that 'proper incentives' for farmers are needed to encourage 'good land use',[16] over 10 years before a similar call was adopted in Article 11 of the Biodiversity Convention. The 1981 Charter also recognised that 'Certain land-tenure structures may constitute an obstacle to the adoption of sound soil management measures on farms' and called for reforms, compatible with farmers' property rights, to address this.[17] On the other hand, the document is wholly anthropocentric and there is no reference to soils being unique and important ecosystems in their own right. Instead, the 1981 Charter only states that soil degradation can impact on the environment.[18]

In 2015, the UN's International Year of Soils, the FAO adopted a Revised World Soil Charter.[19] Building on major developments in international environmental law, the Revised Charter must still be described as anthropocentric, as it uses the language of ecosystem services to frame soil conservation in terms of its importance to maintaining human society.[20] However, it also recognises not only that soil is 'integral to ecosystems'[21] but that soil is itself an important habitat for biodiversity that must be protected.[22] The Revised Charter therefore represents an important step forward in advancing agroecology as it includes soil per se, as well as the species that maintain its ecological health, within the regulation of agriculture's socioecological networks.

Other features of the Revised Charter also have an agroecological element. Of note is Principle 6:

> The implementation of soil management decisions is typically made locally and occurs within widely differing socioeconomic contexts. The development of specific measures appropriate for adoption by local decision-makers often requires multi-level, interdisciplinary initiatives by many stakeholders. A strong commitment to include local and indigenous knowledge is critical.

14 N. Fromherz, 'The Case for a Global Treaty on Soil Conservation, Sustainable Farming, and the Preservation of Agrarian Culture' (2012) 39 *Ecology Law Quarterly* 57, 57.
15 Text available at: https://www.fao.org/3/p8700e/p8700e.pdf (last accessed 20/04/2023).
16 1981 Charter, Principle 6.
17 1981 Charter, Principle 8.
18 1981 Charter, Principle 4.
19 Text available at: https://www.fao.org/documents/card/en/c/e60df30b-0269-4247-a15f-db564161fee0/ (last accessed 20/04/2023).
20 Revised Charter, Principles 3, 4 and 5.
21 Revised Charter, Principle 3.
22 Revised Charter, Principle 8.

This emphasis on engaging different stakeholders in soil management is carried into the Charter's Guidelines for Action. Recommended activities for individuals and the private sector, the scientific community, governments and international organisations are outlined.[23] The actions for scientists, governments and international organisations are typical of other international instruments. Scientists are called on to share information on soil conservation; governments are recommended to, inter alia, support research into soil conservation, incorporate soil management into other relevant policies and impose regulations to ensure soil quality; and international organisations are requested to facilitate the sharing of best practice and capacity-building efforts. More interesting is what the Revised Charter says in relation to the role of individuals:

> All individuals using or managing soil must act as stewards of the soil to ensure that this essential natural resource is managed sustainably to safeguard it for future generations.

The idea of humanity as stewards of the environment offers the potential to bridge alternative, if not necessarily competing, cultural understandings of humanity's relationships with nature. A notion of stewardship reflects indigenous cultures that see humanity's role as that of a cultivator or gardener of nature, whereby use is intended to enhance nature as well as benefit society;[24] an idea which has been adopted by ecocentric theorists.[25] At the same time, it reflects the emergence in Western legal traditions of an idea of environmental responsibility inherent to property rights over land.[26] Rodgers has observed this in agricultural land management. He suggests that as landowners, farmers may choose to adopt any method of farming on their land, but after doing so are required to pursue that method in a way that, at the very least, minimises its environmental impacts.[27] There is space to take this idea of responsibility for land further, particularly in wider land-use planning policies,[28] but at a minimum it reveals a degree of common ground between world philosophies which, in other contexts, have proven difficult to reconcile.[29]

23 The 1981 Charter also contains Guidelines for Action, but these were limited to actions by governments and international organisations.

24 This is a broad generalisation and it is important to recognise that views of indigenous communities on humanity's place within nature vary – B. Richardson and D. Craig, 'Indigenous Peoples, Law and the Environment', in B. Richardson and S. Wood (eds), *Environmental Law for Sustainability* (Hart Publishing, 2006).

25 A. Pelizzon, 'Earth Laws, Rights of Nature and Legal Pluralism', in M. Mahoney and P. Burdon (eds), *Wild Law – In Practice* (Routledge, 2014).

26 S. Coyle and K. Morrow, *The Philosophical Foundations of Environmental Law: Property, Rights and Nature* (Hart Publishing, 2004) 167–169.

27 C. Rodgers, 'Agenda 2000, Land Use, and the Environment: Towards a Theory of "Environmental" Property Rights', in J. Holder and C. Harrison (eds), *Law and Geography* (OUP, 2003) 255–256.

28 J. Holder and D. McGillivray, 'Recognising an Ecological Ethic of Care in the Law of Everyday Shared Spaces' (2020) 29 *Social & Legal Studies* 379.

29 We saw this in ch 2 in relation to the acceptability of traditional knowledge and science in the Intergovernmental Science-Policy Platform on Biodiversity and Ecosystem Services.

Interestingly, Hamilton suggests it was the absence of a moral obligation of stewardship that led to soil conservation being neglected in the latter half of the 20th century.[30]

The Revised Charter is a central feature of the FAO's work on soil governance,[31] but its work on soil is much broader than this. Through the Global Soils Partnership, the FAO is coordinating action on ten issues relevant to the conservation of soils:

- Awareness raising
- Soil biodiversity
- Capacity building
- Soil information
- Soil erosion
- Soil fertility
- Soil governance
- Soil pollution
- Soil salinity
- Soil organic carbon[32]

Each of these has merit in terms of agroecology. The 2019 Global Symposium on Soil Erosion, for example, adopted recommendations for the design and implementation of national measures to prevent soil erosion, which focus on building connections between stakeholders.[33] Also worth mentioning is the Global Assessment of Soil Pollution, which sets out the anthropogenic sources of soil pollution, including in agricultural, urban and industrial areas, the consequences of this for maintaining ecological health and human society and measures that reduce soil pollution.[34]

The FAO's work on soil comprehensively addresses the environmental, social and economic impacts of deteriorating soil health, identifying this as the foundation of agricultural systems and related communities. While it is largely grounded in nature's anthropocentric values, increasing recognition is also being given to the role soil plays in supporting the wider natural world, as the Revised World Soil Charter illustrates, and that soil hosts its own unique biodiversity that warrants protection. It only takes the form of guidelines and recommendations, however.

Also relevant is the Biodiversity Convention. In 2006, at the eighth Conference of the Parties (COP), the International Initiative for the Conservation and Sustainable Use of Soil Biodiversity was launched.[35] Central to this is the mainstreaming of

30 N. Hamilton, 'Needed: A New Commitment to Soil Conservation – Can Addressing Soil Health and Climate Change Re-Energize This Work?' (2021) 52 *University of the Pacific Law Review* 599, 617.

31 https://www.fao.org/global-soil-partnership/areas-of-work/soil-governance/en/ (last accessed 20/04/2023).

32 https://www.fao.org/global-soil-partnership/en/ (last accessed 20/04/2023).

33 FAO, *Outcome Document of the Global Symposium on Soil Erosion* (FAO, 2019) 12–15.

34 FAO and UNEP, *Global Assessment of Soil Pollution: Report* (FAO, 2021).

35 Decision VIII/23, Agricultural biodiversity, UNEP/CBD/COP/DEC/VIII/23, 15 June 2006, Part B, Annex

soil conservation into other policies and programmes operating at international and national levels and facilitating collaboration between stakeholders.[36] This is now being taken forward through the 2020–2030 Plan of Action, which was adopted at COP-15 and is reflective of core principles of agroecology.[37] It is grounded in the ecosystem approach[38] and explicitly recognises the role of different stakeholders in maintaining soil biodiversity, including 'smallholders, small-scale food producers, family farmers, peasants, landowners, land managers, foresters, ranches, indigenous peoples [and] local communities'.[39] Specific global actions to be pursued are similarly compatible with agroecology and include, for example:

> Promote both in-situ and ex-situ conservation, restoration and sustainable use activities and management practices while strengthening the systems of knowledge of indigenous peoples and local communities.[40]

The reference to local knowledge systems is particularly important, as it may help to avoid situations such as that observed in Bali, where reforms to traditional agricultural methods were made without appreciating the complex socioecological networks that had evolved out of the water temples, leading to a range of negative environmental and social impacts.[41]

While only soft law, the Plan of Action is still a positive development. It goes further than the original Soil Biodiversity Initiative in calling for actual conservation measures for soil ecosystems,[42] with the original scheme primarily emphasising the gathering of data and sharing of best practices.[43] As we discussed in chapter 4, building connections between stakeholders is important, not least because this is central to supporting the relationships between different actors in the same socio-ecological network, but this should not be seen as a substitute for more direct conservation action.[44]

### A Soil Treaty?

The limits of soft law approaches to conservation typified by the Biodiversity Convention's non-binding programmes of work have been well-documented.[45] Calls have consequently been made for sustainable soil management to be addressed

36 ibid section B.
37 Decision 15/28, Biodiversity and agriculture, CBD/COP/DEC/15/28, 19 December 2022, Annex.
38 ibid para 16.
39 ibid para 18.
40 ibid para 20(j).
41 J. Lansing, *Perfect Order: Recognizing Complexity in Bali* (Princeton University Press, 2006) 6–10.
42 Decision 15/28 (n 37) para 21.
43 Decision VIII/23 (n 35) section C.
44 S. Harrop, 'Biodiversity and Conservation', in R. Falkner (ed) *The Handbook of Global Climate and Environment Policy* (John Wiley & Sons, 2013) 49.
45 E.g., S. Harrop and D. Pritchard, 'A Hard Instrument Goes Soft: The Implications of the Convention on Biological Diversity's Current Trajectory' (2011) 21 *Global Environmental Change* 474.

through a binding legal instrument. In 2000, the IUCN World Conservation Congress passed the Amman Resolution on Soils, stating that the ecological health of the world's soils depended on the existence of appropriate legal strategies at global, regional and national levels, and instigated work to explore a new global soils instrument with binding obligations.[46] The form such obligations might take can be seen in Article VI of the 2003 Revised African Convention on the Conservation of Nature and Natural Resources.[47] It is worth considering this provision in full due to its relevance to agroecology:

1. The Parties shall take effective measures to prevent land degradation, and to that effect shall develop long-term integrated strategies for the conservation and sustainable management of land resources, including soil, vegetation and related hydrological processes.
2. They shall in particular adopt measures for the conservation and improvement of soil, to, inter alia, combat its erosion and misuse as well as the deterioration of its physical, chemical and biological or economic properties.
3. To this end:
   a. they shall establish land-use plans based on scientific investigations as well as local knowledge and experience and, in particular, classification and land-use capability;
   b. they shall, when implementing agricultural practices and agrarian reforms,
      i. improve soil conservation and introduce sustainable farming and forestry practices, which ensure long-term productivity of the land,
      ii. control erosion caused by land misuse and mismanagement which may lead to long-term loss of surface soils and vegetation cover,
      iii. control pollution caused by agricultural activities, including aquaculture and animal husbandry;
4. Parties shall develop and implement land tenure policies able to facilitate the above measures, inter alia by taking into account the rights of local communities.

The first point to note is that Article VI locates soil conservation in its wider ecological context by requiring soil conservation measures to be adopted alongside the management of other natural resources as part of long-term, integrated strategies. It thereby reflects the systems-analysis approach of agroecology that requires natural elements to be considered in the context of related agro- and ecosystems. With regard to soil specifically, paragraph 2 sets out both positive, i.e. to actively improve soil, and negative, i.e. to prevent the erosion and deterioration of soil, conservation obligations. Also interesting is that the obligation to prevent deterioration applies separately to the soil's biological and economic qualities. This means that any degradation in soil quality does not have to result in any direct economic harm

46 IUCN World Conservation Congress, Amman Resolution on Soils, 2.59, October 2000.
47 Maputo, 11 July 2003, in force 23/07/2016. Text available at: https://au.int/en/treaties/african-convention-conservation-nature-and-natural-resources-revised-version (last accessed 20/04/2023).

before states are required to act. In other words, the public interest in maintaining long-term soil health is considered just as important as the short-term economic interests of private landowners. This is also reflected in the requirement that agricultural practices and reforms should have as their goal the long-term productivity of land.

Further, Article VI emphasises the need to engage with communities in the design and implementation of soil-related policies. Importantly, Article VI(3)(a) recognises the legitimacy of local knowledge, which may not necessarily accord with strict scientific doctrine. This contrasts with the apparent approach being taken to knowledge relating to ecosystem services through the Intergovernmental Science-Policy Platform on Biodiversity and Ecosystem Services, highlighted in the previous chapter, where local and traditional knowledge appears marginalised.[48] As we discussed in chapter 2, such knowledge should be considered essential to decision-making processes, particularly in the context of agroecology. Different actors in a socioecological network will have different experiences and understandings of, and relationships with, its constituent natural elements and it is only by incorporating these that a true systems-level analysis of individual decisions and broader strategies and policies can be conducted. States are also encouraged to take the rights of local communities into account when developing and implementing land tenure policies. Note, though, that this provision is contingent on local communities having relevant rights in national law, and 'taking into account' is not the same as giving meaningful effect.

From an agroecological perspective, the 2003 African Convention contains a positive soil provision. At the time of writing, however, it has only been ratified by 17 states and so is of limited application, even in Africa.[49] As noted above, due to the fundamental importance of soil to ecological health and a range of human concerns, calls have been made for a global soils treaty to be adopted. Fromherz is one advocate of this and proposes a treaty that would address five issues relevant to soil: urban growth boundaries; erosion control; nutrient depletion control; irrigation reform; and restrictions on contamination.[50]

Urban growth boundaries are essentially a land-use development mechanism, through which states limit the lateral expansion of cities into arable lands, instead taking advantage of the opportunities many cities have for vertical expansion.[51] This could be taken further by explicitly accounting for ecosystem services in

48 U. Brand and A. Vadrot, 'Epistemic Selectivities and the Valorisation of Nature: The Cases of the Nagoya Protocol and the Intergovernmental Science-Policy Platform on Biodiversity and Ecosystem Services (IPBES)' (2013) 9 *Law, Environment and Development Journal* 204, 215.

49 (n 47). The earlier 1968 African Convention on the Conservation of Nature and Natural Resources (Algiers, 15 September 1968, in force 9 October 1969, 1001 UNTS 3) has 32 ratifications, but a less comprehensive soils provision.

50 Fromherz (n 14) 109–112.

51 D. Judd, 'Cities and the Environment', in R. Vogel (ed), *Handbook on Research on Urban Politics and Policy in the United States* (Greenwood Press, 1997) 399, cited in Fromherz (n 14) 110.

urban land-use planning policies, so that they enhance, rather than merely avoid damage to, natural infrastructure.[52]

For erosion control, Fromherz proposes imposing obligations on states to regulate activities that are known to contribute to soil erosion.[53] No further details on what form these might take are given, but a potential model is environmental assessment legislation. In short, environmental assessment subjects certain activities to an assessment to identify their likely environmental impacts on the area in question and then, depending on the strength of the mechanism, will only permit those activities to proceed if the results of the assessment have been taken into account, or compensatory measures have been adopted.[54] In combination with Monteduro's proposals for agricultural zoning,[55] a similar approach could be taken so that activities that result in soil erosion are either prohibited or strictly controlled in agricultural areas. This might prove more effective than other environmental assessment mechanisms. A common criticism of these is that they fail in their objective of preventing environmentally harmful land-uses because socioeconomic interests too easily outweigh environmental concerns.[56] Here, however, there would be a more direct socioeconomic interest, coupled with a powerful public interest in maintaining long-term soil health, being protected through the assessment mechanism.

More controversial are the proposals on nutrient depletion. The first step here would be to require states to monitor and report on the quality of their soils to an international body. While this would be very burdensome, particularly on developing states, work is already being done by the Desertification Convention to support data collection on land degradation issues. Once submitted, these reports would be reviewed by an international body, which, under Fromherz's model, would have the power to recommend a temporary suspension of agricultural activity in at-risk areas. Suspending economic activity in pursuit of a conservation objective is not unheard of in international law. Under the Convention on International Trade in Endangered Species (CITES),[57] a state's trading rights in CITES-listed species may be suspended in the event of serious or persistent non-compliance.[58] A ban on trade in certain species, however, is very different from shutting down food production in part of a state. Due to their potential impacts on the livelihoods of farmers and a state's food security, and consequent extreme political controversy, Fromherz suggests that such measures would only come into effect with the approval of the

52 J. Ruhl, 'Beyond Green Infrastructure – Integrating the Ecosystem Services Framework into Urban Planning Policy' (2020) 4 *Journal of Comparative Urban Law and Policy* 218.

53 Fromherz (n 14) 110.

54 See ch 9.

55 M. Monteduro, 'From Agroecology and Law to Agroecological Law? Exploring Integration between *Scientia Ruris* and *Scientia* Iuris' in M. Monteduro and other (eds) *Law and Agroecology: A Transdisciplinary Dialogue* (Springer, 2015) 79–80.

56 R. Amos, 'Assessing the Impact of the Habitats Directive: A Case Study of Europe's Plants' (2021) 33 *Journal of Environmental Law* 365, 372–374.

57 Washington, 3 March 1973, in force 1 July 1975, 993 UNTS 243.

58 Resolution Conf. 14.3 (CITES Compliance Procedures) para 30.

state concerned,[59] but it is difficult to envisage the circumstances in which a state would give this consent.

For irrigation control, the soil treaty would set out a number of principles to guide national policies:

- The water and saline content of soil should be monitored to ensure efficient water use and so that excessive salinisation can be identified at an early stage.
- Irrigation that delivers directly to crops' root systems should be favoured over standard sprinkler irrigation. Where this is not possible, crops should be watered at night to reduce wastage through evaporation.
- Appropriate drainage systems should be installed to reduce the impacts of agricultural run-off.

These are all sound management practices but would depend on states having sufficient resources and technical expertise to be effective. Fromherz suggests that any state that fails to implement them would be subject to sanctions,[60] but arguably measures to facilitate compliance would be the more appropriate response to such non-compliance issues, at least initially. This approach has been taken in other contexts, including CITES, and is considered to be an important factor in such treaties' success.[61]

Finally, with regard to preventing contamination by agricultural chemicals, Fromherz proposes establishing a cap-type mechanism, similar to that adopted in the Kyoto Protocol to the UN Framework Convention on Climate Change (UNFCCC),[62] which would limit the amount of certain chemicals that states could release into the environment.[63] There would be practical difficulties with such approaches, however, as monitoring and enforcing any caps might be beyond the means of developing states. Experience from the EU also suggests that limiting chemical usage in certain areas would be politically contentious.[64]

Notwithstanding the flaws in some of Fromherz's proposals, it is clear that a soil treaty could deliver on multiple aspects of agroecology. Soil conservation would be integrated into other land-uses policies and steps would be taken to maintain soil quality and quantity so that it could continue to meet the needs of society and the natural world. There is a question of whether a brand-new treaty is required or the more appropriate avenue would be to develop a soil protocol under the Biodiversity Convention, which benefits from an established institutional

59 Fromherz (n 14) 110–111.

60 ibid.

61 E. Goodwin, 'The World Heritage Convention, the Environment, and Compliance' (2009) 20 *Colorado Journal of International Environmental Law and Policy* 157, 181–185.

62 Kyoto, 11 December 1997, in force 16 February 2005, 37 ILM 22 (1998); New York, 9 May 1992, in force 24 March 1994, 1771 UNTS 107.

63 Fromherz (n 14) 112.

64 E.g., Case C-293/97 *R v Secretary of State for the Environment, ex parte Standley* [1997] ECR I-2603. See ch 10.

architecture. Ultimately though, the case for a legally binding instrument on soil conservation, both in terms of protecting soils as a specific objective and advancing agroecology, is a strong one.

### Land Degradation and Desertification

The conservation of soil should be seen as an important element of the wider issue of land degradation and desertification, with other contributory factors caused by agricultural activity including land salinisation, vegetation degradation and water erosion.[65] A useful working definition of land degradation is provided in Article 1 of the Desertification Convention, the third treaty to come out of the 1992 Rio Conference on Environment and Development:[66]

> "land degradation" means reduction or loss, in arid, semi-arid and dry sub-humid areas, of the biological or economic productivity or complexity of rainfed cropland, irrigated cropland, or range, pasture, forest and woodlands resulting from land uses or from a process or combination of processes, including processes arising from human activities and habitation patterns, such as:
>
> - soil erosion caused by wind and/or water;
> - deterioration of the physical, chemical and biological or economic properties of soil; and
> - long-term loss of natural vegetation.

As we will see in chapter 8, land degradation can have major social and economic consequences, as it forces communities to relocate from areas that are no longer ecologically capable of supporting them.[67] Soil conservation and other responses to the drivers of desertification are one way to prevent this type of environmental migration. At the same time, it is important to remember that deserts, arid and semi-arid regions constitute important biomes in their own right, hosting a diverse range of flora and fauna specifically adapted to thrive in what appear to be extremely hostile environments. When adjacent to farmlands, these species should be considered vital elements of agrobiodiversity and agriculture's socioecological networks. To give just one example, arid lands are home to many snake species, which prey on rats and other agricultural pests.[68]

The main global instrument concerned with preventing and mitigating the impacts of desertification is the Desertification Convention. Enjoying near-universal

65 H. Dregne, 'Land Degradation in the Drylands' (2002) 16 *Arid Land Research and Management* 99.

66 The other two being the Biodiversity Convention and UNFCCC.

67 E.g., R. Reuveny, 'Climate Change-Induced Migration and Violent Conflict' (2007) 26 *Political Geography* 656, 663–667.

68 https://www.farmersweekly.co.za/farming-basics/how-to-crop/how-snakes-can-help-farmers/ (last accessed 20/04/2023).

participation, with 197 Contracting Parties at the time of writing,[69] this treaty has a number of merits in terms of agroecology. It locates local desertification in the context of other global environmental and social challenges,[70] recognising that meaningful action towards solving one global problem will only be successful if meaningful action is taken towards solving all of them.[71] This corresponds to the systems-level analysis of problems and their potential solutions that have been strongly associated with agroecology,[72] and wider literature on the SDGs.[73]

The approach of the Convention is bottom-up, i.e. it focuses on encouraging and facilitating community responses to the drivers of desertification through national action programmes, rather than calling for the top-down designation of certain areas and species for protection, which are typical approaches in other environmental agreements.[74] Arguably, and notwithstanding the arguments in favour of more robust legal frameworks for conservation,[75] this is a more appropriate legal model for advancing agroecology. It does not prescribe specific actions to be taken, leaving individual actors free to respond to their own human and natural communities' socioecological conditions.

That a novel management approach has been adopted in the Desertification Convention may in part be attributable to it having a different remit to other conservation agreements. While treaties such as the Biodiversity Convention are primarily intended to preserve nature, which arguably requires prescriptive measures such as creating protected areas and prohibiting certain activities as the principal means of implementation,[76] the Desertification Convention's main objective of limiting the socioeconomic impacts of the expansion of deserts depends on the involvement of those communities affected by those impacts.[77] Bottom-up approaches carry a number of agroecological advantages. They are typically based on local community engagement in policy design and implementation, which has benefits not just in terms of having policies that reflect the cultures and interests of affected socioecological networks, but also in the wider context of delivering environmental

69 https://www.unccd.int/convention/ratification (last accessed 20/04/2023).

70 Article C.

71 S. Way, 'Examining the Links between Poverty and Land Degradation: From Blaming the Poor toward Recognising the Rights of the Poor', in P. Johnson and others, *Governing Global Desertification: Linking Environmental Degradation, Poverty and Participation* (Routledge, 2006).

72 E. Noe and H. Alrøe, 'Regulation of Agroecosystems: A Social Systems Analysis of Agroecology and Law', in Monteduro and others (n 55).

73 E.g., P. Carvalho and C. Spataru, 'Advancing the Implementation of SDGs in Brazil by Integrating Water-Energy Nexus and Legal Principles for Better Governance' (2018) 3 *Sustainability in the Environment* 277.

74 K. Danish, 'International Environmental Law and the 'Bottom-Up' Approach: A Review of the Desertification Convention' (1995) 3 *Indiana Journal of Global Legal Studies* 133.

75 R. Amos, *International Conservation Law: The Protection of Plants in Theory and Practice* (Routledge, 2020) 57–62.

76 In practice, a conservation strategy will need to comprise both top-down and bottom-up approaches if it is to be successful – ibid 216–221.

77 Desertification Convention, Article 2.

justice for these communities and building local support for what might otherwise be controversial restrictions on natural resource use.[78] On the other hand, doubts have been raised over whether bottom-up approaches to regulation are capable of delivering the required level of action to deliver on environmental goals. While broad public engagement in decision-making is important, it may also make it harder to find consensus on environmental policies because there will be wider scope for these to be rejected as contrary to the cultural or economic interests of different stakeholders.[79] This has been observed in relation to the Desertification Convention.[80]

These limits of bottom-up approaches to regulation underpin arguments that environmental policies can only be effective if they are imposed by a central authority capable of enforcing them.[81] They are linked to the criticism of sustainable development as a policy framework highlighted previously, namely that while it is easy to find consensus on broad policy goals, finding consensus on the means to achieve these is more challenging.[82] This in turn relates to Parker's observation that it is not enough for a society to identify green values with which everyone can agree; they need to be values which everyone can respect.[83] It is for these reasons that Wilkinson casts doubt over whether genuinely sustainable laws can be adopted through liberal democratic processes. His solution is for ecological imperatives to be embedded in pre-democratic structures, such as constitutions, so that decision-making processes are framed by an ecological backstop.[84] For advancing agroecology, these democratic structures perform a similar role as the principle of ecological sustainability would if it were adopted as the overarching framework for international law and policy. Namely, they would frame trade-offs between competing environmental, social and economic goals in the ecological integrity of affected ecosystems.

Related to the concern that the Desertification Convention's bottom-up approach is incapable of instigating the action necessary to combat desertification is that it

78 See various contributions in A. Lawrence (ed), *Taking Stock of Nature: Participatory Biodiversity Assessment for Policy, Planning and Practice* (CUP, 2010).

79 A. Tal and J. Cohen, 'Bringing "Two-Down" to "Bottom-Up": A New Role for Environmental Legislation in Combating Desertification' (2007) 31 *Harvard Environmental Law Review* 163, 215.

80 W. Burns, 'International Convention to Combat Desertification: Drawing a Line in the Sand' (1995) 16 *Michigan Journal of International Law* 831, 879–881.

81 Tal and Cohen (n 79) 215.

82 M. Lee, *EU Environmental Law, Governance and Decision-Making* (2nd edn, Hart Publishing, 2014) 59.

83 J. Parker, 'Enabling Morally Reflective Communities: Towards a Resolution of the Democratic Dilemma of Environmental Values in Policy', in Y. Guerrier and others (eds) *Values and the Environment: A Social Sciences Perspective* (Wiley, 1995) 45.

84 D. Wilkinson, 'Using Environmental Ethics to Create Ecological Law', in J. Holder and D. McGillivray (eds), *Locality and Identity: Environmental Issues in Law and Society* (Dartmouth, 1999) 17–18. This can already be observed in the constitutions of a broad range of states – J. May and E. Daly, *Global Environmental Constitutionalism* (CUP, 2015).

lacks positive commitments for states to pursue.[85] Instead, there are preambular references to vague goals, such as achieving sustainable development. Actual conservation action is dependent on the provision of technological and financial assistance to developing states, which has so far not been forthcoming at a level that would enable meaningful action.[86] Further, while the Convention takes a holistic perspective on the connections between land degradation and other global challenges,[87] this is undermined by its wholly anthropocentric focus. Nothing in Article 4, which lists the general obligations of the Contracting Parties, relates to the conservation of desert or dryland biodiversity per se, with the only reference to environmental protection being a requirement for affected states to cooperate in the conservation of land and water resources. Instead, priority is given to addressing the poverty and economic implications of desertification, which although important, are not its only impacts. This has implications for the utility of the Desertification Convention as an instrument to advance agroecology, as the success of efforts to support the socioeconomic interests of stakeholders in a socioecological network will be conditioned on the health and functioning of the natural elements of that network, in the same way that all human society ultimately depends on ecological health. This includes agricultural ecosystems and the arid and semi-arid ecosystems connected to these.

The lack of positive commitments in the Desertification Convention can be attributed to two factors. First, as with all agricultural issues, attempts to restrain state activities that contribute to desertification must be reconciled with the implications this has for state sovereignty. The Convention's preamble reaffirms Principle 2 of the Rio Declaration on Environment and Development,[88] which sets out the peremptory norm of states' permanent sovereignty over natural resources,[89] and none of the obligations in the Desertification Convention can be read as imposing, or even encouraging, any kind of limitation on states' right to freely develop or exploit land.

Second, when negotiating the treaty, states were keen to avoid conflict with other conventions that had similar remits, notably the Biodiversity Convention.[90] This argument would be valid had the Biodiversity Convention been developing a comprehensive programme for the conservation of desert and arid biodiversity. However, the Contracting Parties to the Biodiversity Convention did not adopt

85 M. Bowman and others, *Lyster's International Wildlife Law* (2nd edn, CUP, 2010) 632.

86 ibid 634.

87 A. Tal, 'Degraded Commitments: Reviving International Efforts to Combat Desertification' (2007) 13 *Brown Journal of World Affairs* 187, 189.

88 31 ILM 874 (1992).

89 I.e., that states may utilise the natural resources within their jurisdiction in any manner they wish, subject to this being sustainable – N. Schrijver, *Sovereignty Over Natural Resources: Balancing Rights and Duties* (CUP, 1997) ch 4.

90 Bowman and others (n 85) 632.

the Programme of Work on dry and sub-humid lands until COP-5 in 2000.[91] This consists of two elements: assessments and targeted actions. Specific conservation and sustainable use actions are listed in Activity 7 of the Programme. In addition to standard conservation measures seen throughout international conservation instruments, including protected areas and the rehabilitation of degraded ecosystems, these contain a number of actions relevant to agriculture and agricultural practices:

(d) The sustainable management of dry and sub-humid land production systems;
(e) The appropriate management and sustainable use of water resources;
...
(g) The economic valuation of the biological diversity of dry and sub-humid lands, as well as the development and the use of economic instruments and the promotion of the introduction of adaptive technologies that enhance productivity of dry and sub-humid lands ecosystems;
(h) The sustainable use or husbandry of plant and animal biomass, through adaptive management, bearing in mind the potential population fluctuation in dry and sub-humid lands, and the support by Parties of national policies, legislation and land-use practices, which promote effective biodiversity conservation and sustainable use;

While theoretically sound, the actions in the Programme of Work lack sufficient detail to be easily implemented at the national level. There is no guidance, for example, on how economic instruments should be designed so as to promote and support the conservation of dryland habitats, although as we saw in the previous chapter, this has been addressed by the Biodiversity Convention in other contexts.[92] The Programme of Work also explicitly mentions other multilateral environmental agreements and how there is a need to coordinate action with each to ensure the successful conservation of different elements of the natural world:

(l) Cooperation with the Ramsar Convention on Wetlands and the Convention on the Conservation of Migratory Species with regard to, inter alia, integrated catchment management incorporating wetlands ecosystems as integral parts of dry and sub-humid lands, and the creation of migratory-species corridors across dry and sub-humid lands during seasonal periods, as well as with the Convention on International Trade in Endangered Species (CITES) with regard to rare and endangered species in dry and sub-humid lands.

Had a similar provision to this been included in the Biodiversity Convention, a more integrated and coherent body of international conservation law could have

91 Decision V/23, Consideration of options for conservation and sustainable use of biological diversity in dryland, Mediterranean, arid, semi-arid, grassland and savannah ecosystems, UNEP/CBD/COP/DEC/V/23, 22 June 2000, Annex.
92 https://www.cbd.int/incentives/positive.shtml (last accessed 20/04/2023).

evolved.[93] This would also have facilitated the pursuit of agroecology through international law. As this book illustrates, sustainable agriculture requires consideration of a range of issues that are subject to international regulation, within and beyond the specific field of conservation. Similarly, enabling the more holistic pursuit of different, potentially conflicting, policy goals is one of the principal rationales of the SDGs, which explicitly recognise policy synergies and trade-offs, but the extent to which the Goals can deliver on this in practice, notwithstanding their potential in this regard, is debatable.[94]

### *A Land-Degradation Neutral World*

Taking the above into account, there are limits to how far global conservation instruments can go in advancing agroecology with regard to mitigating the socio-economic impacts of advancing deserts and arid lands while also protecting these ecosystems so that related agrobiodiversity, such as predators of agricultural pests, can continue to play its role in socioecological networks. Given the overall weaknesses in the Desertification Convention's approach, calls have been made for action at combatting desertification to be targeted towards a new goal of a land-degradation neutral world (LDNW).[95] The Desertification Convention Secretariat responded in 2013 by adopting the goal of achieving net-zero land degradation by 2030,[96] which has subsequently been included in SDG-15.3. It constitutes an explicit recognition that to support the livelihoods of farmers, it is essential that the soil that is protected is also sufficiently healthy and capable of supporting agricultural and related ecosystems.[97]

Also referenced in the 'The Future We Want',[98] the Outcome Report of the 2012 Rio+20 Conference, LDNW focuses on the restoration of land, or an equivalent area of land, that is degraded or lost either to natural or anthropogenic causes.[99] LDNW is now a central action area for the Desertification Convention, with considerable work being done to support states in devising and implementing national targets. In particular, the Convention's Global Mechanism,[100] in cooperation with

93 Developing stronger connections between individual agreements has been identified as a key way in which the overall effectiveness of international environmental law can be improved, particularly in the context of conservation – W. Bradnee Chambers, *Interlinkages and the Effectiveness of Multilateral Environmental Agreements* (UNUP, 2008) ch 6 and 7.

94 R. Amos and E. Lydgate, 'Trade, Transboundary Impacts and the Implementation of SDG 12' (2020) 15 *Sustainability Science* 1699.

95 P. Chasek and others, 'Operationalizing Zero Net Land Degradation: The Next Stage in International Efforts to Combat Desertification' (2014) 112 *Journal of Arid Environments* 5.

96 Secretariat to the CCD, *A Stronger UNCCD for a Land-Degradation Neutral World* (2013).

97 A. Telesetsky and others, *Ecological Restoration in International Environmental Law* (Routledge, 2017) 102.

98 A/RES/66/288, 11 September 2012, para 206.

99 S. Welton and others, 'Legal & Scientific Integrity in Advancing a "Land Degradation Neutral World"' (2015) 40 *Columbia Journal of Environmental Law* 39.

100 https://www.unccd.int/actions/ldn-target-setting-programme (last accessed 20/04/2023).

its Science-Policy Interface,[101] has developed a checklist of key features that should be included in any LDNW national policy:

- Ensuring transformation and innovation by translating the [Land Degradation Neutrality (LDN)] Scientific Conceptual Framework into practice,[102] including the LDN response hierarchy (avoid, reduce and reverse land degradation) and the principle of counterbalancing (losses are balanced by gains in land-based natural capital).
- Promoting responsible and inclusive governance, including gender equality, inclusiveness, accountability and transparency.
- Ensuring sustainability, including a conducive policy environment; delivering multiple environmental, economic and social benefits and enhancing (sub) national ownership and capacity.
- Leveraging innovative finance, especially from the private sector.[103]

The added value of these points is debatable. Balancing losses in productive land with gains in other land-based natural capital, while uncontroversial in theory, is likely to prove ineffective in practice. There is evidence from other biodiversity offsetting mechanisms showing that like-for-like replacements are virtually impossible to achieve. Alternative sites will have very different ecological systems and connections to sites that have been degraded or lost, and the planting of 100 saplings will take decades, if not centuries, before they replicate the ecological functions of 100 mature trees, for example.[104] Requiring compensatory measures to go beyond mere equivalence is one response to this, although there is still doubt over whether this is a suitable trade-off for the loss of already productive ecosystems.[105]

The other three points are grounded in the language and objectives of the SDGs. They reflect, therefore, the principal strength of the SDGs, i.e. the holistic consideration of a range of environmental, social and economic issues and the recognition that these must be advanced simultaneously if meaningful progress in any one area is to be achieved.[106] This also means that the Global Mechanism's checklist shares the SDGs' main weakness. Its contents are based on the mainstream,

101 https://knowledge.unccd.int/science-policy-interface (last accessed 20/04/2023).

102 The Framework provides practical, science-based information to aid states in achieving land degradation neutrality – B. Orr and others, *Scientific Conceptual Framework for Land Degradation Neutrality: A Report of the Science-Policy Interface* (UNCCD, 2017).

103 https://www.unccd.int/land-and-life/land-degradation-neutrality/projects-programmes/guidance-developing-tpp (last accessed 20/04/2023).

104 R. Morris and others, 'The Creation of Compensatory Habitat – Can It Secure Sustainable Development?' (2006) 14 *Journal for Nature Conservation* 106.

105 D. McGillivray, 'Compensatory Measures Under Article 6(4) of the Habitats Directive: No Net Loss for Natura 2000?', in C. Born and others (eds), *The Habitats Directive in Its EU Environmental Law Context: Nature's Best Hope?* (Routledge, 2015) 105.

106 R. Amos and others, *Living Sustainability in Higher Education: Connecting Communities, Learning and Justice* (2025, forthcoming) Introduction.

anthropocentric, understanding of sustainable development, which has proven incapable of shifting human activities on to a more sustainable trajectory.[107]

As with other areas of international conservation law, the work of the Desertification Convention in relation to LDNW can be criticised for pursuing outputs at the expense of outcomes. Its Global Support Programme for LDNW does not support states in pursuing LDNW activities but in submitting reports.[108] Reporting obligations are always important when responding to environmental challenges. As we discussed in relation to adaptive management approaches to conservation in chapter 1, assessing and reporting on the current state of biodiversity and the impacts of conservation activities is essential if those activities are to be adapted in a timely and meaningful manner.[109] To devote too much attention to reports, however, risks the only action being taken under treaties such as the Desertification Convention being the documenting of the gradual decline of nature, and therefore of related socioecological networks as well.[110]

## Conclusions

Soil has been shown to be critically important, not just for agriculture but in supporting virtually all ecological and human systems. That it is being continually degraded by agricultural and other anthropogenic activities is therefore concerning, as this raises challenges not only for pursuing agroecology but the international community's wider sustainable development agenda represented by the SDGs. The work of the FAO shows some progress. The 1981 Soils Charter, while flawed as an anthropocentric instrument, was nevertheless innovative in certain respects, and the 2015 Revised Charter is an important agroecological document. In particular, it places greater emphasis on maintaining soil health as a prerequisite to other ecological and socioeconomic policy goals.

A limiting factor of the FAO Charters is that they are non-binding. The same applies to the Biodiversity Convention's Plan of Action for soil biodiversity. An argument can therefore be made in favour of a binding soil agreement, either as a new protocol to the Biodiversity Convention or as a separate instrument. A soil agreement along the lines proposed by Fromherz could be a powerful tool to advance agroecology in international law. Control of urban expansion, if coupled with the integration of other environmental goals into land-use planning policies,

107 L. Kotzé and D. French, 'The Anthropocentric Ontology of International Environmental Law and the Sustainable Development Goals: Towards an Ecocentric Rule of Law in the Anthropocene' (2018) 7 *Global Journal of Comparative Law* 5.

108 https://www.unccd.int/land-and-life/land-degradation-neutrality/projects-programmes (last accessed 20/04/2023).

109 M. Wells and T. McShane, 'Integrating Protected Area Management with Local Needs and Aspirations' (2004) 33 *Ambio* 513, 516. See also N. Salafsky and R. Margoluis, 'Threat Reduction Assessment: A Practical and Cost-Effective Approach to Evaluating Conservation and Development Projects' (1999) 13 *Conservation Biology* 830.

110 Harrop makes a similar point in relation to the Biodiversity Convention – (n 44).

could ensure that the growth of cities no longer comes at the expense of the land needed to feed those cities' populations. Similarly, the proposals on erosion control represent promising new approaches to the oft-critiqued mechanism of environmental assessment. More controversial are the proposals to sanction states that fail to implement the principles on irrigation and to allow an international body to propose suspending agricultural activity in areas suffering from severe nutrient depletion. Conditioning such restrictions on state consent overcomes this problem but also renders the proposal meaningless.

The decline in soil quantity and quality is one of the main drivers of land degradation and desertification, alongside other impacts caused, in part, by agriculture. Recognising the consequences of this, especially for remote and poorer communities' ability to support themselves, the Desertification Convention emphasises bottom-up measures. As such, this is potentially an important mechanism for advancing agroecology in international law, as it places the communities that form agriculture's socioecological networks at the heart of decision-making and implementation. As the Desertification Convention itself demonstrates, however, in most cases, meaningful conservation will only be pursued if there is also a central authority imposing top-down regulation to prohibit or otherwise minimise certain harmful activities.

The Desertification Convention's adoption of LDNW as a new objective may be construed as a recognition that measures to address the impacts of desertification under the treaty have, to date, fallen short. However, because the Convention's approach to LDNW is grounded in the SDGs, whether this will be any more successful is, I suggest, doubtful. Until the broader weaknesses in sustainable development, particularly its inability to give proper weight to ecological imperatives in decision-making processes, are addressed, progress in achieving sustainable agriculture along agroecological lines will be limited.

# 7 Water Conservation

## Our Changing Perceptions of Water

Fresh water is fundamental to all life on Earth. Even in some of the harshest deserts, life persists because there is some kind of water supply. In the Atacama Desert of South America, where it may only rain once every 50 years, the adjacent cold waters of the Pacific bring regular mists that provide enough water and nutrients to sustain an array of plant life, which in turn allows other species to survive in what would otherwise be an uninhabitable environment.[1] It should also go without saying that society depends on there being a sufficient supply of quality fresh water for a host of different reasons. One of the, if not the, most important of these is the growing of crops and other agricultural products. Agriculture places huge demands on finite water resources, however, to the extent that it has been suggested that there is not enough water to irrigate more than half of the world's crops.[2]

The Secretariat to the Biodiversity Convention[3] suggests that by 2025, up to 1.8 billion people will live in a region that suffers from absolute water scarcity,[4] with water consumption increasing at more than twice the rate of the global population growth.[5] This in turn is having significant impacts on the natural world, with nature's capacity to support diverse ecosystems across a range of biomes and deliver the water-based and other ecosystem services associated with these, being increasingly eroded due to the lack of water.[6]

Against this backdrop, global perspectives on the relationships between water and biodiversity are changing. In the past, undermining biodiversity was seen as an acceptable trade-off against what were seen as more important socioeconomic uses of water. To the extent that biodiversity extracted water, it was considered to

1 A. González and others, 'Bromeliad Growth and Stoichiometry: Responses to Atmospheric Nutrient Supply in Fog-Dependent Ecosystems of the Hyper-Arid Atacama Desert, Chile' (2011) 167 *Oecologia* 835.

2 T. Walker, *Plant Conservation: Why It Matters and How It Works* (Timber Press, 2013) 190.

3 Rio de Janeiro, 5 June 1992, in force 29 December 1993, 31 ILM 822 (1992).

4 Secretariat of the Convention on Biological Diversity, *Water and Biodiversity – Natural Solutions for Water Security* (2013) 9.

5 ibid 24.

6 ibid 27–45.

DOI: 10.4324/9781003435174-10

be in conflict with society;[7] a further demonstration of the dangerous anthropocentricity of sustainable development as a decision-making framework. In 2013, however, when the International Day for Biodiversity was dedicated to Water and Biodiversity to coincide with the UN International Year for Water Cooperation, the Secretariat to the Biodiversity Convention put forward a new model to guide long-term water management and conservation strategies. The emphasis was no longer on biodiversity's depletion of water but on how it contributed to global, regional and local hydrological cycles, summarised by the phrase 'Ask not what water can do for biodiversity; ask what biodiversity can do for water'.[8] In other words, the last decade has seen much greater emphasis being placed on how conserving biodiversity can support water, and, therefore the ecosystem services that water provides.

This shift in focus aligns with the Biodiversity Convention's ecosystem approach, discussed in chapter 1. It also reflects the more positive interactions that occur between the natural and human constituents of the socioecological networks that underpin agricultural systems. It is not a case of biodiversity removing already depleted water resources from a system, thereby undermining the livelihoods of farmers and the security of local communities. Rather, biodiversity has a central role in maintaining the quality and quantity of fresh water and is consequently critical in ensuring that freshwater systems can deliver ecosystem services for society.

This chapter will explore whether this new emphasis is being delivered in practice through relevant laws and policies, in a manner that is compatible with agroecology. I begin by considering how water and its usage relate to core agroecological norms and practices through the concept of natural water infrastructure. Attention then turns to instruments that cover freshwater ecosystems, where we will see that criticisms relating to the prioritisation of anthropocentric concerns again apply. Finally, I discuss aquaculture and how its current regulation offers both opportunities and challenges for the advancement of agroecology through the law.

## Natural Water Infrastructure

The maxim, 'Ask not what water can for biodiversity; ask what biodiversity can do for water', while an important recognition of how diverse ecosystems and their constituent species contribute to water quality and quantity, glosses over the critical need to address what humans can do for water and biodiversity. An overly simplistic answer to this is that humans could use less water, and this will not be achieved without changes to how agriculture utilises water resources.

Globally, agricultural activities consume around three-quarters of the water extracted for anthropogenic use.[9] It is therefore unsurprising that water usage is

7 ibid 9.
8 ibid 17.
9 UN-Water, *Summary Progress Update 2021 – SDG 6 – Water and Sanitation for All* (UN-Water, 2021) 23.

increasingly recognised as a key indicator of the sustainability of agricultural operations.[10] The situation is more complex than this, however, as activities that might otherwise be considered positive, even essential, from a sustainability perspective become unsustainable due to their water demands. One response to the soil erosion and desertification discussed in the previous chapter is the mass planting of trees to restore the integrity of subterranean structures and support soil ecosystems, while also helping to combat climate change. China is pursuing this to such an extent, however, that concerns have been raised over the pressures that are being placed on water resources,[11] to the point that some scientists now advocate discontinuing the programme.[12]

It has also been suggested that the water demands of biofuels render them unsustainable,[13] despite their potential as an alternative to fossil fuels.[14] Biofuels are a useful illustration of how a socioecological network can be traced from the local to the global, across multiple issues, and the consequent need to adopt a holistic, systems-level approach when analysing the potential impacts of policies and decisions. For example, a farmer decides to switch from growing food crops to biofuels, in response to a government scheme that offers subsidies for biofuel production as part of a climate change mitigation strategy. At the local level, this could reduce food security due to the reduction in the availability of food crops. It could also impact the resilience of local ecosystems if the change in crops resulted in a net loss of biodiversity. Depending on how many farmers took advantage of the scheme, there could also be national implications. In addition to impacts similar to those that might occur at the local level, the reduction in food supply could push up prices, which would in turn incentivise the conversion of land so that new crops could be grown to meet demand. If this land is primary habitat, the resulting conversion could cancel out any reduction in carbon emissions that were achieved through the biofuel subsidies.[15]

Due to the challenges of needing to feed an increasing global population and more frequent droughts associated with the changing climate, simply mandating reductions in water use is not a realistic solution. What is instead required is the more efficient and sustainable use of finite water resources, and one means to achieve this is to develop natural water infrastructure. Natural infrastructure is another way of (de)constructing complex ecological processes so that they are

10 M. Forouzani and E. Karami. 'Agricultural Water Poverty Index and Sustainability' (2011) 31 *Agronomy for Sustainable Development* 415.

11 X. Feng and others, 'Revegetation in China's Loess Plateau Is Approaching Unsustainable Water Resource Limits' (2016) 6 *Nature Climate Change* 1019.

12 J. Ge and others, 'Impact of Revegetation of the Loess Plateau of China on the Regional Growing Season Water Balance' (2020) 24 *Hydrology and Earth System Sciences* 515.

13 Walker (n 2) 192.

14 O. Edenhofer and others (eds), *Climate Change 2014: Mitigation of Climate Change, Contribution of Working Group III to the Fifth Assessment Report of the Intergovernmental Panel on Climate Change* (IPCC, 2014) 12.

15 R. Amos, 'Bioenergy Carbon Capture and Storage in Global Climate Policy: Examining the Issues' (2016) 4 *Carbon & Climate Law Review* 187, 188–189.

more compatible with the limitations of law and policymaking.[16] The increasing attention that the concept is receiving highlights the fallacy of weak understandings of sustainability, i.e. that natural capital can be substituted by technology.[17] A recent report on natural water infrastructure in the United States shows that artificial water infrastructure has been unable to keep pace with growing demand and ecological changes, demonstrating that even where alternative technology appears to exist, it is neither viable nor sustainable in the long term.[18]

Like ecosystem services, the concept of natural infrastructure emphasises the importance of protecting and enhancing ecological integrity. Habitats and species are commonly understood to fall within definitions of natural capital, but in an agroecological context, in which the human is as important as the natural, we might expand this to related human capital, such as the local and traditional knowledge of farmers.[19] Protecting natural infrastructure therefore serves multiple aspects of agroecological, and wider sustainability, agenda. Regarding natural water infrastructure,[20] protecting watersheds has been shown to be a more cost-efficient way to maintain water quality than treatment plants, while also benefitting associated ecosystems.[21] Protecting and restoring wetlands similarly supports biodiversity, building greater diversity into local agroecological networks while reducing the risk of flooding in agricultural and other areas.[22] Other flood control benefits result from maintaining coastal ecosystems, which also helps to reduce erosion, improve the food security of coastal communities[23] and enhance the resilience of local economies.[24] In other words, natural water infrastructure supports

16 Related to this is the idea of nature-based solutions, i.e. utilising ecosystems in a way that enhances nature's resilience – UNEP-DHI and others, *Nature-Based Solutions for Water Management: A Primer* (UNEP, 2018). Research suggests, however, that despite being widely recognised in national policymaking, this has yet to translate into concrete actions to respond to environmental problems – OECD, *Nature-Based Solutions for Adapting to Water-Related Climate Risks* (OECD Publishing, 2020).

17 For a critique of weak and strong understandings of sustainability, see W. Beckerman, '"Sustainable Development": Is It a Useful Concept?' (1994) 3 *Environmental Values* 191.

18 American Rivers, *Naturally Stronger: How Natural Water Infrastructure Can Save Money and Improve Lives* (2017). Available at: https://medium.com/naturally-stronger (last accessed 20/04/2023).

19 See ch 2.

20 In reality, it is not easy to distinguish natural water infrastructure from other categories of natural infrastructure. Forests, for example, may be considered natural water infrastructure due to their role in regulating hydrological cycles.

21 J. Salzman, 'A Field of Green? The Past and Future of Ecosystem Services' (2006) 21 *Journal of Land Use and Environmental Law* 133, 139–140.

22 K. Suttles and others, 'Upstream Solutions to Downstream Problems: Investing in Rural Natural Infrastructure for Water Quality Improvement and Flood Risk Mitigation' (2021) 13 *Water* 3579.

23 S. Cunniff, 'Scaling Protection and Restoration of Natural Infrastructure to Reduce Flood Impacts and Enhance Resilience' (2019) 87 *Shore & Beach* 51.

24 M. Spalding and others, 'The Role of Ecosystems in Coastal Protection: Adapting to Climate Change and Coastal Hazards' (2014) 90 *Ocean & Coastal Management* 50.

both natural and human members of socioecological networks, as well as the relationships between them.

Supporting natural water infrastructure is a central feature of the Biodiversity Convention's work on inland waterways, with the Revised Programme of Work on Inland Water Biological Diversity comprising three elements: conservation, sustainable use and benefit-sharing; institutional and socioeconomic enabling environment; and knowledge assessment and monitoring.[25] As is typical of programmes of work under the Biodiversity Convention, each element has its own goals, sub-goals and supporting activities. Overall, these reflect core features of an agroecological approach to the regulation of freshwater environments, identifying the need to integrate the conservation and sustainable use of freshwater ecosystems into other policy areas;[26] ensure that economic incentives promote, rather than discourage, the conservation of biodiversity;[27] and engage local and indigenous communities in decisions that may impact freshwater ecosystems, including the cultures that are connected to these.[28] The principal weakness of the Programme of Work, as it is for much of the Biodiversity Convention regime, is that positive frameworks are not being implemented to the necessary degree at the national level. A review into the Programme of Work concludes that while it remains a useful framework to direct action, greater efforts need to be made to implement it.[29] In particular, the review identifies the need to more fully integrate water issues into other policy areas, on the basis of a clearer recognition of the contribution that healthy freshwater systems make to the sustainable development agenda.[30] The review therefore underscores that regardless of the merits of the legal framework, progress in shifting society towards a more sustainable track will be limited if sufficient steps are not taken to implement it. This applies to agroecology as much as it does to the wider sustainability agenda represented by the Sustainable Development Goals (SDGs).[31]

## Protecting Freshwater Ecosystems in International Law

That the world's fresh water is found almost exclusively under the jurisdiction of states means that national law is the primary source of regulation.[32] Two treaties have, however, been adopted for freshwater bodies that cross international borders: the 1992 UNECE Convention on the Protection and Use of Transboundary

25 Decision VII/4, Biological diversity of inland water ecosystems, UNEP/CBD/COP/DEC/VII/4, 13 April 2004, Annex.

26 ibid Goals 1.1 and 2.1.

27 ibid Goal 2.3.

28 ibid Goal 3.3.

29 Decision X/28, Inland waters biodiversity, UNEP/CBD/COP/DEC/X/28, 29 October 2010, para 6.

30 ibid.

31 N. Eisenmenger and others, 'The Sustainable Development Goals Prioritize Economic Growth Over Sustainable Resource Use: A Critical Reflection on the SDGs from a Socio-Ecological Perspective' (2020) 15 *Sustainability Science* 1101.

32 E. Brown Weiss, 'The Coming Water Crisis: A Common Concern of Humankind' (2012) 1 *Transnational Environmental Law* 153, 153.

Watercourses and International Lakes[33] and the 1997 Convention on the Law of the Non-Navigational Uses of International Watercourses.[34] The significance of these treaties is clear when we consider that there are around 300 transboundary river basins, comprising approximately 80% of the world's rivers, but many of these are not subject to a bespoke bi- or multilateral agreement.[35] It should be noted, however, that at the time of writing the 1992 Convention only has 49 parties,[36] and the 1997 Convention just 37,[37] so their application is relatively limited.

### *The 1997 Watercourses Convention*

As we saw in chapter 1, while an ecosystem approach can be identified in the 1997 Watercourses Convention, it is undermined by the qualified nature of its environmental protection provisions in Articles 20–23. Salman views this Convention as manifesting a wider tension in international watercourses law between the 'no harm' rule, on the one hand, and the principle of equitable and reasonable utilisation on the other, with downstream states favouring the former and upstream states the latter.[38] In brief, the 'no harm' rule, a peremptory norm of international law, requires states to avoid any serious harmful transboundary environmental effects resulting from activities conducted in their territory.[39] It should, though, be considered an obligation of due diligence, i.e. to take reasonable steps to prevent harm, rather than an obligation of result,[40] with specific obligations on states considered to be those of assessing potentially harmful activities and notifying and consulting states likely to be impacted by them.[41] The principle of equitable and reasonable utilisation requires the rights of watercourse states to be determined on the

33 Helsinki, 17 March 1992, in force 6 October 1996, 31 ILM 1312 (1992).

34 New York, 21 May 1997, in force 17 August 2014, 36 ILM 700 (1997).

35 World Commission on Dams, *Dams and Development: A New Framework for Decision-Making* (Earthscan, 2000) 15, cited in S. Salman, 'Freshwater Resources', in L. Rajamani and J. Peel (eds), *The Oxford Handbook on International Environmental Law* (2nd edn, OUP, 2021) 513. For an overview of the regional agreements that have been adopted, see M. Fitzmaurice, 'The Relationship Between the Law of International Watercourses and Sustainable Development', in M. Fitzmaurice and others (eds), *Research Handbook on International Environmental Law* (2nd edn, Edward Elgar, 2021).

36 https://treaties.un.org/Pages/ViewDetails.aspx?src=TREATY&mtdsg_no=XXVII-5&chapter=27&clang=_en (last accessed 20/04/2023).

37 https://treaties.un.org/Pages/ViewDetails.aspx?src=IND&mtdsg_no=XXVII-12&chapter=27&clang=_en (last accessed 20/04/2023).

38 Salman (n 35) 518.

39 *Trail Smelter Case (United States v Canada)*, Award, 1941, 3 UNRIAA 1905, 1965.

40 A. Boyle and C. Redgwell, *Birnie, Boyle and Redgwell's International Law and the Environment* (4th edn, OUP, 2021) 153. In contrast, see T. Meshel, 'Unmasking the Substance Behind the Process: Why the Duty to Cooperate in International Water Law is Really a Substantive Principle' (2018) 47 *Denver Journal of International Law and Policy* 29.

41 G. Handl, 'Transboundary Impacts', in D. Bodansky and others (eds), *The Oxford Handbook of International Environmental Law* (OUP, 2007) 540–544.

basis of all relevant circumstances in a given case.[42] It is not considered to contain a substantive environmental protection element, beyond the extent to which its interpretation is influenced by sustainable development and other developments in international environmental law.[43] Neither is the term 'equitable' linked to ideas of intergenerational equity, as might be argued in other international environmental legal contexts.[44] Instead, it merely relates to the fair resolution of disputes between states.[45] Salman contends that in the Convention, it is the principle of equitable and reasonable utilisation that has greater status over the 'no harm' rule.[46] While the exact relationship between the two norms is contested,[47] it is notable that Article 7, which sets out the 'no harm' obligations of states in this context, is qualified by references to the provisions on equitable and reasonable utilisation.[48] The point is also made that the International Court of Justice has previously indicated that equitable and reasonable utilisation is the primary rule governing international watercourses.[49]

Neither the principle of 'no harm' nor of equitable and reasonable use is incompatible with a system of law that promotes agroecology. As has been observed in this work, agroecology recognises the importance of protecting socioeconomic values and interests such as those reflected in the principles: the reasonable exploitation of natural resources and preventing harm to states' capacity to pursue that exploitation. Two criticisms can nevertheless be made of how these principles operate in the context of transboundary freshwater bodies. First, the wrong balance has been struck between them. What is equitable and reasonable should be determined in the bounds of likely significant harm, i.e. harm that breaches the 'no harm' rule should not be considered reasonable, rather than the 'no harm' rule being qualified by what is considered to be equitable and reasonable use. This reflects the criticism of sustainable development for failing to frame trade-offs between environmental protection, social equity and economic development in ecological limits.[50] As noted above, ecological health is not a substantive element of the 'no harm'

42 X. Fuentes, 'Sustainable Development and the Equitable Utilization of International Watercourses' (1998) 69 *British Yearbook of International Law* 119, 119.

43 ibid 199–200.

44 E. Brown Weiss, 'Intergenerational Equity: A Legal Framework for Global Environmental Change', in E. Brown Weiss (ed), *Environmental Change and International Law: New Challenges and Dimensions* (UN University Press, 1992).

45 Fuentes (n 42) 200.

46 Salman (n 35) 519. Note that the 'no harm' rule also aligns with anthropocentric understandings of sustainable development, as it has been interpreted to mean no harm to the rights and interests of states, rather than no harm to the environment per se – *Corfu Channel Case (United Kingdom v Albania)*, Judgment of 15 December 1949, [1949] ICJ Reports 4, 22.

47 L. Caflisch, 'Regulation of Uses of International Watercourses', in S. Salman and L. Boisson de Chazournes (eds), *International Watercourses – Enhancing Cooperation and Managing Conflict* (World Bank Technical Paper No 414, 1998) 15, cited in Salman (n 35) 518.

48 Salman (n 35) 519.

49 ibid 522. E.g., *Gabčikovo-Nagymaros (Hungary/Slovakia)* (1997) ICJ Reports 7, 150.

50 R. Amos, *International Conservation Law: The Protection of Plants in Theory and Practice* (Routledge, 2020) 226–227.

rule, which is our second criticism of how these principles have been applied in international freshwater law. The failure to account for how society's utilisation of fresh water impacts freshwater and related ecosystems is contrary to theories of agroecology, as it ignores the reality that the socioeconomic priorities pursued through that utilisation ultimately depend on those ecosystems enjoying a certain standard of health and integrity.

More recent international judgments suggest that greater attention is being paid to the ecological impacts of states' use of freshwater bodies. The *Kishenganga Arbitration*[51] is considered to be a strong statement of the importance that international courts now attach to maintaining the ecological health of riparian systems.[52] Of particular note is the Permanent Court of Arbitration's (PCA) finding that it was necessary to maintain an 'environmental flow' in the Kishenganga to prevent 'significant harm' to Pakistan.[53] Such judgments should not be read as a new 'no ecological harm' rule asserting itself against the principle of equitable and reasonable use in the law of international watercourses. In its ruling, the PCA made it clear that its role was not that of policymaker, whereby it would require environmental considerations to overrule the explicit rights set out in the Indus Waters Treaty[54] between India and Pakistan regarding the river's socioeconomic uses.[55] Decisions such as this may, however, represent the principle of equitable and reasonable use being given a more robust interpretation in line with ongoing developments in international environmental law, principal among these being the ecosystem approach.[56] If carried through in future developments, this would create more space to advance agroecology through the law. It would constitute continued recognition that the equitable and reasonable use of fresh water is essential for human activities, including agriculture, but how that use is assessed would have a clearer, if not stronger, ecological content. More desirable still would be for determinations of what is equitable and reasonable to be made on the basis of predominately ecological criteria, but there is little to suggest that international watercourses law is currently evolving in that direction.

51 *Indus Waters Kishenganga Arbitration (Pakistan v India)*, Final Award of the Court of Arbitration, 20 December 2013.

52 O. McIntyre, 'Protection and Preservation of Freshwater Ecosystems (Articles 20–23)', in L. Boisson de Chazournes and others (eds), *The UN Convention on the Law of the Non-Navigational Uses of International Watercourses: A Commentary* (OUP, 2018) 207.

53 *Kishenganga Arbitration* (n 51) 112.

54 Indus Waters Treaty Between the Government of India, the Government of Pakistan and the International Bank for Reconstruction and Development, 19 September 1960, in force 12 January 1961, 419 UNTS 216.

55 *Kishenganga Arbitration* (n 51) 112. The PCA's freedom was restricted in this case because the treaty expressly limits the extent to which other sources of law can be applied in the event of a dispute.

56 R. Brooks and others, *Law and Ecology: The Rise of the Ecosystem Regime* (Ashgate, 2002) ch 10. The *Kishenganga Arbitration* provides an illustration of this, as the PCA held that Pakistan's wider assessment of how reducing the river's flow would impact on the ecosystem was considered more appropriate than India's assessment of how it would impact on certain fish species – (n 51) 100.

### *The 1992 UNECE Convention on the Protection and Use of Transboundary Watercourses and International Lakes*

The 1992 UNECE Convention is arguably a stronger conservation instrument than the 1997 Convention,[57] and potentially a more appropriate instrument for pursuing agroecology as well. In addition to the 'no harm' and equitable and reasonable use principles,[58] when taking action to prevent, control and reduce transboundary impact resulting from their use of a shared freshwater body, states must be guided by three further principles of environmental law: the precautionary principle; the polluter pays principle; and the principle of intergenerational equity.[59] Each of these facilitates the advancement of agroecology in the law.

As we discussed in chapter 3, precaution is inherent to risk assessment processes, and both these and the precautionary principle (or approach) have a role in maintaining the ecological and social integrity of agricultural processes. Questions remain over whether a more environmentally appropriate definition of the precautionary principle should be adopted,[60] and there are valid concerns over the implications of its ambiguous nature when being applied in decision-making,[61] but at the very least it provides space for different actors in a socioecological network to engage in discussions about decisions that will impact that network.[62]

Simply defined, the polluter pays principle requires that the costs of remedying harms caused by pollution, or of preventative measures, fall on the party or parties responsible for that pollution.[63] It has found expression in numerous environmental treaties, with Principle 16 of the Rio Declaration on Environment and Development reflecting both its environmental and economic aspects:

> National authorities should endeavour to promote the internalisation of environmental costs and the use of economic instruments, taking into account the approach that the polluter should, in principle, bear the cost of pollution, with due regard to public interest and without distorting international trade and investment.[64]

How the polluter pays principle relates to agroecology is interesting. De Sadeleer suggests that the principle's main function in regulation is redistribution. It seeks to

57 Amos (n 50) 113–114.

58 1992 UNECE Convention Articles 2(1) and 2(2)(c).

59 1992 UNECE Convention Article 2(5).

60 E.g., C. Sunstein, 'Irreversible and Catastrophic' (2006) 91 *Cornell Law Review* 841.

61 J. Scott and E. Vos. 'The Juridification of Uncertainty: Observations on the Ambivalence of the Precautionary Principle within the EU and the WTO', in C. Joerges and R. Dehousse (eds), *Good Governance in Europe's Integrated Market* (OUP, 2002).

62 M. Lee, *EU Environmental Law, Governance and Decision-Making* (2nd edn, Hart Publishing, 2014) 5–6.

63 P. Schwartz, 'The Polluter-Pays Principle', in M. Fitzmaurice and others (eds), *Research Handbook on International Environmental Law* (Edward Elgar, 2011).

64 31 ILM 874 (1992).

ensure that the costs of remediating pollution, which would otherwise be borne by public authorities and society in general, fall on those responsible for it.[65] It therefore responds to the problem that ecosystem services, including the disposal of pollution, are common goods, the exploitation of which provides a direct benefit to the individual concerned, but the costs are shared by society as a whole.[66] In terms of industrial actors, this argument is sound. However, farmers, who will also be polluters, are producing a public good, i.e. food, albeit for private profit. While wider society therefore still carries the burden of the pollution, either in terms of accepting the consequent environmental harm or having to pay to rectify that harm, they also benefit from that pollution through, in general terms, greater food security.

This raises the question of who is a polluter? Traditionally, the answer to this has been the party responsible for releasing the harmful or foreign substance into the environment,[67] which would suggest that the farmer is responsible for any pollution resulting from his activities regardless of any benefit to society. An alternative approach, however, would be to apply a 'user pays' principle, under which those responsible for the consumption of a natural resource are required to account for that usage.[68] This would underpin an argument in favour of sharing the costs of pollution resulting from agricultural activities across society. The farmer would bear no specific or additional responsibility, assuming they acted lawfully.[69] It has been suggested that a user pays principle would contribute more to the achievement of sustainable development than the polluter pays principle,[70] a position that is reinforced by the inclusion of responsible consumption and production in SDG-12. It is possible to read in this Goal an emphasis on the wider responsibility of society in ensuring the sustainable consumption of resources, with SDG-12.3 calling for a reduction of food waste, including at the consumer level, and SDG-12.8 highlighting the need to ensure that everyone has the information required to pursue sustainable lifestyles. This underscores that consumers of agricultural products, i.e. the public, may not only be considered part of agriculture's socioecological networks but are just as responsible for maintaining the ecological and social integrity of those networks as those involved in the production of agricultural goods.

Finally, intergenerational equity is considered a core component of sustainable development[71] and may potentially be an emerging principle of international law in

65 N. de Sadeleer, *Environmental Principles: From Political Slogans to Legal Rules* (2nd edn, OUP, 2020) 43–44.
66 See ch 5.
67 Schwartz (n 63) 247.
68 De Sadeleer (n 65) 51.
69 This relates to the curative function of the polluter pays principle, i.e. it provides a rationale for permitting civil liability claims to be brought where pollution has either been discharged unlawfully or is lawful under public law, e.g. because it is pursuant to a statutory duty, but the resulting harm is considered too great an infringement on a private person's enjoyment of their property. For further discussion on this latter point, see B. Pontin, *Nuisance Law and Environmental Protection* (Lawtext Publishing, 2013) ch 2.
70 De Sadeleer (n 65) 51.
71 Boyle and Redgwell (n 40) 121–123.

its own right.[72] At its most progressive, intergenerational equity considers current generations to be trustees of the natural world, responsible for ensuring that, at the very least, they leave it in no worse state for future generations than that in which they inherited it.[73] Invoking the concept of trusteeship raises the questions of whether future generations may be said to have rights, and, if accepted, how these might be discerned and accounted for in legal processes. While controversial, such questions are now being addressed through the law, with Wales's Well-being of Future Generations Act 2015 being one of the clearest examples.[74] More practicable, though, is the language of options; current generations should maximise the options of future generations so that they are in the strongest possible position to deal with their own challenges.[75] Protecting the diversity and resilience of agricultural systems and the natural world, in accordance with agroecology, is arguably the best way to do this.

The UNECE Convention also goes further than the 1997 Watercourses Convention in incorporating an ecosystem approach, which again makes it a stronger agroecological instrument. This is evident when we analyse the 'appropriate measures' that states are encouraged to adopt under Article 2. Article 2(b) calls on states 'To ensure that transboundary waters are used with the aim of ecologically sound and rational water management…', but more interesting is Article 2(d). This requires states 'To ensure [the] conservation and, where necessary, restoration of ecosystems'. The first point to note is that while the obligation of ecologically sound management is only an 'aim' of state action, no such qualification is applied to the need to conserve and restore ecosystems. Notwithstanding the overall discretionary nature of Article 2, there does appear to be a reasonably clear substantive element to paragraph (d). These obligations are ambiguous, however. 'Conservation' is not defined,[76] and simply compiling an inventory of species in a watercourse would arguably meet the requirements of Article 2. Restoration is also not defined, but that it is listed separately suggests that it means something different to conservation. One way to read Article 2(d) would therefore be for conservation to relate to a negative obligation of preventing further degradation to freshwater bodies and maintaining their capacity to deliver ecosystem services and restoration as a positive obligation of actively assisting in their ecological recovery. This

72 E. Brown Weiss 'Implementing Intergenerational Equity', in Fitzmaurice and others (n 63) 103–108. See also the comments of Judge Cançado Trindade in his Separate Opinion to *Whaling in the Antarctic (Australia v Japan: New Zealand Intervening)* (2014) ICJ Reports 226, 41–45.

73 Brown Weiss ibid 102. See also M. Wood, *Nature's Trust: Environmental Law for a New Ecological Age* (CUP, 2014).

74 In brief, this requires public bodies in Wales to consider, inter alia, the long- and short-term implications of its actions, particularly where short-term needs are being met in a manner that carries significant long-term implications (s.5). See further H. Davies, 'The Well-Being of Future Generations (Wales) Act 2015: Duties or Aspirations?' (2016) 18 *Environmental Law Review* 41.

75 Brown Weiss (n 44) 402–404.

76 The 1992 UNECE Convention is not alone in failing to provide a precise definition for 'conservation'. I have made a similar observation in relation to the Biodiversity Convention – Amos (n 50) 25.

would be in line with the Society for Ecological Restoration's definition of ecosystem recovery,[77] which is frequently used in international policymaking.[78]

A final point to note in relation to the UNECE Convention is its definition of 'transboundary impact':

> "Transboundary impact" means any significant adverse effect on the environment resulting from a change in the conditions of transboundary waters caused by a human activity... Such effects on the environment include effects on human health and safety, flora, fauna, soil, air, water, climate, landscape and historical monuments or other physical structures or the interaction among these factors; they also include effects on the cultural heritage or socioeconomic conditions resulting from alterations to those factors.[79]

This definition is similar to that of 'impact' in Article 1(vii) in the Convention on Environmental Impact Assessment in a Transboundary Context[80] and to the factors that must be assessed under the EU's Environmental Impact Assessment regime.[81] Agricultural activities clearly have the potential to result in such impacts, either through excessive extraction of water or through pollution. Equally, agriculture may be affected by such impacts, and not just in terms of the environmental quality and productivity of agricultural land. An argument can be made that this definition of 'transboundary harm' also includes the cultural aspects of agriculture. In certain conventions, cultural heritage is broadly equated to physical structures. Under the World Heritage Convention, for example, cultural heritage is defined in terms of monuments, groups of buildings and particular sites.[82] That the UNECE Convention lists cultural heritage separately from physical buildings suggests that in this context, heritage goes beyond physical infrastructure and might be said to include intangible heritage, such as agricultural knowledge and traditional ways of doing. Any use of a transboundary freshwater body that threatens significant harm to a local community's traditional farming practices, or might result in a com-

77 Society for Ecological Restoration International Science & Policy Working Group, *The SER International Primer on Ecological Restoration* (Society for Ecological Restoration, 2004) 1.

78 A. Telesetsky and others, *Ecological Restoration in International Environmental Law* (Routledge, 2017) 23.

79 1992 UNECE Convention, Article 1(2).

80 Espoo, 25 February 1991, in force 10 September 1997, 30 ILM 802 (1991). See Ch 9 for discussion.

81 Initially set out in Article 3 of Directive 85/337/EC on the assessment of the effects of certain public and private projects on the environment [1985] OJ L 175 and most recently described in Directive 2011/92/EU [2012] OJ L 26, as amended by Directive 2014/52/EU [2014] OJ L 124.

82 Paris 16 November 1972, in force 17 December 1975, 27 UST 37, 11 ILM 1358 (1972) Article 1. Operational Guidelines 2021, para 47. While traditional practices may not per se be protected under the World Heritage Convention, Articles 4 and 5 call on states to take measures to, inter alia, conserve and protect world heritage sites and this may conceivably include steps to protect cultural practices if these are inextricably linked with the reasons why a site is considered to host heritage that is of outstanding universal value. Also relevant here is the Convention for the Safeguarding of Intangible Cultural Heritage, Paris, 17 October 2003, in force 20 April 2006, 2368 UNTS 3.

munity having to abandon the area in which their unique agricultural knowledge is centred, would therefore appear to be contrary to the UNECE Convention. To that extent, the Convention may also be said to advance agroecological approaches in the law, as it provides some protection to the cultural diversity of agricultural systems.

The UNECE regime has been enhanced by the adoption of the 1999 Protocol on Water and Health.[83] As might be expected, this is primarily concerned with ensuring universal access to sufficient and safe drinking water, but the Protocol also recognises the necessity of protecting freshwater ecosystems if this is to be achieved.[84] Action under the Protocol is framed by the same three principles as the UNECE Convention: precaution, polluter pays and intergenerational equity.[85] In terms of sustainable development, the Protocol on Water and Health is yet another example of the law's failure to frame policy trade-offs within ecological limits, with Article 5(g) stating:

> Water has social, economic and environmental values and should therefore be managed so as to realise the most acceptable and sustainable combination of those values;

This is, however, balanced to an extent by Article 5(j):

> Water resources should, as far as possible, be managed in an integrated manner on the basis of catchment areas, with the aim of linking social and economic development to the protection of natural ecosystems and of relating water-resource management to regulatory measures concerning other environmental mediums.

While this cannot be read as conditioning the socioeconomic development of freshwater resources on maintaining their ecological integrity, it does at least reinforce the ecosystem approach in the 1992 regime. Although not explicit, Article 8(j) also calls for a systems-level approach to water resource management, as this is arguably the only way that the desired integration will be achieved.

## Aquaculture

Aquaculture is the farming of plants and animals in freshwater and marine environments.[86] It is a global and growing industry, with most states engaging in some form of aquacultural activity, either to meet local demand or for international markets.[87]

83 London, 17 June 1999, in force 4 August 2005, 38 ILM 1708 (1999).
84 Protocol on Water and Health, Articles 1 and 4(c).
85 Protocol on Water and Health, Articles 5 (a), (b) and (d).
86 https://www.fao.org/fishery/en/aquaculture (last accessed 20/04/2023).
87 F. Asche and others, 'Future Trends in Aquaculture: Productivity Growth and Increased Production', in M. Holmer and others (ed), *Aquaculture in the Ecosystem* (Springer, 2008). It should be noted

The primary products of aquaculture are fish, but reptiles, shellfish and aquatic plants are all reared for a variety of purposes.[88] It has been suggested that aquaculture is a solution to several complex social challenges, and as such may advance multiple aspects of agroecology. Most obvious are those that relate to food security and the vulnerability of wild fish stocks.[89] While the 1995 Fish Stocks Agreement has some merit as a conservation instrument,[90] the FAO estimates that a growing number of fish stocks are being exploited at unsustainable levels.[91] Aquaculture can relieve pressure on wild populations by shifting consumption to farmed sources, providing what could be a more reliable source of protein to a significant part of the world's population in the process. It has been estimated that aquaculture now supplies half the fish that is consumed by humans.[92] Algae could also help address global hunger; it has long been a staple food in its own right and is now also processed into a range of meat- and dairy-free products.[93] To date, however, most interest in algae in the context of aquaculture has been its role in tackling climate change. Algae is potentially a more efficient source of biofuel than land-based crops, as the production of algae-based biofuels does not consume as much fresh water and would not reduce the land available for food-crop production. There is also growing interest in using algae as carbon sinks, due to its significant capacity to absorb carbon dioxide.[94]

Aquaculture therefore has a role in supporting agroecological responses to global challenges. Notably, aquacultural systems constitute a further layer of diversity to food production systems, especially if they are themselves diverse in what they produce and how they produce it. Their potential impacts on the environment and associated socioecological networks should not be underestimated, however, and call into question how far aquaculture can go in remedying society's problems. With regard to aquaculture as a source of protein, for example, the farming of popular but predatory species, such as salmon, requires huge amounts of protein-based

that the nature and size of the global market varies according to the aquacultural product in question. E.g., there is no real global market for farmed oysters due to a range of environmental and regulatory supply-side issues – R. Botta and others, 'A Review of Global Oyster Aquaculture Production and Consumption' (2020) 117 *Marine Policy* 103952.

88 FAO, *The State of World Fisheries and Aquaculture: Sustainability in Action* (FAO, 2020) 21.

89 S. Stetkiewicz and others, 'Seafood in Food in Security: A Call for Bridging the Terrestrial-Aquatic Divide' (2022) 5 *Frontiers in Sustainable Food Systems* 703152.

90 New York, 4 December 1995, in force 11 December 2001, 34 ILM 1542 (1995). Boyle and Redgwell (n 40) 747–762.

91 FAO, *The State of World Fisheries and Aquaculture: Towards Blue Transformation* (FAO, 2022) 46. See also FAO (n 88) part 1.

92 J. Cai and X. Zhou, 'Contribution of Aquaculture to Total Fishery Production: The 50-percent Mark' (2019) 60 *FAO Aquaculture Newsletter* 43.

93 J. Stapelberg, 'Algae: A Key to a Greener Future?' TEDx Talk, University of Praetoria, 30 October 2019. Available at: https://www.youtube.com/watch?v=SpjVsIK33SM (last accessed 20/04/2023).

94 D. Dah-Wei Tsai and others, 'Carbon Sequestration by Alga Ecosystems' (2015) 84 *Ecological Engineering* 386.

fish feed, limiting the extent to which aquaculture relieves pressures on wild fish populations.[95]

Another critical issue is the pollution resulting from fish-farming activities. This includes nutrient loading when feed and antibiotic inputs into fish farms leach into the wider ecosystem, as aquacultural infrastructure is not designed to prevent such escapes,[96] as well as other waste products.[97] One study found that in areas immediately adjacent to fish farms, there can be a layer of sediment as much as a kilometre thick due to the amount of waste produced.[98] A related problem is the escape of non-native farmed species and the consequent impacts these alien species have on surrounding ecosystems.[99] Similar concerns have been raised over how the mass production of algae can fundamentally alter local ecosystems.[100]

These challenges are not insurmountable, particularly if an agroecological approach is adopted in the regulation and management of aquaculture. A systems-level analysis of salmon production would reveal the extent to which meeting the industry's demands for protein-based feed is undermining efforts to reduce pressures on wild fish populations. Precaution also has a role to play, although the regulatory manifestation of this through risk assessments has proven just as controversial in aquaculture as it has for other agricultural issues,[101] due to the prioritisation of expert opinion over public concerns.[102] Addressing such issues is the basis of the FAO's Blue Transformation, a roadmap to enhance the sustainability of aquatic food production by 2030.[103] This complements and builds on the 2021 Declaration for Sustainable Fisheries and Aquaculture produced by the FAO Committee on Fisheries, which represents a new vision for developing aquaculture-based solutions to, inter alia, global hunger, poverty and climate change, and a forum for scientific and public engagement.[104]

95 R. Goldburg and R. Naylor, 'Future Seascapes, Fishing, and Fish Farming' (2005) 3 *Frontiers in Ecology and the Environment* 21, 23.

96 ibid 25.

97 C. Moore, 'Rapidly Increasing Plastic Pollution from Aquaculture Threatens Marine Life' (2014) 27 *Tulane Environmental Law Journal* 205.

98 R. Wu, 'The Environmental Impact of Marine Fish Culture: Towards a Sustainable Future' (1995) 31 *Marine Pollution Bulletin* 159, cited in J. Roderburg 'Marine Aquaculture: Impacts and International Regulation' (2011) 25 *Australian and New Zealand Maritime Law Journal* 161, 165.

99 E. Cook and others, 'Non-Native Aquaculture Species Releases: Implications for Aquatic Ecosystems', in M. Holmer and others, *Aquaculture in the Ecosystem* (Springer, 2008). For discussion of regulatory responses to marine biological invasions, see Amos (n 50) 180–185.

100 M. Silver and others, 'Toxic Diatoms and Domoic Acid in Natural and Iron Enriched Waters of the Oceanic Pacific' (2010) 107 *Proceedings of the National Academy of Sciences* 20762. See R. Abate and A. Greenlee, 'Sowing Seeds Uncertain: Ocean Iron Fertilization, Climate Change, and the International Environmental Law Framework' (2010) 27 *Pace Environmental Law Review* 555.

101 See ch 3.

102 A. Lee and P. Cloutier de Repentigny, 'Farming the Sea, a False Solution to a Real Problem: Critical Reflections on Canada's Aquaculture Regulations' (2019) 50 *Ottawa Law Review* 29.

103 FAO, *Blue – Transformation – Roadmap 2022–2030: A Vision for FAO's Work on Aquatic Food Systems* (FAO, 2022).

104 Text available at: https://www.fao.org/documents/card/en/c/cb3767en/ (last accessed 20/04/2023).

'Blue Transformation' is defined as a 'targeted effort' by a range of stakeholders, including governments, international organisations and local communities, to reorientate the utilisation of aquatic food systems towards an ecosystem approach, recognising that our exploitation of these systems has both ecological and socio-economic impacts.[105] On the one hand, the deliberate emphasis of an ecosystem approach is welcome, not least because, as observed previously, this aligns closely with agroecological approaches to the regulation and management of human activities.[106] There is also a recognition that aquatic food systems operate in overlapping socioecological networks, and that ensuring their sustainable utilisation can lead to benefits for the natural world and support the livelihoods of a range of communities in a more just manner than current consumption patterns.[107]

On the other hand, it is possible to question the extent to which an ecosystem approach is embedded in the Blue Transformation, and whether it constitutes a genuinely new approach to the management of aquatic food chains. A bespoke definition of 'ecosystem approach' is not provided in the Blue Transformation, and while reference is made to the 'ecosystem approach to fisheries' concept that has been developed to guide states in fisheries management,[108] this does not fully capture the range of challenges that arise in aquaculture, or reflect the need to adopt holistic solutions to its complex environmental and socioeconomic impacts.[109] Further, the guiding principles that have been developed to inform the Blue Transformation are almost exclusively concerned with reforming governance processes for anthropocentric reasons. There is a strong emphasis on human rights and justice, for example. The only mention of the environment in the principles is a call for action to achieve the Blue Transformation to 'balance socioeconomic and environmental outcomes', which suggests that this is merely another manifestation of the failed model of sustainable development rather than a genuine new framework for the management of aquatic food systems. This does not mean that the principles are devoid of agroecological content, however. They include respect for traditional and local knowledge and reflect an adaptive management approach to implementation by calling for the continual improvement in mechanisms that evaluate ongoing actions to deliver the transformation.

The roadmap itself comprises three areas: aquaculture, fisheries and value chains. Our focus here is on aquaculture, for which five targets have been identified.[110] These, as well as the priority actions intended to deliver them, are typical of international environmental programmes. Target A1, for example, calls for global and regional cooperation in the design, dissemination and implementation of good

105 FAO (n 103) 4.
106 See ch 1.
107 FAO (n 103) 4.
108 ibid 10. FAO Fisheries Department, *The Ecosystem Approach to Fisheries* (FAO / FAO Technical Guides for Responsible Fisheries, 2003).
109 C. Carter, *The Politics of Aquaculture: Sustainability Interdependence, Territory and Regulation in Fish Farming* (Routledge, 2018).
110 FAO (n 103) 8–9.

aquacultural practice. In terms of the environment, the most important target is A4, which aims to minimise the environmental impacts of aquaculture and ensure the efficient use of resources. This requires action to improve the management of biosecurity issues, which, as noted above, is a particular concern in the operation of aquacultural installations.[111] There is again, however, evidence indicating that the Blue Transformation is not a radical agenda for change. Target A2 calls for the development of technology to support the intensification of aquaculture. As we discussed in the book's introduction, new technologies are legitimate components of an agroecological framework, but that technologies are emphasised in the context of intensification, in the absence of a corresponding target to consider whether some uses of aquatic systems may per se be unsustainable, suggests that the Blue Transformation is built on a weak understanding of sustainability.

Despite these concerns, the Blue Transformation offers some opportunities to advance agroecology in the regulation of aquaculture. While it can be criticised for lacking a strong ecological content, the emphasis on delivering justice and food security for a broad range of communities is still important in supporting socioecological networks.[112] It is possible to question whether a sufficiently robust regulatory framework exists to deliver the Blue Transformation, however. It has been suggested that aquaculture represents a gap in regulation because it cannot properly be classified as agriculture, animal husbandry or fisheries.[113] That the natural systems on which aquaculture depend are considered, in some cases, to be at the point of collapse, suggests that major reforms are therefore needed to how the law addresses aquaculture.[114] Roderburg believes that a dedicated treaty is required due to the global nature of aquacultural issues. This would, in her view, address the problems arising from the fragmentation of aquacultural issues,[115] which have to date only been addressed in an ad hoc fashion.[116] I am not convinced this would add anything of substance to what it already found in pre-existing international regulation, and might instead lower international standards because, as in the case of agriculture, there would be significant sovereignty implications. Instead, efforts should be made to integrate those elements of agroecology that are compatible with pre-existing international norms and principles in relevant regimes, particularly those that locate aquaculture systems in the wider environment.

Arguably, the FAO is not the most appropriate forum for this. Instead, renewed efforts should be made to deal specifically with the environmental impacts of

111 ibid.

112 See ch 12.

113 FAO, *Preliminary Review of Selected Legislation Governing Aquaculture* (ADCP/REP/89/42), drawing on African Regional Aquaculture Centre, *Introduction to Aquaculture* (ARAC/87/WP/11).

114 FAO, *The State of the World's Land and Water Resources for Food and Agriculture: Systems at Breaking Point* (FAO, 2021) ch 1.

115 Roderburg (n 98) 178.

116 See D. VanderZwaag, 'The International Law and Policy Seascape for Aquaculture: Navigating Tangled Currents', in N. Bankes and others, *Aquaculture Law and Policy: Global, Regional, and National Perspectives* (Edward Elgar, 2016).

aquaculture through the Biodiversity Convention. As we saw in chapter 1, the Biodiversity Convention has developed a reasonably strong understanding of an ecosystem approach, which would provide a more ecologically appropriate framework for regulatory responses than the Blue Transformation's guiding principles, notwithstanding the importance and noted role of the justice-oriented guiding principles in advancing agroecology as well.

Guidance on specific measures that could be pursued through either a new programme of work or a binding protocol under the Biodiversity Convention can be found in an FAO review of aquacultural regulatory frameworks, which provides examples of regulatory practice at the national level.[117] Many of these are typical of regimes designed to respond to the environmental impacts of activities. They include subjecting aquaculture proposals to environmental impact assessment to ensure that any impacts on local ecosystems are identified and at least mitigated,[118] and requiring operators to go through a permitting process so that there is transparency and accountability in the aquacultural industry.[119] The review is also useful in identifying responses to challenges that are specific to aquaculture. On the issue of escapement, for example, it not only highlights national rules on preventing and responding to escapes from aquacultural installations to avoid ecological damage but also on ownership over escaped animals.[120] As was observed in relation to the Biodiversity Convention's Programme of Work on Inland Water Biological Diversity, however, regardless of how 'good' a framework is in terms of establishing an agroecological approach to the regulation of aquaculture, it will be of minimal effect if not properly implemented at the national level.

## Conclusions

In many ways, water is the most important subject in this book. It is a useful illustration of how the natural and the human are connected through sociological networks. Sufficient fresh water is essential if nature is to thrive. Nature will then be able to provide the range of ecosystem services, including for agricultural purposes, on which society depends. The shift in international law from seeing biodiversity's use of fresh water as a problem to a critical step in maintaining the health and functioning of the natural world is welcome. What is missing from discussions, whether these are framed in terms of natural water infrastructure or a similar policy

117 P. Talla Takoukam and K. Erikstein, *Aquaculture Regulatory Frameworks: Trends and Initiatives in National Aquaculture Legislation* (FAO, 2013). See also J. Kyrönviita and others, 'Achieving Blue Growth Post-Weser: A Study of Aquaculture Regulation in the Nordic Region' (2021) 18 *Journal of European Environmental & Planning Law* 256, which examines the difficulties that the European aquaculture industry face due to disparate national regulations.

118 Talla Takoukam and Erikstein, ibid 13.

119 ibid 10–12. See also, J. Vince and M. Haward, 'Hybrid Governance of Aquaculture: Opportunities and Challenges' (2017) 201 *Journal of Environmental Management* 138, which examines the role of communities in monitoring the aquaculture industry in Australia.

120 Talla Takoukam and Erikstein (n 117) 16–17.

concept, is a sufficient focus on how human behaviours need to change to ensure that increasingly scarce freshwater resources are utilised in a sustainable manner.

Both the 1992 UNECE Convention and the 1997 Convention have the potential to advance agroecological approaches to the conservation of water. The fundamental principles of international water law on which they are based – equitable and reasonable utilisation and 'no harm' – are compatible with agroecology, which recognises legitimate anthropogenic uses of water. Arguably, however, the relationship between these needs to be recast so that it is equitable and reasonable use that is qualified by the 'no harm' principle, rather than understandings of 'no harm' being conditioned by equitable and reasonable use. Recent developments in the law are nevertheless encouraging, with the emphasis on ecological standards in the *Kishenganga Arbitration*, while not constituting a 'no ecological harm' rule, demonstrating a greater awareness of ecological concerns in this area of the law.

A further observation that was made in relation to both the Biodiversity Convention's Programme of Work and the freshwater conventions is that proposed solutions to global water challenges, even those that purport to be radical new approaches, are grounded in weak understandings of sustainability. The emphasis is on technological solutions rather than fundamental behavioural change so that human pressures on finite water resources are reduced. This is particularly evident in the FAO's Blue Transformation for the aquaculture industry. There are again positive aspects to this agenda from an agroecological perspective, including the recognition of the need to engage a wide range of stakeholders in the design and implementation of policies. While the specific challenges will vary according to the aquacultural product, production methods and state of the local and global markets in question, overall the Blue Transformation can be read as simply another iteration of sustainable development. As such, while it may provide some answers to the challenges in ensuring that aquaculture is sustainable, it will not do so in such a way that would protect and enhance the integrity of aquatic ecosystems, and therefore adequately support the socioecological networks that have evolved out of aquaculture.

# 8 Climate Change

## Agriculture and Climate Change

Climate change epitomises the indivisibility of nature and society, and the consequences of how humanity's actions have degraded the health and integrity of the natural world. The anticipated impacts of climate change are well known. Sea-level rise is perhaps most associated with it, but just as destabilising are the more fundamental changes to ecosystems.[1] Increasing temperatures can alter habitats, rendering them uninhabitable for species that are then forced to migrate, but not all will be able to do so easily. Alpine plants are an obvious example, as their potential for relocation is limited by their reproduction method and, ultimately, the height of their mountain.[2] Even if a species can migrate, there is no guarantee that other species on which it depends, such as for pollination or prey, will follow, or that substitutes will be found in their new range. Species that must migrate due to climate change will also be alien species in any area they colonise, and their impacts on these new ecosystems can be exacerbated if the integrity of these has already been undermined by climate change.[3]

Climate change's impacts on agriculture mirror its wider environmental effects.[4] This is unsurprising given agriculture's reliance on healthy ecosystems, but how these effects manifest in a socioecological network varies according to context. California, for example, produces around half of the fruit and nuts consumed in the United States, and as these must grow for several years before they can be harvested are especially vulnerable to extreme weather events caused by climate change.[5] For farmers in Tanzania, in contrast, it is the persistent rise in annual

1 M. Harm Benson and R. Kundis Craig, *The End of Sustainability: Resilience and the Future of Environmental Governance in the Anthropocene* (Kansas University Press, 2017) ch 1.

2 J. Good and D. Millward, *Alpine Plants: Ecology for Gardeners* (Batsford, 2007) 158.

3 E. Brown Weiss, 'Intergenerational Equity: A Legal Framework for Global Environmental Change', in E. Brown Weiss (ed), *Environmental Change and International Law: New Challenges and Dimensions* (UN University Press, 1992) 402–403. Although see F. Pearce, *The New Wild: Why Invasive Species Will Be Nature's Salvation* (Icon Books, 2015), which discusses the role of alien species in restoring degraded ecosystems.

4 J. Santilli, *Agrobiodiversity and the Law* (Earthscan, 2012) ch 3.

5 T. Pathak and others, 'Climate Change Trends and Impacts on California Agriculture: A Detailed Review' (2018) 8 *Agronomy* 25.

DOI: 10.4324/9781003435174-11

temperatures that is of greatest concern, as these put pressure on limited water supplies and increase the risk of pest and disease outbreaks.[6] In both cases, the proposed mitigation measures draw on agroecology. There is an emphasis on promoting diversity within and between agrosystems to enhance their resilience and in facilitating stakeholder participation in discussions regarding associated strategies.

Agriculture is a major driver of climate change, although the individual footprint of farmers again varies according to the nature and scale of their activities.[7] That the clearing of primary forests for agricultural purposes contributes to carbon emissions is uncontested, but the extent to which more mundane agricultural activities are a 'problem' is more controversial. There is scientific debate, for example, over whether livestock methane emissions are as problematic as has been suggested,[8] particularly with research suggesting that this may be resolved through the selective-breeding of animals that produce less methane.[9] The agricultural industry also has an important role in combatting climate change,[10] particularly if it follows agroecology. Diverse agrosystems that follow agroecology have significant carbon storage capacity, although at present this cannot match the carbon emissions from industrial agricultural production.[11]

The purpose of this chapter is not to revisit the scholarship examining the links between human activities and climate change, or the international frameworks intended to address these.[12] For context, a brief overview of the UN Framework Convention on Climate Change[13] (UNFCCC) regime is provided, focusing specifically on its work on adaptation. Instead, I focus on how agroecology can enhance the resilience of agricultural systems and the communities these support so that they are better able to adapt to the inevitable impacts of climate change. Framing this discussion will be a case study on Kiribati. Kiribati has been selected for several reasons. First, as a small island developing state, Kiribati is a prime example of the inherent injustice of climate change, i.e. that it is those communities that have

6 R. Kangalawe and others, 'Climate Change and Variability Impacts on Agricultural Production and Livelihood Systems in Western Tanzania' (2017) 9 *Climate and Development* 202.

7 FAO, *Greenhouse Gas Emissions from Agrifood Systems: Global, Regional and Country Trends 2000–2020* (FAOSTAT Analytical Brief Series No. 50, 2022). Connected to this is the carbon emissions from the international transportation of food – M. Li and others, 'Global Food-Miles Account for Nearly 20% of Total Food-Systems Emissions' (2022) 3 *Nature Food* 445.

8 S. Liu and others, 'Rethinking Methane from Animal Agriculture' (2021) 2 *CABI Agriculture and Bioscience* 22.

9 O. González-Recio and others, 'Novel Methods and Perspectives for Modulating the Rumen Microbiome through Selective Breeding as a Means to Improve Complex Traits: Implications for Methane Emissions in Cattle' (2023) 269 *Livestock Science* 105171.

10 FCCC/CP/2022/10/Add.1, Decision 3/CP.27.

11 M. Altieri and C. Nicholls, 'The Adaptation and Mitigation Potential of Traditional Agriculture in a Changing Climate' (2013) 140 *Climate Change* 33.

12 See instead C. Carlarne and others (eds), *The Oxford Handbook of International Climate Change Law* (OUP, 2016).

13 New York, 9 May 1992, in force 24 March 1994, 1771 UNTS 107.

contributed least to climate change that are most at risk from its consequences.[14] Second, it represents a relatively contained socioecological network but one that also reveals how such networks are nevertheless impacted by, and impact on, the wider world. Finally, the effects of climate change on Kiribati are not hypothetical but happening now. The country therefore constitutes a very real warning of our continued failure to exploit the natural world sustainably.

## The UN Framework Convention on Climate Change

Adopted in 1992, the UNFCCC aims to stabilise atmospheric concentrations of greenhouse gases 'at a level that would prevent dangerous anthropogenic interference with the climate system'.[15] The Convention itself does not contain specific obligations, but instead a series of overarching principles and commitments.[16] Regarding the former, arguably the most important of these is common but differentiated responsibilities (CBDR), the idea that while all states must take action to reduce their emissions, developed states have a responsibility to go further, faster.[17] While reflecting the respective capacities of different socioecological networks, CBDR is not uncontroversial and may be seen as legitimising developing states' pursuit of the same environmentally harmful activities that have caused the climate crisis.[18] The commitments in Article 4(1) of the Convention are similarly broad, with some links to agroecology. They include promoting the sustainable management of ecosystems and developing integrated plans for the management of agriculture, although it took some time before this received substantive attention from state parties.[19]

The 1997 Kyoto Protocol[20] and 2015 Paris Agreement,[21] which set out specific mechanisms for how the UNFCCC's emission reductions are to be achieved, have, for their own reasons, fallen short in instigating the level of action needed to keep the global temperature rise below the stated target of 2°C.[22] For the Kyoto Protocol, the exclusion of China and India from its mandatory emission reduction targets

14 In 2021, Kiribati emitted 71,533 tonnes of carbon dioxide, while the United States released 5.01 billion tonnes – https://ourworldindata.org/co2/country/kiribati?country=KIR~USA#what-are-the-country-s-annual-co2-emissions (last accessed 20/04/2023). K. Odeku, 'Climate Injustices Due to the Unequal and Disproportionate Impacts of Climate Change' (2022) 11 *Perspectives of Law and Public Administration* 103.

15 UNFCCC, Article 2.

16 UNFCCC, Articles 3 and 4.

17 P. Cullett, 'Common But Differentiated Responsibilities', in M. Fitzmaurice and others (eds), *Research Handbook on International Environmental Law* (2nd edn, Edward Elgar, 2021).

18 A. Boyle and C. Redgwell, *Birnie, Boyle and Redgwell's International Law and the Environment* (4th edn, OUP, 2021) 401–402.

19 B. O'Sullivan and C. Streck, 'Forestry and Agriculture under the UNFCCC: A Jigsaw Waiting to be Assembled?', in Carlarne and others (n 12).

20 11 December 1997, in force 16 February 2005, 37 ILM 22 (1998).

21 22 April 2016, in force 4 November 2016, C.N.92.2016.TREATIES-XXVII.7.d.

22 Paris Agreement, Article 2.

led to resentment in developed states and a corresponding reluctance to see it extended beyond its first commitment period.[23] A fundamentally different approach was consequently adopted in the Paris Agreement, centred on all states producing nationally determined contributions of emission reductions.[24] While this represents an important shift towards the 'common' aspect of CBDR and away from the 'differentiated', it has so far not delivered the level of commitment necessary to prevent the global temperature rise from exceeding 2°C, and the catastrophic ecological change that will result from this.[25] The UNFCCC regime consequently demonstrates the Catch-22 of international environmental law. Treaties dealing with global environmental problems require near-universal participation if they are to be effective, but securing such participation requires substituting the specific, enforceable and ambitious obligations that could drive progress with more ambiguous standards.[26]

With efforts to prevent and mitigate climate change falling dangerously short, an increasingly important aspect of the UNFCCC's work is adaptation. This is a core objective of the regime, with Article 2 of the Convention stating that efforts to stabilise atmospheric greenhouse gas concentrations 'should be achieved within a time frame sufficient to allow ecosystems to adapt naturally to climate change, to ensure that food production is not threatened and to enable economic development to proceed in a sustainable manner'. Despite this reference to ecosystems, meaningful efforts to coordinate the work of the UNFCCC and the Convention on Biological Diversity[27] to protect biodiversity from climate change, as a conservation goal and for purposes of adaptation, were not made until 2010.[28]

It was not until the 2015 Conference of the Parties (COP), following significant lobbying by developing states, that adaptation was identified as an equal priority to mitigation in the UNFCCC regime.[29] It is reflected throughout the Paris Agreement, with Article 7(1) establishing 'enhancing adaptive capacity, strengthening resilience and reducing vulnerability to climate change' as a global goal of adaptation.[30] Progress has since stalled (again), however. Discussions on defining the global adaptation goal intended for the 2022 COP were postponed and developed states were unwilling to move forward on their 2021 commitment to double

23 Boyle and Redgwell (n 18) 391.

24 Paris Agreement, Articles 4 and 6. B. Mayer, 'Article 4: Mitigation', in G. Van Calster and L. Reins (eds), *The Paris Agreement on Climate Change: A Commentary* (Edward Elgar, 2021).

25 H. Lee and others, *Synthesis Report of the IPCC Sixth Assessment Report* (IPCC AR6 SYR, 2023) 23–27.

26 L. Rajamani, 'Addressing the 'Post-Kyoto' Stress Disorder: Reflections on the Emerging Legal Architecture of the Climate Regime' (2009) 58 *International and Comparative Law Quarterly* 803.

27 Rio de Janeiro, 5 June 1992, in force 29 December 1993, 31 ILM 822 (1992).

28 R. Amos, *International Conservation Law: The Protection of Plants in Theory and Practice* (Routledge, 2020) 120–122.

29 P. Sands and J. Peel, *Principles of International Environmental Law* (4th edn, CUP, 2018) 325.

30 Adaptation is also recognised in Articles 4–6 and 9–14 of the Agreement.

adaptation financing by 2025.[31] On the other hand, there was a breakthrough on the issue of loss and damage resulting from climate change,[32] which has been one of the most controversial issues in international climate change negotiations.[33]

The reference to resilience in the global goal highlights the importance of agroecology to climate change adaptation. As we discussed in the book's introduction, natural and human systems will be more resilient, i.e. better able to cope with detrimental change, if they are diverse.[34] Agroecology promotes this diversity, as well as the integration of land management policies, stakeholder engagement and knowledge exchange considered prerequisites to resilience.[35] As the following case study on Kiribati demonstrates, the UNFCCC's support for adaptation is going to be increasingly important. Achieving this for those communities most at risk is extremely challenging but will arguably be more likely if lessons are drawn from agroecology.

## Climate Change Adaptation in Kiribati

### *Agriculture in Kiribati*

Located in the central Pacific, Kiribati is not one island but a collection of 33, 21 of which are currently inhabited.[36] Most are low-lying atolls, leaving them especially vulnerable to rising sea levels. Even if the rise is not sufficient to entirely submerge an island, it may still be enough to contaminate freshwater supplies with seawater, reduce the land available for agriculture and habitation and leave communities exposed to major weather events.[37] Kiribati's total land area is just 811 $km^2$, spread across 3.5 million $km^2$ of ocean, with the island of Kiritimati constituting over 70% of its landmass.[38] In 2023, the population was estimated at approximately 115,000,[39] around half of which reside on the main islands of South Tarawa.[40]

Soil in Kiribati is exceptionally poor and mostly ill-suited for crops.[41] The inhabitants consequently rely on imports of basic foodstuffs, notably rice and flour, leaving them exposed to global events that increase prices. Agriculture nevertheless

31 https://www.wri.org/insights/cop27-key-outcomes-un-climate-talks-sharm-el-sheikh (last accessed 20/04/2023). FCCC/PA/CMA/2021/10/Add.1, 8 March 2022, Decision 1/CMA.3, para 18.

32 FCCC/PA/CMA/2022/10/Add.1, 17 March 2023, Decision 2/CMA.4.

33 C. Voigt, 'Climate Change and Damages', in Carlarne (n 12).

34 B. Walker and D. Salt, *Resilience Thinking: Sustaining Ecosystems and People in a Changing World* (Island Press, 2006) ch 1.

35 N. Webb and others, 'Land Degradation and Climate Change: Building Resilience in Agriculture' (2017) 15 *Frontiers in Ecology and the Environment* 450.

36 https://www.kiribatitourism.gov.ki/kiribati-pacific-ocean-location/ (last accessed 20/04/2023).

37 Ministry of Environment, Lands and Agriculture Development (MELAD), *Kiribati Agriculture Strategy (KAS 2020–2030)* (March 2020) 2.

38 (n 36).

39 https://www.cia.gov/the-world-factbook/countries/kiribati/summaries (last accessed 20/04/2023).

40 MELAD (n 37) 2.

41 ibid 9

accounts for 20% of Kiribati's economy.[42] Principal products include livestock, as well as coconuts and a variety of fruit and vegetables that are grown for subsistence and export.[43]

Ensuring the long-term viability of Kiribati's agricultural industry is increasingly challenging. The land that is available for agricultural production is decreasing, falling from 53% of the country's total land area in 1964 to just 42% in 2016, largely due to erosion and sea-level rise.[44] Related to this are the restrictive rules on land tenure, which further reduces the land that is available for cultivation.[45] Water is similarly increasingly scarce, again due to rising sea levels but also because of unsustainable usage.[46]

Globalisation has also had an impact. Major socioeconomic changes in Kiribati society during the 20th century have led to the diet of much of the population now comprising imported food. This has undermined Kiribati's food security, as demand for imported food has resulted in a corresponding drop in demand for local produce, meaning that even if domestic agricultural production could be increased, it would be of little economic benefit to the farmers.[47] As I explore in chapter 12, this raises questions over whether globalised systems that purport to deliver food security merely embed food insecurity in the world's most vulnerable communities.[48] That demand for local food has fallen also means that the traditional knowledge of how to produce, prepare and preserve that food is being lost.[49] Another related challenge is the country's geography. That the population is dispersed over so many islands over such a large area makes supporting the internal economy difficult. The reliance on imports, as well as frequent visits from tourists, also mean that the islands' ecosystems are vulnerable to outbreaks of invasive/alien species and disease.[50]

### *Climate Change's Impacts on Kiribati*

The above is just an overview of the challenges that Kiribati faces in supporting its agricultural industry. Although not explicitly mentioned in the 10-year agriculture strategy that Kiribati has adopted, it is encouraging that this nevertheless reflects key agroecological principles. It is built on stakeholder engagement, from all levels of society, in the design, implementation and review of measures intended to

42 ibid 3.
43 ibid 9.
44 ibid 9–10.
45 ibid 9.
46 ibid 10.
47 ibid 12
48 A. Saab, 'An International Law Approach to Food Regime Theory' (2018) 31 *Leiden Journal of International Law* 251, 258–264.
49 Kiribati Climate Change Policy (2019) 9. Available from https://www.president.gov.ki/resources/information-library.html (last accessed 20/04/2023).
50 MELAD (n 37) 12.

support domestic agricultural production.[51] There is also an emphasis on education to shift demand towards domestic produce, which will help protect the traditional knowledge associated with this, and to share best practices with other Pacific Island states in maintaining their natural resource base.[52]

By far the most significant challenge with which Kiribati's agricultural sector, and wider society, must contend is climate change.[53] Since the 1950s, average temperatures have increased in Kiribati by 0.1–0.2°C each decade and could potentially reach 3°C by 2100.[54] Local higher temperatures threaten Kiribati's agriculture through the heightened risk of disease, as well as by reducing crop yields and increasing stresses on livestock.[55] Global temperature rises, on the other hand, mean that many of its islands are threatened with being partially or wholly submerged and that most are less than 2 km wide means that retreating inland is not a viable option. Of most concern is the prediction that up to half of Tawara, the most populated island, may disappear.[56]

Admittedly, these are estimates of worst-case scenarios. It is not just gradual sea-level rise that threatens Kiribati and other low-lying states, however. In 2015, Cyclone Pam hit the South Pacific and while Kiribati was not in its path, the resulting storm surge caused significant damage to its agricultural and other infrastructure.[57] Cyclone Pam was the first tropical storm to affect Kiribati, and its impacts were exacerbated by climate change.[58]

Agroecology not only represents a framework for sustainable agriculture, but a more sustainable society as well.[59] Kiribati's experiences illustrate the urgency of society transitioning towards greater sustainability, but also the limitations of what even immediate reform can achieve. Speaking at a TED talk in 2015, the then-President of Kiribati, Anote Tong, made the point that for his country, climate change is happening *now*.[60] What may appear dry scientific statistics relating to seemingly small increases in temperature, or rising sea levels, are the everyday, lived experiences of Kiribati's communities.[61] A comprehensive policy has been developed to guide Kiribati's efforts to adapt to climate change, with priority areas including

51 ibid 12–13.
52 ibid.
53 N. Fiertz and others, *Climate Risk Summary Report: Tawara, Kiribati* (Stimson Centre, 2022).
54 The World Bank Group, *Climate Risk Country Profile: Kiribati* (2021) 5 and 8.
55 MELAD (n 36) 10–11.
56 Fiertz and others (n 53) 4.
57 Vanuatu was worst impacted by the cyclone – https://reliefweb.int/disaster/tc-2015-000020-vut (last accessed 20/04/2023).
58 R. Hoeke and others, 'Severe Flooding in the Atoll Nations of Tuvalu and Kiribati Triggered by a Distant Tropical Cyclone Pam' (2020) 7 *Frontiers in Marine Science* 539646.
59 See the introduction to this book.
60 A. Tong, *My Country Will Be Underwater Soon – Unless We Work Together* (November 2015). Available at: https://www.ted.com/talks/anote_tong_my_country_will_be_underwater_soon_unless_we_work_together?language=en (last accessed 20/04/2023).
61 Kiribati Climate Change Policy (n 49) 8.

food security, water security and environmental resilience.[62] The reality, though, is that Kiribati cannot adapt its way out of all the challenges it faces.[63] Relocating the population may ultimately be the only realistic solution, but this raises a host of ecological, legal, social and economic questions, for the people that are migrating and the regions to which they move, to which there are no easy answers.

#### *Climate Change Migration and International Law*

There are two types of migration: internal to a state and external, i.e. cross-border migration. Perhaps counter-intuitively, internal migration has received more attention in international law. At the global level, the UN Guiding Principles on Internal Displacement set out the rights and protections that states are expected to provide displaced persons.[64] While these do not explicitly refer to environmental displacement, the requirement in Principle 5 that 'All authorities and international actors shall respect and ensure respect for their obligations under international law… so as to prevent and avoid conditions that might lead to displacement of persons' must be read as including their climate change obligations. Although non-binding, the Guiding Principles reflect other binding rules of international law[65] but present the management of internally displaced people primarily as a matter for the state in question rather than an international concern.[66]

Stronger instruments have been adopted at the regional level. The Convention for the Protection and Assistance of Internally Displaced Persons in Africa (Kampala Convention) is one example.[67] This not only defines 'refugee' in a manner that includes those forced to relocate due to climate change[68] but also requires states to 'take measures to protect and assist persons who have been internally displaced due to natural or human made disasters, including climate change'.[69] While vague on the type of measures that should be adopted, it is notable that this obligation is expressed in imperative language.

Agreeing laws concerning external migration has proven more challenging at the international level, particularly migration that is associated with climate change. This is in part due to migration being a politically controversial topic in many Western states, but also because it raises questions that the law appears ill-equipped to answer. Campbell draws two important distinctions, between climate

62 ibid.

63 J. Kupferberg, 'Migration and Dignity – Relocation and Adaptation in the Face of Climate Change Displacement in the Pacific – A Human Rights Perspective' (2021) 25 *International Journal of Human Rights* 1793, 1807.

64 Available at: https://www.unhcr.org/uk/protection/idps/43ce1cff2/guiding-principles-internal-displacement.html (last accessed 20/04/2023).

65 J. McAdam, 'Climate Change-Related Displacement of Persons', in Carlarne (n 12) 529.

66 Principle 3.

67 Kampala, 23 October 2009, in force 6 December 2012, 3014 UNTS 3.

68 Kampala Convention, Article 1(k).

69 Kampala Convention, Article V(4).

migration and climate change migration, and between induced and forced migration.[70] Regarding the former, environmental degradation that is not necessarily associated with climate change is often at least partially behind a person's decision to relocate from their home region,[71] particularly if this affects a region's agricultural systems.[72] Climate change migration, in contrast, is a direct result of either the gradual changes to a region caused by climate change or a one-off event that is attributed to climate change. Drawing such causal links is difficult, but the difference between climate and climate change migration may soon be redundant given the increasing scale and frequency of climate change's global impacts.

What will become more salient in political discourse, I suggest, is Campbell's second distinction between induced and forced migration. Induced migration is where individuals choose to relocate in response to how climate change is affecting their homes at a time when remaining where they are is still a feasible option. This may even form part of an adaptation strategy if it is in response to a policy encouraging people to move to reduce pressures on fragile but still-functioning ecosystem services. With forced migration, as the name suggests, there is no choice involved and the environmental conditions are such that a person or community has no option but to relocate.[73]

Significant time and effort have been spent debating what label should be attached to those that have been displaced by climate change. One term commonly used in the literature is 'climate refugee'. The difficulty with this is that 'refugee' has a specific legal meaning in international law, with the 1951 Refugee Convention defining it in relation to fear of persecution.[74] Climate change impacts cannot easily be read into this, except possibly in circumstances where environmental degradation is used as a means of persecution.[75] While the Convention could be reopened, there appears little political appetite to do so and a new agreement on climate change migration is similarly unfeasible.[76]

Debates over language are important, as definitions determine the law's scope. The danger is that these substitute discussions of measures that must be taken to support those who are displaced by climate change. In the absence of a treaty on climate change migration, recourse must be made to non-binding instruments. In

70 J. Campbell, 'Climate-Change Migration in the Pacific' (2014) 26 *The Contemporary Pacific* 1, 9–11.

71 R. Reuveny, 'Climate Change-Induced Migration and Violent Conflict' (2007) 26 *Political Geography* 656, 663–667.

72 FAO, *Migration, Agriculture and Climate Change: Reducing Vulnerabilities and Enhancing Resilience* (2017).

73 Campbell (n 70) 11.

74 Geneva, 28 July 1951, in force 22 April 1954, 189 UNTS 137, Article 1(2).

75 McAdam (n 65) 522.

76 J. McAdam, *Climate Change, Forced Migration, and International Law* (OUP, 2012) ch 7. Although see D. Hodgkinson and L. Young '"In the Face of Looming Catastrophe" – A Convention for Climate-Change-Displaced Persons', in M. Gerrard and B. Wannier (eds), *Threatened Island Nations: Legal Implications of Rising Seas and a Changing Climate* (CUP, 2013).

2018, the UN adopted the Global Compact for Migration,[77] which calls for coordinated approaches to environmental migration, including in response to climate change.[78] Another important framework is the strategy on climate change migration adopted by the International Organisation for Migration (IOM).[79] Both these instruments have merit. The Compact has been broadly welcomed as a first step in changing the nature of the debate over migration, through its emphasis on the long-term benefits that migrants bring to their host states and how these align with sustainable development.[80] Central features of the IOM's strategy are also compatible with agroecology. Its guiding principles emphasise, for example, the need for broad stakeholder engagement in the design and implementation of measures that support displaced persons, and for the food, water and environmental security of migrants to be guaranteed.[81] That the Compact and IOM strategy are non-binding, however, means that in the short-term at least their value lies more in their political positioning than their legal force.[82]

Part of the reason why a treaty has yet to emerge on external climate migration is because it raises exceptionally complex issues. Host communities may face their own ecological vulnerabilities, which would be put under further stress by the sudden influx of a large number of people. Agricultural systems would be particularly at risk, as they would need to meet greater demand, potentially with less space and less water depending on where the displaced persons settled. Similar concerns can be raised over other aspects of the host society. Additional pressures would be placed on health and education services, for example, and consideration would also have to be given to the impacts on the employment and welfare sectors. All this speaks to the objective of ensuring that displaced communities integrate with their new society. Although considered necessary for the success of any relocation, and an important step in preventing the discrimination and persecution of climate refugees/migrants that has previously been witnessed in the Pacific,[83] it must be balanced with the need to respect and protect the cultures of displaced communities. This is especially relevant to Pacific Islanders and others residing in regions with histories of colonialism,[84] highlighting the essential human rights dimension of climate (change) migration.[85]

77 Available at: https://refugeesmigrants.un.org/migration-compact (last accessed 20/04/2023).

78 Global Compact, para 18(h)-(l).

79 IOM, *Institutional Strategy on Migration, Environment and Climate Change 2021–2030* (IOM, 2021).

80 M. Klein Solomon and S. Sheldon, 'The Global Compact for Migration: From the Sustainable Development Goals to a Comprehensive Agreement on Safe, Orderly and Regular Migration' (2018) 30 *International Journal of Refugee Law* 584.

81 IOM (n 79) ch 3.

82 V. Chetail, *International Migration Law* (OUP, 2019) 392–394.

83 Kupferberg (n 63) 1805.

84 ibid 1798.

85 S. Atapattu, 'Justice for Small Island Nations: Intersections of Equity, Human Rights, and Environmental Justice', in R. Abate (ed), *Climate Justice: Case Studies in Global and Regional Governance Challenges* (ELI Press, 2016).

***Kiribati and Climate Change Migration***

Migration is part of the cultural identity of many Pacific Island communities, with the ocean seen as a pathway, not a barrier.[86] Increasingly, however, internal migration within Kiribati is being driven by people's desire for the security offered by the major population centre of South Tarawa, which is more resilient than the outlying islands to the environmental impacts of climate change and offers greater access to healthcare and education. The resulting overcrowding is only exacerbating the pressures on Kiribati's agricultural industry, with settlements expanding into water catchment areas.[87]

Managed properly, facilitating internal migration can form part of a state's strategy to adapt to climate change.[88] Fiji, for example, is able to relocate communities at risk from rising sea levels inland and to higher elevations. The three approaches behind their 2018 Planned Relocation Guidelines incorporate principles and practices that are associated with agroecology. Community engagement in decision-making underpins the human-centred and human rights-based approaches,[89] highlighting the greater emphasis on human rights in international climate change law following the adoption of the Paris Agreement.[90] The livelihood-based approach reflects 'that the planned relocation process needs to be sensitive to the types of communities and households that may be on the move and to their specific needs', thereby acknowledging that different communities will have their own expectations, needs and challenges, including in relation to agriculture.[91]

A similar policy of adaptation through internal migration has been adopted by Kiribati. The Temaiku Land and Urban Development Project aims to develop 300 hectares of currently uninhabitable land so that it is 2 m above the anticipated sea-level rise.[92] In theory, there is a lot to commend this project. It would allow the i-Kiribati to remain in their own country, thereby protecting the cultural links between the people and the land,[93] and raises fewer legal questions than alternatives that have been considered, such as artificial floating islands.[94] Delivering the project is proving challenging, however, notwithstanding the progress to date. The costs are unaffordable for Kiribati alone and so recourse has had to be made to

86 M. Jolly, 'On the Edge? Deserts, Oceans, Islands' (2001) 13 *The Contemporary Pacific* 417, 419.

87 Fiertz and others (n 53) 5.

88 J. Barnett and M. Webber, 'Migration as Adaptation: Opportunities and Limits', in J. McAdam (ed), *Climate Change and Displacement: Multidisciplinary Perspectives* (Hart Publishing, 2010).

89 Fiji Ministry of Economy, *Planned Relocation Guidelines: A Framework to Undertake Climate Change Related Relocation* 2018) 8.

90 S. Atapattu, 'Climate Change, Human Rights, and COP 21' (2016) 17 *Georgetown Journal of International Affairs* 47.

91 Fiji Ministry of Economy (n 89) 8.

92 https://www.jacobs.com/projects/kiribati (last accessed 20/04/2023).

93 J. Campbell, 'Climate-Induced Community Relocation in the Pacific: The Meaning and Importance of Land', in McAdam (n 88).

94 Tong (n 60). These questions include where the islands should be located; how this might affect their jurisdiction over marine resources; and who would be liable for maintaining the islands.

international partners and funding bodies. More problematic is that seven projects on this scale would be required to accommodate Kiribati's estimated population growth.[95]

The wider sustainability of the project has also been called into question. The Temaiku region is already overpopulated, resulting in pollution, lack of access to water and corresponding impacts on health, and pressures on the community's agricultural systems.[96] The Global Environment Facility Small Projects Grants Programme has funded work to resolve these issues, including educating the public on water conservation and sanitation, the installation of water infrastructure and, reflecting the links between biodiversity and water discussed in the previous chapter, encouraging local communities to enhance the area's ecological health through the cultivation of native plants and crops.[97]

In light of the predicted effects of climate change, and the limitations of the Temaiku Development Project, external migration from Kiribati appears inevitable,[98] but this would not be a new phenomenon. In his TED talk, Tong discusses visiting a community in the Solomon Islands that emigrated from Kiribati in the 1960s following a severe drought. What he observed was that their language had begun to evolve away from the Kiribati dialect and that they had developed their own customs and behaviours.[99] In and of itself, this is not a bad thing, and may even be considered positive from an agroecological perspective if it enhances cultural diversity in a socioecological network. It also shows, however, that diversity may also be lost if entire communities are forced to relocate from the physical and cultural spaces in which specific traditions have evolved.[100]

Prior to a change in government in 2016, voluntary cross-border relocation was the country's principal adaptation strategy, under the label of 'Migration with Dignity' (MWD).[101] Kiribati bought 20 km$^2$ of land on the Fijian island of Vanua Levu for this purpose, and so a programme based on MWD remains an option. The rationale behind MWD relates back to Campbell's distinction between induced and forced migration. It involved i-Kiribati choosing to migrate to an area that is culturally and ecologically similar to Kiribati, and where concerns over the land rights

95 Kupferberg (n 63) 1801.

96 https://sgp.undp.org/spacial-itemid-projects-landing-page/spacial-itemid-project-search-results/spacial-itemid-project-detailpage.html?view=projectdetail&id=26098 (last accessed 20/04/2023).

97 ibid. See also G. Kiddle and others, 'Nature-Based Solutions for Urban Climate Change Adaptation and Wellbeing: Evidence and Opportunities From Kiribati, Samoa, and Vanuatu' (2021) 14 *Frontiers in Environmental Science* 723166.

98 Kupferberg (n 63) 1801.

99 Tong (n 60).

100 C. Yow Mulalap, '"To Preserve the Heritage of the Past, and to Protect the Promise of the Future": Intergenerational Equity Challenges from Climate Change in the Federated States of Micronesia', in Abate (n 85) 324–325.

101 https://www.rnz.co.nz/international/pacific-news/296669/kiribati-climate-induced-migration-to-start-in-five-years?utm_content=buffer2afbf&utm_medium=social&utm_source=twitter.com&utm_campaign=buffer (last accessed 20/04/2023).

of displaced persons have at least been partially answered by their government's purchasing of Fijian land.

MWD is not without its own weaknesses, however. Alongside the logistical difficulties in relocating large numbers of people, Tong's visit to the Solomon Islands shows that moving to a new country eventually leads to a dilution of culture, which would undermine the traditions that are central to Kiribati's socioecological networks, notwithstanding that these would be substituted with new knowledge and practices. A more immediate problem is that while the land that has been purchased for MWD could technically accommodate the entire population of Kiribati, doing so would leave no room for agricultural production.[102] In other words, there is room for Kiribati's people, but not its society.

A combination of MWD and the Temaiku development project could, however, be an effective adaptation strategy for Kiribati, one that retained, to a degree, the links with their traditional lands that are central to Kiribati culture and the integrity of their socioecological networks. It would also provide a solution to the 'disappearing state' issue.[103] Article 1 of the Convention on the Rights and Duties of States sets out four criteria for an entity to be a state: a permanent population; a defined territory; a government; and the capacity to enter relations with other states.[104] Questions have been raised over how the first two of these in particular would be met if a state's entire territory is affected by climate change to the extent that its population can no longer reside there. Maintaining functioning communities on part of a state's territory addresses these concerns and while there are a host of other issues that would have to be addressed for states that found themselves operating ex situ,[105] the debate over these would to an extent be one of practicality rather than legal technicality.

### *Summary – Climate Change Migration, Sustainable Development and Agroecology*

The purpose of relocation, as part of an adaptation policy or not, is to secure the livelihood and futures of those communities that are impacted by climate change. On one level, defining this is straightforward. As Fiji's Relocation Guidelines make clear, it means respect for displaced communities' human rights and ensuring that they have the means and opportunities to pursue their livelihoods in accordance with their cultures and traditions.[106] Drawing on Nickel's analysis of

102 Kupferberg (n 63) 1805–1806.

103 J. Grote Stoutenburg, 'When Do States Disappear? Thresholds of Effective Statehood and the Continued Recognition of "Deterritorialized" Island States', in Gerrard and Wannier (n 76).

104 Montevideo, 26 December 1933, in force 26 December 1934, 165 LNTS 19.

105 A. Torres Camprubí, *Statehood Under Water: Challenges of Sea-Level Rise to the Continuity of Pacific Island States* (Brill Nijhoff, 2016).

106 Fiji Ministry of Economy (n 89) 3.

the 1948 Universal Declaration of Human Rights,[107] Kupferberg identifies certain basic needs that are necessary for 'the minimally good life', including food and water security, shelter and access to education and healthcare.[108]

Although not discussed in these terms, there is an overlap between the idea of a 'minimally good life' and understandings of sustainable development. It indicates what could be meant by the term 'needs' in the Brundtland definition and, if this is accepted, reveals the extent to which current generations are utilising natural resources beyond the level necessary for this.[109] The elements of a 'minimally good life' also reflect the 17 targets of the Sustainable Development Goals, and how these are mutually dependent on each other.[110] As the chapters in this part of the book have illustrated, protecting the natural resources on which agriculture, and therefore society, depends requires holistic approaches to be taken in the management of the environment and the design and implementation of all policies. Agroecology, due to its emphasis on ecological integrity and respecting and protecting cultures that are as much at risk from climate change as the lands from which they have evolved, is arguably the most appropriate framework to deliver this. It will be just as important in supporting communities as they adapt to and rebuild from climate change as it is in mitigating its impacts.

## Conclusions

Climate change is already having severe impacts on agricultural systems around the world. Extreme weather events are destroying crops, while rising temperatures leave them more vulnerable to pests and disease and increase pressure on already limited freshwater supplies. Some progress in combating climate change has been made through the UNFCCC, although the landmark agreements have yet to deliver the emission reductions necessary to keep the global temperature rise to below 2°C. It has consequently been suggested that the law's role in responding to climate change is limited, with social and technological changes more likely to be decisive.[111] The law can nevertheless drive these changes along more sustainable tracks.[112]

This chapter has shown through the case study on Kiribati that even if for some communities it is too late to prevent the worst impacts of climate change, agroecology is still an important framework in enhancing the resilience of their agricultural

107 J. Nickel, *Making Sense of Human Rights: Philosophical Reflections on the Universal Declaration of Human Rights* (University of California Press, 1987). Declaration available at https://www.un.org/en/about-us/universal-declaration-of-human-rights (last accessed 20/04/2023).

108 Kupferberg (n 63) 1798.

109 World Commission on Environment and Development, *Our Common Future (The Brundtland Report)*, A/42/427, 4 August 1987, 54.

110 A/RES/70/1, 21 October 2015.

111 Boyle and Redgwell (n 18) 357.

112 S. Vernile, 'Agriculture, Climate Change and Law', in M. Monteduro and others (eds), *Law and Agroecology: A Transdisciplinary Dialogue* (Springer, 2015).

systems and wider society, and in mapping a way forward if the land in which those socioecological networks is grounded must be abandoned. Whether the policy is to remain in place and transform the land, migrate with dignity or a combination of both, a community's resilience in the face of this fundamental change will be enhanced through greater biodiversity, agrodiversity and the cultures and traditions that connect the two.

What is also becoming evident in our examination of international law is that there are structural flaws that appear to not only frustrate efforts to advance core aspects of agroecology but actually embed environmental degradation in society. It is to this issue that we turn to in Part 3.

# Part 3

# Agroecology in a Globalised World

# 9 Environmental Assessment

## The Origins of Environmental Assessment

Environmental assessment is often described as a coalescence of environmental regulation and ecological science.[1] Its contemporary forms can be traced to the United States' National Environmental Policy Act 1969 (NEPA).[2] By requiring decision-makers to consider the environmental consequences of their actions in an interdisciplinary manner, NEPA established a link between understandings of the natural world and how it is impacted by administrative decision-making.[3]

The term 'environmental assessment' covers a diverse range of assessment types, and this chapter begins with an overview of these. In brief, environmental impact assessment (EIA), the original and most common form of environmental assessment, examines the likely impacts of specific projects and activities on the environment. Strategic environmental assessment (SEA), which was developed in response to the limitations of EIA, concerns the likely impacts of wider plans and programmes. More recently, different forms of sustainability impact assessment (SIA) have been established, recognising that all decisions carry environmental, economic and social impacts that should be considered holistically if sustainable development is to be achieved.

Our focus when reviewing these forms of environmental assessment will be EU law.[4] The EU has established arguably the most sophisticated environmental assessment regime[5] and provides a useful illustration of how environmental assessment has evolved. Environmental assessment mechanisms, and their respective strengths and weaknesses, vary according to context, however, and other regimes

1 R. Brooks and others, *Law and Ecology: The Rise of the Ecosystem Regime* (Ashgate, 2002) 156–161.

2 42 U.S.C. ss 4321–4347. B. Karkkainen, 'NEPA and the Curious Evolution of Environmental Impact Assessment in the United States', in J. Holder and D. McGillivray (eds), *Taking Stock of Environmental Assessment: Law, Policy and Practice* (Routledge-Cavendish, 2007).

3 Brooks and others (n 1) 159.

4 Specifically, Directive 2011/92/EU on the assessment of the effects of certain public and private projects on the environment [2012] OJ L 26/1, as amended by Directive 2014/52/EU [2014] OJ L 124/1 (the EIA Directive); and Directive 2001/42/EC on the assessment of the effects of certain plans and programmes on the environment [2001] OJ L 197/30 (the SEA Directive).

5 L. Ognjanoska 'Environmental Impact Assessment in the Context of the Environmental Law and Policy of the European Union: Evolvement and Future Perspectives' (2021) *Regional Law Review* 163.

DOI: 10.4324/9781003435174-13

discussed later in the chapter offer their own opportunities and limitations in relation to agroecology.

The purported grounding of ecological science in environmental assessment suggests that there is significant scope for using these regimes to advance agroecology. By accounting for the environmental impacts of decisions, and the respective interests of different members of a socioecological network, environmental assessment should allow for the socioeconomic development of that network in a way that is cognisant of its ecological foundations. As we shall see, however, rather than protect the natural world's ecological integrity, environmental assessment perpetuates the critical flaws of sustainable development by allowing socioeconomic interests to be prioritised. Nevertheless, ecological reforms to environmental assessment, discussed at the end of this chapter, could potentially lead to a fundamental shift in our understanding of sustainable development so that the law is not only better able to advance agroecology but also deliver genuine sustainability.

## Defining Environmental Assessment

### *Theories of Environmental Assessment*

Before examining specific forms of environmental assessment, it is necessary to consider the theoretical space that it occupies, as this reveals environmental assessment's potential for advancing agroecology in the law. Information theories reflect a point already made in this work: that 'better' decisions are reached if decision-makers have access to a wide range of information.[6] Environmental assessment seeks to provide this through obligations to collect and present information on the proposed project or programme, and measures on public participation. The information included in an environmental assessment may not be purely technical in nature. Properly constructed, environmental assessment provides an avenue through which the values and cultures of different constituencies can be taken into account in a way that other decision-making processes, notably risk assessment, do not.[7] In theory at least, it offers a mechanism that responds to the different interests of all actors in a socioecological network, while also maintaining that network's ecological foundations.

The provision of a broad range of environmental information, and even obligations to take this into account, does not inevitably lead to 'greener' decisions, however. While conceptually EIA is seen as a way of inserting ecological science into environmental decision-making, its contemporary forms may better be described as a regulatory manifestation of the weaknesses of the three-pillar conceptualisation of sustainable development. Environmental assessment, especially EIA, demonstrates how sustainable development allows socioeconomic interests to be

6 J. Steele, 'Participation and Deliberation in Environmental Law: Exploring a Problem-Solving Approach' (2001) 21 *Oxford Journal of Legal Studies* 415.

7 J. Holder, *Environmental Assessment: The Regulation of Decision Making* (OUP, 2004) 24. See ch 3.

prioritised over ecological imperatives.[8] That environmental assessment perpetuates unsustainable regulatory behaviours may be attributed to its position between two theories of regulatory decision-making. The procedural nature of environmental assessment obligations is considered to respond to rational choice theory.[9] Ostrom and Ostrom identify basic assumptions about individuals: that they are self-interested, rational, will seek to maximise their own advantages and will act in a way that corresponds to the level of information that they have in the given situation.[10] Applying this to environmental assessment, a developer will present their project in a manner that best serves their personal interests, by downplaying likely impacts and emphasising the proposed activity's benefits, rather than in a way that facilitates informed decision-making.[11]

On the other hand, environmental assessment draws from deliberation theories of public participation. Since its inception, public participation has been central to environmental assessment, and environmental assessment is an early example of public rights of participation being written into law.[12] Public participation may be seen as 'democratising' planning procedures, as it allows for the information presented by a project's proponents to be challenged and alternative views to be discussed.[13] Where this participation extends beyond mere consultation to genuine deliberation,[14] there is the potential for individuals to set aside, or at least redefine, their self-interest to reach a decision that more closely reflects a common good.[15]

It is not enough, however, for diverse information to be provided to decision-makers. Decision-makers must also critically engage with this information with the specific intention of avoiding and mitigating environmental impacts. Evidence suggests, however, that decision-makers often approach their EIA obligations with the primary goal of minimising the scope for future litigation, rather than a genuine concern for the environment.[16] The proper design and implementation of environmental assessment procedures may itself be a response to this, according to culture

8 R. Amos, 'Assessing the Impact of the Habitats Directive: A Case Study of Europe's Plants' (2021) 33 *Journal of Environmental Law* 365, 372–373.

9 E. Van der Zee, 'How Insights on Bounded Rationality Could Inform the International Law of Environmental Assessment' (2022) 23 *German Law Journal* 395, 396.

10 V. Ostrom and E. Ostrom, 'Public Choice: A Different Approach to the Study of Public Administration' (1971) 31 *Public Administration Review* 203, 204–206, drawing on Herbert Simon, *Administrative Behaviour: A Study of Decision-Making Processes in Administrative Organisations* (Macmillan, 1964).

11 Van der Zee (n 9) 396.

12 R. Macrory, 'Environmental Regulation as an Instrument of Constitutional Change', in R. Macrory, *Regulation, Enforcement and Governance in Environmental Law* (2nd edn, Hart Publishing, 2014) 231.

13 Holder (n 7) 18–19.

14 J. Stacey, 'The Deliberative Dimensions of Modern Environmental Assessment Law' (2020) 43 *Dalhousie Law Journal* 865 and S. Arnstein, 'A Ladder of Citizen Participation' (1969) 35 *Journal of the American Institute of Planners* 216.

15 Holder (n 7) 197–199.

16 T. Yang, 'The Emergence of the Environmental Impact Assessment Duty as a Global Legal Norm and General Principle of Law' (2019) 70 *Hastings Law Journal* 526, 536.

theories of environmental assessment. In short, it is suggested that by requiring environmental concerns related to the public good to be systematically taken into account, this will eventually become an automatic and self-evidently necessary part of decision-making procedures, rather than merely a response to a legislative prompt.[17]

Culture theories view environmental assessment as a means of reforming administrative processes so that they reflect ecological rationality. Whereas other forms of rationality that typically dominate decision-making, namely economic and technical rationality, seek to achieve specific goals in the most efficient way possible, ecological rationality mandates that the structure and functions of administration correspond to the environment in and on which that society is based.[18] Importantly, ecological rationality is not considered to be an alternative to other forms of rationality but is instead the context that conditions how technical, economic and other types of rationality should be applied. Bartlett makes the point that ecological rationality should be seen as the priority because a system that operates in conflict with ecological rationality through its administrative procedures will see those procedures, and the system itself, eventually collapse.[19] We see here parallels with a comparison made earlier in this work between sustainable development and ecological sustainability as the principal frameworks for decision-making. Technical and economic rationality justify the environmentally harmful decisions that are made in the name of sustainable development, whereas ecological rationality is the manifestation of the ecological safeguards envisaged by the principle of ecological sustainability.

Bartlett argues that by requiring those involved in decision-making processes to consciously and repeatedly address the environmental values that are raised in environmental assessment, either as legislative standards or through public consultations, environmental assessment gradually embeds ecological rationality into administrative structures.[20] It is possible, however, to question the value of environmental assessment as a so-called 'worm in the brain' of decision-makers.[21] In Western states, environmental assessment has been in place for decades and there is little indication that administrative cultures have evolved what might be called an environmental subconscious. The reasons why this is the case are complex, and beyond the scope of this work. Broadly, it may be a reflection of the wider and constantly shifting policy and political contexts in which environmental assessment operates. Opening a new coal mine may be thought anathema to a state that

17 R. Bartlett, 'Ecological Reason in Administration: Environmental Impact Assessment and Green Politics', in R. Paehlke and D. Torgerson (eds) *Managing Leviathan: Environmental Politics and the Administrative State* (Broadview Press, 2005) 54–56.

18 ibid 49–50.

19 ibid 50, drawing on J. Dryzek, *Rational Ecology: Environment and Political Ecology* (Basil Blackwell, 1987) 58–59.

20 ibid 55.

21 ibid 54.

has committed to reducing its carbon emissions by 100% by 2050,[22] but this is precisely what the United Kingdom has approved, in part due to the implications of the war in Ukraine for the British steel industry's coal supply.[23] This suggests that while EIA has proven a useful tool in challenging decisions that appear environmentally or procedurally flawed, it has yet to embed ecological rationality into administrative structures.

### *Environmental Impact Assessment*

EIA exists in most national legal systems and various international regimes as well.[24] The composition of the EIA obligations varies depending on the context in which they are applied and the nature of the legal system in question but typically comprises five elements.

The first stage is screening, i.e. determining whether a proposed project is likely to have significant impacts and should therefore be subject to an EIA. EIA has consequently been described as a circular process: the only way to determine whether a proposal should be subject to an assessment of its impacts is to conduct an initial assessment of its impacts.[25] This is mitigated to an extent by various regulatory techniques, with some regimes making pre-determinations about whether a project is likely to have significant impacts. In the EU, certain projects, including the large-scale rearing of poultry and pigs, are automatically subject to EIA requirements,[26] while other projects may fall under EIA rules if they meet specific thresholds.[27] Importantly, these thresholds not only relate to the scale of the proposed project but, inter alia, its location, use of natural resources and the nature of its likely impacts as well.[28]

Including such criteria in the screening process recognises that even very small projects can have significant impacts if they are in environmentally sensitive areas. However, the ambiguous nature of some of the Annex II categories has proven problematic when it comes to application, particularly in the context of agriculture. This is illustrated in the case of *Alford*.[29] Here, the defendant had taken up the lease of a neglected farm and spread manure and calcified seaweed over several fields so that they could be used as pasture, destroying the natural habitat that had evolved on the site. Annex II of the EIA Directive, which lists project categories that may

22 Climate Change Act 2008 (UK), s.1.

23 https://assets.publishing.service.gov.uk/government/uploads/system/uploads/attachment_data/file/1122625/22-12-07_Whitehaven_-_Decision_Letter_and_IR.pdf (last accessed 20/04/2023).

24 Yang (n 16) 545

25 Holder (n 7) 36.

26 EIA Directive, Annex I, para 17.

27 EIA Directive, Annex II.

28 EIA Directive, Annex III.

29 *Department for Environment, Food and Rural Affairs v Alford* [2005] EWHC 808 (Admin). For analysis, see D. McGillivray, 'Case Law Analysis – Restricting the Application of EIA for Agricultural Projects' (2005) 17 *Journal of Environmental Law* 395.

require an assessment, includes 'Projects for the use of uncultivated land or semi-natural areas for intensive agricultural purposes', and the defendant was prosecuted for failing to take the required steps under the then-Environmental Impact Assessment (Uncultivated Land and Seminatural Areas) (England) Regulations 2001 to determine whether an EIA was required.

A successful appeal was brought by the defendant on the grounds that their actions did not constitute 'intensive agricultural purposes'. In reaching its decision, the High Court stated:

> [A]lthough we remind ourselves that the EIA Directive has a wide scope and a broad purpose, we do not consider that its framers intended it to catch a project that was concerned only to bring land back to a normal level of agricultural productivity.[30]

The Court defined 'intensive' in relation to 'normal' agriculture rather than extant conditions and uses of the site. This was problematic in three respects. First, what constitutes normal agriculture can only be determined on a case-by-case basis. The use of large quantities of pesticides may be normal in a region that predominately grows genetically modified crops, but would be an aberration in an organic agricultural area. Second, as McGillivray observes, the implication of the High Court's judgment is that 'normal' agricultural activity is not intensive; a position which does not bear scrutiny.[31] Related to this is the third point, which is that the Court's ruling appears contrary to the central purpose of the EIA Directive, i.e. to ensure that projects that are 'likely have significant effects on the environment' are assessed. This construction, typical of EIA regimes, is deceptively simple and belies the complex nature of significance as a regulatory concept.[32] What is clear, however, is that significance does not relate to how the proposed project compares to some abstract average level of activity. Instead, determinations of significance must be spatially and culturally located and will be influenced as much by subjective values as it is by objective standards.[33] This is vital if EIA is to be used to advance agroecological approaches to agriculture through the law. The diversity of agricultural networks will only be maintained if it is the unique characteristics, cultural and ecological, that are the starting point for any determinations of significance. The specific problem arising from *Alford* was addressed in the 2006 revision to the 2001 Regulations, which made it clear that any project to enhance the productivity of uncultivated or semi-natural land constituted 'intensive agricultural

30 *Alford*, ibid para 27.
31 McGillivray (n 29) 409.
32 Holder (n 7) 103.
33 ibid 103–104, drawing on B. Sadler, *Environmental Assessment in a Changing World: Evaluating Practice to Improve Performance*, Final Report of the International Study of the Effectiveness of Environmental Assessment and Canadian Environmental Assessment Agency, Ministry of Supply and Services (1996).

purposes'.[34] The case illustrates, however, that the utility of EIA as a mechanism for both protecting the environment and advancing agroecology depends as much on sympathetic judicial interpretation as it does legislative implementation.

If a project is deemed to fall under the applicable EIA regulations, it must undergo the second stage, scoping. This is the main assessment phase and essentially involves the compilation of an environmental statement, usually by the developer or someone contracted by them, that pulls together information about the project and its likely impacts. Under the EU's system the environmental statement must contain, inter alia, a description of the project, its processes and likely pollution; an outline of the main alternatives considered by the developer; a description of its environmental impacts, especially on 'fauna, flora, soil, water, air, climatic factors, material assets, including the architectural and archaeological heritage, landscape and the interrelationship between the above factors; and intended mitigation measures'.[35]

These requirements reveal further opportunities and limitations of using EIA as a means of advancing agroecology. They emphasise the importance of assessing impacts in their wider socioecological contexts, with the inclusion of landscape particularly interesting. As we observed in chapter 4, this is a difficult concept to define but is as much related to interactions between land and people as it is to physical features.[36] A proposed project may have minimal direct environmental impacts, and therefore seem unobjectionable, but if it were to restrict or radically alter a practice that created and sustains the area's landscape, the effects on the local community and their environment could nevertheless be significant. Requiring consideration of the interactions between different factors is also a reflection of agroecology's perception of natural and human factors being inherently linked through sociological networks.

On the other hand, it is notable that the environmental statement need only contain information about alternatives studied by the developer. This may be a pragmatic approach, but given that developers have a central, arguably even determinative role, in EIA procedures, it raises concerns over the extent to which the views of other stakeholders are addressed.[37] This links to the third common feature of EIA: public participation.[38] From an agroecological perspective, this helps to ensure that the interests of all members of a socioecological network are taken into account when decisions that will affect that network are made. However, it is important to recognise the inherent power imbalances in administrative decision-making. Regardless of how liberal participation measures may be, there will be

34 C. Rodgers, 'Environmental Impact Assessment: Mapping the Interface between Agriculture, Development and the Natural Environment?' (2011) 13 *Environmental Law Review* 85, 97.

35 EIA Directive, Annex IV.

36 J. Holder, 'Hedgerows, Laws and Cultural Landscapes', in J. Holder and D. McGillivray (eds), *Locality and Identity: Environmental Issues in Law and Society* (Dartmouth Publishing, 1999).

37 Holder (n 7) 97–99.

38 EIA Directive, Article 6(2)-(4). Consultations with relevant public authorities are also often required – Article 6(1).

some groups in society less capable of engaging in them than others.[39] Particular concerns have been raised over the ability of indigenous peoples to participate in EIA, raising questions over the extent to which their unique understandings of local landscapes and ecosystems are included in decision-making.[40]

The environmental statement and the results of consultations feed into the fourth stage of EIA: the decision. Under most systems, decision-makers are merely required to take all this information 'into consideration in the development consent procedure',[41] and publish how they have reached their decision.[42] Decision-makers are not required to reject a proposal in response to a negative EIA, leading commentators to criticise EIA and other environmental assessment mechanisms for only being procedural in nature, and therefore not a positive instrument of environmental protection.[43] The line between the procedural and the substantive is increasingly blurred, however, particularly at the international level, not least due to the development of the law of environmental assessment and related principles.[44] Nevertheless, it is the case that EIA often fails to prevent even the most destructive of activities from proceeding. This is despite studies also indicating that EIA is an important factor in decision-making.[45] It is therefore possible to question how far environmental assessment is embedding itself into decision-making and introducing a new ecological rationality into administrative structures.

What may enhance EIA in this regard is post-project analysis, which was introduced in the EU in 2014 and is increasingly common in other regimes. The rationale behind post-project analysis is twofold. First, it provides an opportunity for additional mitigatory measures to be adopted should the environmental impacts of a project turn out to be more severe than anticipated. The advantages of this are obvious when we consider that mitigatory and compensation measures proposed as part of an ex-ante assessment usually fall short of the required standard.[46] However, environmental harms can take years, if not decades, to manifest, raising questions over how long any monitoring should last and who should bear the responsibility for remedying any harms if the original developer no longer exists. It is also

39 T. Richardson, 'Environmental Assessment and Planning Theory: Four Short Stories About Power, Multiple Rationality and Ethics' (2005) 25 *Environmental Impact Assessment Review* 341, 344–347. I return to this point in the context of food justice in ch 12.

40 F. Dhiksawan and others, 'Involvement of Indigenous People in Environmental Impact Assessment' (2018) 48 *Environmental Policy and Law* 307.

41 EIA Directive, Article 8.

42 EIA Directive, Article 9.

43 C. Jones and others, 'Environmental Assessment: Dominant or Dormant?', in Holder and McGillivray (n 2) 17.

44 J. Brunnée, 'Harm Prevention', in L. Rajamani and J. Peel (eds), *The Oxford Handbook of International Environmental Law* (2nd edn, OUP, 2021) 274–276.

45 Jones and others (n 43) 30–35.

46 D. McGillivray, 'Compensatory Measures under Article 6(4) of the Habitats Directive: No Net Loss for Natura 2000?', in C. Born and others (eds), *The Habitats Directive in its EU Environmental Law Context: European Nature's Best Hope?* (Routledge, 2015).

reactive, responding to harms rather than preventing them, and therefore at odds with the principal purpose of EIA and other norms of environmental law.[47]

This is not the case with the second rationale, which is that if it is properly implemented, post-project analysis creates a body of information that can be used to strengthen EIA as a tool for predicting and preventing future environmental harms.[48] It transforms EIA from a linear procedure with each assessment being treated as a singular, isolated event, to a circular and connected learning process. The experiences from one assessment regarding the requisite standards for environmental statements, the reliability and accuracy of methodologies and the effectiveness of mitigatory measures inform the content and evaluation of future environmental statements and provide an evidence base for challenging decisions.[49] Post-project analysis is consequently a means of reforming EIA so that it becomes a tool for adaptive management in the regulation of environmentally harmful activities.[50] It strengthens EIA as a means of advancing agroecology through the law, as it constitutes a better way of protecting the integrity of socioecological networks and the interests of all stakeholders within these.

***Strategic Environmental Assessment***

EIA's scope is limited to individual proposals which, while problematic at the local level, may be part of a wider plan or programme.[51] The difficulties this can create, both for the environment and local communities, are illustrated in a study of the Nairobi Expressway. While performing an important function, Kosgei and Kioko-Mutinda observe that the Expressway's EIA failed to capture the broader, cumulative impacts of Kenya's transport policy, and reduced the public to mere objectors. By the time the EIA was being conducted, it was too late for the public to play a positive role in the formulation of the wider policy of which it was part.[52]

Such realities led to the development of SEA, which assesses the impacts of plans and programmes. SEA mechanisms typically comprise similar stages to EIA.[53] Plans and programmes for certain industries are automatically subject to SEA, while others undergo a screening process. A report is produced that, under

47 Particularly the principle of prevention, i.e. that it is better to prevent environmental harms rather than respond to them.

48 N. Craik, *The International Law of Environmental Impact Assessment* (CUP, 2008) 196.

49 K. Arabadjieva, "Better Regulation' in Environmental Impact Assessment: The Amended EIA Directive' (2016) 28 *Journal of Environmental Law* 159, 167–168.

50 See ch 1.

51 M. Cordonier Segger and A. Khalfan, *Sustainable Development Law: Principles, Practices and Prospects* (OUP, 2004) 181.

52 L. Kosegi and M. Kioko-Mutinda, 'EIA as a Tool for Balancing Economic, Social & Environmental Considerations in Infrastructure Development: The Case of the Nairobi Expressway' (2019) *East African Law Journal* 82. See also R. Thomé and J. Ribeiro, 'Community Participation in the Analysis of the Environmental Impact Assessment as a Democratic Mechanism to Insure Social-Environmental Rights' (2016) 13 *Veredas do Direito* 69.

53 See S. Kingston and others, *European Environmental Law* (CUP, 2017) 403–407.

EU law, should contain information relating to issues such as the main objectives of the plan or programme, the current state of the environment and how it is likely to evolve in the absence of the plan or programme, the likely significant environmental effects, including on cultural heritage and landscapes, and any mitigatory measures.[54] Consultations with various stakeholders, including the public, are again required, and Article 6 of the SEA Directive also obliges states to give environmental NGOs early and effective opportunities to express their views on the plan or programme.

Like EIA, SEA is primarily procedural in nature,[55] with decision-makers only required to take the environmental report and subsequent consultations 'into account' before the plan or programme is formally adopted.[56] There are also key differences. The environmental report must set out 'reasonable alternatives' to the proposed plan or programme, not just those alternatives that have been considered by its proponents,[57] and the courts have been willing to accept challenges to plans and programmes on the grounds that this requirement has not been sufficiently addressed.[58] There is therefore more space in SEA, at least in the European acquis, for the vested interests of those who want a particular plan or programme to proceed to be challenged by members of the socioecological network(s) that will be affected.[59]

### *Sustainability Impact Assessment*

The focus of EIA and SEA is on the environmental impacts of projects, plans and programmes, which is limiting in two respects. Environmental impacts, while an essential aspect of administrative decision-making, are not the only consequences of decisions. Socioeconomic, cultural and other factors are just as likely to be impacted and are legitimate issues for consideration.[60] While each could be subject to a bespoke assessment, the holistic underpinnings of sustainable development, and the costs involved in conducting multiple assessments of the same project, plan or programme, mean that a single SIA offers significant advantages.[61] Second, projects, plans and programmes may be the result of policies, adopted by national,

54 SEA Directive, Article 5 and Annex I.

55 W. Howarth, 'Substance and Procedure under the Strategic Environmental Assessment Directive and the Water Framework Directive', in Holder and McGillivray (n 2) 157–158.

56 SEA Directive, Article 8.

57 SEA Directive, Article 5(1).

58 D. Elvin QC, 'The Role of Alternatives in the SEA Directive', in G. Jones QC and E. Scotford (eds), *The Strategic Environmental Impact Assessment Directive: A Plan for Success* (Hart Publishing, 2017).

59 That is not to say that the procedures for adopting plans and programmes do not raise their own issues regarding vested interests and power relations.

60 J. Benson, 'What's the Alternative? Impact Assessment Tools and Sustainable Planning' (2003) 21 *Impact Assessment and Project Appraisal* 261.

61 K. Jacob, 'Regulatory Impact Assessment and Sustainable Development: Towards a Common Framework' (2010) 3 *European Journal of Risk Regulation* 276, 277.

devolved or local government, and these are as much a valid subject of impact assessment as the targets of EIA and SEA. SIA responds to these weaknesses by allowing for the assessment of a broad range of impacts at the policy level.[62]

Explicitly recognising the need to integrate the objectives of one policy area into all others is at the heart of sustainability. It is also reflected in the Sustainable Development Goals (SDGs).[63] States' experiences in trying to deliver this in practice demonstrate how challenging it can be,[64] and SIA is one mechanism that could assist with this. SIA could also be a way of advancing agroecology in the law. As set out in the introduction to this work, one of agroecology's basic premises is the indivisibility of the natural and the human, and SIA responds to the reality that environmental impacts are also economic impacts, social impacts, human rights impacts and so on.

There are challenges in designing an effective system of SIA, however. From a practical perspective, the assessment of different types of impact requires different types of expertise, which can be challenging to access.[65] Secondly, different impacts will materialise over different timescales, with negative environmental effects often appearing much later than short-term economic gains, which has implications for any post-project analysis that is conducted. This highlights the challenge of maintaining environmental integrity through sustainable development frameworks and reinforces arguments for conditioning decision-making processes on basic ecological safeguards.

## Environmental Assessment in International Law

While environmental assessment originated in national legal systems, it is now found throughout international law. It is recognised as a core concept of global environmental law, i.e. a body of law that is grounded in common national regulatory approaches that have been expressed through international agreements and subsequently informed the ongoing development of national legal systems.[66] The proliferation of international environmental assessment mechanisms has led to debates over whether a duty of EIA in particular has achieved an elevated legal status. It

62 SIA can also be applied at the project, plan and programme levels, which raises similar challenges as those discussed here in relation to SIA of policies.

63 A/RES/70/1, 21 October 2015.

64 R. Amos and E. Lydgate, 'Trade, Transboundary Impacts and the Implementation of SDG 12' (2020) 15 *Sustainability Science* 1699.

65 E.g., the EU's approach to SIA has been criticised for failing to adequately address the potential impacts that a trade agreement can have on human rights – S. Velluti, 'The Promotion and Integration of Human Rights in EU External Trade Relations' (2016) 32 *Utrecht Journal of International and European Law* 41.

66 T. Yang and R. Percival, 'The Emergence of Global Environmental Law' (2009) 36 *Ecology Law Quarterly* 615, 623. See also O. Elisa and M. Wong, 'Environmental Impact Assessment', in M. Fitzmaurice and others (eds), *Research Handbook on International Environmental Law* (2nd edn, Edward Elgar, 2021).

is now widely, although not universally,[67] accepted that EIA constitutes a rule of customary international law, not least because of judgments by the International Court of Justice (ICJ) to that effect. In *Pulp Mills*, the Court held that states have an obligation to conduct an EIA of an activity that is likely to have a transboundary effect, but only to the extent that EIA was required by their domestic law.[68] The ICJ has consequently been criticised for establishing a rule of customary international law that lacks an international content.[69] Subsequent developments, while not remedying this specific issue, can be seen as providing guidance on how the customary rule of EIA operates. In the *Kishenganga Arbitration*, the Permanent Court of Arbitration held that Pakistan's holistic assessment of the potential impacts that a dam would have on the Kishenganga river's ecosystem was more appropriate than India's more narrow assessment of the impacts on certain fish species.[70] This ruling does not mean that states are now required to undertake broad ecosystem assessments of proposed projects' transboundary impacts. It does suggest, however, that where there are competing assessments of a project's likely impacts, priority will be given to the one that is more ecologically coherent.[71] This would indicate that an assessment that takes an agroecological approach, i.e. one that addresses impacts across a socioecological network, would be viewed more favourably by the courts than one that only considers individual aspects of it.

### *The Convention on Environmental Impact Assessment in a Transboundary Context*

To find more specific international obligations for environmental assessment, it is necessary to consider the mechanisms that have been developed by treaty regimes and international organisations. One of the most important is the Espoo Convention on Environmental Impact Assessment in a Transboundary Context.[72] In many respects, this is a typical EIA mechanism, although as its name suggests, one that only applies to transboundary impacts. This reflects the centrality in international law of concepts of territory and boundaries, grounding EIA even more firmly in

67 J. Knox, 'The Myth and Reality of Transboundary Environmental Impact Assessment' (2002) 96 *American Journal of International Law* 291.

68 *Pulp Mills on the River Uruguay (Argentina v Uruguay)* (1997) ICJ Reports 7 111, para 204–205. See also *Responsibilities and Obligations of States Sponsoring Persons and Entities with Respect to Activities in the Area* (Advisory Opinion), Case No. 17, 1 February 2011, in which the International Tribunal for the Law of the Sea stated that 'the obligation to conduct an environmental impact assessment is… a general obligation under customary international law' (at 145).

69 P. Sands and J. Peel, *Principles of International Environmental* Law (4th edn, CUP, 2018) 678–679.

70 *Indus Waters Kishenganga Arbitration (Pakistan v India)*, Final Award of the Court of Arbitration, 20 December 2013, 99.

71 R. Amos, *International Conservation Law: The Protection of Plants in Theory and Practice* (Routledge, 2020) 12–13.

72 Espoo, 25 February 1991, in force 10 September 1997, 30 ILM 802 (1991).

ideas of administrative, rather than ecological, space.[73] Nevertheless, the Convention has proven successful at streamlining complex and lengthy regulatory processes for major infrastructure projects that cross multiple jurisdictions in a way that allows consideration of factors both of common concern and unique to a single state.[74]

The Contracting Parties, of which there are 45 at the time of writing,[75] are required to subject any activity listed in Appendix I 'likely to cause [a] significant adverse transboundary impact' to an EIA.[76] This list includes deforestation of 'large areas' but not agricultural activities. These may, however, be covered by Article 2(5), which calls for an assessment of activities not covered by Appendix I but are nevertheless 'likely to cause [a] significant adverse transboundary impact'. Note that this provision is only triggered if agreement is reached between the state in which the activity originates and a Concerned Party, i.e. a state affected by an EIA, which limits its application and creates a further opportunity for socioeconomic considerations to override environmental concerns.

Appendix III provides guidance on when non-Appendix I activities should be subject to an EIA under the Espoo Convention, based on their size, location and effects. The latter two criteria highlight the Convention's potential to facilitate agroecological approaches to the assessment of projects.[77] In terms of location, in addition to activities that would take place in or close to areas of 'special environmental sensitivity or importance',[78] states are also called on to apply EIA to non-Appendix I activities that would occur in 'locations where the characteristics of proposed development would be likely to have significant effects on the population'. 'Effects' is not defined in the Convention, but drawing on the definition of 'impact' in Article 1, it is clear that effects on cultures that are inherently linked to environmental factors that may be impacted are included. A proposal to cultivate a genetically modified crop in a location that may impact an organic farming community in a neighbouring state would therefore seem to be a legitimate subject for EIA under the Espoo Convention. Even if the predicted environmental impacts of the cultivation were considered to be negligible, the cultural and socioeconomic consequences of the organic farming community's crops becoming contaminated would appear to demand proper assessment.

Public participation is addressed in Article 2(6) of the Espoo Convention and Appendix II, which sets out the information that should be included in the

73 G. Handl, 'Transboundary Impacts', in Daniel Bodansky and others, *The Oxford Handbook of International Environmental Law* (OUP, 2007) 532.

74 C. Redgwell, 'Contractual and Treaty Arrangements Supporting Large European Transboundary Pipeline Projects: Can Adequate Human Rights and Environmental Protection Be Secured?', in M. Roggenkamp and others (eds), *Energy Networks and the Law: Innovative Solutions in Changing Markets* (OUP, 2012) 114–115.

75 https://treaties.un.org/Pages/ViewDetails.aspx?src=TREATY&mtdsg_no=XXVII-4&chapter=27&clang=_en#1 (last accessed 20/04/2023).

76 Espoo Convention, Article 3(2).

77 On size, states are merely encouraged to assess projects 'which are large for the type of activity'.

78 I.e., sites that are protected under international or national law, including for historical, cultural or archaeological reasons.

documentation produced as part of an EIA. Much of this is typical of the information required by EIA regimes, but one point warrants highlighting. Subparagraph (g) of Appendix II says that EIA documentation should include: 'An identification of gaps in knowledge and uncertainties in compiling the required information'. From a practical perspective, requiring EIA documentation to identify gaps and uncertainties addresses concerns that EIA processes can become captured by project proposers by compelling them to identify where the information they are submitting is either incomplete or based on assumptions. It also underscores the unavoidable role of precaution in environmental assessment.[79] How the precautionary principle is applied is critical in determining the effectiveness of environmental assessment as a means of protecting the environment and of advancing agroecology in the law. This was recognised by the Court of Justice of the European Union in the *Waddenzee* case,[80] although subsequent analysis suggests that subsequent application of this decision at the national level has reduced the protection it affords to the environment.[81]

Another positive aspect of the Espoo Convention is the inclusion of post-project analysis in Article 7, which was not a common feature of EIA mechanisms when the Convention was negotiated. As noted above, post-project analysis can be an example of adaptive management approaches to regulation.

Notwithstanding these agroecological merits, the Espoo Convention is open to criticism, especially regarding the strength of its obligations. Consideration of alternatives, which is a key aspect of environmental assessment regimes,[82] is only required 'where appropriate'.[83] In contrast to similar language used in the Biodiversity Convention,[84] it has been suggested that this phrasing is legitimate in the Espoo Convention. By allowing states to determine whether it is appropriate for alternatives to be considered during an EIA, the Espoo Convention does not impose burdens on projects that have potential transboundary impacts that might not be required by a state's national law on those that have purely internal impacts, thereby ensuring its compatibility with the legal principle of non-discrimination.[85] This is problematic in two respects, however. First, one of the principal achievements of international environmental law is how it has influenced the development of environmental regulation and more democratically accountable decision-making at the national level.[86] The Espoo Convention's requirements on public

79 G. Tucker and J. Treweek, 'The Precautionary Principle in Impact Assessment: An International Review', in R. Cooney and B. Dickson (eds), *Biodiversity & the Precautionary Principle: Risk and Uncertainty in Conservation and Sustainable Use* (Earthscan, 2005).

80 Case C-127/02 *Landelijke Vereniging tot Behoud van de Waddenzee v Staatssecretaris van Landbouw, Natuurbeheer en Visserij* [2004] ECR I-7405.

81 P. Scott, 'Appropriate Assessment: A Paper Tiger?', in G. Jones QC (ed), *The Habitats Directive: A Developer's Obstacle Course?* (Hart Publishing, 2012).

82 Holder (n 7) 15–18 and Ch 5, and Elvin (n 58).

83 Espoo Convention, Appendix II, sub-para (b).

84 Rio de Janeiro, 5 June 1992, in force 29 December 1993, 31 ILM 822 (1992). See ch 1.

85 Craik (n 48) 139–149.

86 E. Fisher and others, *Environmental Law: Text, Cases and Materials* (2nd edn, OUP, 2019) 414–415.

participation are itself an example of this.[87] From this perspective, it would be better if the Convention called for national laws to adapt so that consideration of alternatives is required regardless of transboundary impact, rather than give way in states that do not require them to be considered. Second, ignoring alternatives is environmentally questionable and undermines one of the main components of environmental assessment.[88]

***Sustainability Assessment of Food and Agriculture Systems***

Assessing the impacts of food systems and value chains is an important part of the work of the UN Food and Agriculture Organisation. Established in 2013 following a five-year consultation and development process, SAFA provides guidance to assist stakeholders in this task.[89] The principal difference between SAFA and the other environmental assessment mechanisms discussed above is that SAFA is not intended to facilitate the external review of proposed plans and activities by decision-makers and the public with a view to granting or challenging permission for them to proceed. Instead, SAFA is a tool for internal evaluation and learning[90] and is therefore part of a wider trend towards promoting corporate accountability in private entities in international law.[91] The SAFA Guidelines are targeted at food and agriculture enterprises, i.e. actors in agricultural and related sectors, enabling them to perform self-assessments of their operations and supply chains, and identify areas for improvement. That being said, they are also a tool for NGOs and communities to monitor the impacts of agricultural activities, and to aid government bodies in the design and implementation of policies.[92]

The SAFA Guidelines are premised on four dimensions of sustainability: good governance, environmental integrity, economic resilience and social wellbeing.[93] These are a more nuanced understanding of sustainable development than the three-pillar conceptualisation. The focus on environmental *integrity*, rather than environmental *protection*, suggests a greater concern for maintaining ecological health than is seen in other mechanisms discussed in this work that purport to deliver sustainable development. Similarly, economic resilience, i.e. building eco-

87 Decision III/8, Guidance on public participation in environmental impact assessment in a transboundary context, ECE/MP.EIA/6, 13 September 2004.

88 M. Herz, 'Parallel Universes: NEPA Lessons for the New Property' (1993) 93 *Columbia Law Review* 1668–1737, 1679.

89 FAO, *SAFA: Sustainability Assessment of Food and Agriculture Systems Guidelines: Version 3.0* (FAO 2014)

90 ibid 5.

91 F. Cafaggi, 'Regulation through Contracts: Supply-Chain Contracting and Sustainability Standards' (2016) 12 *European Review of Contract Law* 218.

92 FAO (n 89) 5.

93 ibid section 3. A similar model for SIA is proposed by Bachev, who is responding to a specific governance gap in Eastern Europe, based on ideas of ecological, social and economic sustainability – H. Bachev, 'Defining and Assessing the Governance of Agrarian Sustainability' (2016) 4 *Journal of Advanced Research in Law and Economics* 797.

nomic structures capable of withstanding economic shocks such as the COVID-19 pandemic, is arguably a greater priority than economic growth. This again suggests that SAFA has more space for ecological concerns than other interpretations of sustainable development, as economic resilience ultimately depends on ecological health.

Each dimension comprises a series of themes and sub-themes, providing template sustainability performance indicators that those conducting a SAFA adapt to the food system or enterprise in question.[94] Many of these themes and sub-themes are relevant to the ecological, cultural and social aspects of agroecology. The ecological integrity dimension, for example, includes soil improvement practices (Indicator E 3.1.1), diversity of production (Indicator E 4.2.4) and genetic diversity in wild species (Indicator E 4.3.4).[95] There is nevertheless scope for improvement from an agroecological perspective. While Indicator E 4.3.5 on saving seeds and livestock breeds recognises that farmers have traditionally exchanged seeds to promote crop genetic diversity, its specific benchmarks only relate to allowing farmers to save seed for future use. It is therefore of limited use in addressing the restrictions that intellectual property rights have placed on farmers' exchange of seeds that were discussed in chapter 2.

A SAFA comprises four phases. Step 1, mapping, involves compiling various types of information to build an accurate picture of the entity being assessed and the goal of the assessment. Mapping includes the location and character of the entity, details about the relevant sector in which it operates and, most significantly from an agroecological perspective, its so-called 'sphere of influence'.[96] This focus on broader value supply chains is another distinguishing feature of SAFA and responds to criticisms of other forms of legal oversight of commercial enterprises, which typically focus on the impacts of individual contractual relationships.[97]

An entity's sphere of influence must be assessed in relation to its temporal and spatial boundaries and the direct and indirect impacts of its operations.[98] In theory, therefore, SAFA does not share the weaknesses of being confined to physical borders and timescales that are amenable to project developers, rather than allow for a proper assessment of the potential impacts a project may have on a site's ecological integrity, that undermine other forms of environmental assessment. The SAFA Guidelines recognise the inherent challenges in defining an entity's sphere of influence due to the interconnected nature of value supply chains and the natural and human capital that feed into them,[99] but also give pragmatic guidance on how to set the limits of an assessment in such a way as to capture, as much as possible, these relationships. They advise that:

94 FAO, *SAFA Sustainability Assessment of Food and Agriculture Systems Indicators* (FAO, 2013).

95 Reflecting issues discussed in Chs 6, 3 and 2 respectively.

96 FAO (n 89) 26.

97 F. Cafaggi and P. Iamiceli, 'Supply Chains, Contractual Governance and Certification Regimes' (2014) 37 *European Journal of Law and Economics* 131, 136–137.

98 FAO (n 89) 26–27.

99 ibid 26.

The scope of a SAFA assessment should include all processes:

- that are part of production, processing or distribution, relevant to inputs (e.g. fertilisers, feed and irrigation water, wages at processing facilities);
- that generate significant upstream and downstream impacts on sustainability in the surrounding environment and in the community (e.g. decisions regarding use of fresh water, waste management); and
- over which the assessed entity has control or significant influence in terms of financial and operating policies and practices (e.g. the activities of any subsidiaries, other members in a producer group or procurement policy for inputs and suppliers).[100]

This indicates that a SAFA is intended to capture impacts across a socioecological network, and its constituent parts. SAFA therefore represents the systems-level approach to assessment that was identified in this book's introduction as a key way that agroecology can be advanced in the law.

Having established the nature of the entity and the purpose of the SAFA, the next step is to select and contextualise the sub-themes and default indicators listed in the SAFA Guidance so that they can be applied in a manner that is relevant to the entity in question. It is not the case that every SAFA will address all the sub-themes;[101] there would be little need for a farm that does not keep livestock to consider animal health (Indicator E 6.1.2), for example.

For the indicators, it is necessary for additional information to be gathered so that they can be applied in the specific context of the assessment. To know whether an entity is extracting groundwater from a particular resource faster than its natural renewal rate (Indicator E 2.1.3), it is necessary to identify factors such as local annual rainfall, other water sources that feed that resource and other sources of extraction. The SAFA Guidelines then apply a colour-code system. For ground and surface water extraction, a dark green score applies where the enterprise does not contribute to water scarcity, either for ecosystems or human communities, at any point in its operations, while a red score is given if it is over-exploiting a water resource.[102] Performing this for all the sub-themes selected during the contextualisation phase allows the entity to build a visualisation of the sustainability impacts of their operations and supply chains.[103]

The final SAFA stage is reporting: summarising the purpose and scope of the assessment and identifying areas in which the enterprise needs to improve.[104] An important element of this is facilitating critical review. The SAFA report should contain sufficient details and information so that it can be peer-reviewed.[105] This is

100 ibid 29.
101 ibid 39
102 ibid.
103 E.g., ibid 69.
104 ibid 70.
105 ibid 70–71.

key in ensuring the transparency, and therefore legitimacy, of SAFA assessments, and it also enhances them as adaptive management tools. Related to this is SAFA's encouragement for the communication and sharing of SAFA assessments, so that other entities and stakeholders can learn best practices for both performing SAFA assessments and building sustainability into their operations. From an agroecological perspective, this also reinforces the connections in and between socioecological networks. Sharing assessments creates opportunities for actors in the same network to collaborate. One entity may be able to take advantage of another's waste products, for example, thereby establishing elements of a circular economy, or actors may find ways to cooperate in their management of a shared natural resource, improving the efficiency of their activities and reducing their environmental impacts.

## (Re)Introducing Ecology to Environmental Assessment

Environmental assessment is presented as means of achieving sustainable development[106] but is one of the clearest examples of how sustainable development legitimises unsustainable activities.[107] One reason for this is that, despite originally being seen as grounding environmental regulation in ecological science, environmental assessment has developed in a way that fails to reflect ecological realities.[108] This is particularly true of EIA. There is, for example, no requirement to use ecological characteristics to determine the boundaries of the site that is subject to an impact assessment. Instead, these are usually determined in accordance with the arbitrary delimitations of property ownership.[109] Similarly, the timescales are set so as to accommodate the interests of the developer, not so that proper baselines can be established and the effectiveness, or otherwise, of any mitigatory measures accurately assessed.[110] Most significantly, and notwithstanding requirements for decision-makers to consider 'the interaction' that exists within and between humanity and the natural world,[111] EIA methodologies are reductionist, treating entities such as species and habitats in isolation rather than as part of an integrated whole.[112] In other words, EIA fails to adopt the systems-level analysis necessary to maintain the integrity of socioecological networks.

In response to these issues, Holder proposes a series of reforms to EIA. It is suggested that the boundaries of an assessment could be based on ecological units rather than property ownership.[113] Similarly, the timeframes of EIA could be lengthened so that a clearer understanding is gained of the character of the ecosystem that

106 J. Connah and S. Hall, 'From SA to SEA: Sustainability Appraisals and Strategic Environmental Assessment', in Jones and Scotford (n 64) 141–143.

107 Amos (n 8).

108 J. Holder, 'The Prospects for Ecological Impact Assessment', in Holder and McGillivray (n 2) 267.

109 ibid 259.

110 ibid 259.

111 E.g., EIA Directive, Article 3(d).

112 Holder (n 108) 271–275. See also Holder (n 7) 83–86.

113 Holder (n 108) 281–282.

is likely to be impacted.[114] Post-project analysis goes some way in implementing this, although that it comes after a project has been allowed to proceed means that its value is more in the lessons learnt rather than the harms prevented.

Adapting the spatial and temporal boundaries of EIA so that they better reflect ecology is appealing in theory, but challenging in practice.[115] Issues such as the artificial boundaries of property law are not insurmountable, but there is still the question of where to draw the line of any assessment. If a proposed project will affect a river, should the developer be expected to consider the potential impacts on the entire riparian system and every community that utilises it? If not, then wherever the line is drawn will defeat the ecological purpose of the exercise. Holder's proposals are not the only way that a system of ecological impact assessment can be devised, however.

Early definitions presented sustainable development as a process. For the World Commission on Environment and Development, sustainable development constituted a process of development that did not undermine the ability of future generations to meet their own needs.[116] Under the three-pillar conceptualisation, sustainable development was first presented as a process through which gains in one of the pillars of environmental protection, social equity and economic development automatically led to gains in the others, and is now more accurately understood as a process of balancing these overlapping goals.[117] In contrast, more recent constructions present sustainable development as a destination as well as an ongoing process. This is most evident in several of the SDGs. The concept of 'Goals' implies that sustainable development is something to be achieved through policy and action, with the objective of '*zero* hunger' in SDG-2 being a clear example. Sustainable development may now, therefore, be considered to be about what can be gained, neatly summarised by the use of the term 'prosperity' in SDG documentation.[118] Gains, however, require a starting point, so that progress in achieving them can be measured. Following this reasoning, we can begin to see sustainable development as a standard of non-regression: sustainable development is development that does not (further) degrade the ecological integrity of natural systems.

Goodwin explores similar ideas in relation to the Ramsar Convention on Wetlands of International Importance and its core concept of 'wise use'.[119] This has typically been read as an obligation of conduct rather than of result; to act wisely is to take into account as much information about the proposed activity and

114 ibid 278–280.
115 J. Treweek, *Ecological Impact Assessment* (Blackwell Science, 1999) ch 10.
116 World Commission on Environment and Development, *Our Common Future (The Brundtland Report)*, A/42/427, 4 August 1987, 54.
117 E. Lydgate 'Sustainable Development in the WTO: From Mutual Supportiveness to Balancing' (2012) 11 *World Trade Review* 621.
118 (n 63).
119 Ramsar, 2 February 1971, in force 21 December 1975, 996 UNTS 245, Article 3.

its likely effects on the target site as possible.[120] Goodwin argues, however, that to be able to judge whether the use of a wetland is 'wise', it is necessary to have an end goal in mind and this introduces a substantive element. To be clear, there is no suggestion that obligations of wise use should be reinterpreted as ones of result. There is an important distinction between an obligation of conduct or procedure with an understanding of the desired outcome of that conduct, and an obligation to deliver that desired outcome.

This raises the question of what is the end goal that the procedural obligations are seeking to achieve? For Ramsar sites this is relatively easy to answer. States are required to ensure that listed wetlands are monitored so that they can be informed of any changes in their ecological character,[121] defined as 'the combination of the ecosystem components, processes and benefits/services that characterise the wetland at a given point in time'.[122] It would appear, therefore, that wise use means use of a wetland that does not degrade these characteristics as they existed at the point of listing. Or, in other words, the procedural obligation must be carried out with the aim of maintaining those characteristics.[123]

For listed Ramsar sites, identifying specific characteristics for each site is straightforward because they are set out in the listing documentation submitted by states to the Ramsar Secretariat. More difficult is identifying characteristics that could perform the same role for sites subject to EIA. That they are being considered for development that falls under EIA regulations suggests that the sites concerned will possibly be unprotected, and consequently there is unlikely to be a pre-existing assessment of their ecological values. It is, however, possible to identify suitable values to form a sustainable development baseline in EIA procedures using the principle of ecological sustainability. While this can be just as vague as sustainable development, I have argued elsewhere that it can also be defined in such a way as to be a clear, operable framework for policymaking, based, inter alia, on concepts such as ecological integrity and carrying capacity.[124] Even so, a principle of ecological sustainability per se would still be too high-level to serve as site-specific characteristics that should not be compromised following any EIA procedure. It could, however, form the starting point for reforming each stage of the EIA process so that site-specific characteristics are identified and protected:

1. During the screening process, site-specific values are identified through the application of an ecological sustainability framework.[125]

120 E. Goodwin, 'The "Wise Use" of Wetlands', in R. Gardner and others (eds), *Wetlands and International Environmental Law: The Evolution and Impact of the Ramsar Convention* (Edward Elgar, 2023, forthcoming).

121 Ramsar Convention, Article 3(2).

122 Ramsar Convention Secretariat, *Wise Use of Wetlands: Concepts and Approaches for the Wise Use of Wetlands* (4th edn, Ramsar Convention Secretariat, 2010) 14.

123 Goodwin (n 120). The moment of listing is the given definition for 'at a given point in time', ibid.

124 Amos (n 71) 228–234.

125 The SAFA sub-themes and indicators, discussed above, is one example of how this might work.

2. The environmental statement produced at the scoping stage includes an assessment of how the proposed activity will impact on those site-specific values.
3. The public and relevant public bodies are consulted on whether the alleged benefits of the proposal outweigh the values that would be lost or otherwise impacted should permission be granted.
4. Decision-makers are required to not only explain how they have taken the environmental statement and consultations into account but, if granting permission for the activity to proceed, why they believe its anticipated benefits outweigh the specific ecological and/or cultural values that are considered necessary for delivering ecological sustainability that would be adversely affected.

How this might work in practice is as follows. A developer wishes to build a new factory on an old industrial site next to a river, which is a thriving habitat. An ecological sustainability planning framework, similar to SAFA, lists certain quality and quantity standards considered necessary to maintain the ecological integrity of waterways, which are identified as applicable during the screening process. In the developer's environmental statement, it is explicitly stated that the waste disposal methods of the factory will breach the ecological sustainability standards for waterways. As well as their thoughts on the overall proposal, the local community is consulted specifically on the predicted loss of the ecological integrity of the river's habitat.

These reforms would not alter the fundamentally procedural nature of EIA. Decision-makers would not be obligated to refuse permission for a project that would breach an ecological sustainability standard. Instead, the reforms may be seen as introducing a legal definition of *unsustainable* development based on ideas of non-regression, and a rebuttable presumption against this.[126] The onus would be on those who support an unsustainable decision to justify it, rather than those who wish to challenge that decision to explain why it is procedurally flawed. Ultimately an unsustainable activity may still be allowed to proceed, but the procedure through which that decision was made would contain much stronger ecological safeguards than currently exist in EIA.

Reforming EIA in the manner proposed would serve agroecology in two ways. First, as argued in the introduction to this work, agroecology and ecological sustainability are inherently linked. Both emphasise the importance of maintaining the ecological integrity of the natural systems on which society depends. Implementing ecological sustainability through EIA would therefore create a more compatible regulatory framework for agroecology. Second, core tenets of agroecology could be incorporated into the ecological sustainability framework from which site-specific values are drawn. These include conserving biodiversity, maintaining the diversity of agricultural systems and protecting local cultures, practices and knowledge that are linked to those systems and their wider landscapes. Promoting agroecology would, in other words, become a specific objective of EIA.

126 Amos (n 71) 232.

## Conclusions

Environmental assessment is one of the, if not the, most important mechanisms for advancing agroecology in international law. Properly constituted, it represents a regulatory manifestation of a socioecological network by allowing its members to express their views on proposed activities and their environmental impacts while maintaining the network's ecological foundations.

It is debatable whether environmental assessment has succeeded in embedding an ecological rationality into administrative structures. There is no doubt, however, that environmental assessment has had a demonstrable impact on decision-making processes. There has also been a proliferation of environmental assessment mechanisms in international law, responding to specific issues and challenges. As an example of SIA, SAFA demonstrates the value of holistically assessing the impacts of agricultural activities and supply chains.

However, despite, in theory at least, being the meeting point between ecology and environmental law, environmental assessment is undermined because it facilitates the worst excesses of sustainable development. For a multitude of reasons, including the central role played by project proponents and the lack of substantive obligations on decision-makers, environmental assessment legitimises the prioritisation of socioeconomic interests over the health and integrity of ecosystems.

At the same time, environmental assessment offers opportunities to redefine sustainable development. If we accept that sustainable development now constitutes a goal as well as an ongoing process, this introduces the idea of sustainable development as a standard of non-regression, which inserts a substantive objective into environmental assessment's procedural obligations. Adapting a framework of ecological sustainability to inform this would add a genuine ecological element to environmental assessment, allowing us to develop legal understandings of unsustainable development and strengthen the position of stakeholders in challenging the approval of environmentally harmful activities. Equally, due to the overlaps between ecological sustainability and agroecology, and that the stakeholders referred to would ultimately be the members of affected socioecological networks, such reforms would deliver on environmental assessment's agroecological potential.

# 10 Transboundary Pollution

## Agriculture and Pollution

That an environmental impact assessment has been conducted does not mean that the activity in question will have no adverse effects on the environment. Indeed, carrying out an assessment is an acknowledgement that there *will* be some harmful impact, as no environmental assessment regime absolutely prohibits an activity in the event of a negative assessment. Equally, many activities may simply fall outside environmental assessment legislation but still result in pollution harming the environment, either following a one-off incident, such as when the *Amaco Cadiz* ran aground in 1978 and the resulting oil spill polluted 200 miles of the French coast,[1] or through the cumulative effects of individual actions over a period of time.[2]

The relationships between agriculture and pollution are complex. That a farm cannot be isolated from its surrounding ecosystems means that it will inevitably be impacted if those ecosystems are polluted. These impacts vary according to the nature of the pollution incident in question but generally include direct damage to crops and contamination of soil and water supplies.[3] They also carry implications for global and national food security. Between 1980 and 2010, for example, pollution is believed to have reduced wheat and rice yields in India by 36%, with that figure rising in some parts of the country to as much as 50%.[4]

It is also true that agriculture can be a major contributor to local and global pollution. In the United Kingdom, livestock farms were reported to have polluted rivers 300 times during 2021,[5] and the pollution caused by pesticide and fertiliser

1 An overview of this and other major oil pollution incidents is provided in J. Woodruff, 'Does International Trade Really Trump Environmental Law? A Maritime Perspective' (2000) 9 *Currents: International Trade Law Journal* 17.

2 Driving a petrol or diesel car is an illustration of this. This is not per se unlawful, and driving a car is not subject to any environmental regulation, but doing so contributes to global carbon emissions.

3 A useful summary of how different types of pollution affect crops can be found at: https://www.ontario.ca/page/effects-air-pollution-agricultural-crops (last accessed 20/04/2023).

4 J. Burney and V. Ramanthan, 'Recent Climate and Air Pollution Impacts on Indian Agriculture' (2014) 111 *PNAS* 16319.

5 https://www.bbc.co.uk/news/science-environment-63961659 (last accessed 20/04/2023).

DOI: 10.4324/9781003435174-14

runoff is known to be a leading cause of algal blooms in aquatic ecosystems.[6] A well-known incident of this is the annual 'red tides' that appear in the Gulf of Mexico. These are caused by the algae species *Karenia brevis*, which produces neurotoxins that poison a variety of marine life and have severe impacts on human health. This includes people who have no direct contact with the algae but instead consume shellfish reared in contaminated water.[7] Addressing the causes of algal blooms has proven politically contentious. This is in part due to the difficulties in establishing a causal link between farmers' activities and the presence of common pollutants in the environment.[8] It is also because solutions require farmers to change how they operate, which can constitute a risk to their operations and therefore their livelihoods.[9]

Pollution varies considerably in terms of the media affected (land, water, air), the type of pollution (e.g. solid waste, atmospheric-loading) and the means of dispersion (e.g. through natural means such as air currents and deliberate actions of humans). Its capacity to spread far beyond an initial site and remain in the environment, potentially forever, has long been accepted in scientific discourse and administrative decision-making.[10] Addressing it is consequently recognised as a prerequisite to the success of a range of international projects, including the Sustainable Development Goals.[11] For our purposes, pollution helps to define agriculture's socioecological networks. The pervasiveness of pollution underscores that these networks are intrinsically linked through their ecological connections. Polluting one ecosystem can lead to contamination of another, and an action that may appear to be only local in character can have global repercussions. It is therefore critical that a systems-level approach is taken when considering how to protect

6 S. Chakraborty and others, 'Effects of Fertilizers Used in Agricultural Fields on Algal Blooms' (2017) 226 *The European Physical Journal Special Topics* 2119.

7 https://oceanservice.noaa.gov/hazards/hab/gulf-mexico.html (last accessed 20/04/2023).

8 E.g., C-293/97 *R v Secretary of State for the Environment, ex parte Standley* [1997] ECR I-2603.

9 G. Hoselton and M. Boerngen, 'Awareness of Nutrient Loss Among Illinois Corn Farmers' (2021) 76 *Journal of Soil and Water Conservation* 387.

10 In the United Kingdom, measures were taken to address poor air quality in London as far back as the 13th century – L. Cass, 'Air Pollution and Acid Rain: Early Action and Slowing Progress', in P. Harris (ed), *Routledge Handbook of Global Environmental Politics* (2nd edn, Routledge, 2022) 406.

11 UNGA Resolution, *Transforming Our World: The 2030 Agenda for Sustainable Development*, A/RES/70/1, 21 October 2015. B. Lode and others, 'Clean Air for All by 2030? Air Quality in the 2030 Agenda and International Law' (2016) 25 *Review of European, Comparative and International Environmental Law* 27. See also K. Rain, 'Establishing Sound Chemicals Management – A Prerequisite for Achieving the Millennium Development Goals' (2005) 6 *Sustainable Development Law & Policy* 27. Concerns have been raised over states' apparent inability to decisively address air pollution, with Robinson noting it was identified as a priority by the World Commission on Environment and Development in 1987 (A/42/427, 4 August 1987, Ch 9) – N. Robinson, 'Legal Redress of Transboundary Air Pollution through Environmental Cooperation', in S. Jayakumar and others (eds), *Transboundary Pollution: Evolving Issues of International Law and Policy* (Edward Elgar, 2015) 367–369.

the environment from toxic substances.[12] Pollution's persistence, on the other hand, shows that we cannot just conceive of socioecological networks in spatial terms. They are also temporal constructs, with the actions of one generation having a direct bearing on the quality of the natural systems that future generations will inherit, and the scale of environmental challenges that they will have to overcome.

To illustrate how international law responds to these challenges, and the extent to which those responses reflect agroecology, this chapter focuses on two regimes adopted to deal with pollution: the 1979 Convention on Long-Range Transboundary Air Pollution (LRTAP)[13] and the 2001 Convention on Persistent Organic Pollutants (the POPs Convention).[14] These are just two of a suite of international agreements that although targeted at reducing pollution, nevertheless have an important role in conserving the ecological integrity of natural systems, and therefore of agriculture's socioecological networks as well.[15] To conclude, I consider proposals for a more unified approach to pollution and whether this would be a better framework for advancing agroecology.

## Transboundary Air Pollution

Regarding relations between states, there are two strands to international law's response to transboundary air pollution.[16] The first, litigation, can be seen in the seminal *Trail Smelter* case, a dispute between the United States and Canada over the damage being caused to the former's environment by pollution emanating from a Canadian smelter. Finding in favour of the United States, the tribunal held that states have a legal duty to prevent activities in their jurisdiction from harming the territory, or any property therein, of another state.[17] This established the customary 'no harm' rule of international law, which has subsequently been linked to other principles of international environmental law.[18]

Also relevant is the *Aerial Herbicide Spraying Case* brought by Ecuador in response to severe transboundary damage being caused by Colombia's spraying of herbicides close to the border to destroy illegal drug plantations.[19] This was settled prior to oral arguments. Colombia agreed to cease spraying within an exclusion zone and the parties established a joint mechanism to manage any such opera-

12 E. Howard, 'Pollution Prevention in the Watershed: Protect the Land to Protect the River' (1996) 5 *Review of European Community and International Environmental Law* 116.

13 Geneva, 13 November 1979, in force 16 March 1983, 18 ILM 1442 (1979).

14 Stockholm, 22 May 2001, in force 17 May 2004, 40 ILM 532 (2001).

15 M. Bowman and others, *Lyster's International Wildlife Law* (2nd edn, CUP, 2010) ch 21.

16 A further dimension to this issue is the human rights implications of transboundary air pollution – see A. Boyle, 'Transboundary Air Pollution: A Tale of Two Paradigms', in Jayakumar and others (n 11) 248–256.

17 *Trail Smelter Case (United States, Canada)* (1938 and 1941) 3 RIAA 1905, at 716.

18 C. Redgwell, 'Transboundary Pollution: Principles, Policy and Practice', in Jayakumar and others (n 11).

19 *Aerial Herbicide Spraying (Ecuador v Colombia)* (2008) – https://www.icj-cij.org/en/case/138 (last accessed 20/04/2023).

tions in the future,[20] illustrating that where causation is relatively easy to establish, litigation may be the most effective means of stopping incidents of transboundary air pollution.[21]

Despite never reaching a final judgment, the *Aerial Herbicide Spraying Case* is still useful in showing how agroecology may be advanced in international law. It was noted in chapter 4 that some of the harm suffered by indigenous communities might have been avoided had Colombia sought to engage these stakeholders over how their spraying activities would be conducted. There are limits to what litigation can achieve, however. By definition, the number of parties involved is small, the issues at stake are generally narrow, and while valuable in progressively developing the meaning and application of principles of international environmental law, disputes tend to be more concerned with the past actions of one state without necessarily being an influence on the future behaviours of others.

Consequently, more relevant to agroecology is the second strand of international law's response to transboundary air pollution: multilateral agreements. Principal among these is the LRTAP, the catalyst for which was mounting evidence of how sulphur dioxide and nitrogen oxides, emitted alongside carbon dioxide in the burning of fossil fuels, were causing acid rain in Europe.[22] In terms of agricultural impacts, acid rain strips soil of magnesium and calcium, the absence of which deprives plants of essential nutrients, and releases metals into the soil, preventing roots from developing and absorbing water.[23] It consequently damages crops that are in situ and renders soil unsuitable for future cultivation. Initial concern over acid rain was far from universal, with the United States, United Kingdom and West Germany being particularly sceptical about whether an international response was warranted,[24] but there was sufficient political will for states in Europe and North America to agree a framework convention.

The treaty itself contains only vague obligations, which at the time of its adoption led critics to question whether anything meaningful had been achieved.[25] Exemplifying this is Article 2:

> The Contracting Parties taking due account of the facts and problems involved, are determined to protect man and his environment against air pollution and

20 ibid Order of 13 September 2013.

21 Boyle (n 16) 235–236.

22 E. Cowling, 'Acid Rain: An Emerging Ecological and Public Policy Issue' (1982) 5 *Canada-United States Law Journal* 23.

23 Cass (n 10) 407.

24 J. McCormick, *Acid Earth: The Global Threat of Acid Pollution* (Earthscan, 1990) 76, cited in A. Byrne, 'Trouble in the Air: Recent Developments under the 1979 Convention on Long-Range Transboundary Air Pollution' (2017) 26 *Review of European, Comparative and International Environmental Law* 210.

25 A. Boyle and C. Redgwell, *Birnie, Boyle and Redgwell's International Law and the Environment* (4th edn, OUP, 2021) 367.

> shall endeavour to limit and, as far as possible, gradually reduce and prevent air pollution including long-range transboundary air pollution.

Measures to achieve this include information exchange,[26] internal reviews of policies and scientific measures,[27] and consultations with affected states,[28] all of which supports the development of strategies and air quality management systems. These, however, are only required to the extent that they are 'compatible with balanced development' and employ the best available technologies that are 'economically feasible'.[29]

The references to 'balanced development' and 'economically feasible' technologies are, from an environmental perspective, problematic. While they cannot be labelled as symptoms of the inherent flaws of sustainable development highlighted elsewhere in this work, as the LRTAP was negotiated before this concept had entered common usage, they still speak to the broader issue of how ecological imperatives are too easily traded off against economic interests in policymaking.[30] Despite this, the treaty is not without merit, with Article 1 defining 'air pollution' as:

> the introduction, by man, directly or indirectly, of substances or energy into the air resulting in deleterious effects of such a nature as to endanger human health, *harm living resources and ecosystems* and material property and impair or interfere with amenities *and other legitimate uses of the environment.*' (emphasis added)

The early reference to ecosystems is notable, and 'other legitimate uses of the environment' appears sufficiently broad to include agriculture. We might also read 'impair or interfere with' as meaning that it is not just physical harm that is covered by the treaty. Arguably, frustrating or preventing the pursuit of a traditional agricultural practice constitutes impairment and interference. If accepted, this would mean that the LRTAP offers some protection to agricultural cultures and not just its natural and physical infrastructure.

The true value of the LRTAP regime lies in how it has subsequently evolved through its protocols. To date, eight protocols have been adopted,[31] most of which

26 LRTAP, Article 3.
27 LRTAP, Article 4.
28 LRTAP, Article 5.
29 LRTAP, Article 6.
30 See also R. Amos, *International Conservation Law: The Protection of Plants in Theory and Practice* (Routledge, 2020) 225–228.
31 https://unece.org/protocols (last accessed 20/04/2023). For an overview, see P. Sands and J. Peel, *Principles of International Environmental Law* (4th edn, CUP 2018) 262–271.

address specific types of air pollution,[32] and a number of these have proven effective at reducing, or at least controlling, emissions of the targeted pollutants. The 1985 Sulphur Protocol[33] required states to reduce sulphur emissions by 30% no later than 1993, using 1980 as the baseline.[34] By 1993, states party to the Protocol had collectively achieved cuts of 50%, with 11 reporting reductions in excess of 60%.[35] While there is debate over how much of this is attributable to the Protocol and how much was driven by industrial changes that were inevitable as a result of political and economic upheaval in Eastern Europe, the consensus is that the Protocol made some contribution to the reductions.[36]

Notwithstanding its success, the construction of the 1985 Protocol can be criticised for failing to account for differing circumstances and capacities of states; the 30% target applied equally to all parties. This was not repeated in later protocols, with the most recent, the 1999 Gothenburg Protocol, which covers sulphur, nitrogen oxides, ammonia and volatile organic compounds (VOCs), differentiating between parties on the basis of the environmental impacts of their emissions and the relative ease with which those emissions can be reduced.[37] The 1999 Protocol was updated in 2012.[38] In addition to expanding its scope to include additional matters, most notably black carbon, which is a major contributor to climate change, it extended parties' obligations regarding the four substances beyond 2020 and sought to consolidate the LRTAP regime by replacing the protocols on nitrogen oxides and VOCs.

The evolution of the LRTAP through a series of protocols dealing directly with substances that cause transboundary pollution stands in marked contrast to the Convention on Biological Diversity.[39] This is also a framework convention, but as noted in chapter 1 the only two protocols that have been adopted relate to the transboundary movement of living-modified organisms and access to genetic resources,[40] which although important, are not key drivers of biodiversity loss.[41] Also notable

32 The exception being the Protocol on Long-Term Financing of the Cooperative Programme for Monitoring and Evaluating the Long-Range Transmission of Air Pollutants in Europe, Geneva, 28 September 1984, in force 28 January 1988, 2 SMTE 285, which ensures funding for the Cooperative Programme for the Monitoring and Evaluation of the Long-Range Transmission of Air Pollutants in Europe (EMEP). The EMEP, established by Article 9 of the LRTAP, oversees the monitoring of air pollutants through a series of monitoring stations throughout the states party to the convention and develops common monitoring procedures.

33 Helsinki, 8 July 1985, in force 2 September 1987, 2 ILM 1077 (1987).

34 1985 Protocol, Article 2.

35 Sands and Peel (n 31) 263.

36 Byrne (n 24) 212.

37 Gothenburg, 30 November 1999, in force 17 May 2005, UN Doc. EB.AIR/1999.

38 4 May 2012, in force 7 October 2019, ECE/EB.AIR/114, 6 May 2013.

39 Rio de Janeiro, 5 June 1992, in force 29 December 1993, 31 ILM 822 (1992).

40 Protocol on Biosafety, Cartagena, 29 January 2000, in force 11 September 2003, 39 ILM 1027 and Protocol on Access to Genetic Resources and the Fair and Equitable Sharing of Benefits Arising from Their Utilization, Nagoya, 29 October 2010, in force 12 October 2014, C.N.782.2010.TREATIES-1.

41 Amos (n 30) 36–37.

is the relative progress of states towards the overarching objective of the LRTAP – 'to limit and… gradually reduce and prevent air pollution'[42] – compared with the consistent failure of states to meet the goals of the Biodiversity Convention – to conserve biodiversity and ensure its sustainable use.[43] Explanations for these differences are provided by Dai. Drawing on political theory, Dai suggests that different issues appeal to different national constituencies, and governments focus on those groups who possess more 'political clout', i.e. are more likely to be engaged in political processes.[44] The 1985 Protocol to the LRTAP provided a mechanism through which governments could take action to address a concern of key demographics, i.e. acid rain, and therefore reflected a national priority.[45] Arguably, the Biodiversity Convention lacks a sufficiently powerful domestic constituency, due to biodiversity loss's lack of direct impact on individuals; people can tell when acid rain is falling on them, but not when a species becomes extinct. Whether this remains the case as the ecological harms resulting from degraded ecosystems and the consequences this will have for human society become more apparent has yet to be seen.

For Boehmelt and Spilker, the success that has been achieved under the LRTAP highlights the importance of developing interactions between different international environmental regimes, not only to ensure coherence in the law but to facilitate its development through the dissemination of innovative regulatory design. States learn from experience, and so something adopted in one regime is likely to be employed in another if it can be shown to be effective without incurring an unacceptable infringement on state sovereignty.[46] Mechanisms, norms and concepts that reflect agroecology in one regime may therefore migrate into others if they can be shown to respond to critical environmental and social challenges, even between regimes that at first glance appear to have little or no connection. To date, though, this migration in design characteristics has only been observed in relation to soft law. Models for hard law obligations, due to their clearer implications for sovereignty, appear not to transfer across multilateral agreements,[47] which may explain why we have not seen the LRTAP's, and other pollution regimes',[48] expansive use of binding protocols deployed under the Biodiversity Convention.

42 LRTAP, Article 2.

43 Biodiversity Convention, Article 1. Secretariat to the Convention on Biological Diversity, *Global Biodiversity Outlook 5* (2020).

44 X. Dai, 'Why Comply? The Domestic Constituency Mechanism' (2005) 59 *International Organization* 363.

45 ibid 385–387.

46 T. Bohmelt and G. Spilker, 'The Interaction of International Institutions from a Social Network Perspective' (2016) 16 *International Environmental Agreements: Politics, Law and Economics* 67.

47 ibid 85.

48 E.g., the Protocol on Substances that Deplete the Ozone Layer, Montreal, 16 September 1987, in force 1 January 1989, 26 ILM 154 (1987) to the Convention for the Protection of the Ozone Layer, Vienna, 22 March 1985, in force 22 September 1988, 26 ILM 1529 (1985).

The sharing of information is identified as one way in which the good practice of one treaty regime might translate across to another.[49] Reciprocity in information sharing is also key in developing partnerships between non-state actors within socioecological networks. This means not only that decision-makers should consider information from a wide range of stakeholders but also that decision-makers should explain to those stakeholders how that information has been taken into account.[50] As well as improving the confidence of environmental groups in particular, due to the disadvantages they typically face in engaging with decision-makers compared to industry bodies, in what can otherwise be obscure decision-making processes,[51] greater sharing of information through both vertical (state and private actor) and horizontal (state and state; private actor and private actor) relationships can help to ensure that all members of a socioecological network are meaningfully engaged in measures intended to support that network's ecological and social foundations. This is particularly relevant to commercial entities' place in these networks, especially if they are major polluters. The challenges in ensuring that companies internalise the inherent externalities of their operations, i.e. the costs to society of their pollution, have been well-documented,[52] and manifested in regulation through various expressions of the polluter pays principle.[53]

Commercial entities' destabilising impact on socioecological networks is not just a result of the direct harm they cause to the environment through pollution. States' desire to attract foreign investment to support their economies has been linked to a so-called 'race to the bottom' in environmental standards, although the evidence for this is far from conclusive.[54] Zimmer's solution is for states to adopt common baselines for environmental protection through multilateral environmental agreements.[55] This would mean that the only competition in environmental standards is upward.[56] An example of this can be found in Article 193 of the Treaty on the Functioning of the European Union, which allows Member States to adopt stricter environmental protections than those found in EU law, provided that they are compatible with the Treaties.

A further difficulty in regulating commercial entities is that while there is a consensus on what basic fundamental human rights are, and therefore common

49 Bohmelt and Spilker (n 46) 71–73.

50 E. Baar, 'Partnerships in the Development and Implementation of Canadian Air Quality Regulation' (1992) 14 *Law & Policy* 1,

51 ibid 12 and 23–29.

52 R. Macrory, 'Regulating in a Risky Environment', in M. Freeman (ed), *Current Legal Problems 2001* (OUP, 2002) 619.

53 P. Schwartz, 'The Polluter-Pays Principle', in M. Fitzmaurice and others (eds), *Research Handbook on International Environmental Law* (Edward Elgar, 2010).

54 M. Rauscher, 'International Trade, Foreign Investment, and the Environment', in K. Mäler and J. Vincent (eds), *Handbook of Environmental Economics: Economywide and International Environmental Issues* (North Holland, 2005).

55 M. Zimmer, 'Governing the Sulphur Dioxide Emissions of Multinational Corporations: Putting the Brakes on the Race-to-the-Bottom' (2010) 19 *Dalhousie Journal of Legal Studies* 64, 77.

56 ibid 79.

levels of protection across most states, no such consensus exists over what constitutes a 'good' environment or (un)acceptable levels of pollution.[57] In addition to frustrating efforts to agree common baseline standards, these cultural differences also mean that there is often a failure by stakeholders to perceive the connections between what they consider to be legitimate but environmentally harmful socio-economic activities at a local level, and impacts on the global socioecological networks of which they are part.

That perceptions of pollution are grounded in culture means that it is not enough for international negotiators or national decision-makers to merely develop a series of mechanisms, such as those devised under the LRTAP, to respond to it. Consideration must also be given to how regulatory tools might be applied, and how effective they might be, in different local contexts. It is not just differing technical and financial capacities that will influence how a community engages with a regulatory approach, but their perceptions of the legitimacy of that approach and of the seriousness of the problem it is trying to solve.[58] As we observed in the failed efforts to modernise Bali's agricultural system in chapter 4, without understanding the cultural context in which a law will operate, its pursuit by well-meaning but ill-informed policymakers may result in more damage to the socioecological network in question than the issue that is being addressed.

The cultural limitations of the LRTAP model in addressing transboundary air pollution are evident in Asia, where transboundary air pollution is now a greater issue than it is in Europe.[59] In South Korea, improvements in air quality resulting from the regulation of domestic industries are being undermined by transboundary air pollution emanating primarily from China.[60] Reflecting the broader trend in North East Asian states against reaching regional agreements on environmental matters, South Korea is pursuing discussions between government ministers and scientific cooperation as the primary means to address transboundary pollution.[61] The problem is that this approach is not comprehensive enough to respond to the multiple environmental and health challenges that have emerged as a consequence of the region's rapid economic development,[62] leading Henry et al to call for a

57 ibid 77–78.

58 J. Scholtes, 'The Siren Sounds for Nitrogen' (2008) 38 *Environmental Law Reporter* 10253, 10256. See also N. Castells and J. Ravetz, 'Science and Policy in International Environmental Agreements: Lessons from the European Experience on Transboundary Air Pollution' (2001) 1 *International Environmental Agreements: Politics, Law and Economics* 405–425.

59 This is not to say that air pollution is no longer a problem in Europe, with ClientEarth being especially proactive in holding decision-makers to account if they fail to meet legally mandated air quality standards – https://www.clientearth.org/what-we-do/priorities/air-pollution/ (last accessed 20/04/2023).

60 L. Henry and others, 'From Smelter Fumes to Silk Road Winds: Exploring Legal Responses to Transboundary Air Pollution over South Korea' (2012) 11 *Washington University Global Studies Law Review* 565, 568.

61 ibid 568–569.

62 ibid 570.

formal agreement between South Korea, Japan and China that contains binding commitments to tackle air pollution.[63]

A model for this agreement can be found in the Association of South East Asian Nations (ASEAN) 2002 Agreement on Transboundary Haze Pollution.[64] What is interesting about this agreement is that it demonstrates that even where there is a reluctance, based either on cultural traditions or concerns over sovereignty, to agree formal environmental standards, domestic pressures can compel governments to engage with multilateral fora. The illegal burning of forests for palm oil plantations in Indonesia has long been recognised as a source of transboundary air pollution in South East Asia. For Indonesia, this was purely an internal matter, and calls from other states to deal with it were met with allegations of interfering with Indonesia's sovereignty. As pollution-related problems increased in Indonesia, however, domestic pressures grew and in 2014 Indonesia finally ratified the Haze Agreement.[65]

The Haze Agreement broadly follows the model of the LRTAP. There is an overall objective to 'prevent and monitor' transboundary haze pollution,[66] with the principal obligations relating to monitoring pollution, sharing information and engaging in consultations with affected states.[67] What is missing is the series of more specific protocols that drove progress in Europe. This, coupled with its reliance on under-resourced national institutions to ensure implementation and compliance,[68] means that the Agreement is having only a marginal impact on transboundary air pollution in South East Asia.[69]

An alternative approach to dealing with South East Asia's transboundary air pollution problem is what Robinson calls 'biological remedies'. He argues that rather than bespoke pollution treaties, states should increase their efforts to implement agreements concerned with nature conservation. The burning of forests would not be an issue if these were designated under a robust system of protected areas.[70] While attractive in theory, and aligned with agroecology's focus on supporting the integrity of ecological and human systems, enhancing nature protection measures to prevent air pollution would present similar challenges regarding implementation

63 ibid 625–626.

64 Kuala Lumpur, 10 June 2002, in force 25 November 2003. Text available at https://asean.org/wp-content/uploads/2021/01/ASEANAgreementonTransboundaryHazePollution-1.pdf (last accessed 20/04/2023).

65 Robinson (n 11) 362–363.

66 Haze Agreement, Article 2.

67 Haze Agreement, Article 4.

68 It is for this reason that Byrne cautions the use of the LRTAP as a template for other regions – A. Byrne, 'The 1979 Convention on Long-Range Transboundary Air Pollution: Assessing its Effectiveness as a Multilateral Environmental Regime after 35 Years' (2015) 4 *Transnational Environmental Law* 37, 64.

69 L. Syarif, 'Evaluating the (In)Effectiveness of ASEAN Cooperation Against Transboundary Air Pollution', in Jayakumar and others (n 11).

70 Robinson (n 11) 382 et seq.

and enforcement,[71] and may prove more controversial than solutions presented as pollution mechanisms. As noted, it was domestic pressure that led to Indonesia joining the Haze Agreement, similar to how internal political considerations were a key factor in European states' implementation of the 1985 Sulphur Protocol.[72] That illegal deforestation remains a consistent problem in Indonesia suggests that a sufficiently strong domestic constituency to drive positive changes in how the forests are managed has yet to emerge.

**Persistent Organic Pollutants**

The LRTAP responds to how one type of pollution impacts agriculture. As noted at the start of this chapter, agricultural activities are also a major cause of environmental pollution. A key issue is the use of certain pesticides that are particularly harmful to the natural world and human health, and that persist in the environment for long periods of time. Together with other pollutants, a small number of pesticides are addressed through the 2001 Convention on Persistent Organic Pollutants (the POPs Convention), the principal objectives of which are to protect the environment and human health from their impacts.[73]

The impacts of POPs vary according to the chemical in question but have commonly been found to result in diseases, reproductive and development abnormalities and unnatural behaviours in humans and other animals.[74] These are exacerbated by the ease with which POPs traverse different environmental media, their bioaccumulative nature, i.e. they build up in an organism over time as more of the substance is ingested, and that they may be passed on by mothers to their offspring both pre- and post-natal.[75] Once in the environment, they can be exceptionally difficult to eradicate. Many take a long time to naturally degrade, and others can only be destroyed through processes such as incineration.[76]

POPs became a matter of international concern in the 1980s, when scientists discovered significant concentrations of toxins in the Arctic Circle; an area where levels had been expected to be low due to the relative lack of production and use of these substances.[77] Subsequent research found POPs throughout the environment,

71 Bowman and others (n 15) ch 4.

72 Dai (n 44).

73 POPs Convention, Article 1. For an overview, see D. Downie and J. Templeton, 'Persistent Organic Pollutants: Managing Threats to Human Health and the Environment', in P. Harris (ed), *Routledge Handbook of Global Environmental Politics* (Routledge, 2022).

74 https://www.epa.gov/international-cooperation/persistent-organic-pollutants-global-issue-global-response (last accessed 20/04/2023).

75 Downie and Templeton (n 73) 472.

76 ibid.

77 E. Dewaiily and C. Furgal, 'POPs, the Environment, and Public Health', in D. Downie and T. Fenge (eds), *Northern Lights against POPs: Combatting Toxic Threats in the Arctic* (McGill-Queens University Press, 2003). See also H. Selin and N. Eckley, 'Science, Politics, and Persistent Organic Pollutants: The Role of Scientific Assessments in International Environmental Co-Operation' (2003) 3 *International Environmental Agreements: Politics, Law and Economics* 17.

including in food chains of a variety of species and communities.[78] Most notable among these are cetaceans,[79] underscoring the interconnectedness of the natural world. Species that at first glance have no connection with agriculture must still, if a true systems-level approach is to be taken in decision-making, be considered part of a farm's socioecological network.

The POPs Convention operates through a series of Annexes, with Annex A listing POPs that should be eliminated and Annex B containing substances that should be restricted.[80] At the time of writing, Annex A lists 26 chemicals, 16 of which are pesticides. Annex B contains DDT and perfluorooctane sulfonic acid.[81] Measures that states should take to deliver the elimination and reduction of these substances are set out in Article 3. This has been criticised for the use of soft language, with states' obligations phrased as ones of conduct (to take measures to eliminate and reduce) rather than as ones of result (to actually eliminate and reduce), and is consequently an illustration of the tensions in international negotiations on hazardous substances.[82]

These tensions are also evident in Article 4, which establishes a register for country-specific exemptions that allow a state to continue using listed substances for the uses listed in the Annexes. Part VI of Annex A, for example, permits the continued production and use of the pesticide endosulfan to control pests of a variety of major crops. To take advantage of one of the exemptions for five years, a state must inform the Convention's Secretariat. At the end of that period, the state must reapply and that this is subject to review suggests that their application could theoretically be rejected.[83] If no state requests to take advantage of an exemption, it is removed from the register and may not be reactivated in the future. These exemptions will therefore eventually expire.

There are a number of strengths of the POPs Convention that align with principles and practices of agroecology. First, the treaty is another example of a living instrument.[84] Allowing new substances to be included in the Annexes means that the Convention is adaptable in the face of changing scientific knowledge and

78 E.g., H. Kuhnlein and others, 'Canadian Arctic Indigenous Peoples, Traditional Food Systems, and POPs', in Downie and Fenge, ibid.

79 A detailed account of how pesticides have impacted cetaceans and the wider marine environment is provided in L. Charles (ed), *Marine Environments: Diversity, Threats and Conservation* (Nova, 2020).

80 Annex C lists substances for which states must take the measures list in Article 5 to reduce releases from anthropogenic sources; Annexes D–F provide more information on the process for listing a new substance, and Annex G sets out dispute settlement procedures.

81 https://www.pops.int/TheConvention/ThePOPs/AllPOPs/tabid/2509/Default.aspx (last accessed 20/04/2023).

82 P. Lallas, 'The Stockholm Convention on Persistent Organic Pollutants' (2001) 95 *American Journal of International Law* 692, 702.

83 Boyle and Redgwell (n 25) 459–460.

84 See the discussion of the 2001 International Treaty on Plant Genetic Resources for Food and Agriculture, Rome, 3 November 2001, in force 29 June 2004. Text available at: https://www.planttreaty.org/index_en.htm (last accessed 20/04/2023) in ch 1.

circumstances, thereby reflecting that socioecological networks are in a state of constant flux as new technologies are developed and deployed. Listing additional substances is a lengthy and complex process,[85] but that 14 have been added to the original 12 shows that, to date at least, it has functioned reasonably well. Questions have been raised over whether this trend will continue, however. Sands and Peel note that the regime's attention is now turning to substances for which there is more scientific debate over their levels of toxicity, and whose regulation would come at greater socioeconomic cost.[86]

The precautionary principle will therefore take on an increasingly important role. In contrast to other regimes concerned with hazardous substances and pollutants,[87] precaution is embedded in the POPs Convention's text. While the Contracting Parties have merely stated that they are 'mindful' of the need to adopt a precautionary approach,[88] its explicit incorporation in the treaty text legitimises COP discussions about whether decisions to delay or refuse the listing of a substance are justifiable in light of compelling, if inconclusive, scientific evidence.[89]

These two issues – the balancing of socioeconomic costs with environmental benefits in the context of uncertain science and the extent to which the precautionary principle can inform that balancing – mean that stakeholder engagement in decisions about what and how to regulate is vital.[90] There are numerous obstacles at the national level to facilitating the broad participation needed to ensure that all members of a socioecological network are represented in those decisions, however. In particular, there has been insufficient financial support. The Global Environment Fund (GEF) serves as the financial mechanism referred to in Article 13(6) of the POPs Convention, responsible for supporting developing states and states with economies in transition in their implementation of the treaty. Difficulties are twofold. First is the overall lack of sufficient finance. This problem has only increased with the addition of more substances to the Annexes, which has increased the burden that the POPs Convention imposes on parties.[91] Second, while the GEF has been reasonably forthcoming in providing funds to support the development of national implementation plans, actual projects require co-financing, which developing states

85 POPs Convention, Article 8.

86 Sands and Peel (n 31) 583.

87 Most notably the Rotterdam Convention (n 105) below.

88 POPs Convention, Article 1.

89 S. Maguire and J. Ellis, 'Redistributing the Burden of Scientific Uncertainty: Implications of the Precautionary Principle for State and Nonstate Actors' (2005) 11 *Global Governance* 505.

90 The negotiation of the POPs Convention itself has been commended for the diverse range of stakeholders that were involved, although power imbalances between the large and well-funded delegations from developed states and the smaller delegations of developing states were also observed – P. Lallas 'The Role of Process and Participation in the Development of Effective International Environmental Agreements: A Study of the Global Treaty on Persistent Organic Pollutants (POPs)' (2000) 19 *UCLA Journal of Environmental Law and Policy* 83.

91 Boyle and Redgwell (n 25) 462.

have struggled to secure.[92] To date, therefore, greater emphasis has typically been placed on implementation planning rather than implementation per se.[93] Planning is of course an essential step in all decision-making processes and a key stage in the adaptive management approaches we have identified as central to agroecology. However, it also reflects observations made in relation to international biodiversity law in chapter 1, where there is a similar emphasis on outputs over outcomes and a corresponding failure to deliver on the law's principal objectives.

It is not just a lack of financial resources that undermine developing states' efforts to implement the POPs Convention. Banning or otherwise controlling the production and use of substances requires the construction of physical infrastructure to safely store and dispose of chemicals, regulatory reform comprising positive and negative incentive measures to compel users to comply, and administrative systems to monitor any changes to the treaty's Annexes and coordinate action across multiple government departments.[94] There are therefore limitations, due to its design and implementation, to how far the POPs Convention may advance agroecological approaches to managing the use of toxic pesticides and other harmful substances. It should be remembered, however, that agroecology promotes diversity between agricultural systems as well as within them. Farms that rely on pesticides contribute to this diversity and to ensuring the food security that is just as an important and legitimate a goal as protecting the environment, although not, prima facie at least, at the expense of an ecosystem's integrity if we follow an agroecological philosophy. For some communities, and in light of how climate change is facilitating the spread of invasive/alien species,[95] the use of pesticides is considered to be the most cost-effective way of protecting their crops.

Snyder and Li have observed this in relation to eight toxic pesticides commonly used in agriculture in China. They argue that the best way to at least ensure that they are used in a more environmentally responsible manner is to present pesticide governance as an issue of public health and advance this message through a comprehensive education programme targeted at both individuals and corporations.[96] This raises an interesting question as to whether framing agroecological approaches in more anthropocentric terms, such as a matter of public rather than ecological health, would improve the likelihood of them being adopted more widely. I have suggested elsewhere that it is laws that reflect (most) states' anthropocentric perceptions of the value of nature that tend to enjoy stronger legal status

92 P. Kohler and M. Ashton. 'Paying for POPs: Negotiating the Implementation of the Stockholm Convention in Developing Countries' (2010) 15 *International Negotiations* 459.

93 ibid 480.

94 M. AlÁfghani and D. Paramita, 'Regulatory Challenges in the Phasing-Out of Persistent Organic Pollutants in Indonesia' (2018) *International Chemical Regulatory and Law Review* 12 and S. Yadav and K. Lian, 'The Management of Persistent Organic Pollutant Pesticides in Nepal' (2009) 6 *Macquarie Journal of International and Comparative Environmental Law* 217.

95 See ch 2.

96 F. Snyder and L. Ni, 'A Tale of Eight Pesticides: Risk Regulation and Public Health in China' (2017) 8 *European Journal of Risk Regulation* 469.

and higher levels of implementation.[97] The risk, as observed in relation to a possible agriculture protocol to the Biodiversity Convention in chapter 1, is that linking obligations to protect the environment to an anthropocentric agenda might legitimise the neglect, if not deliberate targeting, of those elements of nature that do not appear directly related to those agenda.

### Unified Approaches to Hazardous Substances and Pollutants

A common criticism of the current international system for regulating hazardous chemicals such as pesticides is that it follows a problem-by-problem approach.[98] If new substances are identified as toxic and do not fit within a pre-existing regime, an entirely separate treaty regime must be negotiated in response. This has resulted in critical gaps in the types of substances covered[99] and a fragmented and largely uncoordinated approach for those that are.[100] In response, the Strategic Approach to International Chemicals Management (SAICM) was adopted in 2006,[101] following calls in the 2002 Johannesburg Plan of Implementation for the international community to reduce the impact of hazardous substances on the environment.[102] In terms of agroecology, the SAICM should be commended for its inclusion of a broad range of stakeholders and for adopting a systems-level approach in its proposals for dealing with chemicals and their environmental effects.[103] As a legal instrument, however, its utility has been undermined by it being a non-binding framework and the general unwillingness of states to commit to its more ambitious agenda.[104]

More successful has been the so-called TripleCOPs between the POPs Convention, the Basel Convention on the Control of Transboundary Movements of Hazardous Wastes and Their Disposal and the Rotterdam Convention on the Prior Informed Consent Procedure for Certain Hazardous Chemicals and Pesticides in International Trade.[105] Holding these meetings simultaneously is more than just convenient. It has been found to maximise synergies and minimise discrepancies across the regimes, with decisions adopted under one treaty likely to be agreed

97 Amos (n 31) ch 1.

98 K. Kummer Peiry, 'International Chemicals and Waste Management', in M. Fitzmaurice and others (eds), *Research Handbook on International Environmental Law* (2nd edn, Edward Elgar, 2021).

99 E.g., electronic materials – Boyle and Redgwell (n 25) 464.

100 K. Kummer Peiry, 'The Chemicals and Waste Regime as a Basis for a Comprehensive International Framework on Sustainable Management of Potentially Hazardous Materials?' (2014) 23 *Review of European, Comparative and International Environmental Law* 172, 174.

101 https://www.saicm.org (last accessed 20/04/2023).

102 Para 23. Available at: https://www.un.org/esa/sustdev/documents/WSSD_POI_PD/English/WSSD_PlanImpl.pdf (last accessed 20/04/2023).

103 Kummer Peiry (n 100) 175.

104 ibid 175.

105 Basel, 22 March 1989, in force 5 May 1992, 28 ILM 657 (1989); Rotterdam, 11 September 1998, in force 24 February 2004, 38 ILM 1 (1999). See Boyle and Redgwell (n 25) 487–500 and 456–459, respectively.

for the other two as well. Greater scope for compromise has also been found in negotiations, with states showing a willingness to give way on an issue under one treaty in return for a concession under another. Providing developing states the opportunity to negotiate together across common issues also addresses some of the power imbalances between developed and developing delegations, although this is qualified by the greater time constraints imposed by having to work through three agenda simultaneously, which tends to favour the larger delegations of developed states.[106]

The TripleCOPs are consequently a positive, but not unproblematic, development, and calls have long been made for a single entity to oversee the international response to toxic pollution.[107] It is argued that this would enhance technical and scientific collaboration between the regimes, avoid duplication of effort and help to streamline the provision of financial support and non-compliance procedures.[108] On the other hand, there are no guarantees that a new oversight body would be able to resolve the challenges identified in the implementation of international rules on chemicals management.[109]

Notwithstanding this scholarly debate, there is little to suggest that the international community intends to depart from the issue-by-issue approach seen to date. In 2013, the Mercury Convention was adopted.[110] Its approach is similar to the other treaties discussed in this chapter,[111] with the regime's principal objectives being to 'protect human health and the environment from anthropogenic emissions and releases of mercury and mercury compounds',[112] and key measures including the phasing out of mercury mining and the use of mercury in products and production processes.[113]

Like other pollution instruments, the Mercury Convention may be criticised for expressing certain obligations as ones of conduct rather than of result, most notably in relation to mercury emissions in Article 8. In other respects, however, it is stronger than other hazardous substance regimes and a better instrument to facilitate agroecological approaches to the management of pollutants. While states may again take advantage of certain exemptions to use restrictions, these may only be extended once.[114] It has also been noted that when it comes to supporting the imple-

106 J. Allan and others, 'Experimenting with TripleCOPs: Productive Innovation or Counterproductive Complexity?' (2018) 18 *International Environmental Agreements: Politics, Law and Economics* 557, 564–566.

107 E.g., J. Krueger and H. Selin, 'Governance for Sound Chemical Management: The Need for a More Comprehensive Global Strategy' (2002) 8 *Global Governance* 323.

108 K. Rain, 'The Need for an Independent Entity to Manage Global Chemicals Agreements' (2006) 6 *Sustainable Development Law & Policy* 17, 19.

109 ibid 19–20.

110 Kumamoto, 10 October 2013, in force 16 August 2017, C.N.244.2015.TREATIES-XXVII.17.

111 H. Eriksen and F. Perrez, 'The Minamata Convention: A Comprehensive Response to a Global Problem' (2014) 23 *Review of European, Comparative and International Environmental Law* 195.

112 Mercury Convention, Article 1.

113 Mercury Convention, Articles 3–5.

114 Mercury Convention, Article 6.

mentation of the Convention, rather than distinguishing between developed and developing states, all states are called on to provide financial resources, within their capabilities.[115] Most significant, and again in contrast to other substance regimes, the treaty attempts to regulate all stages of mercury's life cycle – extraction, storage, utilisation and disposal. This should be considered a prerequisite to the successful adoption of a systems-level approach to environmental management that is central to agroecology. It will not be possible to understand how a substance such as mercury affects all natural and human stakeholders in a socioecological network without also being aware of its impacts at each stage of its life cycle.

The Mercury Convention consequently has some merit but does nothing to address concerns related to the proliferation of separate substance regimes. These are only going to be exacerbated following the international community's decision to negotiate a new agreement under the UN Environment Programme (UNEP), this time on plastic pollution.[116] The impacts of plastics on the marine environment have been well-documented,[117] although the international response to this to date has fallen short.[118] Marine plastic pollution is a critical issue, but framing plastics as an issue of marine pollution has arguably frustrated efforts to adopt a more holistic, life cycle approach that focuses as much on the production and use of plastic as it does on plastic waste.[119] It is only relatively recently that attention has turned to the toxic effects it has on terrestrial ecosystems and society.[120] The impacts on these systems are just as severe as they are on the oceans, affecting processes central to ecosystem functioning and impacting the health of a range of species and their associated food webs.[121] Agriculture is again both a victim and cause of plastic pollution, particularly in soils. Up to half of microplastics in soil were introduced by the fertilisation of crops.[122] This has implications for all natural and human members of agriculture's socioecological networks, including the consumers of agricultural products.[123]

115 Mercury Convention, Article 13. Boyle and Redgwell (n 25) 463–464.
116 UNEP/EA.5/Res.14, 7 March 2022.
117 S. Morath, 'Our Plastic Problem' (2019) 33 *Natural Resources & Environment* 45.
118 M. McMahon, 'Tides of Plastic: Using International Environmental Law to Reduce Marine Plastic Pollution' (2022) 28 *Hastings Environmental Law Journal* 49.
119 G. Carlini and K. Klein, 'Advancing the International Regulation of Plastic Pollution Beyond the United Nations Assembly Resolution on Marine Litter and Microplastics' (2019) 27 *Review of European, Comparative and International Environmental Law* 234.
120 E. Goodwin, 'Biodiversity and Plastics', in E. Kirk and others (eds), *Research Handbook on Plastics Law* (Edward Elgar, 2024, forthcoming).
121 A. de Souza Machado and others, 'Microplastics as an Emerging Threat to Terrestrial Ecosystems' (2018) 24 *Global Change Biology* 1405.
122 J. Stubenrauch and F. Ekardt, 'Plastic Pollution in Soils: Governance Approaches to Foster Soil Health and Closed Nutrient Cycles' (2020) 7 *Environments* doi:10.3390/environments7050038, 3–5.
123 G. Conti and others, 'Micro- and Nano-Plastics in Edible Fruit and Vegetables. The First Diet Risks Assessment for the General Population' (2020) 187 *Environmental Research* 109677.

In some respects, plastic pollution is more difficult to address than other toxic substances. While certain single-use products, epitomised by the plastic straw,[124] are being banned in some states, that plastic is ubiquitous in everyday life means that eradication will not be possible without fundamental societal reform. Monast and Virdin believe that lessons can be learnt from how the international community has used economic measures as one response to climate change. They propose imposing a cost on producers, either in the form of a tax or a more ambitious cap-and-trade system, to incentivise manufacturers to reduce the amount of plastic that they use and to also raise revenue to fund clean-up efforts and research into alternatives.[125] These ideas are interesting and benefit from economic measures already being used to address society's use of plastic.[126] They also have the advantage of tackling plastic usage throughout society, as they could incentivise both producers and consumers to search for cheaper alternatives.[127] Much has been written about the limitations of market mechanisms as tools of environmental regulation,[128] however, and without global participation, particularly in a cap-and-trade system, it is difficult to see how the use of plastic in production will be reduced, rather than merely relocated to states that are outside the system.

It is too early at the time of writing to know what form the new UNEP plastics agreement will take. As the above discussion indicates, economic measures could have a role to play, but I suggest that it is unlikely that anything as ambitious as a cap-and-trade system will be introduced, not least because of the complexities that would be involved.[129] To address the impacts that plastic pollution has on agriculture, it is essential that states go beyond what they have agreed in earlier hazardous substance treaties and adopt ambitious obligations of result to eradicate and otherwise reduce the use of plastic. This is because the impacts of plastic on the soil and aquatic ecosystems that support agriculture are as much due to the quantity of plastic in the environment as its harmful effects on species.[130] As noted, an ambitious programme of elimination would be politically and practically difficult due to plastic being *everywhere* in modern life, but it is also true to say that research into greener alternatives is meeting with success, including for agricultural uses of plastics.[131] There is also evidence to suggest, in some developed states at least, that

124 M. Mosquera, 'Banning Plastic Straws: The Beginning of the War Against Plastics' (2019) 9 *Environmental and Earth Law Journal* 5.

125 J. Monast and J. Virdin, 'Pricing Plastics Pollution: Lessons from Three Decades of Climate Policy' (2022) 54 *Connecticut Law Review* 345.

126 Charging for the use of plastic bags in supermarkets in the United Kingdom being one example.

127 This would depend on, inter alia, the technological and financial viability of alternatives.

128 E. Fisher and others, *Environmental Law: Texts, Cases and Materials* (2nd edn, OUP, 2019) 256–259.

129 What sectors would be covered? Would it apply to the type of plastic or the type of product? What unit would be used to measure plastic and how would you calculate the price of that unit in such a way as to incentivise reductions in usage?

130 Stubenrauch and Ekardt (n 122).

131 Sustainable Soils Alliance, 'Avoidable Plastic Pollution to Soil in the UK' (Briefing Note, January 2023), available at: https://sustainablesoils.org/our-work/projects/micro-plastics-in-soil (last accessed 20/04/2023).

governments are willing to impose strict legal obligations on the use of plastics in products intended for release into the environment, notably organic fertilisers.[132] From an agroecological perspective, this is an important first step in protecting agricultural systems and their associated socioecological networks from plastic pollution, which needs to be coupled with restrictions on the production of plastics.

## Conclusions

Pollution illustrates the indivisibility of natural and human systems, and the value of adopting systems-level approaches when considering how the actions of one actor may impact on all the others across interconnected socioecological networks.

This is illustrated by the issue of transboundary air pollution. Although limited in application, the international disputes concerning this highlight the importance of legal principles in governing transboundary pollution, and the value of agroecology in protecting all stakeholders in an affected system. As a multilateral agreement, the LRTAP enjoys a greater scope and has proven relatively successful in reducing the emission of substances that were causing significant damage to agricultural, and other, systems. It is therefore unfortunate that the model of a framework convention coupled with a series of specific, binding protocols is not being adopted in Asia, where transboundary air pollution is now a much greater concern. While agroecology requires any legal response to be conscious of and compatible with the cultures in which it is being applied, it is evident that the deference that is being shown to national sovereignty in the ASEAN region, and the emphasis that is being placed on cross-border scientific cooperation in North East Asia, is not delivering the same improvements that have been witnessed in Europe.

Agriculture is also a major source of pollution, with the impacts of pesticides being especially harmful to the environment and human health. There are consequently compelling reasons to rapidly reduce and eliminate their production and use, but these must be balanced against the increasingly important role they play, due to climate change, in ensuring food security for certain communities. Given the difficulties developing states in particular face in implementing the various international hazardous substance regimes, and that this problem is only going to increase as more agreements are reached, calls have been made for a more unified approach. TripleCOPS and the SAICM go some way in answering these calls. The SAICM is another example of how different stakeholders may be brought together in ways that reflect agroecological principles of systems-level analysis of problems and broad stakeholder engagement, although is limited by its non-binding nature. TripleCOPS, on the other hand, have served to maximise synergies between the POPs, Rotterdam and Basel Conventions and facilitated negotiations, but are not without their own administrative weaknesses, especially for the smaller delegations of developing states.

132 Stubenrauch and Ekardt (n 122).

Taking the more radical step of bringing all the relevant treaties within the remit of a single body, with streamlined procedures for providing financial and technical support and non-compliance, seems unlikely, and in any event might only serve to relocate, rather than resolve, the implementation challenges that developing states face. Instead, states continue to address substances on a problem-by-problem basis, with negotiations currently underway on a new plastic pollution treaty. This will only exacerbate the difficulties of developing states. That plastic has contaminated every ecosystem on the planet, and is now found in the food chains of a huge variety of species, including humans, means, however, that this new instrument also has the potential to be hugely consequential in protecting agricultural, natural and human systems, connected through socioecological networks. Both pre-existing hazardous substance and climate change regimes provide some guidance on what form the obligations in this new instrument could take. States should look to go beyond these and agree binding obligations of result to eliminate and reduce the production and use of plastic to protect the natural systems on which agriculture and society depend.

# 11 International Trade

## Neoliberalism and Agroecology

A central argument of this work is that sustainable development is inherently flawed from an environmental perspective, and consequently unsuited to advancing agroecological approaches to agriculture and humanity's wider relationships with the natural world. This is because, as the chapter on environmental assessment illustrated, sustainable development legitimises the prioritisation of economic interests over ecological imperatives in decision-making procedures. This was never inevitable, however. While the way in which sustainable development has been implemented has enabled an economic hegemony, its leading policy sources, such as the World Commission on Environment and Development's report and its reference to the Earth's ecological limits,[1] could have led to a paradigm much closer to a principle of ecological sustainability. Why it did not can be linked to a second dominant framing of international and national policymaking: neoliberalism.[2]

Neoliberalism built on the preceding capitalist agenda of free markets by driving dramatic increases in the scale and scope of economic activity and in the number of people and communities involved in it, coupled with the emergence of new transnational economic actors and the deliberate pursuit of deregulation.[3] In the international legal order, neoliberalism has manifested in the World Trade Organisation (WTO), but its influence can be traced throughout the law. Relevant to this work is how neoliberal thought has transformed conservation policy, evidenced in measures that commodify nature, or justify its conservation in economic terms.[4] Like sustainable development, neoliberal conservation is presented as delivering 'win-win-win' policies for economic growth, social equity and environmental protection.[5] Also like sustainable development, it neglects the inevitable trade-offs

1 World Commission on Environment and Development, *Our Common Future (The Brundtland Report)*, A/42/427, 4 August 1987, 24.

2 C. Okereke, *Global Justice and Neoliberal Environmental Governance: Ethics, Sustainable Development and International Co-operation* (Routledge, 2008) ch 9.

3 D. Brockington and others, *Nature Unbound: Conservation, Capitalism and the Future of Protected Areas* (Earthscan, 2008) 190–191.

4 G. Holmes and C. Cavanagh, 'A Review of the Social Impacts of Neoliberal Conservation: Formations, Inequalities, Contestations' (2016) 75 *Geoforum* 199.

5 ibid 202.

DOI: 10.4324/9781003435174-15

between these objectives,[6] and that the ability of different communities to take advantage of the opportunities that neoliberal policies present often depends on the extent to which they are already part of neoliberal society.[7] From an agroecological perspective this is critical, because it undermines disadvantaged and marginalised stakeholders in socioecological networks, thereby reducing the diversity of agricultural producers.

Support for neoliberalism has never been universal.[8] In the 1970s, resistance centred around the *Limits to Growth* hypothesis, i.e. the belief that the Earth does not possess the ecological carrying capacity to sustain continuous economic growth and human population increases.[9] More recently, popular rejection of dominant economic power structures is framed in part by the language of the climate and ecological emergency. Like proponents of agroecology, those who demand action in response to this are seeking fundamental change in society's relationships with the natural world.

This chapter focuses on the principal legal arena in which these tensions between neoliberalism and non-economic public values must be reconciled: international trade. I begin by considering how the relationship between environmental protection and free trade as competing policy objectives has evolved, and the space for agroecology in that relationship. On the one hand, that the WTO largely remains a 'closed shop' to non-state, non-trade stakeholders means that the full range of interests present in agriculture's socioecological networks is unrepresented in global trade decision-making. On the other, the advantages that WTO rules enjoy in comparison to international environmental law means that it has the potential to drive agroecological reforms.

Attention then turns to the WTO's Agreement on Agriculture.[10] Here, the focus is the extent to which non-trade values associated with agroecology, such as protecting environmental and cultural diversity and ensuring communities' food security, may be used to justify restrictions on trade in agricultural products.

Finally, we will examine the consequences of international trade, and the broader pursuit of globalisation, for the health of the planet and society. COVID-19 has put beyond doubt what the costs will be of our destructive behaviours. After evaluating the agroecological merits of international rules on wildlife trade, the concept of One Health, which has received renewed attention in the wake of the pandemic, is discussed. The chapter concludes by looking at how COVID-19

6 D. Roe and M. Walpole, 'Whose Value Counts? Trade-Offs between Biodiversity Conservation and Poverty Reduction', in Nigel Leader-Williams and others (eds), *Trade-Offs in Conservation: Deciding What to Save* (ZSL / Wiley-Blackwell, 2010).

7 Holmes and Cavanagh (n 4) 206–207.

8 J. Holder and M. Lee, *Environmental Protection, Law and Policy: Texts and Materials* (2nd edn, CUP, 2007) 306–307.

9 D. Meadows and others, *The Limits to Growth* (Potomac Associates/Club of Rome, 1972).

10 Text available at: https://www.wto.org/english/docs_e/legal_e/14-ag_01_e.htm (last accessed 20/04/2023).

reshaped, albeit temporarily, society's connection with nature and what this means for advancing agroecology.

## Agroecology, Trade and the Environment in the WTO

The environment and trade as objectives of public policy are often presented as being in conflict.[11] Proponents of free trade see environmental protection as disguised protectionism and environmental advocates view trade as perpetuating unsustainable behaviours. This polarisation conceals a significant degree of nuance, however.[12] It is not the case that all trade policies are harmful to the environment, or that all environmental measures undermine free trade.[13] The relationship between international environmental and international trade law is also continuously evolving and, in certain regards at least, has passed through a period of confrontation to one of mutually beneficial partnership.[14] This crystallised with the adoption of the Sustainable Development Goals (SDGs),[15] core to which is the idea of collaboration and enhanced partnerships as both prerequisites to and objectives of sustainable development.[16]

We have seen examples in this work of how these partnerships are developing at the sub-national level and between epistemological communities.[17] Less evident, especially in the context of trade, are efforts by states with different interests to build similar collaboration into domestic policies that have an extra-territorial effect. Evidence shows how states typically disregard collaborative initiatives in pursuit of short-term economic gain through trade,[18] contrary to otherwise universally accepted positions such as Principle 12 of the Rio Declaration,[19] which is considered a focal point for reconciling trade and environmental objectives.[20] Research

11 M. Trebilcock and others, *The Regulation of International Trade* (4th edn, Routledge, 2013) 656.

12 O. Perez, *Ecological Sensitivity and Global Legal Pluralism: Rethinking the Trade and Environment Conflict* (Hart Publishing, 2004) ch 1.

13 R. Amos, *International Conservation Law: The Protection of Plants in Theory and Practice* (Routledge, 2020) 139.

14 D. Olawuyi, 'Environment', in D. Bethlehem and others (eds), *The Oxford Handbook on International Trade Law* (2nd edn, OUP, 2022) 676–683. This confrontation was epitomised by controversial decision by the WTO Dispute Panel in *United States – Restrictions on Imports of Tuna (United States – Tuna I)*, DS21/R – 39S/155, 3 September 1991 (not adopted). See T. Goplerud, 'The Struggle to "Green" GATT: Free Trade and Environmental Responsibility in the Wake of the United States-Mexico Tuna-Dolphin Dispute' (1993) 17 *William and Mary Journal of Environmental Law* 215 for contemporary analysis of the ruling.

15 A/RES/70/1, 21 October 2015.

16 E.g., ibid para 39. See also SDG-17 (Strengthen the means of implementation and revitalise the Global Partnership for Sustainable Development).

17 E.g., the Satoyama Initiative discussed in ch 4 – https://satoyama-initiative.org (last accessed 20/04/2023).

18 N. Robinson, 'Legal Redress of Transboundary Air Pollution through Environmental Cooperation', in S. Jayakumar and others (eds), *Transboundary Pollution: Evolving Issues of International Law and Policy* (Edward Elgar, 2015) 371–372.

19 A/CONF.151/26 (Vol. I) 12 August 1992.

20 A. Boyle and C. Redgwell, *Birnie, Boyle & Redgwell's International Law and the Environment* (4th edn, OUP, 2021) 776.

has demonstrated this in the context of SDG-12: responsible consumption and production. SDG-12 seeks to decouple environmental degradation and resource use from economic growth and is consequently central to sustainable development.[21] This can only be achieved if states take a systems-level approach to assessing the environmental impacts of their consumption patterns. In particular, developed states must account for how their high rates of consumption are driving environmentally harmful activities in developing producer states. Few developed states consider their extra-territorial footprint, however,[22] and a recent report reveals that two regions, Europe/North America and Eastern/South-Eastern Asia, account for 70% of global domestic material consumption of natural resources.[23] This failure to properly assess the (un)sustainability of global supply chains means that developed consumer states are not only frustrating their own efforts to achieve the SDGs but the wider international community's.[24] Putting this in an agroecological context, it means that developed states are doing little to address how their actions undermine the position of other members in global socioecological networks, namely communities in developing states and the natural entities that are being exploited for the benefit of distant consumers.

Notwithstanding these concerns, the renewed emphasis on harmonising international environmental and trade rules in pursuit of sustainable development suggests that space might exist for greater levels of stakeholder engagement, if not actual participation, in WTO decision-making. This in turn would allow for more account to be taken of the diverse interests of members of agriculture's socioecological networks. However, without reform to WTO structures and processes, the scope for developing this engagement is limited.[25]

There is no 'trade or the environment' dichotomy underpinning WTO decision-making. While true that the environment does not enjoy a general level of protection in WTO law, neither is it the case that free trade is automatically or inevitably prioritised over environmental protection.[26] This is most evident in the WTO Appellate Body's seminal judgment in the *United States – Shrimp* dispute, in which it was made clear that states could and should pursue policies that protect the environment and that these can be justified under WTO rules even if they have the effect of restricting trade.[27]

A more pertinent observation is that the characteristics of the WTO regime, specifically that it is almost uniformly expressed in binding terms and is supported by a

21 UN, *The Sustainable Development Goals Report 2022* (UN, 2022) 48.

22 R. Amos and E. Lydgate, 'Trade, Transboundary Impacts and the Implementation of SDG 12' (2020) 15 *Sustainability Science* 1699, 1700–1701.

23 UN (n 21) 50.

24 Amos and Lydgate (n 22) 1703.

25 Holder and Lee (n 8) 310.

26 Boyle and Redgwell (n 20) 777.

27 *United States – Import Prohibition of Certain Shrimp and Shrimp Products (United States – Shrimp)* WT/DS58/AB/R, adopted 6 November 1998, para 185. See Amos (n 13) 148–153.

system of mandatory dispute settlement that is largely respected by states,[28] lead to it being the forum in which disputes over potential conflicts between trade and the environment are raised.[29] There is a lack of expertise in international environmental law in the WTO dispute bodies, however.[30] This adds to concerns raised throughout this book about sustainable development. Having the principal forum for resolving conflicts between trade and the environment as one that has the promotion of free trade as its objective is merely going to reinforce this flawed paradigm.[31]

The WTO has demonstrated its awareness of the need to find a different balance between free trade and environmental protection. A significant development was the creation of the Committee on Trade and Environment (CTE) in 1995. Its purpose is to promote synergies between trade and the environment as a way of pursuing sustainable development, but the CTE's success in this is limited. Work on an Environmental Goods Agreement, which would remove tariffs on a range of environmental commodities,[32] has been hampered by the same conflicting interests of states that characterise the Agreement on Agriculture, discussed below.[33]

On the other hand, by opening WTO processes to representatives from environmental instruments, the CTE has facilitated closer cooperation between the WTO and environmental secretariats.[34] This relates to the point made in the previous chapter that developing links between regimes can lead to the dissemination of regulatory norms.[35] The value of this in promoting agroecology is evident in the CTE through the granting of observer status in WTO procedures for certain environmental organisations,[36] resulting in a greater range of stakeholders at least being present at those discussions. It is important not to overstate the influence that international environmental law is exerting over the still largely closed processes of the WTO, however. Developing states have traditionally been reluctant to permit environmental NGOs and similar groups a more formal position in the WTO because these groups tend to represent the Global North, and consequently do not accurately represent their positions.[37] These concerns are valid, but environmental

28 That WTO Members have established the Multi-party Interim Appeal Arbitration mechanism demonstrates a need for a two-tier dispute settlement system in the WTO, notwithstanding ongoing disagreements about whether and how that system should be reformed – D. Unterhalter and E. Schneidereit, 'Institutions', in Bethlehem and others (n14) 916–918.

29 M. Bowman and others, *Lyster's International Wildlife Law* (2nd edn, CUP, 2012) 668.

30 Olawuyi (n 14) 686.

31 Boyle and Redgwell (n 20) 812.

32 https://www.wto.org/english/tratop_e/envir_e/ega_e.htm (last accessed 20/04/2023).

33 Olawuyi (n 14) 680–681.

34 Bowman and others (n 29) 668.

35 T. Bohmelt and G. Spilker, 'The Interaction of International Institutions from a Social Network Perspective' (2016) 16 *International Environmental Agreements: Politics, Law and Economics* 67.

36 Bowman and others (n 29) 668.

37 G. Shaffer, 'The Word Trade Organization under Challenge: Democracy and the Law and Politics of the WTO's Treatment of Trade and Environment Matters' (2001) 25 *Harvard Environmental Law Review* 1, 61–68.

groups could nevertheless still play an important role, as they do in national decision-making fora, in ensuring that environmental issues are part of the discussion.[38]

The de facto priority that states afford to trade rules over environmental obligations, coupled with the limited scope for stakeholder engagement, constitutes a barrier to reforming WTO rules and procedures along lines that would be more compatible with agroecology. At the same time, however, the institutional and structural advantages of WTO law mean that it could be an important avenue through which agroecological reforms could be advanced, and arguably space already exists in the WTO to achieve these.

An important starting point for such reform is the preamble to the WTO Agreement, which recognises that states' trade and economic policies should be conducted in a manner that is compatible with sustainable development.[39] Those who considered the explicit reference to sustainable development to be a major step in incorporating the environment into the WTO regime were vindicated when the Appellate Body specifically referred to it in *United States – Shrimp*.[40] Significantly, the Appellate Body used the Preamble as an interpretative guide for Article XX of the General Agreement on Tariffs and Trade (GATT), noting that WTO law must be read 'in the light of contemporary concerns' of the international community and, taking this into account, the meaning of the term 'natural resources' is 'by definition, evolutionary'.[41] It follows that the meaning of sustainable development, which has no specific definition in international trade,[42] is also evolutionary. What this suggests is that if a new interpretation of sustainable development that enjoyed wide and diverse international support was to emerge, the WTO dispute bodies would be open to taking that interpretation into account when applying WTO law.

I have proposed in this work that sustainable development should be replaced by a principle of ecological sustainability. While it cannot be said that this is attracting widespread support, there is evidence that ideas related to it are gaining prominence, particularly in international judgments.[43] If the WTO dispute bodies were to follow these rulings, it would be a step towards facilitating agroecological approaches in the law and in ensuring that WTO law was not a barrier to responses to global environmental challenges.[44]

38 Holder and Lee (n 8) 310.

39 Marrakesh, 15 April 1994, in force 1 January 1995, 33 ILM 1125 (1994), Recital 1. This incorporated the General Agreement on Tariffs and Trade, Geneva, 30 October 1947, 55 UNTS 194, in force provisionally since 1 January 1948 under the 1947 Protocol of Application, 55 UNTS 308.

40 E.g., J. Cameron, 'The GATT and the Environment', in P. Sands (ed), *Greening International Law* (Earthscan, 1993). *United States – Shrimp* (n 27) para 129.

41 *United States – Shrimp* (n 27) para 129, drawing on *Namibia (Legal Consequences) Advisory Opinion* (1971) ICJ Rep 31, para 53, in which the International Court of Justice stated that concepts embedded in treaties are 'by definition, evolutionary'.

42 E. Lydgate, 'Sustainable Development in the WTO: From Mutual Supportiveness to Balancing' (2012) 11 *World Trade Review* 621, 623.

43 E.g., *Indus Waters Kishenganga Arbitration (Pakistan v India)*, Final Award of the Court of Arbitration, 20 December 2013.

44 Boyle and Redgwell (n 20) 811–812.

## The WTO's Rules on Agricultural Trade

If there is one issue where there has been significant resistance from states to the expansion of neoliberalism it is trade in agricultural products. Agriculture is arguably the most prominent, and controversial, issue in international trade negotiations, and has been since before the establishment of the WTO.[45] Its unique status is largely attributable to the historic strength of domestic farming lobbies, particularly in the United States and EU Member States, and the political sway these groups hold in those states' democratic traditions.[46] It is also because of the political imperative for states in ensuring that they can feed their populaces.[47]

Arguments justifying the special treatment of agriculture in international trade law focus on what the OECD has termed agriculture's multifunctionality, i.e. that its role in society is more than merely producing commodities to be traded.[48] Agriculture is also about food security, environmental protection and supporting the livelihoods and cultures of farming communities,[49] which cannot easily be accounted for in the operation of a global market.[50] Multifunctionality reflects aspects of agroecological agenda, as these examples illustrate. Regarding environmental protection, it has been argued that government support of local farmers that use a diverse range of crops is necessary so that they remain viable against larger commercial farms that plant monocultures,[51] thereby maintaining the diversity of agricultural systems. Similar arguments are made in relation to protecting the traditional knowledge and diversity in local farming cultures.[52]

More complex is the issue of food security. Again, proponents of protectionist measures highlight the importance of maintaining strong national agriculture industries to ensure that states can continue to feed their populations in the event of a disruption to global markets. This is largely uncontentious, given that states agreed to explicitly permit this in the GATT.[53] It is not a universal position, however. Anderson argues that food security can be enhanced by states taking advantage of global markets in agricultural goods by diversifying their international supplies.[54] This too is compatible with agroecological thinking; it promotes

45 M. Margulis, 'The Forgotten History of Food Security in Multilateral Trade Negotiations' (2017) 16 *World Trade Review* 25.

46 Trebilcock and others (n 11) 447–448.

47 B. Hoekman and M. Kostecki, *The Political Economy of the World Trading System: WTO and Beyond* (2nd edn, OUP, 2001) 210–212.

48 OECD, *Multifunctionality in Agriculture: Evaluating the Degree of Jointness, Policy Implications* (OECD, 2008).

49 ibid.

50 G.A. Wilson, *Multifunctional Agriculture: A Transition Theory Perspective* (CABI, 2007) ch 4 and 5.

51 Trebilcock and others (n 11) 443.

52 ibid.

53 GATT 1994, Article XI(2)(a).

54 K. Anderson, 'Agriculture's 'Multifunctionality' and the WTO' (2000) 44 *Australian Journal of Agricultural and Resource Economics* 475, 483. See also K. Cross, 'King Cotton, Developing Countries and the 'Peace Clause': The WTO's Cotton Subsidies Decision' (2006) 9 *Journal of International Economic Law* 149, 159–162.

diversity in socioecological networks, this time in relation to the diversity of supply rather than production.

The validity of arguments connecting free trade in agricultural commodities with food security does not detract from the importance of supporting local farmers that may otherwise be unable to compete in a globalised industry so that they too contribute to the diversity of global food networks. It does, though, highlight the importance of striking a balance between opening global agricultural markets by ensuring free, or at least freer, trade and protecting small-scale local farmers, and their knowledge and traditions, through trade restrictions. Whether the WTO has succeeded in striking this balance in the right place from an agroecological perspective is debatable. The principal instrument governing trade in agricultural products in the WTO is the Agreement on Agriculture (AoA). Adopted in 1995 following contentious negotiations,[55] the AoA focuses on three issues: market access, domestic support for agricultural industries and export competition.[56] What is clear from the following analysis is that the law fails to appreciate that rules regarding a level-playing field between states impact the integrity of local socioecological networks. Protection is afforded to farmers, but this is contingent on their conformity with neoliberal practices.

### *Market Access*

Market access for agricultural products is promoted by the AoA limiting the types of import restrictions that states may impose. Non-tariff measures, such as quantitative restrictions and minimum import prices, had to be converted to tariffs,[57] and tariffs themselves had to be reduced over the Agreement's six-year implementation period beginning in 1995.

While concerns have been raised over how some states, and in particular the EU, engaged in a so-called 'dirty tariffication' process by inflating the value of their non-tariff restrictions so that they converted into a higher tariff level and thereby offered greater protection to domestic agricultural industries,[58] the AoA's measures on market access are generally considered to favour free trade over non-trade values such as food security and environmental protection.[59] This is partly due to how the Agreement has subsequently been confirmed by the WTO Appellate Body as applying to all non-tariff import restrictions. In the *Chile – Price Band System* dispute the Appellate Body held that Chile's price band system for certain imports was covered by Part III of the AoA,[60] despite this never being directly addressed

55 Trebilcock and others (n 11) 447–450.
56 Parts III, IV and V of the Agreement.
57 AoA, Article 4.2.
58 M. Ingco, 'Tariffication in the Uruguay Round: How Much Liberalisation?' (1996) 19 *World Economy* 425, 433–442.
59 F. Smith, 'Trade in Agriculture', in Bethlehem and others (n 14) 559.
60 *Chile – Price Band System and Safeguard Measures Relating to Certain Agricultural Products* WT/DS207/AB/R, 23 September 2002.

in the Uruguay Round negotiations, the relatively vague description of the type of measures that had to be converted to tariffs in the footnote to Article 4.2 of the AoA and that other states maintained similar price band systems.[61] In this respect, the AoA limits the extent to which states can protect the diversity of their domestic agricultural industries and other non-trade priorities associated with agroecology.

There are caveats to this, however. First, Article 5 of the Agreement sets out special safeguard measures, which allow states to impose additional, but time-limited, duties on imports in the event that either the quantity of the import of a certain product exceeds a trigger level, or the import price of a product falls below a trigger level.[62] While the quantitative nature of these means that they are of limited value in supporting states in protecting the environment, they do offer some means of protecting small-scale local farmers from the excesses of global markets, and thus help to maintain diversity within a state's agricultural industry.

Second, while the WTO Appellate Body has been uncompromising in the type of trade restrictions that must be converted to tariffs under Article 4.2 of the AoA, it has also recognised the potential legitimacy of arguments based on GATT Article XX justifying states' decisions to exempt specific measures for this requirement.[63] The dispute settlement bodies have also confirmed that states may pursue non-trade values through agricultural policy,[64] underpinning developing states' demands for a broader reconsideration of how non-trade values are balanced against the benefits of opening market access.[65] International consensus on this remains elusive, however, with some states believing that the law already goes too far in allowing market access to be restricted.[66]

***Domestic Support***

The above discussion indicates that the ability of states to pursue agroecological approaches to agriculture through its policies on market access largely rests on whether they can successfully defend such policies in the WTO dispute settlement process. They enjoy more discretion under the AoA's rules on domestic support to pursue policies in line with agroecology through, in particular, the so-called green box of domestic support measures. These are exempt from the general obligation

61 K. Bagwell and A. Sykes, 'Chile- Price Band System and Safeguard Measures Relating to Certain Agricultural Products' (2004) 3 *World Trade Review* 507, 527–528.

62 See *European Communities – Measures Affecting the Importation of Certain Poultry Products* WT/DS69/AB/R, 13 July 1998.

63 E.g., *Indonesia – Importation of Horticultural Products, Animals and Animal Products* WT/DS477/AB/R and WT/DS478/AB/A, 9 November 2017, although note that Indonesia was unsuccessful in arguing that Article XX applied in this dispute.

64 E.g., ibid and *Indonesia – Measures Concerning the Importation of Chicken Meat and Chicken Products* WT/DS484/R, 17 October 2017, in which the Dispute Panel recognised that policies designed to ensure a state's food security are not in and of themselves contrary to WTO law – para 7.679.

65 Smith (n 59) 562.

66 ibid 562–563.

to reduce domestic support on the grounds that they have only a minimal effect on trade.[67] Guidance on what measures are exempt is in Annex 2 of the Agreement and includes policies that support farmers to engage in environmental research programmes,[68] stockpile food for purposes of food security[69] and pursue conservation and other environmental objectives.[70] Permitting states to provide domestic support to farmers for such purposes clearly facilitates agroecological policies.

The WTO Dispute Panel and Appellate Body are receptive to arguments challenging trade-restrictive domestic support measures. A leading dispute on this issue is *United States – Subsidies on Upland Cotton*.[71] In brief, Brazil challenged long-standing domestic support and export control measures that benefitted cotton producers in the United States, the essence of their argument in relation to the domestic support measures being that they did not qualify as green box measures, and were therefore not protected from challenge under the Agreement on Subsidies and Countervailing Measures (the SCM Agreement)[72] by Article 13 of the AoA.[73] These arguments were broadly upheld by the Appellate Body.

The rejection of the United States' arguments in *United States – Subsidies on Upland Cotton* led Cross to suggest that the dispute might be a starting point for a realignment in the WTO in favour of developing states.[74] This has not materialised, at least not in relation to domestic support for agricultural production. In 2020, the International Institute for Sustainable Development (IISD) released a report on WTO Members' use of domestic support measures.[75] While the report acknowledges the importance of measures such as those contained in the green box, and that some states need to invest more to ensure that agricultural production is environmentally and socially sustainable,[76] it is also critical of the AoA's rules on domestic support and the way in which some states use them. It notes, for example, that direct payments to farmers to engage in activities permitted by the green box gives those farmers an unfair advantage over producers in other countries, and that the AoA overall has failed to achieve a significant reduction in the levels of domestic support provided by states.[77]

67 AoA, Article 6.
68 AoA, Annex 2, para 2(a).
69 ibid para 3.
70 ibid para 12.
71 WT/DS267/AB/R, 3 March 2005.
72 Text available at: https://www.wto.org/english/docs_e/legal_e/24-scm.pdf (last accessed 20/04/2023).
73 Article 13 is described as the 'peace clause' of the AoA, and is part of a compromise attributed with reconciling key differences between the United States and EU that threatened to end the negotiations without an agreement – Hoekman and Kostecki (n 47) 215–216.
74 Cross (n 54) 194.
75 J. Glauber and others, *What National Farm Policy Trends Could Mean for Efforts to Update WTO Rules on Domestic Support* (IISD, 2020).
76 ibid 31
77 ibid 29.

The IISD report can be criticised for focusing on the benefits of international trade and its role in assisting states in achieving the SDGs without recognising legitimate concerns over its negative environmental and socioeconomic impacts. On the other hand, from an agroecological perspective, the IISD's arguments are sound. It has been nearly 30 years since the AoA was adopted, and in that time society's understanding of the ecological crises it is facing, and the technology that drives and mitigates those crises, has evolved.

***Export Competition***

As with the rules on market access, an emphasis on free trade over other concerns can be seen in the AoA's provisions on export competition. Article 9 sets out export subsidies that were subject to reduction obligations for the implementation period, with limited scope for states to use export policies to pursue non-trade objectives.[78] Export subsidies are generally presented as contrary to the economic interests of importing and exporting states, due to how they distort ordinary commercial activity.[79] However, Janow and Staiger observe that the AoA adopts a slightly different position on who benefits from reductions in export subsidies. Noting the reference to 'the possible negative effects of the implementation of the reform programme on least-developed and net food-importing developing countries' in the Agreement's preamble, they suggest that increasing export competition by reducing subsidies is more in the interests of net exporters than net importers.[80] Their argument is based on an economic analysis showing how allowing states to apply export subsidies would harm the interests of competing net exporters but is advantageous to net importers. If their domestic markets could sustain the increased exports, their consumers would gain from the competition, and if they could not, then measures such as countervailing import tariffs would mitigate the impact of the subsidies while providing new revenue.[81] From an agroecological perspective, the advantage of such policies is that supporting local farmers to engage with global markets maintains the diversity of national agricultural systems by providing another means through which small farmers can be commercially viable in a globalised world, and increases the diversity, and therefore resilience, of global agricultural networks.

That the AoA calls for action that primarily benefits developed state net exporters reflects a broader tension in WTO agricultural policy between developed and developing states. The AoA's principal response to this is Article 16, which asks

78 E.g., *United States – Subsidies on Upland Cotton* (n 81) para 605–628. AoA, Article 10 and Annex L of the Draft Modalities for Agriculture TN/AG/W/4Rev.4, 6 December 2008. See further B. Karapinar, 'Defining the Legal Boundaries of Export Restrictions: A Case Law Analysis' (2012) 15 *Journal of International Economic Law* 443.

79 E.g., GATT, Article XVI. For analysis of the WTO's rules on export subsidies, see M. Janow and R. Staiger, 'Canada – Measures Affecting the Importation of Dairy Products and the exportation of Milk' (2004) 3 *World Trade Review* 277.

80 ibid 279–280

81 ibid 281.

states to implement the AoA in a manner that is compatible with the Marrakesh Decision on Measures Concerning the Possible Negative Effects of the Reform Programme on Least-Developed and Net Food-Importing Developing Countries.[82] The scope of this Decision is limited, however, and focuses primarily on the Agreement's implications for food aid programmes. Work continues improving the position of least-developed and net importing developing states, but progress remains slow.[83] In contrast, and evidencing the priority that is given to the interests of developed states under the WTO's agricultural rules, in 2015 a WTO Decision calling for the abolition of agricultural export subsidies was adopted.[84]

***Local and Indigenous Farmers***

Addressing the position of developing states under WTO agricultural rules is important, but limiting discussion of these rules' impact to the macroeconomic position of states fails to reflect that agriculture's socioecological networks are grounded at the local level. The measures described above offer some protection to local, indigenous and other small-scale farmers but it is only to the extent that they are able and willing to adapt their operations to align with the globalised market.[85] This is contrary to key elements of agroecological thinking, including promoting diversity in and between agricultural systems and protecting those systems' distinct knowledge and cultural bases.

Smith's proposal to enhance the position of indigenous farmers in the WTO is to recognise their role in protecting biodiversity and contributing to food security, and their corresponding rights to practice agriculture in their chosen manner, in the WTO's rules.[86] Although appealing in theory, in practice there would be significant obstacles. First, WTO law is primarily about the rights and obligations of states. While there has been some academic discussion of applying a doctrine of direct effect similar to that which characterises the EU's Single Market,[87] and there is growing debate over the extent to which WTO law should incorporate international human rights law,[88] there is nothing to suggest that a substantive body of individual rights is emerging in the WTO. Second, although in recent decades there has been greater recognition of the rights of indigenous peoples,[89] including in an

82 Text available at: https://www.wto.org/english/docs_e/legal_e/35-dag_e.htm (last accessed 20/04/2023).

83 G/AQ/W/227, 29 November 2022.

84 WT/MIN(15)/45 – WT/L/980, 19 December 2015.

85 F. Smith, 'Indigenous Farmers' Rights, International Agricultural Trade and the WTO' (2011) 2 *Journal of Human Rights and the Environment* 157, 168.

86 ibid 176.

87 H. Ruiz Fabri, 'Is There a Case – Legally and Politically – for Direct Effect of WTO Obligations?' (2014) 25 *European Journal of International Law* 151.

88 L. Bartels, 'Trade and Human Rights', in D. Bethlehem and others (eds), *Oxford Handbook on International Trade Law* (OUP, 2009).

89 S. Anaya and L. Rodríguez-Piñero, 'The Making of the UNDRIP', in J. Hohmann and M. Weller (eds), *The UN Declaration on the Rights of Indigenous Peoples: A Commentary* (OUP, 2018).

agricultural context,[90] this is another politically contentious area at the international level.[91] Third, while indigenous communities are an important constituency in agroecology, these are not the only small-scale farmers that are neglected in the WTO system. Protecting the rights of other local and subsistence farmers is just as important in promoting agroecology, but how you would define these entities in a legal instrument is unclear.

Instead, WTO agricultural rules, particularly on export competition and market access, should be rebalanced in favour of state discretion so that they can deliberately support agroecological policies. This could be achieved by including in the AoA specific exemptions from its obligations for measures intended to protect biodiversity, promote diversity in national agricultural networks and maintain local and indigenous knowledge, without necessarily engaging in the language of rights. The potential for abuse would remain, but the WTO dispute settlement bodies have, on balance, demonstrated an ability to properly scrutinise state policies so that those that genuinely pursue non-trade objectives are upheld.

Going further, it is necessary to more forcefully locate WTO law in its proper global and international legal context,[92] rather than accept its apparent primacy due to it being unashamedly about economic development and therefore reflective of states' priorities.[93] This has been made easier by the adoption of the SDGs, which present a more holistic vision of how society should develop.[94] Trade is inevitably an important part of this, and is directly relevant to several of the Goals,[95] but notably was not afforded a Goal itself.[96] Coupled with the comments above on how a revised principle of ecological sustainability could be advanced through WTO disputes and, as a corollary to this, wider international trade law, this would ensure that rules on trade in agricultural commodities actively facilitate agroecology.

## Regulating the Drivers of Zoonotic Disease

One consequence of the neoliberal transformation of the world order that has been pursued since the end of the Second World War is that international trade is no longer limited to the mere cross-border movement of goods. Instead, it

90 E.g., International Treaty on Plant Genetic Resources for Food and Agriculture, Rome, 3 November 2001, in force 29 June 2004, Article 9. Text available at: www.fao.org/plant-treaty/overview/texts-treaty/en/ (last accessed 20/04/2023).

91 See ch 2.

92 Boyle and Redgwell (n 20) 785.

93 N. Eisenmenger and others, 'The Sustainable Development Goals Prioritize Economic Growth Over Sustainable Resource Use: A Critical Reflection on the SDGs from a Socio-Ecological Perspective' (2020) 15 *Sustainability Science* 1101.

94 (n 15) Preamble.

95 E.g., SDGs 8 (decent work and economic growth); 10 (reduced inequalities); and 12 (responsible consumption and production).

96 SDG-17.10, however, calls for 'a universal, rules-based, open, non-discriminatory and equitable multilateral trading system under the World Trade Organisation'.

encompasses nearly every conceivable economic activity and sector.[97] This has negatively impacted the interactions between humans and other species. Scientists have long warned what the costs of this disturbance to the health and integrity of complex ecological systems might be,[98] including as a result of the negative environmental impacts of harmful agricultural practices.[99] Their concerns were realised in an almost sci-fi manner with the outbreak of COVID-19. While the precise origins of this virus remain contested, the most likely explanation appears to be that the virus first infected humans in a wildlife market in the Chinese province of Wuhan.[100] From there, it rapidly spread as a result of the movement of people between countries in a globalised world,[101] the virus's high mutation rate,[102] and a fatal combination of scientific uncertainty and political indecisiveness.[103]

In addition to the significant human and socioeconomic costs, the pandemic also revealed the limitations of international law in both preventing and responding to the global outbreak of a zoonotic disease. Multiple international organisations have the prevention of and response to zoonotic diseases as part of their remit.[104] Principal among these is the World Health Organisation (WHO). Following the more limited SARS pandemic, the WHO's 2005 International Health Regulations were adopted.[105] These have been criticised, however, for focusing more on

97 D. McRae, 'The Development of the Regulation of International Trade: The Past and the Future', in Bethlehem and others (n 14) 22.

98 E.g., O. Emre Can and others, 'Dealing in Deadly Pathogens: Taking Stock of the Legal Trade in Live Wildlife and Potential Risks to Human Health' (2019) 17 *Global Ecology and Conservation* e00515 and E. Balogun and others, 'Global Warming and the Possible Globalization of Vector-Borne Diseases: A Call for Increased Awareness and Action' (2016) 44 *Tropical Medicine and Health* 38.

99 T. Allen and others, 'Global Hotspots and Correlates of Emerging Zoonotic Diseases' (2017) 8 *Nature Communications* 1124, 5.

100 WHO-Convened Global Study of Origins of SAS-CoV-2: China Part, Joint WHO-China Study, 14 January–10 February 2021, available at: https://www.who.int/emergencies/diseases/novel-coronavirus-2019/origins-of-the-virus (last accessed 20/04/2023). An alternative hypothesis is presented in Office of the Director of National Intelligence, *Updated Assessment on COVID-19 Origins* (2021).

101 S. Keita, 'Air Passenger Mobility, Travel Restrictions, and the Transmission of the COVID-19 Pandemic Between Countries' (2020) *Covid Economics* 80.

102 K. Nguyen, 'Containing the Spread of COVID-19 Virus Facing to its High Mutation Rate: Approach to Intervention Using a Nonspecific Way of Blocking Its Entry into the Cells' (2022) 41 *Nucleosides, Nucleotides & Nucleic Acids* 778.

103 V. Singh, 'The Human Costs of COVID-19 Policy Failures in India' (2021) 5 *Nature Human Behaviour* 810; John Boswell and others, 'The Comparative 'Court Politics' of COVID-19: Explaining Government Responses to the Pandemic' (2021) 28 *Journal of European Public Policy* 1258; and A. Lavazza and M. Farina, 'The Role of Experts in the COVID-19 Pandemic and the Limits of Their Epistemic Authority in Democracy' (2020) 8 *Frontiers in Public Health* doi: 10.3389/fpubh.2020.00356.

104 A summary of different measures, and the wider political context in which they operate, is provided in J. Childs, 'Pre-Spillover Prevention of Emerging Zoonotic Diseases: What Are the Targets and What Are the Tools?', in J. Childs and others (eds), *Wildlife and Emerging Zoonotic Diseases: The Biology, Circumstances and Consequences of Cross-Species Transmission* (Springer, 2007).

105 WHO, *International Health Regulations (2005)* (3rd edn, 2016).

response than prevention.[106] While Article 2 includes 'to prevent [and] protect against' the international spread of disease in the purpose of the Regulations, the substantive measures it sets out primarily concern identification, notification and information-sharing.[107] Prevention is addressed in terms of preventing the spread of disease, rather than preventing their emergence.[108] The same can be said of the non-binding standards developed by the World Organisation for Animal Health to control zoonotic diseases.[109] The emphasis on preventing the spread of a disease, rather than its emergence, has led to measures that are not directly linked to activities that are undermining the ecological integrity of key natural systems.

That international trade in wildlife has been identified as a driver of zoonotic disease suggests that regulations controlling that trade might be of greater use in preventing their emergence and spread. In international environmental law, the most relevant instrument in this respect is the Convention on International Trade in Endangered Species of Fauna and Flora (CITES).[110] This operates through a listing mechanism whereby trade in species is prohibited or controlled depending on the Appendix in which it has been included.[111] CITES is of limited use in preventing the outbreak and spread of zoonotic diseases for three reasons, however. First, CITES only covers *international* trade in species,[112] and consequently has no relevance to the local wildlife market in which COVID-19 is suspected to have originated. Second, its listing criteria are primarily based on a species' extinction risk. There is no basis in CITES for restricting trade in a species because it is a potential source of zoonotic disease. This links to the third reason, which is that CITES' scope is limited to trade; it does nothing to directly address other human activities that increase the likelihood of a zoonotic disease emerging.[113]

Given the relative strengths of the WTO system compared to most environmental instruments, arguably the most significant agreement addressing the intersections between wildlife products, health and trade is the WTO Agreement on Sanitary and Phytosanitary Measures (SPS Agreement).[114] The SPS Agreement builds on the exception in Article XX(b) of the GATT by setting out conditions on which states may restrict trade for the purposes of protecting plant, animal and human

106 K. Woolaston, *Ecological Vulnerability: The Law and Governance of Human-Wildlife Relationships* (CUP, 2022) 201.

107 Parts II, III and V of the WHO Regulations (n 105).

108 E.g., ibid part IV.

109 https://www.woah.org/en/what-we-do/standards/codes-and-manuals/ (last accessed 20/04/2023).

110 Washington, 3 March 1973, in force 1 July 1975, 993 UNTS 243.

111 See Bowman and others (n 29) ch 15.

112 CITES, Article I(c).

113 Although it may indirectly address these, e.g. by reducing (lawful) demand for a species and thereby removing the incentive for people to engage in habitat disturbance and hunting to acquire specimens.

114 Text available at: https://www.wto.org/english/tratop_e/sps_e/spsagr_e.htm (last accessed 20/04/2023).

life and health.[115] Central to the Agreement is the need for a risk assessment,[116] taking into account relevant scientific principles,[117] and complemented by rules on international standards,[118] equivalence,[119] transparency,[120] and certification and inspections.[121]

Like the AoA, the SPS Agreement's risk assessment mechanism, and the way in which it has been applied by the WTO Appellate Body, has prioritised trade liberalisation over the ability of states to pursue other policy objectives through trade restrictions.[122] There must be 'sufficient scientific evidence' of a potential risk before states may adopt SPS measures.[123] If such evidence is not available, provisional measures may be adopted 'on the basis of available pertinent information' while the state acquires the information necessary to enable an 'objective assessment of [the] risk'.[124] Such measures must be reviewed 'within a reasonable time period'. Any SPS measures that are adopted must 'take into account the objective of minimising negative trade effects' and must not be 'more trade-restrictive than required to achieve their appropriate level of sanitary or phytosanitary protection, taking into account technical and economic feasibility'.[125] If another state considers an SPS measure to be unjustified on the basis of an objective assessment of the risk, the state imposing the measure must justify that measure.[126]

From an agroecological perspective, the SPS Agreement can be criticised in two respects. First, its approach to risk assessment denies the link between food products and local and traditional food cultures, instead emphasising the importance of objective scientific information.[127] As we saw in chapter 3, the concept of risk is more complex than this and is as much an exercise in political judgement as it is in scientific assessment. While true that the WTO's understanding of risk has matured in recent years, through recognition of the concepts of risk management and risk communication, these only go so far as to allow states to take into account

115 SPS Agreement, Article 2.1.
116 SPS Agreement, Article 5.
117 SPS Agreement, Article 2.2.
118 SPS Agreement, Article 3.
119 SPS Agreement, Article 4.
120 SPS Agreement, Annex B.
121 SPS Agreement, Annex C.
122 E.g., *European Communities – Measures Concerning Meat and Meat Products (Hormones)* WTDS26/AB/R; WT/DS48/AB/R, 16 January 1998. Note though that this does not mean that the Appellate Body is unaware of the limitations in requiring a scientific justification for policies intended to protect non-technical public values – M. Lee, *EU Regulation of GMOs: Law and Decision Making for a New Technology* (Edward Elgar, 2008) 202–203.
123 SPS Agreement, Article 2.2.
124 SPS Agreement, Article 5.7.
125 SPS Agreement, Articles 5.4 and 5.6.
126 SPS Agreement, Article 5.8.
127 M. Echols, 'Food Safety: Balancing SPS Scientific Principles and Article XX(b) Sovereignty', in Bethlehem and others (n 14) 699.

practices related to fair trade and not other non-trade public values based, inter alia, on cultural and environmental concerns.[128]

Similarly, the principal sources of international standards with which national SPS measures are encouraged to comply do not reflect the full range of values that agroecology identifies in agricultural systems and communities. Article 3.4 of the SPS Agreement lists these sources as the World Organisation for Animal Health, which as noted above is of limited use in protecting ecosystem integrity, the 1997 International Plant Protection Convention,[129] which focuses only on the economic values of (agro)biodiversity,[130] and the Codex Alimentarius Commission. The Codex, which is a joint initiative between the WTO and the UN Food and Agriculture Organisation (FAO) established in 1962, comprises a series of international food standards, compliance with which will generally protect the corresponding national measures from challenge under WTO law.[131] Consequently, and despite being non-binding, the Codex has consequently exerted considerable influence over national and regional food safety standards.[132] Standards have been adopted for a huge range of agricultural and food products.[133] In the past, these were commended for being agreed through a robust consultative process with states,[134] but more recent analysis identifies significant concerns with the Commission's procedures. George, for example, notes that the food industry is over-represented at Commission meetings, including in the delegations from developed states, and other groups, most notably consumer groups and developing states, lack the capacity to effectively engage with the negotiations.[135]

A further difficulty in relation to zoonotic disease is that again the Codex is of limited use when it comes to preventing the emergence of new diseases. Standards have been adopted for the handling of meat in wildlife markets as part of the Code of Hygienic Practice for Meat,[136] for example, which specifically address the risk

128 ibid 698.

129 In force 2 October 2005, amending the 1951 Convention (Rome, 6 December 1951, in force 3 April 1952, 150 UNTS 67, as revised by the FAO Conference in 1979). Text available at: https://www.ippc.int/en/core-activities/governance/convention-text/ (last accessed 20/04/2023).

130 See ch 2.

131 E.g., Article 2.4 of the Agreement on Technical Barriers to Trade – https://www.wto.org/english/docs_e/legal_e/17-tbt_e.htm (last accessed 20/04/2023).

132 A. Toma-Bianov, 'The Role of Codex Alimentarius Commission in Regulating Food Security at International and European Level' (2011) *Law Annals from Titu Maiorescu University* 71.

133 https://www.fao.org/fao-who-codexalimentarius/codex-texts/list-standards/en/ (last access 20/04/2023).

134 S. Shubber, 'The Codex Alimentarius Commission under International Law' (1972) 21 *International and Comparative Law Quarterly* 631.

135 A. George, 'An Unwelcome Seat at the Table: The Role of Big Food in Public and Private Standard-Setting and Its Implications for NCD Regulation' (2018) 18 *QUT Law Review* 156, 166. See also K. Pruchniewicz and T. Srogosz, 'The Codex Alimentarius Standards Decision-Making: Some Critical Remarks on an Ongoing Discussion' (2020) 6 *European Food and Feed Law Review* 571.

136 CAC/RCP 58-2005.

of zoonoses, but the application of these is limited to cross-border trade.[137] This observation applies equally to the broader measures in the SPS Agreement. Trade-related activities carrying an ecological and public health risk that occur within the territory of a single state largely escape international regulation.

***One Health***

The weaknesses of the international law and policy intended to prevent the emergence of zoonotic diseases have led to calls for a more unified and coherent policy response. These have resulted in renewed attention being given to the concept of One Health. Central to this is an understanding of the indivisibility of human, animal and environmental health, and the consequent need to address all three holistically in health decision-making.[138] This aligns clearly with agroecology and the recognition that agricultural systems comprise both natural and human entities that exert direct and indirect influence over each other. The high degree of compatibility between One Health and agroecology is further illustrated by the 2004 Draft Manhattan Principles on One World, One Health. These Principles highlight the importance of maintaining healthy and functioning ecosystems so as to prevent, rather than merely control, the outbreak of zoonotic diseases. They also call for the use of adaptative management approaches in environmental health policies and for broad stakeholder engagement in the development of these.[139]

The One Health concept has been adopted by a range of international organisations and an increasing number of national governments.[140] This includes the FAO, which considers the adoption of the One Health approach in food and agricultural policies to be essential if a future pandemic is to be avoided.[141] Various areas of the law are identified, but while each of these are important for pursuing One Health, and agroecology, what the FAO says about them suggests that there is little prospect of the reform necessary to put the ideas of One Health into meaningful effect. The FAO condones the SPS Agreement and its approach to risk, for example, which as shown limits states' ability to pursue non-trade agricultural policies and account for non-technical considerations in decision-making processes.[142] It also calls for the mainstreaming of biodiversity into food and agricultural policies and explicitly mentions agroecology in this regard. What the FAO fails to recog-

137 D. Taylor, 'Improving Wet Market Regulation to Control the Spread of Disease' (2021) 23 *Asian-Pacific Law and Policy Journal* 97, 113–114.

138 A. Davis and J. Sharp, 'Rethinking One Health: Emergent Human, Animal and Environmental Assemblages' (2020) 258 *Social Sciences & Medicine* 113093, 2.

139 https://oneworldonehealth.wcs.org/About-Us/Mission/The-Manhattan-Principles.aspx (last accessed 20/04/2023).

140 Woolaston (n 106) 204–208.

141 FAO and others, *White Paper: Build Back Better in a Post-COVID-19 World – Reducing Future Wildlife-Borne Spillover of Disease to Humans: Sustainable Wildlife Management (SWM) Programme* (FAO, 2020) Ch 2.

142 FAO, *One Health Legislation: Contributing to Pandemic Prevention through Law* (July 2020) 2–3.

nise, however, is the barriers to advancing agroecology through international law, including in instruments that it is responsible for, such as the International Treaty on Plant Genetic Resources for Food and Agriculture.[143]

More broadly, the One Health concept has been criticised for typically being defined in a way that takes no account of different communities' knowledge, traditions and experiences of agriculture, the wider environment and how these frame health policies. Davis and Sharp have consequently argued that as the concept is developed following the pandemic, greater efforts need to be made to locate understandings of One Health in local communities.[144] Building on this, it is possible to frame the One Health approach in more ecocentric terms, which to date has not been fully explored in the literature. There are numerous theories that reject the anthropocentricity that underpins social structures, including the law,[145] and humanity's wider perceptions of the natural world.[146] Most relevant to the current discussion is Lovelock's Gaia theory.[147] In brief, Lovelock presents the Earth as a single entity, comprising all living and non-living aspects of nature. Some of these aspects constitute Earth's vital organs, the proper functioning of which we undermine at our peril, in the same way that we risk our individual health if we damage our own vital organs.[148]

Taking this analogy forward, and without wishing to trivialise the human cost of the pandemic, it is possible to conceive COVID-19 as the Earth's immune system responding to the real virus that is harming the Earth – humanity's excesses. In certain respects, the virus proved effective at constraining these, at least in the short term. Air pollution and the emission of greenhouse gases were significantly, if only temporarily, reduced around the world as a result of lockdowns and the overall drop in human activity.[149] The reality is of course much more complex than this, and presenting COVID-19 as a response to human's effects on the natural world ignores that it is those states and communities that have the smallest environmental impact that have been worst affected by the pandemic.[150] Gaia theory does serve to underscore the cause-and-effect relationship between humanity's actions and the natural world, however.[151] It also speaks to a further point relevant to agroecology. Ideas of 'connection with nature', i.e. a person's awareness of the connections between themselves and their natural world and a wider affinity to nature,

143 ibid 5. See Chs 1 and 2.
144 Davis and Sharp (n 138).
145 Amos (n 13) Ch 1.
146 See Holder and Lee (n 8) 47–57.
147 J. Lovelock, *Gaia: A New Look at Life on Earth* (reprint edn, OUP, 2009).
148 ibid 119. Specific examples are given in ch 4–7.
149 Z. Venter and others, 'COVID-19 Lockdowns Cause Global Air Pollution Declines' (2020) 117 *PNAS* 18984.
150 C. Brockett and K. Woolaston, 'Environmental Justice and the Post-COVID-19 Regulation of Wildlife Trade and Markets' (2022) 13 *Journal of Human Rights and the Environment* 371.
151 Lovelock (n 147) 132.

are implicit in framings of agroecology's socioecological networks that comprise natural and human entities.

Ensuring that people have sufficient access to nature is important in terms of supporting their mental health and wellbeing,[152] but also in promoting the recognition of nature's non-anthropocentric values.[153] It may therefore be considered as laying the groundwork for the shift away from the anthropocentrism in wider societal perceptions of nature that is a prerequisite to the broader acceptance of the legitimacy of the principle of ecocentric theories, if not their details, and, perhaps more importantly, of driving reform of sustainable development towards ecological sustainability.[154]

One of the few positives of the lockdowns that were widely imposed to control the spread of COVID-19 is that they appeared to drive a renaissance in people's connection with nature. While the evidence is mixed on whether there has been a corresponding shift in environmental attitudes,[155] as noted, there is a clear link between a person's connection with nature and their perceptions of it.[156] Studies indicating that people's connection with nature increased during lockdowns, in part because of the restrictions on movement and indoor socialising,[157] suggest that there was potentially political space to begin to redefine the priorities for public policy as they are expressed through the economic hegemony of sustainable development, which could in turn have led to a reconsideration of the natural world's place within that paradigm.

Regrettably, this opportunity seems to have passed, at least in the United Kingdom. Natural England, the statutory body responsible for supporting the government's nature conservation policies, tracked peoples' attitudes towards and engagement with nature over the course of the pandemic through the People and Nature Survey.[158] Of particular relevance to the current discussion are the questions concerning connection with nature. Participants were asked how much they agreed or disagreed with three statements:

152 F. Williams, *The Nature Fix: Why Nature Makes Us Happier, Healthier, and More Creative* (W.W. Norton & Company, 2017).

153 S. Gagnon Thompson and M. Barton, 'Ecocentric and Anthropocentric Attitudes Toward the Environment (1994) 14 *Journal of Environmental Psychology* 149.

154 Amos (n 13) 234–239.

155 A. Colléony and others, 'Impacts of Nature Deprivations During the COVID-19 Pandemic: A Pre-Post Comparison' (2022) 268 *Biological Conservation* 109520.

156 C. Bruni and others, 'Measuring Values-Based Environmental Concerns in Children: An Environmental Motives Scale' (2012) 43 *Journal of Environmental Education* 1.

157 S. Friedman and others, 'Understanding Changes to Children's Connection to nature During the COVID-19 Pandemic and Implications for Child Well-Being' (2022) 4 *People and Nature* 155; P. Selvaraj and others, 'COVID-19: A Crisis or Fortune? Examining the Relationship between Nature Relatedness and Mental Wellbeing During the Pandemic' (2022) 8 *Heliyon* E09327; and S. Labib, 'Nature's Contributions in Coping with a Pandemic in the 21st Century: A Narrative Review of Evidence During COVID-19' (2022) 833 *Science of the Total Environment* 155095.

158 https://www.gov.uk/government/collections/people-and-nature-survey-for-england (last accessed 20/04/2023).

- Being in nature makes me happy
- I feel part of nature
- I am taking more time to notice and engage with everyday nature (e.g. listening to bird song, noticing butterflies)

In May 2020, at which point the United Kingdom had been in lockdown for approximately 10 weeks, 23% of respondents completely agreed that being in nature made them happy; 13% completely agreed that they felt part of nature; and 20% completely agreed that they were taking more time to notice and engage with nature. Only 1% of those who participated completely disagreed with each of the statements.[159] In April 2022, when the United Kingdom had been free from lockdown and virtually all other COVID regulations for nine months, 18% completely agreed that being in nature made them happy and 2% completely disagreed, 11% completely agreed that they felt part of nature and 3% completely disagreed, and 14% completely agreed that they took more time to notice nature and 3% completely disagreed.[160] There has been, therefore, a small but measurable decrease in the public's connection with nature.

The figures cited above are snapshots from a much larger data set. What they indicate, however, is that since life in the United Kingdom has returned to something resembling normality, the general public has grown more distant from the natural world. In some respects, this is understandable. With the pandemic 'over' in much of the world, in the sense that society has learnt how to live with the virus, attention has shifted to accountability for COVID-19 decision-making, particularly where this is perceived to have gone wrong, economic recovery for individuals, sectors and states, and other issues, not least the war in Ukraine. Reverting back to business-as-usual, however, which is contrary to both the One Health concept and agroecology, means that nature will continue to decline and that another zoonotic pandemic is virtually inevitable. Evidence also suggests that there is a positive correlation between an individual's connection with nature and the likelihood that they would comply with COVID regulations.[161] From a public health response perspective, it is therefore also in states' interest to actively support people's ability to connect with nature, and thereby foster the change in attitudes that would facilitate a wider societal shift towards accepting ecological sustainability, rather than sustainable development, as the paradigm for law and policy.

159 Data available from: https://www.gov.uk/government/statistics/the-people-and-nature-survey-for-england-monthly-indicators-with-specific-weight-for-april-2020-march-2021-official-statistics (last accessed 20/04/2023).

160 Data available from: https://www.gov.uk/government/statistics/the-people-and-nature-survey-for-england-monthly-indicators-for-march-2022-official-statistics (last accessed 20/04/2023).

161 S. Haasova and others, 'Connectedness with Nature and Individual Responses to a Pandemic: An Exploratory Study' (2020) 11 *Frontiers in Psychology* doi: 10.3389/fpsyg.2020.02215.

## Conclusions

The relationship between international trade and environmental concerns is often portrayed as a conflict. In reality, it is one of nuance, an observation that is just as relevant when considering whether international trade law is a help or a hindrance to advancing agroecology.

Following *United States – Shrimp*, there is no doubt space for states to justify agroecological policies that are contrary to their international obligations to ensure free trade. Further, that the Appellate Body has made it clear that WTO obligations can be reinterpreted in light of wider developments in international law suggests that if sustainable development was redefined in terms closer to ecological sustainability, this could influence the application of international trade rules in the future. The difficulty is that the broader legal and political structures of the WTO are not conducive to the wider principles and practices of agroecology. Efforts to open WTO decision-making processes to a broader range of stakeholders have produced little meaningful change, and international trade rules remain predominately focused on technical questions of economic effects.

This is evident in the AoA, the priority of which is not protecting the environment, maintaining the integrity and diversity of states' agricultural industries, or supporting individual farmers. Rather it is unashamedly intended to facilitate free trade in agricultural products, albeit while accepting that states pursue other legitimate priorities. What the AoA also reveals is the power imbalances inherent to international trade rules that undermine developing states and local communities in both global and sub-national socioecological networks. Ultimately, what we may conclude is that international trade law is relatively benign to environmental protection, and so in that respect may, conditionally, be said to support the ecological sustainability aspect of agroecology. What it does not do sufficiently, however, is promote the diversity in and between socioecological networks that is also central to theories of agroecology.

Legalistic debates over whether states can and should be able to exercise discretion to impose trade restrictions to achieve other policy objectives mask the more fundamental question of what international trade law reveals about society's fractured relationships with the natural world. International trade is a symptom of the neoliberal and sustainable development paradigms that have defined those relationships. The consequences of how unsustainable practices have undermined the ecological health and integrity of the planet became clear with COVID-19. While not comprehensive, the analysis in this chapter indicates that pre-existing rules focus too much on preventing the spread of zoonoses, and not enough on tackling the dangerous human behaviours that lead to those diseases emerging in the first place. Renewed attention on the One Health concept and its holistic approach to public and environmental health is therefore welcome, but evidence suggests that the way in which it is being taken forward, with reliance on pre-existing legal rules, will not lead to more systemic reform that could drive and be driven by agroecology. History may come to judge the greatest tragedy of the pandemic to be society's collective failure to transform that brief moment of reconnection with nature into a more sustained and fundamental realignment of humanity's relationships with the natural world.

# Part 4

# Agroecology in Society

# 12 Tracing a Path from Food Security to Food Justice

## Food (In)Security and International Law

Through its discussions of different features of the globalised world – transboundary environmental impacts, pervasive and persistent pollution and international trade – Part 3 revealed a system of laws that are driving ecological destructive behaviours to which the protection regimes discussed in Parts 1 and 2 appear ill-equipped to respond. This highlights that virtually every area of international law is connected to, and shapes, global and local agricultural networks, and is therefore relevant to the essential challenge of ensuring that everyone has enough to eat.

So far, this work has considered how agroecology might be advanced in international law primarily through a top-down approach. We have taken key areas of the law and considered their compatibility with agroecology, focusing on whether they align with the principle of ecological sustainability, support the natural and cultural integrity of socioecological systems and facilitate a systems-level approach to analysing challenges and their potential solutions. Another way to describe this would be to say that we have focused on processes – legal and ecological – and their implications for creating the local, national and international agricultural systems that can deliver long-term sustainability. In this chapter, a more-bottom-up approach is taken, starting from the position of the individual and considering how pursuing agroecology through the law can best ensure that they always have access to sufficient food. In doing so, the chapter highlights the conceit of labelling the fundamental changes that occurred in the latter half of the 20th century to how the world operates as 'globalisation'. In reality, neoliberal practices impact local communities, including those that are resistant to or marginalised from the globalised world.[1]

Our starting point for this analysis is Goal 2 of the Sustainable Development Goals (SDGs) – to achieve 'zero hunger' by 2030.[2] This is defined as individuals having access to sufficient and nutritious food.[3] Examining the sub-targets, there is a clear role for agroecology in delivering zero hunger. SDG-2.4 highlights

1 W. Twining, 'Law, Justice and Rights: Some Implications of a Global Perspective', in J. Ebbesson and P. Owoka (eds), *Environmental Law and Justice in Context* (CUP, 2009) 93.

2 A/RES/70/1, 21 October 2015.

3 SDGs 2.1 and 2.2.

DOI: 10.4324/9781003435174-17

the importance of 'resilient agricultural practices' that support ecosystems, while SDG-2.3 calls for a doubling in the productivity and income of small-scale and indigenous farmers. Diversity is promoted in SDG-2.5:

> By 2020, maintain the genetic diversity of seeds, cultivated plants and farmed and domesticated animals and their related wild species, including through soundly managed and diversified seed and plant banks at the national, regional and international levels, and promote access to and fair and equitable sharing of benefits arising from utilisation of genetic resources and associated traditional knowledge as internationally agreed.

A deadline of 2020 reflects a similar goal that was included in the Biodiversity Convention's 2020 Strategic Plan for Biodiversity,[4] which was missed,[5] rather than a statement on the urgency of the problem. Further, the target itself is flawed. Crop diversity collapsed during the last century and so to merely maintain, rather than actively develop, crop genetic diversity suggests either a failure to recognise the scale of the problem or an unwillingness to treat it seriously on the part of the international community.[6] Even this lower ambition of maintaining crop diversity has arguably gone unfulfilled, as notwithstanding regional and national differences, the consensus is that the genetic diversity of cultivated plants continues to decline.[7] The same conclusion has been reached regarding wild relatives of crop plants.[8]

The other SDG-2 sub-targets have a deadline of 2030 and so it is too soon to conclude whether they will be met. Current evidence is not encouraging, however.[9] States' apparent failure to deliver on SDG-2 raises fundamental questions about the international legal system. That other conservation targets are frequently missed can be attributed to the low priority that states appear to give their conservation commitments.[10] Ensuring the long-term viability of agriculture, however, relates to states' essential task of feeding their populations, suggesting that there are flaws in the systems through which they seek to achieve this. Biel explores this through the language of path dependency, whereby the failure to implement reforms to agricultural systems so that they become more sustainable is not due to a lack of political will but because actors in those systems have become trapped in

4 Rio de Janeiro, 5 June 1992, in force 29 December 1993, 31 ILM 822 (1992). Decision X/2, The Strategic Plan for Biodiversity 2011–2020 and the Aichi Biodiversity Targets, UNEP/CBD/COP/DEC/X/2, 29 October 2010, Annex, Target 13.

5 Secretariat to the Convention on Biological Diversity, *Global Biodiversity Outlook 5* (2020) 92.

6 See ch 2.

7 FAO, *The State of the World's Biodiversity for Food and Agriculture* (FAO Commission on Genetic Resources for Food and Agriculture, 2019) 115.

8 ibid.

9 FAO and others, *The State of Food Security and Nutrition in the World 2020: Transforming Food Systems for Affordable Health Diets* (FAO, 2020) 3.

10 R. Amos, *International Conservation Law: The Protection of Plants in Theory and Practice* (Routledge, 2020) ch 2.

unsustainable production methods.[11] Saab makes a similar point, arguing that it is neoliberal governance approaches that are undermining efforts to meet the world's food needs sustainably.[12]

The social imperative of ensuring that everyone has enough food has been given numerous labels in scholarship.[13] I focus on four: food security; the right to food; food sovereignty; and food justice.[14] While overlapping in certain respects, each has its own distinct characteristics in relation to its definition, as well as its actual and potential manifestation in international law. The central argument in this chapter is the premise that food security, the right to food, food sovereignty and food justice are progressively linked. Food justice enables the food sovereignty that communities must enjoy if they are to exercise their right to food to achieve food security. Each emphasises a different aspect of agroecological agenda, with the ideal of food justice in particular showing how broader social objectives can be achieved through agricultural policies that are grounded in agroecology.

## Food Security

Food security has been defined by the UN Food and Agriculture Organisation (FAO) as having, at all times, 'access to sufficient, safe and nutritious food that meets… dietary needs'.[15] This is mirrored in typical definitions of food insecurity, i.e. lacking the ability to regularly and safely acquire sufficient, nutritious food.[16] The inclusion of nutrition in food security is important, as it speaks to the quality of food that an individual can access, not just the quantity. In the section on food justice below, the concept of food deserts is raised, with one example being where the only accessible food for a community are convenience foods that are low in nutritional value.[17] Delivering the nutrition aspect of food security depends as much on

11 R. Biel, *Sustainable Food Systems: The Role of the City* (UCL Press, 2016) 75–77. The impact of intellectual property rules on farmers, discussed in Ch 2, is one example of this.

12 A. Saab, 'An International Law Approach to Food Regime Theory' (2018) 31 *Leiden Journal of International Law* 251, 258–264.

13 J. Sun, 'On Right to Adequate Food and Relevant Concepts from the Legal Perspective' (2017) 16 *Journal of Human Rights* 256.

14 Other, equally legitimate, labels include food democracy, food integrity and food access. See, inter alia, N. Orago, 'Commonification of Food as an Approach for the Achievement of Food Security and the Realisation of the Right to Food for All' (2020) 4 *Strathmore Law Journal* 1; G. Steier, *Advancing Food Integrity: GMO Regulation, Agroecology and Urban Agriculture* (CRC Press, 2020) ch 1; and N. Rosenberg and N. Cohen, 'Let Them Eat Kale: The Misplaced Narrative of Food Access' (2018) 45 *Fordham Urban Law Journal* 1091.

15 FAO, *Trade Reforms and Food Security: Conceptualizing the Linkages* (FAO, 2003) 29.

16 S. Anderson, 'Core Indicators of Nutritional State for Difficult-to-Sample Populations' (1990) 120 *Journal of Nutrition* 1555.

17 N. McClintock, 'From Industrial Garden to Food Desert: Demarcated Devaluation in the Flatlands of Oakland, California', in A. Alkon and J. Agyeman (eds), *Cultivating Food Justice: Race, Class, and Sustainability* (MIT Press, 2011).

social reforms as it does on rules regarding the mere provision of food and, as this chapter argues, agroecology is the most appropriate basis for these reforms.[18]

Delivering food security for the world's population is a core mission of the SDGs, relevant not just to the global goal to end world hunger but to the entire agenda.[19] It is therefore concerning, if not unsurprising, that the world is getting further away from achieving this. 1.9 billion people, roughly a quarter of the world's population, face moderate or severe food insecurity,[20] and this number is increasing.[21] Recent spikes in hunger and malnourishment have been attributed to the COVID-19 pandemic and Russia's invasion of Ukraine,[22] but the lack of progress cannot be blamed entirely on these events. A 2020 FAO report was already indicating that by 2030, around 10% of the human population would still suffer from food insecurity.[23] This suggests that there is a more fundamental contradiction in the legal and political structures that frame agricultural production so that measures that purportedly seek to ensure food security actually deliver the opposite.[24] The globalised, neoliberal system, in other words, is working against itself. I would take this further and argue that current systems drive food insecurity because they do not sufficiently support agroecological approaches to agricultural production. This becomes evident when we consider two issues already discussed in this work.

The first is the modernisation of agricultural production through, inter alia, mechanisation, industrialisation and the proliferation of monocultures.[25] As we saw in chapter 2, the Green Revolution succeeded in the short-term in improving impoverished communities' access to nutritious food following the Second World War.[26] It came at the cost, however, of the crop diversity essential for long-term food security, leaving individual farmers and wider food networks at risk from outbreaks of pests and diseases and sudden shifts in climate. Food security has been similarly undermined by the intellectual property rights (IPRs) over the majority of the world's agricultural seed supply being held by a handful of commercial entities, which has limited farmers' right to freely exchange seed to promote crop

18 R. Kerr and others, 'Agroecology and Nutrition: Transformative Possibilities and Challenges', in B. Burlingame and S. Dernini (eds), *Sustainable Diets: Linking Nutrition and Food Systems* (CABI, 2019).

19 R. Amos and others, *Living Sustainability in Higher Education: Connecting Communities, Learning and Justice* (2025, forthcoming) ch 6.

20 https://ourworldindata.org/hunger-and-undernourishment (last accessed 20/04/2023).

21 FAO and others, *The State of Food Security and Nutrition in the World: Repurposing Food and Agricultural Policies to Make Healthy Diets More Affordable* (FAO, 2022) ch 2.1.

22 ibid 10.

23 FAO and others (n 9) 3.

24 T. Gebrehiwot and others, 'Impact of Global Food and Agriculture Laws on Africa's Food Security' (2019) 52 *De Jure* 85.

25 J. Ikerd, 'Farm and Food Policies for a Sustainable Future' (2022) 6 *Business, Entrepreneurship and Tax Law Review* 34.

26 R. Evenson and D. Gollin, 'Assessing the Impact of the Green Revolution, 1960 to 2000' (2003) 300 *Science* 758.

diversity.[27] Changes in agricultural methods, such as the greater use of chemicals, have also had a devastating effect on the ecological systems on which agriculture depends.[28]

Second is the influence that neoliberalism has exerted over virtually all areas of international law and policy, highlighted in the previous chapter. Consequently, agriculture is no longer perceived as producing food to feed people, but to produce food to be traded on global markets. In other words, food has been deliberately commodified by states, with the operation of artificial constructs, i.e. markets, conditioning the very real need to feed people.[29] Coupled with the advantageous position developed states enjoy under international rules on agricultural trade,[30] the resulting distortions in production and supply have embedded food insecurity in some of the world's poorest communities.[31] Gebrehiwot et al., for example, question how global economic rules that have failed to deliver food security for Africa's current population can reasonably be expected to deliver food security for a much larger population in the future.[32]

Reversing these trends requires fundamental reform, with the most promising proposals drawing inspiration from agroecology. Challenging the commodification of food, Orago argues that because food is an asset on which the entire world depends and there is a general understanding of how its (mis)management impacts society as a whole, it is amenable to being governed as a global commons.[33] The value of commons approaches in advancing agroecology was highlighted in our discussion of the International Treaty on Plant Genetic Resources for Food and Agriculture's (PGRT) Multilateral System of Access and Benefit-Sharing.[34] This is the framework through which the genetic material of included crops may be accessed for purposes of the conservation and sustainable use of plant genetic resources for agriculture, with any benefits resulting from that access being shared primarily with farmers in developing countries through the mechanisms set out in Article 13 of the PGRT.[35]

27 S. Mahoney, 'Owning the World's Seed Supply: How Seed Industry Mergers Threaten Global Food Security' (2019) 31 *Georgetown Environmental Law Review* 564.

28 S. Tommasi, 'The Agri-Food Market and Eco-Oriented Consumer Law: Towards a New Model', in M. Monteduro and others (eds), *Law and Agroecology: A Transdisciplinary Dialogue* (Springer, 2015) 322.

29 A. Chadwick, 'World Hunger, the 'Global' Food Crisis and (International) Law' (2017) 14 *Manchester Journal of International Economic Law* 92.

30 F. Smith, 'Trade in Agriculture', in D. Bethlehem and others (eds), *The Oxford Handbook on International Trade Law* (2nd edn, OUP, 2022).

31 Y. Chen, *Trade Food Security, and Human Rights: The Rules of International Trade in Agricultural Products and the Evolving World Food Crisis* (Routledge, 2014) 73.

32 Gebrehiwot and others (n 24).

33 Orago (n 14) 31–37.

34 Rome, 3 November 2001, in force 29 June 2004. Text available at: https://www.planttreaty.org/index_en.htm (accessed 20/04/2023).

35 See ch 2.

The Multilateral System may be described as a regulatory manifestation of the connections between different socioecological networks and the actors within these. By establishing a commons over crop genetic resources, albeit only those in the public domain,[36] it empowers key stakeholders to maintain the diversity, and therefore sustainability, of their own agricultural system while also contributing to the diversity of others. The seminal text on commons is Hardin's *Tragedy of the Commons*, in which he argues that commons management will never be sustainable because the benefits of overexploitation accrue to individuals, while the costs are shared by all other users.[37] Ostrom rejects this, arguing that commons management can be sustainable where robust regulatory systems are in place.[38] The Multilateral System and its use of mandatory standard contracts arguably constitute such a system.

Orago's proposals go further than the Multilateral System as they apply not just to genetic resources but to the entire food production chain. There would consequently be a broader range of stakeholders, and therefore greater scope for conflicting interests, involved in the management of his food resource commons.[39] To overcome the challenges associated with this, Orago advocates grounding decision-making over agricultural production and distribution in local communities.[40] This is more fully explored in relation to food sovereignty below, but at this stage I make two points. First, this is considered a prerequisite in ensuring that commons are managed sustainably, as it ensures that local conditions and cultures are taken into account in decision-making processes.[41] Second, it is a response to the commercialisation of agricultural systems, which has seen small, local farms replaced with large-scale industrialised production.

For Ikerd, supporting local and small-scale farmers is essential in ensuring that agricultural systems have sufficient diversity to deliver long-term food security.[42] Part of this is, as we have seen throughout this work, protecting the distinct knowledge these farmers hold. This does not mean, however, that the ways in which small farms operate cannot themselves be reformed to strengthen the role they play in supporting agroecology. It has been suggested that in Western cultures, social understandings of 'the farm' reflect a White, middle-class and male-dominated stereotype. Support for small-scale, local farms should therefore be delivered in such a way as to maximise the diversity of those involved in agricultural systems,

36 C. Frison, *Redesigning the Global Seed Commons: Law and Policy for Agrobiodiversity and Food Security* (Routledge, 2019) ch 6.

37 G. Hardin, 'The Tragedy of the Commons' (1968) 162 *Science* 1243.

38 E. Ostrom, *Governing the Commons: The Evolution of Institutions for Collective Action* (CUP, 2015) ch 3. See also B. Weston and D. Bollier, *Green Governance: Ecological Survival, Human Rights, and the Law of the Commons* (CUP, 2013).

39 Orago (n 14) 37–38.

40 ibid.

41 Ostrom (n 38) 93–94.

42 Ikerd (n 25).

not just the systems themselves.[43] This is particularly relevant in those countries where there may be legal, cultural and other social barriers, such as lack of health and welfare support, to maximising participation in agricultural production.[44]

It is not just in the production of food where policies oriented towards modern, technological practices are undermining food security.[45] The same has been observed in relation to biodiversity conservation,[46] again as a result of the deliberate pursuit of neoliberal policies.[47] In both cases, it is the exclusion of alternative approaches to perceiving and managing humanity's relationships with the natural world, so that long-term ecological health and integrity are prioritised over short-term economic interests, that is at issue. The weaknesses of food security as a concept, resulting from how it has been implemented, have led some scholars to reject this as the appropriate language to frame discussions of how the goal of food security might be achieved.[48] Focus instead is now placed on concepts that speak more to the inherent links between individuals, communities and agricultural networks and are consequently a better reflection of agroecology.

## The Right to Food

One such concept is the human right to food, which reasserts that food is an essential need of humanity, not just a commodity. Our starting point for considering this right is Article 11 of the International Covenant on Economic, Social and Cultural Rights (ICESCR):

1. The States Parties to the present Covenant recognise the right of everyone to an adequate standard of living for himself and his family, including adequate food, clothing and housing, and to the continuous improvement of living conditions…[49]

It goes on to recognise 'the fundamental right of everyone to be free from hunger' and calls for improvements in the production, conservation and distribution of food

43 R. Rotman and S. Mendelson, 'Food, Freedom, Fairness and the Family Farm' (2022) 125 *West Virginia Law Review* 1.

44 I. Mugabi, 'Inclusive Participation of Persons with Disabilities in Aspects of Agroecology and Agrobiodiversity', in G. Steier and A. Cianci (eds), *Environmental Resilience and Food Law: Agrobiodiversity and Agroecology* (CRC Press, 2020) and J. Ezirigwe, 'Law as a Tool for Ensuring Contributions of Small-Scale Women Farmers to Food Security in Nigeria' (2018) 11 *Law and Development Review* 709.

45 N. Orago, 'Food Security and Access to Food: The Viability of a Rights-Based Approach to Food Sovereignty in Kenya' (2017) *East African Law Journal* 19.

46 K. Wilkinson Cross, 'Technological Innovations Tackling Biodiversity Loss: Solutions or Misdirection?' (2019) 1 *Law, Technology and Humans* 100.

47 G. Holmes and C. Cavanagh, 'A Review of the Social Impacts of Neoliberal Conservation: Formations, Inequalities, Contestations' (2016) 75 *Geoforum* 199.

48 Saab (n 12) 258–264.

49 16 December 1966, in force 3 January 1976, 6 ILM 360 (1967).

to achieve this. The explanatory note for Article 11 reveals a clear overlap with the concept of food security, as it states that the right to food will be realised 'when every man, woman and child, alone or in community with others, have physical and economic access at all times to adequate food or means for its procurement'.[50] It has consequently been suggested that genuine food security will only be delivered when the right to food is universally enjoyed.[51]

There are theoretical and practical issues to achieving this, however. Regarding the theoretical obstacles, doubts have been raised over whether socioeconomic rights qualify as 'proper' legal rights in the same way as civil and political rights, as they lack the same degree of justiciability.[52] This, though, speaks more of the flaws in the international legal system than in the validity of the right to food. Larking argues that ensuring adequate access to socioeconomic goods, such as food, education and housing, requires an approach to the redistribution of advantage that is contrary to the core, free market tenets of neoliberalism.[53] The issue, then, is not the nature of the right to food, but the systems in which it operates, which is evident in a number of countries.[54] In Indonesia, for example, food policies have been found to be inconsistent with the ICESCR's interpretation of the right to food because of the influence of international trade law within that legal system.[55]

The consequences of this incompatibility are evident when we consider the practical difficulties in recognising the right to food. In the same way that the achievement of SDG-2 depends on, and conditions, the achievement of other SDGs,[56] the right to food is inextricably linked to other rights. Many of these, such as the right to water, which was notably not included in Article 11 of ICESCR but has subsequently been read into it,[57] present their own difficulties, particularly in countries where fresh water is increasingly scarce.[58] Ultimately, what links such rights is that they are contingent on humanity's exploitation of the natural world being sustainable,[59] in an ecological sense but also in terms of human wellbeing.

50 CESCR General Comment No. 12: The Right to Adequate Food (Art. 11) (E/C.12/1999/5, 12 May 1999) para 6.

51 N. Lambek and P. Claeys, 'Institutionalizing a Fully Realized Right to Food: Progress, Limitations, and Lessons Learned from Emerging Alternative Policy Models' (2016) 40 *Vermont Law Review* 743

52 A. Neier, 'Social and Economic Rights: A Critique' (2006) 13 *Human Rights Brief* 1. For an overview of this debate, and response specifically in relation to the right to food, see S. Raponi, 'A Defense of the Human Right to Adequate Food' (2017) 23 *Res Publica* 99.

53 E. Larking, 'Human Rights Rituals: Masking Neoliberalism and Inequality, and Marginalizing Alternative World Views' (2017) 32 *Canadian Journal of Law & Society* 1, 7–11.

54 Lambek and Claeys, (n 51).

55 A. Zazili and others, 'Construction of Food Law Based on Rights Approach to Realize the Right to Food' (2022) 30 *Technium Social Sciences Journal* 292, 297.

56 Amos and others (n 19).

57 CESCR General Comment No. 15: The Right to Water (Arts. 11 and 12 of the Covenant) (E/C.12/2002/11, 20 January 2003) para 3.

58 M. Kidd, 'The Right to Access to Water in South Africa', in Y. Le Bouthillier and others, *Poverty Alleviation and Environmental Law* (Edward Elgar, 2012).

59 General Comment 12 (n 50) para 7.

Agricultural policies affect more than just rights to food and water. The use of pesticides impacts the right to health, for example, and rights of access to justice where legal systems are not conducive to holding multinational pesticide producers to account.[60] As we saw in relation to indigenous peoples in chapter 4, there are implications for the cultural rights of marginalised communities as well. Following this reasoning, we can begin to see the wider nexus between different rights, with the right to food at its core, as mirroring the relationships, positive and negative, that exist between the SDGs. This is an idea that is beyond the scope of this work but finds support in literature that identifies common threads in SDG and human rights discourse.[61]

The value of human rights, and the right to food specifically, in advancing agroecology and wider sustainability reforms in agricultural systems is not just contingent on their translation into justiciable legal standards. There is an important distinction between human rights as legal constructs and human rights as a tool in political discourse.[62] Even in the absence of a formally recognised right, to claim that an individual or community's right to food is being violated can rally public support and ultimately lead to policy change.[63] Following this reasoning, and reflecting scholarship that shows human rights,[64] and environmental rights in particular, to be continuously evolving,[65] we can characterise the right to food as it exists in instruments such as the ICESCR as progress to date, while the political discourse represents ambitions for further advancement.

The language of the right to food is consequently a means of empowering disadvantaged members of socioecological networks and wider society to drive the political agenda towards agroecology and greater sustainability. Such reform is contingent on three factors, however. First, the argument of industry lobbyists that using human rights in this way diminishes political debate because of their claim to higher moral authority leaves little room for compromise must be rejected.[66] This is merely a concealed defence of the neoliberal systems that treat access to food as a commodity and not an essential need. Associated with this is the need to reform

60 C. Terwindt and others, 'Health Rights Impacts by Agrochemical Business: Legally Challenging the Myth of Safe Use' (2018) 34 *Utrecht Journal of International and European Law* 130.

61 L. Collins, 'Sustainable Development Goals and Human Rights: Challenges and Opportunities', in D. French and L. Kotzé (eds), *Sustainable Development Goals: Law, Theory and Implementation* (Edward Elgar, 2018).

62 L. Cotula, 'Between Hope and Critique: Human Rights, Social Justice and Re-Imagining International Law from the Bottom Up' (2020) 48 *Georgia Journal of International and Comparative Law* 473.

63 Raponi (n 52) 112.

64 And increasingly non-human rights as well – J. Guayasamin and others, 'Biodiversity Conservation: Local and Global Consequences of the Application of "Rights of Nature" by Ecuador' (2021) 7 *Neotropical Biodiversity* 541.

65 S. Bogojevic and R. Rayfuse (eds), *Environmental Rights in Europe and Beyond* (Hart Publishing, 2018).

66 G. Steier, 'Rights-Based International Agroecological Law', in Steier and Cianci (n 44) 46.

laws and decision-making processes, along lines proposed throughout this book, so that they facilitate agroecological approaches to agriculture.[67]

Third, it is important to not interpret the right to food as a right to be fed, but rather as the right to feed oneself in the manner one chooses.[68] Communities and individuals must enjoy a degree of agency over their food choices if the right to food is to be respected. They must, in other words, enjoy food sovereignty, and it is in the pursuit of this that the necessity of framing agricultural policies in agroecology to achieve genuine food security becomes evident.

## Food Sovereignty

Food sovereignty, perhaps more than any other food concept, has proven difficult to define.[69] This is because it speaks less to whether someone has access to sufficient food and more to how they have access to sufficient food. One definition commonly cited in the literature, and which will form the framework for the analysis in this section, comes from the Declaration of Nyéléni, adopted by the 2007 World Forum for Food Sovereignty (WFFS). It begins by stating:

> Food sovereignty is the right of peoples to healthy and culturally appropriate food produced through ecologically sound and sustainable methods, and their right to define their own food and agriculture systems... It ensures that the rights to use and manage our lands, territories, waters, seeds, livestock and biodiversity are in the hands of those of us who produce food.[70]

Clear from this is that food sovereignty is grounded in the language of rights,[71] of individuals but also of communities. One way to understand food sovereignty, therefore, would be as an individual and community's *capacity* to exercise the right to food. Importantly, this means that communities should not just have agency in agricultural policies, but in all areas that impact their ability to enjoy the right to food.[72]

The characterisation of food sovereignty as being exercised by communities exposes further the limitations of the international legal system in actually delivering food security. As we observed in chapter 4, key human rights instruments have proven resistant to recognising the rights of communities, especially if those communities do not represent an indigenous people. It is this empowering of

67 ibid 45.

68 Raponi (n 52) 102.

69 R. Patel, 'What Does Food Sovereignty Look Like?' (2009) 36 *Journal of Peasant Studies* 663.

70 Text available at: https://nyeleni.org/IMG/pdf/DeclNyeleni-en.pdf (last accessed 20/04/2023).

71 H. Haugen, 'Food Sovereignty – An Appropriate Approach to Ensure the Right to Food?' (2009) 78 *Nordic Journal of International Law* 263.

72 S. Theriault, 'The Food Security of the Inuit in Times of Change: Alleviating the Tension between Conserving Biodiversity and Access to Food' (2011) 2 *Journal of Human Rights and the Environment* 136.

communities, however, that highlights the mutual relevance of food sovereignty and agroecology. Both recognise the role of socioecological networks in managing agricultural processes and the different natural elements on which these depend. That this management should be conducted in a way that does not undermine the health and integrity of agricultural and associated ecosystems further highlights the links between agroecology and food sovereignty.

The emphasis on ecologically sustainable agriculture grounded in local communities has led to food sovereignty being characterised as a response to the limitations of food security resulting from that concept's capture by neoliberal institutions.[73] This perception is reinforced by its critics labelling food sovereignty as merely disguising protectionist policies that hinder free trade[74] and is reflected in the WFFS definition:

> [Food sovereignty] puts those who produce, distribute and consume food at the heart of food systems and policies rather than the demands of markets and corporations… It offers a strategy to resist and dismantle the current corporate trade and food regime, and directions for food farming, pastoral and fisheries systems determined by local producers.[75]

For many scholars, it is this rejection of the neoliberal rules and structures that enable unsustainable practices that is at the heart of food sovereignty. This enabling of unsustainability manifests in different regulatory contexts. In Hungary, for example, significant restrictions on who may purchase legal title over agricultural land, maintained to facilitate a range of social policy objectives, resulted in enforcement action by the European Commission as they were considered to violate the EU's rules on free movement of capital.[76] IPRs over seeds are another example, with Jefferson and Adhikari highlighting how these protect a small number of commercial entities at the expense of the ability of local communities to exercise control over what they produce and how they produce it.[77]

Like the right to food, food sovereignty constitutes a powerful strategy for shaping political discourse to challenge rules that reflect neoliberalism. It has, for example, shaped debates in Ecuador and Nepal so that farmers' right to freely exchange

73 European Coordination Via Campesina, *Food Sovereignty Now! A Guide to Food Sovereignty* (ECVC, 2018) 4–7.

74 I. Marković and M. Marković, 'Agricultural Protectionism of the European Union in the Conditions of International Trade Liberalization' (2014) 61 *Ekonomika Poljoprivede* 423, 424.

75 Declaration of Nyéléni (n 70).

76 M. Csirszki and others, 'Food Sovereignty: Is There an Emerging Paradigm in V4 Countries for the Regulation of the Acquisition of Ownership of Agricultural Lands by Legal Persons?' (2021) 2 *Central European Journal of Comparative Law* 29, 31–34. Case C-235/17 *Commission v Hungary (Usufruct Over Agricultural Land)* ECLI:EU:C:2019:432.

77 D. Jefferson and K. Adhikari, 'Reimagining the Relationship between Food Sovereignty and Intellectual Property for Plants: Lessons from Ecuador and Nepal' (2019) 22 *Journal of World Intellectual Property* 396.

seed is recognised alongside the commercial rights of plant breeders.[78] As we saw in chapter 2, this is an essential step in advancing agroecology through the law. Even in states where IPRs are not qualified in this way, food sovereignty brings together different stakeholders through initiatives that reflect agroecology. Seed libraries in the United States are partnerships between community gardens and farmers, through which farmers 'borrow' crop seed from the library, produce the crop and return some of that seed to the library at the end of the season.[79]

The difficulty with using food sovereignty as a discursive strategy is that on one level, it is inherently contradictory. This is evident in the WFFS definition, as placing 'those who produce [and] distribute... food at the heart of food systems and policies' means including the multinational corporations that are considered responsible for undermining long-term food security and sustainability in discussions of food sovereignty.[80] Following an agroecological understanding of agriculture, however, such entities will inevitably form part of its socioecological networks. The point of pursuing food sovereignty as the means to achieve food security is that the relationship between local communities and globalised corporations would be reversed. Rather than the local having to conform to the demands of neoliberal free markets, regardless of what this means for their cultures, environments and economies, it would be the globalised that would have to adapt so as to accommodate this essential diversity in value-led policymaking and ways-of-doing.

Despite its rejection of neoliberalism, food sovereignty is not wholly incompatible with the current overarching frameworks of law and policy. The WFFS definition draws on key principles and interpretations of sustainable development:

> [Food sovereignty] *defends the interests and inclusion of the next generation.* [It] prioritises local and national economies and markets and empowers peasant and family-driven agriculture, artisanal-fishing, pastoralist-led grazing, and food production, distribution and consumption based on *environmental, social, and economic sustainability.*[81] (emphasis added)

The three-pillar conception of sustainable development has been criticised in this work for legitimising the prioritisation of economic development over environmental protection and social equity. That food sovereignty is a response to the failings of neoliberal policies, however, suggests that references to sustainability in this context should be read as meaning something closer to ecological sustainability, again highlighting the relevance of agroecology. More interesting is the reference to the 'interests and inclusion of the next generation'. 'Interests' suggests something

78 ibid.

79 U. Ramsay, 'Seed Libraries and Food Justice: Cultivating an Effective Legal and Policy Environment' (2018) 25 *Georgetown Journal on Poverty Law and Policy* 193.

80 Patel (n 69) 666–667.

81 Declaration of Nyéléni (n 70)

other than the 'needs' referred to by the World Commission on Environment and Development.[82] Food sovereignty, in other words, requires consideration not just of future generations' basic requirements, but their capacities to meet those requirements in a preferred manner. Following this, 'inclusion' raises the prospect of incorporating the interests of future generations in decision-making so that those capacities can be guaranteed. This presents obvious difficulties but is not unheard of in the law. Section 5 of Wales's Well-being of Future Generations Act 2015 requires public bodies to balance the fulfilment of short-term needs with the long-term sustainability implications of actions taken to achieve these. Although not expressed in the language of sovereignty, this demonstrates that it is possible for the law to mandate the consideration of future generations' interests.[83]

Food sovereignty's adoption of the principle of intergenerational equity introduces further questions of justice and the tensions that may arise when the interests of the present conflict with the interests of the future. A central argument in this book has been that local and traditional agricultural practices should be protected because they contribute to the diversity that is central to agroecology. Some of these cultural practices, however, can be inherently unsustainable. The hunting of bushmeat for subsistence purposes is an illustration of this, with the taking of traditionally targeted but endangered species undermining efforts to conserve biodiversity and exposing society to zoonoses such as Ebola and COVID-19.[84] Practices associated with agroecology again provide a way forward in such scenarios, with evidence showing how engaging with these stakeholders can result in new partnerships that address their contemporary concerns and enhance the biodiversity that is vital to the interests of future generations.[85]

Intragenerational justice is also closely associated with food sovereignty, as the WFFS shows:

> Food sovereignty promotes transparent trade that guarantees just income to all peoples and the rights of consumers to control their food and nutrition. Food sovereignty implies new social relations free of oppression and inequality between men and women, peoples, racial groups, social classes and generations.[86]

Ensuring gender, racial and class equality to enable all people to effectively participate in agriculture's socioecological networks is just as important to the diversity underpinning agroecology as the natural diversity in and between agricultural

82 World Commission on Environment and Development, *Our Common Future (The Brundtland Report)*, A/42/427, 4 August 1987, 54.

83 H. Davies, 'The Well-Being of Future Generations (Wales) Act 2015: Duties or Aspirations?' (2016) 18 *Environmental Law Review* 41.

84 R. Agbor and W. Elangwe, 'Indigenous Peoples and Agrobiodiversity in Africa', in Steier and Cianci (n 66) 86–92.

85 ibid 92–101.

86 Declaration of Nyéléni (n 70).

systems. The WFFS definition goes beyond this, however, and speaks to wider questions of justice between different social demographics. We can criticise legal mechanisms that are hallmarks of neoliberal systems in this regard. In many developing state communities, the principal role of women in agriculture was to own the seed stock. Replacing native crops with genetically modified seeds subject to the IPRs of major commercial entities removed this position of power that women enjoyed in what are otherwise typically patriarchal societies.[87] This reinforces the proposition that food sovereignty, itself a prerequisite of the effective implementation of the right to food that is necessary if people are to have genuine food security, depends on individuals and communities enjoying food justice.

## Food Justice

Food is a focal point for debates over justice and sustainability, particularly in the context of the apparent dichotomy between food sovereignty, which is grounded in empowering 'the local', and the globalised systems that purportedly aim towards food security. Justice, much like sustainability, is in some ways a highly nebulous concept, subject to extensive academic discussion and debate.[88] On the other hand, and again in concert with sustainability, it is relatively simple: justice can be obvious when it exists and conspicuous by its absence when it does not. In this chapter, justice advances our discussion of food sovereignty and concerns over where power over food systems should lie to address the respective capacities of different demographics to exercise that power. It cannot be assumed that just because the right to food has been implemented in a way that gives agency to communities, every member of that community will be able to exercise that agency freely and equally. There are other obstacles, relating to the character of the food system or socioecological network in which a person resides and broader social inequalities that condition an individual's ability to engage with social processes. This is reflected in Just Food's definition of food justice, which, like the definition of food sovereignty discussed above, reflects core elements of agroecology:

> [C]ommunities exercising their right to grow, sell, and eat [food that is] fresh, nutritious, affordable, culturally appropriate, and grown locally with care for the well-being of the land, workers and animals.[89]

87 P. Paul and K. Mukhopadhyay, 'Growth via Intellectual Property Rights Versus Gendered Inequity in Emerging Economies: An Ethical Dilemma for International Business' (2010) 91 *Journal of Business Ethics* 359.

88 For an environmental perspective of some of the principal theories, see S. Coyle and K. Morrow, *The Philosophical Foundations of Environmental Law: Property, Rights and Nature* (Hart Publishing, 2004).

89 justfood.org, cited in J. Agyeman, *Introducing Just Sustainabilities: Policy, Planning and Practice* (Zed Books, 2013) 62. The reference to animals raises the issue of justice for the non-human members of a socioecological network, which I do not have space to explore here. See instead S. Wise,

Food has emerged as one of the principal areas in which the public readily engages in questions of sustainability.[90] This is arguably because how people engage with food on a daily basis is different to their experiences of, for example, the impacts of global biodiversity loss or their carbon footprint.[91] When someone opts to follow a food philosophy, such as veganism, they are doing more than merely following a lifestyle. Such choices reflect their personal values and beliefs and can be a measure of how an individual perceives the universality of justice in society.[92] The role of individuals in socioecological networks is, therefore, not just as the final consumer of agricultural products. Rather, the choices they make influence what is produced, how it is produced and who produces it.

Localism is one food philosophy where this is especially evident. Local food is generally considered to be healthier, more nutritious and entailing a much smaller environmental footprint.[93] It is also linked with enabling consumers to make socially and environmentally ethical choices through the transparency that comes from being able to watch food being produced on the local farm.[94] It is necessary, however, to unpack what it meant by 'local' to fully appreciate its implications for food justice and the wider sustainability of agriculture's socioecological networks.

First, there is nothing inherently just about 'buying local', and rather than respond to social inequalities this may further undermine those who are already disadvantaged in global neoliberal structures. Farmers in developing countries that sell products in developed markets typically enjoy greater wellbeing than their counterparts because of the higher workplace standards expected by Western supermarket chains.[95] Choosing not to purchase imported products in the name of localism consequently risks undermining the welfare of some of the world's poorest farmers.[96] Neither can it be assumed that locally produced food will be more sustainable, as the local family farm can be just as likely to use environmentally harmful methods as the producers of imported food in the supermarket.[97]

There is also a danger that in presenting localism as the alternative to globalisation, the distinctions between local communities, and the different ways they interact with each other and the wider natural and human world, are lost.[98] This reflects

'An Argument for the Basic Legal Rights of Farmed Animals' (2008) 106 *Michigan Law Review First Impressions* 133.

90 Agyeman, ibid 59.

91 Amos and others (n 19).

92 A. Lee, 'The Milkmaid's Tale: Veganism, Feminism and Dystopian Food Futures' (2019) 40 *Windsor Review of Legal and Social Issues* 27.

93 Agyeman (n 89) 60.

94 Tommasi (n 28) 327.

95 P. Cross and others, 'Does Farm Worker Health Vary Between Localised and Globalised Food Supply Systems?' (2009) 35 *Environmental International* 1004.

96 Amos and others (n 19).

97 B. Born and M. Purcell, 'Avoiding the Local Trap: Scale and Food Systems in Planning Research' (2006) 26 *Journal of Planning Education and Research* 195.

98 C. Hinrichs, 'The Practice and Politics of Food System Localization' (2003) 19 *Journal of Rural Studies* 33.

research demonstrating how communities that inhabit the same physical place do not necessarily occupy the same social space.[99] Failing to recognise this can lead to the further marginalisation of vulnerable demographics.[100] There is also significant divergence in the just food movement, with people from different backgrounds demonstrating contrasting, occasionally conflicting, understandings of the principal societal ills and the appropriate remedies. Affluent, typically White, communities tend to focus on ecological issues relevant to their food choices. For poorer ethnic communities, in contrast, discussions of food justice centre on concerns of broader social justice, and how the (un)availability of culturally appropriate and nutritious food constitutes another manifestation of racism and discrimination.[101]

Similar observations can be made in relation to other issues that are closely associated with food systems. There is an important nexus between food, water and energy, as each depends on an overlapping natural resource base,[102] which combined constitute important elements of the ecological basis of agricultural networks. The unsustainable rate at which these resources are being depleted presents a growing barrier to disadvantaged communities to accessing what are considered to be the basic essentials of life.[103]

What this underscores is that food justice, as with the other food concepts discussed in this chapter, is inherently linked to the SDGs. Drawing on environmental justice literature, these links provide further insight into why neoliberal systems are failing to deliver meaningful food security. Food justice is closely associated with environmental justice. Due to the commonalities between the causes of food and environmental injustice, including the unsustainable and inequitable rates of natural resource use referred to above,[104] food justice has been considered as emerging from environmental justice, alongside other concepts such as climate and ecological justice.[105] It is important to remember, though, that the food justice movement has its own unique origins, agenda and challenges, with stakeholders holding different views over the social reforms that would be most effective at improving food justice.[106]

99 P. Street, 'Spaces of Diversity in Diverse Spaces', in J. Holder and C. Harrison (eds), *Law and Geography* (OUP, 2003).

100 Agyeman (n 89) 64.

101 A. Alkon, *Black, White, and Green: Farmers Markets, Race and the Green Economy* (University of Georgia Press, 2012) ch 7.

102 Amos and others (n 19).

103 JRC, *Position Paper on Water, Energy, Food and Ecosystems (WEFE) Nexus and Sustainable Development Goals (SDGs)* (EU, 2018) 13.

104 Others include the systematic racism that was identified in local planning procedures in the United States, where the environmental justice movement first emerged. See United Church of Christ's Commission for Racial Justice, *Toxic Wastes and Race in the United States* (1987).

105 C. Gonzalez, 'Food Justice: An Environmental Justice Critique of the Global Food System', in S. Alam and others (eds), *International Environmental Law and the Global South* (CUP, 2015) 402.

106 N. Hassanein, 'Practicing Food Democracy: A Pragmatic Politics of Transformation' (2003) 19 *Journal of Rural Studies* 77.

A detailed discussion of environmental justice is beyond the scope of this work. For current purposes, it is sufficient to note that it comprises three basic elements: distributive justice, procedural justice and recognition. In a nutshell, the distributive aspect considers whether environmental goods and harms, and the costs of these, are distributed fairly across society; procedural justice relates to who has a say in environmental decision-making and ensuring that decision-making processes facilitate maximum participation; and recognition concerns how the social, cultural and institutional differences within and between communities are accounted for in the pursuit of distributive and procedural justice.[107] We can see examples of each from previous chapters, and how they are linked to food injustices and the failure of international legal systems to adequately address these. A demonstration of how environmental goods and harms are not distributed fairly across society is climate change. As we observed in chapter 8, it is small island and the least developed states that are most at risk from climate change, despite contributing least to its causes.[108] Not only is this undermining the ecological viability of their agricultural systems, but as a consequence is fracturing their wider society through the growing phenomenon of climate migration. Regarding procedural justice, we saw in chapter 9 how different theories on the purpose of public participation underpin environmental assessment.[109] Allowing a broad range of stakeholders to contribute information to administrative processes in a meaningful way, and decision-makers genuinely taking this into account, is central to ensuring that socioecological networks develop in a way that maintains the ecological and cultural diversity on which sustainable agriculture relies. Finally, and returning to the discussion at the start of this section, there is an important distinction between localism as the framing of debates over justice and sustainability in agricultural systems so that the wider connections between socioecological networks, including on a global level, are ignored, and localism as enabling communities to participate in global networks in a manner that recognises and respects their distinct cultures and traditions. Maintaining this diversity, through measures to protect local and traditional knowledge such as those discussed in chapter 2, is again central to agroecology.

Gellers and Cheatham argue that states' implementation of the SDGs has focused more on the distributive aspect of environmental justice and neglected its procedural and recognition aspects.[110] The same can be observed in relation to food justice, with the food security paradigm favoured by neoliberal structures prioritising equal access to food, through the operation of the free market, over deeper questions of how choices made over production and consumption of food

107 D. Schlosberg, *Defining Environmental Justice: Theories, Movements, and Nature* (OUP, 2007) Ch 2.

108 E. Posner and D. Weisbach, *Climate Change Justice* (Princeton University Press, 2020) Ch 1.

109 J. Holder, *Environmental Assessment: The Regulation of Decision Making* (OUP, 2004) 23–29.

110 J. Gellers and T. Cheatham, 'Sustainable Development Goals and Environmental Justice: Realization through Disaggregation' (2019) 36 *Wisconsin International Law Journal* 276.

reflect cultural and social relations.[111] It is therefore necessary to consider how all aspects of food justice might be better achieved so as to add meaning to the food sovereignty necessary for communities to exercise their right to food in a manner that would achieve genuine food security. Various initiatives have been adopted by different communities responding to specific challenges, but what connects them is how they also promote agroecology.

Farmers in some regions of the Western world now grow crops familiar to ethnic communities in their local networks.[112] As well as making commercial sense, this alleviates the problem of food deserts, i.e. areas in which communities have limited or no access to nutritious and culturally appropriate food, typically because they are in low-income or rural areas that are unattractive to supermarkets.[113] From a strictly ecological perspective, the introduction of new crops is potentially problematic. This constitutes the deliberate introduction of an alien species, the impacts of which on native agrobiodiversity will, initially at least, be unknown.[114] Applying agroecology, however, enables us to reconcile such practices with ideas of ecological sustainability because of its emphasis on promoting diversity within agrosystems. Where the introduction of a new crop would enhance the diversity of the agricultural network, this should be recognised as advancing agroecology and food justice. If, on the other hand, there is sufficient evidence indicating that the cultivation of a non-native crop would undermine the ecological integrity of an agricultural system, then regardless of any cultural significance that crop may hold, it should not be grown. The pursuit of food justice, like all social considerations, is conditioned by the need to maintain the ecological integrity of local and global systems.

That some farmers are striving to meet the cultural food needs of all members of associated socioecological networks, even if only for commercial reasons, is welcome, but again focuses more on the distributive aspect of food justice. It is also a narrow response, in the sense that it relies on just one type of actor, and evidence suggests that even where efforts are made to improve access to nutritious and culturally appropriate food, these will fall short if the target communities are not fully engaged so that other barriers they face, which are beyond the control of food producers, are also addressed.[115] Other initiatives reflect more fully the procedural and recognition elements of justice. One example is the creation of local currencies designed to facilitate participation of all communities in food systems,

111 T. Mares and D. Peña, 'Environmental and Food Justice: Toward, Local, Slow, and Deep Food Systems', in Alkon and Agyeman (n 17) 199 and 215.

112 Agyeman (n 89) 67–68.

113 McClintock (n 17).

114 See ch 2.

115 D. Archer and T. Belinfanti, 'We Built It and They Did Not Come: Using New Governance Theory in the Fight for Food Justice in Low-Income Communities of Color' (2016) 15 *Seattle Journal for Social Justice* 307.

while also maximising efficiencies within these systems.[116] Such schemes can also promote agroecology in policymaking. They can, for example, foster links between different stakeholders in a socioecological network, facilitating the sharing of best environmental practices that promote diversity within the system and ensuring the more efficient use of shared natural resources.[117] Local currencies are associated with the transition movement, i.e. supporting society as it moves into a post-fossil fuel age,[118] and so are also relevant to wider sustainability agenda. Perhaps the best-known example of a local currency is the Totnes pound, which was used by the Devonshire town to support the local economy.[119] Sadly, the project was discontinued in 2019 due to the growth in cashless transactions.[120] Local currencies are another response to dominant neoliberal systems, but the demise of the Totnes pound highlights the difficulties in breaking away from these.

## Conclusions

This chapter has sought to highlight the links between international law and the ability of individuals and communities to not only have sufficient food but to have agency in their food choices. SDG-2 calls for zero hunger by 2030, but the food security this would entail appears increasingly difficult to achieve. Recent global events have undoubtedly had an impact, but that success in relation to SDG-2 was looking unlikely prior to the COVID-19 pandemic suggests that there are more fundamental weaknesses in international legal systems.

It has been persuasively argued that the commodification of food, so that it has become just another product on the global market, means that policies intended to deliver food security merely perpetuate food insecurity. IPRs are a clear example of this, as they protect the interests of commercial entities while restricting the ability of farmers to promote the crop diversity needed to ensure the long-term sustainability of agriculture. That food security has been captured by neoliberal structures has led to increased attention being given to alternative food concepts, including the right to food, food sovereignty and food justice. The core argument in this chapter has been twofold: that these concepts are progressively linked, so that the achievement of one depends on the existence of the others; and that they can best be advanced through agroecological frameworks.

The idea of food as a human right is a direct response to the commodification of food and seeks to reassert it as an essential need. In doing so, the language of rights enhances the position of vulnerable members of socioecological networks so

116 M. Angelo and others, 'Small, Slow, and Local: Essays on Building a More Sustainable and Local Food System' (2011) 12 *Vermont Journal of Environmental Law* 353, 402–403.

117 ibid 410–411.

118 L. Russi, *Everything Gardens and Other Stories: Growing Transition Culture* (University of Plymouth Press, 2015) ch 5.

119 N. Longhurst, 'The Totnes Pound: A Grassroots Technological Niche', in A. Davies (ed), *Enterprising Communities: Grassroots Sustainability Innovations* (Emerald Publishing, 2012).

120 https://www.bbc.co.uk/news/uk-england-devon-47471231 (last accessed 20/04/2023).

that they can drive reforms to how food systems operate. There are challenges in recognising the right to food as a formal right, but these are more a consequence of the flaws in neoliberal legal structures than the right itself.

To be truly meaningful, however, the right to food must be implemented in a way that gives individuals and communities agency over their food choices. They must, in other words, enjoy food sovereignty. The WFFS definition of this reveals crossovers between food sovereignty and agroecology. Both recognise the importance of agricultural production being ecologically sustainable and of ensuring that local cultures and traditions in agriculture are protected within international legal systems rather than made to conform with neoliberal rules and practices.

This agency depends on individuals and communities enjoying food justice. Just food movements take multiple forms, reflecting that the experiences of different demographics shape their understanding of the most pressing issues in food systems. For some, it is the ecological footprint of food that is critical, with localism considered the appropriate response. Others, typically ethnic minority and poorer communities, see their lack of access to culturally appropriate and nutritious food as symptomatic of the wider discrimination they face in neoliberal systems that extract an ever-greater amount of limited natural resources. Here, the issue is less about where their food is grown and more about whether they can access food that meets their cultural, as well as nutritional, needs.

Food justice, and therefore food sovereignty, the right to food and food security as well, ultimately depends on broader changes in society and the agricultural systems on which it depends. Agroecology responds to the core demands of each, by emphasising the role that all stakeholders play in agriculture's socioecological networks and the natural and cultural diversity that guarantees their long-term sustainability. Until international law and the structures that implement it are reformed to share these goals, genuine food security on a global scale will remain elusive.

# Conclusion
# Finding Space for Agroecology

At the start of this book, I asked whether there is space in international law to pursue agroecology so that the law could better support the natural and cultural diversity underpinning the relationships within and between socioecological networks. The answer to that question is, on balance, a qualified yes. It does not follow, however, that full advantage is being or will be taken of that space. There are also critical gaps and limitations in the law that require urgent reform if society is going to achieve its ambitious, and essential, sustainability agenda. Core to this agenda is agriculture, highlighted by its importance not only to Goal 2 of the Sustainable Development Goals (SDGs)[1] but many of the other Goals as well.[2]

We began by considering two principal global instruments for the conservation of agrobiodiversity, the Convention on Biological Diversity[3] and the UN Food and Agriculture Organisation's (FAO) International Treaty for Plant Genetic Resources (PGRT).[4] For the Biodiversity Conservation, the programme of work on agricultural biodiversity and the treaty's framework for the ecosystem approach both have agroecological merit.[5] The former recognises the importance of respecting the different cultures embedded in agriculture's socioecological networks, and of adopting adaptive-management approaches to their regulation. Just as important from an agroecological perspective is the more nuanced understanding in the Biodiversity Convention's ecosystem approach of how economic development leads to greater levels of environmental protection. It is not in the short-term exploitation of nature for economic gain, but the long-term protection of its ecological integrity.

There is, however, significant evidence showing how such non-binding approaches to the conservation of nature simply do not work.[6] It is therefore

1 A/RES/70/1, 21 October 2015.

2 Including SDGs-10 (reduced inequalities), 12 (responsible consumption and production) and 13 (climate action).

3 Rio de Janeiro, 5 June 1992, in force 29 December 1993, 31 ILM 822 (1992).

4 Rome, 3 November 2001, in force 29 June 2004. Text available at: https://www.fao.org/plant-treaty/overview/texts-treaty/en/ (last accessed 20/04/2023).

5 Decision III/11, Conservation and sustainable use of agricultural biological diversity, UNEP/CBD/COP/DEC/III/11, 1996; Decision V/6, Ecosystem approach, UNEP/CBD/COP/DEC/V/6, 22 June 2000.

6 E.g., Secretariat to the Convention on Biological Diversity, *Global Biodiversity Outlook 5* (2020).

DOI: 10.4324/9781003435174-18

regrettable that the new Global Biodiversity Framework follows the same flawed approach of setting non-binding global goals.[7] A persuasive argument can be made in favour of a sustainable agriculture protocol to the Convention based on key principles of agroecology, notwithstanding the risks in linking robust conservation obligations with the pursuit of anthropocentric interests. There appears little prospect of a stronger conservation instrument being negotiated, however, and so it appears likely that the integrity of the natural world on which agriculture depends will continue to decline.

A lack of legally binding obligations also limits the extent to which the PGRT can be used to advance agroecology. This applies as much to its provisions on farmers' right to freely exchange seed to enhance the genetic diversity of their crops as it does to its measures on conservation. On the other hand, the Multilateral System for the sharing of crop genetic resources,[8] represented here as a global commons, is an important mechanism for connecting different stakeholders in global and local socioecological networks.[9] While expanding this to cover all species that may be of use to agriculture is arguably unworkable, adding those species that are central to the cultures of some of the world's poorest communities should be considered.

Other international rules relevant to the genetic diversity of crops are deeply problematic from an agroecological perspective. Rather than empower farmers to share seed, as they have done since the advent of agriculture, intellectual property rights (IPRs) prioritise the interests of a handful of commercial entities. This is evident in both the 1991 Act of the Convention for the Protection of New Varieties of Plants[10] and the World Trade Organisation's (WTO) Agreement on Trade-Related Aspects of Intellectual Property Rights.[11]

Related to the restrictions on farmers' right to exchange seed is the relative lack of progress that is being made in the protection of local and traditional agricultural knowledge. This threatens the cultural diversity that is just as important for the long-term sustainability of agricultural production as crop diversity. Negotiations under the World Intellectual Property Organisation remain stalled, due in part to the controversies surrounding how to define 'traditional knowledge' and the level of protection it should be afforded.[12] There has been more success under the Biodiversity Convention's Protocol on Access and Benefit-Sharing,[13] but the scope of this is limited to knowledge over genetic resources and its protection is qualified

7 Decision 15/4, Kunming-Montreal Global Biodiversity Framework, CBD/COP/DEC/15/4, 19 December 2022.

8 PGRT, Part IV. See https://www.fao.org/plant-treaty/areas-of-work/the-multilateral-system/landingmls/en/ (last accessed 20/04/2023).

9 C. Frison, *Redesigning the Global Seed Commons: Law and Policy for Agrobiodiversity and Food Security* (Routledge, 2018) ch 6.

10 Brussels, 2 December 1961, in force 10 August 1968, 15 UNTS 89

11 Marrakesh, 15 April 1994, in force 1 January 1995, 33 ILM 81 (1994).

12 B. Ong, 'Biotechnology Innovations, Genetic Resources and Traditional Knowledge: Current Developments at the World Intellectual Property Organization', in M. Jeffery and others (eds), *Biodiversity Conservation, Law + Livelihoods Bridging the North-South Divide* (CUP, 2008)

13 Nagoya, 29 October 2010, in force 12 October 2014, C.N.782.2010.TREATIES-1.

by references to national law.[14] Ultimately, how far the cultural diversity and integrity of agriculture's socioecological networks are maintained depends on the willingness of states to protect the interests of their local and indigenous communities.

The collapse in genetic diversity has also been driven by the proliferation of monocultures, including of genetically modified organisms (GMOs).[15] Compared with organic agriculture, the place of GMOs in agroecology is disputed. I have argued, however, that they can legitimately form part of agroecological policies as they can contribute to the diversity of wider agricultural networks. There are, though, valid concerns over the risks GMOs present to that diversity if they are allowed to contaminate non-GM crops. This highlights the importance of adopting systems-level analyses when deciding whether to permit their cultivation.

Regulating the risks of GMOs has proven exceptionally controversial, particularly in the EU. Decision-making procedures, central to which are expert risk assessments, are perceived, with some justification, as giving undue weight to technical considerations and ignoring broader public values embedded in agricultural traditions.[16] The failure of regulatory processes to find a politically acceptable way to manage the risks of GMOs has led to rules under EU law and the Biodiversity Convention's Biosafety Protocol that give states discretion to instead prioritise socioeconomic and cultural concerns.[17] Evidence is mixed, however, on whether these will succeed in allowing states to pursue policies that are aligned with agroecology, such as restricting the cultivation of GMOs in a particular region to promote agricultural diversity.

Prohibiting absolutely the cultivation of GMOs is just as contrary to the theory of agroecology as the over-reliance on GM monocultures. Both undermine the essential diversity of agricultural systems. It is also true, however, that there are certain regions where GMO cultivation is culturally and ecologically inappropriate. Protecting such landscapes is important, but compared to species, habitats and ecosystems landscapes have been neglected in international law. Nevertheless, the frameworks that have been adopted advance core aspects of agroecology. The Satoyama Initiative connects key stakeholders in socioecological networks,[18] and

14 R. Amos, *International Conservation Law: The Protection of Plants in Theory and Practice* (Routledge, 2020) 221–223.

15 FAO, *The Second Report on the State of the World's Plant Genetic Resources for Food and Agriculture* (FAO Commission on Genetic Resources for Food and Agriculture Assessments, 2010) 4 and FAO, *Report on the State of the World's Plant Genetic Resources for Food and Agriculture* (1996) 14.

16 M. Lee, 'The Governance of Coexistence Between GMOs and Other Forms of Agriculture: A Purely Economic Issue?' (2008) 20 *Journal of Environmental Law* 193, 199.

17 Directive 2015/412/EU amending Directive 2001/18/EC as regards the possibility for the Member States to restrict or prohibit the cultivation of genetically modified organisms (GMOs) in their territory [2015] OJ L 68/1; Protocol on Biosafety, Montreal, 29 January 2000, in force 11 September 2003, 39 ILM 1027.

18 https://satoyama-initiative.org/about/ (last accessed 20/04/2023). See also the Paris Declaration on the Satoyama Initiative (2010). K. Takeuchi and others, 'Satoyama Landscape as Socio-Ecological System: Historical Changes and Future Perspective' (2016) 19 *Current Opinion in Environmental Sustainability* 30.

the FAO's Globally Important Agricultural Heritage Systems Initiative shows how the ecological and cultural values of agricultural landscapes can be protected.[19] These are again non-binding, however. Technically, the European Landscape Convention does not share this weakness and recognises that landscapes are as much cultural constructs as they are physical ones,[20] but its utility is limited by the vagueness of its obligations.[21]

As well as protecting their natural and cultural diversity, it is also important to adopt integrated approaches to the management of agriculture and its socioecological networks if agroecology is to be advanced through the law.[22] One manifestation of this is the concept of ecosystem services. On the one hand, ecosystem services constitute the law's recognition that society depends on healthy and functioning ecosystems if it is to meet its basic needs. They therefore illustrate the relationships in and between nature and humanity that define socioecological networks.[23] On the other hand, it is possible to question whether a key international body, the Intergovernmental Science-Policy Platform on Biodiversity and Ecosystem Services, reflects non-Western, non-anthropocentric perceptions of the value of nature that are more closely aligned with the principle of ecological sustainability.[24] Similar concerns relate to whether ecosystem services merely justify the deconstruction and commodification of nature, which is again contrary to the more holistic approach of agroecology.[25]

One ecosystem that has received increased attention in recent years is soil, which is not only fundamentally important to agriculture and the natural world but an important biome in its own right. The FAO's Revised World Soil Charter,[26] although anthropocentric, builds on the agroecological strengths of the original 1981 Charter,[27] recognising the importance of systems-level management approaches and of facilitating broad stakeholder engagement in decisions that affect socioecological networks. Both the Charter and the Biodiversity Convention's Plan

19 http://www.fao.org/giahs/en/ (last accessed 20/04/2023). S. Harrop, 'Globally Important Agricultural Heritage Systems: An Examination of Their Context in Existing Multilateral Instruments Dealing with Conservation and Land Tenure' (2009) 12 *Journal of International Wildlife Law & Policy* 127.

20 M. Roe, 'The European Landscape Convention: A Revolution in Thinking about 'Cultural Landscapes'' (2007) 23 *Journal of Chinese Landscape Architecture* 10.

21 Paris, 16 November 1972, in force 17 December 1975, 27 UST 37, 11 ILM 1358 (1972).

22 R. Norgaard and T. Sikor, 'The Methodology and Practice of Agroecology', in M. Altieri, *Agroecology: The Science of Sustainable Agriculture* (2nd edn, Westview Press, 1995).

23 E. Brondizio and others (eds) *Global Assessment Report of the Intergovernmental Science-Policy Platform on Biodiversity and Ecosystem Services* (IPBES, 2019) 359.

24 U. Brand and A. Vadrot, 'Epistemic Selectivities and the Valorisation of Nature: The Cases of the Nagoya Protocol and the Intergovernmental Science-Policy Platform on Biodiversity and Ecosystem Services (IPBES)' (2013) 9 *Law, Environment and Development Journal* 204.

25 V. De Lucia, 'A Critical Interrogation of the Relation between the Ecosystem Approach and Ecosystem Services' (2018) 27 *Review of European, Comparative and International Law* 104, 107.

26 Text available at: https://www.fao.org/documents/card/en/c/e60df30b-0269-4247-a15f-db564161fee0/ (last accessed 20/04/2023).

27 Text available at: https://www.fao.org/3/p8700e/p8700e.pdf (last accessed 20/04/2023).

of Action for soil are non-binding,[28] however, and again a case can be made for a binding soil instrument to drive greater conservation efforts.[29]

Arguably, the most important issue discussed in this work is water. A critical paradigm shift occurred in 2013 when the international community recognised biodiversity's role in supporting water systems.[30] We still need to go further, however, in asking ourselves what society can do for water conservation. Conceptually, the core principles of international fresh water law,[31] i.e. 'no harm' and equitable and reasonable use, are compatible with agroecology. The problem is how the relationship between these two principles has developed. Rather than defining reasonable use in terms of 'no harm', it appears that anything that does not breach the 'no harm' rule typically qualifies as reasonable and equitable use.[32] That 'no harm' relates only to the interests of states, not to the environment per se, also reflects the wider criticism of sustainable development made throughout this work. Ecological concerns are considered as no more than equivalent to economic interests, which is contrary to both ecological sustainability and agroecology. Similar observations were made in relation to the FAO's work on the Blue Transformation of aquacultural industries.[33] That it promotes technological advances rather than fundamental behavioural change indicates that the Blue Transformation is grounded in ideas of weak sustainability.

The consequences of failing to instigate more systematic changes are brought into sharp relief when we consider climate change. For Kiribati, local and global climate change, their contribution to which has been negligible, has fatally undermined the integrity of their agricultural systems and wider society.[34] Kiribati's response is currently one that prioritises adaptation through the Temaiku Land and Urban Development Project.[35] While this has limitations in terms of costs and scale, it also reflects core aspects of agroecology. If successful, the project will enhance the resilience of the i-Kiribati and preserve the culture that has evolved out of their relationships with their natural environment.[36] It seems inevitable,

28 Decision 15/28, Biodiversity and agriculture, CBD/COP/DEC/15/28, 19 December 2022, Annex.

29 N. Fromherz, 'The Case for a Global Treaty on Soil Conservation, Sustainable Farming, and the Preservation of Agrarian Culture' (2012) 39 *Ecology Law Quarterly* 57.

30 Secretariat of the Convention on Biological Diversity, *Water and Biodiversity – Natural Solutions for Water Security* (2013).

31 UNECE Convention on the Protection and Use of Transboundary Watercourses and International Lakes (Helsinki) 17 March 1992, in force 6 October 1996, 31 ILM 1312 (1992); Convention on the Law of the Non-Navigational Uses of International Watercourses (New York) 21 May 1997, in force 17 August 2014, 36 ILM 700 (1997).

32 S. Salman, 'Freshwater Resources', in L. Rajamani and J. Peel (eds), *The Oxford Handbook on International Environmental Law* (2nd edn, OUP, 2021).

33 FAO, *Blue – Transformation – Roadmap 2022–2030: A Vision for FAO's Work on Aquatic Food Systems* (FAO, 2022).

34 Ministry of Environment, Lands and Agriculture Development, *Kiribati Agriculture Strategy (KAS 2020–2030)* (March 2020) 10–11.

35 https://www.jacobs.com/projects/kiribati (last accessed 20/04/2023).

36 J. Kupferberg, 'Migration and Dignity – Relocation and Adaptation in the Face of Climate Change Displacement in the Pacific – A Human Rights Perspective' (2021) 25 *International Journal of Human Rights* 1793, 1800–1801.

however, that a substantial part of the Kiribati population will need to migrate in the foreseeable future as climate change renders many of their islands uninhabitable.[37] Agroecology provides guidance on what displaced communities need to re-establish themselves; it is not just adequate space and security in land rights, but basic needs relating to food, water and environmental security.[38] The diversity that agroecology promotes is the best way to achieve this.

Kiribati's experiences of climate change, and the inadequacies of international law's efforts to prevent and mitigate it, reveal a narrative in which international legal systems are not only failing to deliver the SDGs and other international agenda but are potentially obstacles to its success. Evidence for this can be found in environmental assessment mechanisms. Theoretically, environmental assessment represents the convergence of law and ecology.[39] As well as leading to 'better' decisions by engaging all members of a socioecological network, it embeds an ecological rationality, reflective of ecological sustainability, in regulatory structures.[40] Individual features of environmental assessment also advance different aspects of agroecology. Post-project analysis, for example, transforms environmental impact assessment from a linear, isolated procedure into a circular learning process in which experiences from one assessment inform analyses of future proposals.[41]

In reality, however, environmental assessment epitomises the weakness of sustainable development by legitimising the trading-off of ecological imperatives against economic interests.[42] Reforms are therefore essential if the full potential of environmental assessment to advance agroecology is to be realised. Proposals for ecological impact assessment show how environmental assessment can be properly located in ecology, but are not without practical difficulties.[43] More radical would be to use environmental assessment as a framework for redefining sustainable development in a manner that reflects core aspects of agroecology. Accepting sustainable development as a goal as well as an ongoing process, which certain aspects of the SDGs present it as, introduces a substantive obligation of maintaining pre-existing socioecological values into environmental assessment. This in turn allows us to develop a legal definition of unsustainable development, which would strengthen the position of those members of a socioecological network that wish to protect its long-term ecological values over short-term economic gains.

37 ibid 1807.

38 ibid 1798.

39 R. Brooks and others, *Law and Ecology: The Rise of the Ecosystem Regime* (Ashgate, 2002) 156–161.

40 R. Bartlett, 'Ecological Reason in Administration: Environmental Impact Assessment and Green Politics', in R. Paehlke and D. Torgerson (eds) *Managing Leviathan: Environmental Politics and the Administrative State* (Broadview Press, 2005).

41 K. Arabadjieva, ''Better Regulation' in Environmental Impact Assessment: The Amended EIA Directive' (2016) 28 *Journal of Environmental Law* 159.

42 R. Amos, 'Assessing the Impact of the Habitats Directive: A Case Study of Europe's Plants' (2021) 33 *Journal of Environmental Law* 365, 372–373.

43 J. Holder, 'The Prospects for Ecological Impact Assessment', in J. Holder and D. McGillivray (eds), *Taking Stock of Environmental Assessment: Law, Policy and Practice* (Routledge-Cavendish, 2007).

Environmental assessment responds to the effects of specific policies, plans and projects. However, the cumulative impacts of humanity's everyday activities and the pollution these cause are just as destabilising for agriculture and the natural world.[44] The issue of transboundary pollution adds further dimensions to our understandings of socioecological networks. Pollution's pervasiveness underscores the importance of systems-level analyses of issues, as species and habitats that appear completely unrelated to an activity can nevertheless be impacted by it. Transboundary air pollution is one example of this. The Convention on Long-Range Transboundary Air Pollution (LRTAP) represents a model framework convention, with detailed protocols that are directly relevant to its overall objective being adopted.[45] There is, though, a tension between the pursuit of 'good' international law and agroecology highlighted by the issue of transboundary air pollution. The LRTAP is largely incompatible with the legal cultures in South East and North East Asia, where transboundary air pollution is a growing concern.[46] Agroecology requires these cultures to be respected, not least because ignoring them risks undermining the socioecological networks in which they are located.[47] Responses at the scientific and political level, however, are not delivering the level of change needed in those networks to prevent damage to the regions' agricultural industries and wider environments.[48]

Pollution's persistence is evident in the issue of pesticide and other chemical usage and highlights the need to consider socioecological networks as temporal constructs. Here, a major issue is in supporting developing states with the implementation of the Convention on Persistent Organic Pollutants (POPs Convention).[49] As more substances are regulated, the more difficult it becomes for developing states to adapt their industries and fulfil their international obligations.[50] This reality raises further tensions between short-term economic interests and long-term ecological imperatives. Calls for a more unified approach to the management of hazardous substances have only been partially answered.[51] Instead, the international community appears committed to dealing with these on an issue-by-issue basis, with their

44 https://www.ontario.ca/page/effects-air-pollution-agricultural-crops (last accessed 20/04/2023).

45 Geneva, 13 November 1979, in force 16 March 1983, 18 ILM 1442 (1979). P. Sands and J. Peel, *Principles of International Environmental Law* (4th edn, CUP 2018) 262–271.

46 E.g., L. Syarif, 'Evaluating the (In)Effectiveness of ASEAN Cooperation Against Transboundary Air Pollution', in in S. Jayakumar and others (eds), *Transboundary Pollution: Evolving Issues of International Law and Policy* (Edward Elgar, 2015).

47 As we saw in relation to the Balinese water temples in ch 4 – J. Lansing, *Perfect Order: Recognizing Complexity in Bali* (Princeton University Press, 2006) 6–10.

48 Syarif (n 46).

49 Stockholm, 22 May 2001, in force 17 May 2004, 40 ILM 532 (2001).

50 M. Al'Afghani and D. Paramita, 'Regulatory Challenges in the Phasing-Out of Persistent Organic Pollutants in Indonesia' (2018) *International Chemical Regulatory and Law Review* 12.

51 J. Allan and others, 'Experimenting with TripleCOPs: Productive Innovation or Counterproductive Complexity?' (2018) 18 *International Environmental Agreements: Politics, Law and Economics* 557.

intention to negotiate a new plastics agreement recently announced.[52] This could be of fundamental importance in advancing agroecology, due to the impact plastics have throughout the natural world.[53] Their ubiquitousness also demonstrates how all individuals can affect the ecological integrity of local and global socioecological networks. It is essential that this new agreement commits states to ambitious targets to reduce the production and use of plastics, based on systems-level analyses that prioritise supporting the ecological integrity of the natural world.

The obstacles that international legal systems present to society's pursuit of the SDGs are most apparent in the context of international trade. International trade law's compatibility with agroecology is more nuanced than the supposed trade-environment dichotomy suggests. It is clear that states can pursue agroecological policies through trade restrictions, provided that they can justify these under WTO law.[54] The Appellate Body, although currently defunct, has also proven willing to interpret WTO law in light of developments in international law, including in relation to sustainable development.[55] While it cannot yet be said that a principle of ecological sustainability enjoys sufficient support to be used in this manner by the WTO dispute bodies, there are signs that such a principle may be beginning to emerge in international jurisprudence.[56]

Progress in adopting a more holistic approach to trade and the environment is extremely slow, however, and afforded little apparent urgency by states.[57] It is also legitimate to question whether the WTO is the most appropriate forum, from an agroecological perspective, for resolving conflicts between trade and the environment. It is likely that this will merely perpetuate sustainable development's prioritisation of economic interests. These concerns are compounded by how the WTO's Agreement on Agriculture provides limited space, particularly for developing states, to pursue agroecological policies that conflict with their free trade obligations, and focuses more on the macroeconomic position of states rather than the communities where the impacts of these obligations fall.[58]

Technical discussions over trade rules also obscure the more fundamental issue of how the neoliberal systems that they embody have fractured society's relationships with the natural world. The consequences of this became clear with the outbreak of COVID-19. While debate continues over the precise cause of the pandemic, it is clear that humanity's activities have degraded the environment to a point where

52 UNEP/EA.5/Res.14, 7 March 2022.

53 E. Goodwin, 'Biodiversity and Plastics', in E. Kirk and others (eds), *Research Handbook on Plastics Law* (Edward Elgar, 2024, forthcoming).

54 Amos (n 14) 148–153.

55 *United States – Import Prohibition of Certain Shrimp and Shrimp Products (United States – Shrimp)* WT/DS58/AB/R, adopted 6 November 1998, para 129.

56 E.g., *Indus Waters Kishenganga Arbitration (Pakistan v India)*, Final Award of the Court of Arbitration, 20 December 2013.

57 M. Bowman and others, *Lyster's International Wildlife Law* (2nd edn, CUP, 2012) 668.

58 Text available at: https://www.wto.org/english/docs_e/legal_e/14-ag_01_e.htm (last accessed 20/04/2023). F. Smith, 'Indigenous Farmers' Rights, International Agricultural Trade and the WTO' (2011) 2 *Journal of Human Rights and the Environment* 157.

the emergence of further zoonoses is likely.[59] As with other frameworks, including the Global Biodiversity Framework, the Biodiversity Convention's Action Plan for soil and the FAO's Blue Transformation, the One Health concept reflects agroecology in theory by calling for a holistic approach to ecological, economic and social issues, informed by broad stakeholder engagement.[60] However, the way in which it is being taken forward is merely 'business as usual', with no system-wide reforms so that humanity ceases to undermine the health and integrity of the natural world.

What does all this mean for the communities and individuals at the heart of agroecology's socioecological networks? Delivering global food security is an essential objective of states, central to SDG-2 and the wider sustainable development agenda.[61] International law, however, including through the WTO Agreement on Agriculture, rules on IPRs and the deconstruction of nature through the anthropocentric framework of ecosystem services, merely embeds food insecurity in the most vulnerable communities. It does so because they frustrate efforts to protect the natural and cultural diversity that are essential to long-term sustainability.

That food security as a policy objective has been captured by neoliberalism means that it is necessary to consider alternatives, such as the right to food, food sovereignty and food justice.[62] As well as being progressively linked, each reflects important aspects of agroecology. Presenting food as a human right challenges the commodification of food and empowers vulnerable members of socioecological networks to demand change to policies that adversely affect them.[63] To achieve this, communities must enjoy food sovereignty, i.e. they must have agency over their food choices, and this concept was shown to share common traits with agroecology. Each is grounded in ideas of ecological sustainability and advocates for cultural traditions and practices being recognised in international legal systems, rather than made to conform to neoliberal structures.[64] This agency will only be meaningful in the context of food justice. What this means in practice varies between communities, with the just food movement comprising ecological and social elements, each of which reflects different aspects of agroecology's socioecological networks.[65] Agroecology also reveals certain limits of the food justice movement. Following the principle of ecological sustainability, non-native crops

59 T. Allen and others, 'Global Hotspots and Correlates of Emerging Zoonotic Diseases' (2017) 8 *Nature Communications* 1124.

60 A. Davis and J. Sharp, 'Rethinking One Health: Emergent Human, Animal and Environmental Assemblages' (2020) 258 *Social Sciences & Medicine* 113093

61 R. Amos and others, *Living Sustainability in Higher Education: Connecting Communities, Learning and Justice* (2025, forthcoming) ch 6.

62 T. Gebrehiwot and others, 'Impact of Global Food and Agriculture Laws on Africa's Food Security' (2019) 52 *De Jure* 85.

63 S. Raponi, 'A Defense of the Human Right to Adequate Food' (2017) 23 *Res Publica* 99.

64 H. Haugen, 'Food Sovereignty – An Appropriate Approach to Ensure the Right to Food?' (2009) 78 *Nordic Journal of International Law* 263.

65 J. Agyeman, *Introducing Just Sustainabilities: Policy, Planning and Practice* (Zed Books, 2013) Ch 2.

that are central to a community's culture should not be grown in regions where the cultivation of an alien species could undermine the integrity of local ecosystems.

Agriculture is about more than simply producing food. What we grow and how we grow it speaks to the type of society that we are: the values we hold, our respect for different communities and cultures and our relationships with a desperately fragile natural world. What this book has shown is that society is on the wrong, and a very dangerous, track. Advancing agroecology is therefore about so much more than ensuring the long-term sustainability of agricultural production. It is about redefining our place in nature so that we aid in its cultivation, not hasten its destruction.

# Index


adaptive management 18, 23
*Aerial Herbicide Spraying Case* 88, 191–192
Agreement on Agriculture 210, 216, 224, 230, 260–261; domestic support 217–219; export competition 219–220; local and indigenous farmers 220–221; market access 216–217
agricultural knowledge *see* traditional knowledge
agricultural law 8
agriculture 3–5, 14–15, 26–27, 29, 31, 36, 39, 55, 59, 131–133, 172–173, 234, 262; and climate change 150–151; cultural aspects 7–8, 86, 102; and indigenous communities 50–51; industrialisation 56–58; and international trade 215–216; and pollution 189–191, 207; sustainable agriculture 10, 19, 33, 76, 93–94, 101–102, 243; *see also* organic farming
agrobiodiversity 3, 14–16, 27, 30, 49, 101, 131–132
agroecology 55, 93, 105, 110, 123, 237, 241, 253, 255, 256, 260; and agricultural landscapes 83, 86; agroecological law 8–12; approaches to 18, 243–244; and aquaculture 144, 147–148; and climate change 151, 154, 163–164, 258; and cultures 50; definition 5–8, 12, 25, 58–59, 102; and ecological sustainability 230, 244–245, 250, 257; and environmental assessment 168, 173, 175, 177, 180, 187, 258; examples in law 27, 50, 54–55, 117, 139–141, 159, 160, 200–201, 213; and food security 210, 235–236; and food sovereignty 243, 252, 261; and GMOs 69, 72, 74, 77; and One Health 226, 229, 230, 261; and pollution 192, 199, 202, 207; and socioecological networks 94, 97, 243, 252, 259; and sustainable development 10–12, 102, 135, 156, 163, 233–234; and systems-level analysis 101; and water 137–139, 149; and the WTO 210, 214, 217, 220, 225
aquaculture: Blue Transformation 145–147, 149, 257, 261; and global challenges 143–145; pollution 145

Balinese water temples 79–80, 85, 117
biodiversity *see* agrobiodiversity
biofuels 9, 133
biopiracy 51
biosphere reserves 9

climate change 61, 133, 202, 206, 249, 257–258; adaptation 153–154; impacts of 150–151; resilience 153–154
climate change migration *see* climate migration
climate migration 60–61, 157–159; Convention for the Protection and Assistance of Internally Displaced Persons in Africa 157; and Pacific Islands 160–162; Refugee Convention 158; and sustainable development 162–163; UN Global Compact for Migration 159; UN Guiding Principles on Internal Displacement 157
commercial plant breeders 35, 39–40, 45, 55, 246, 251
common but differentiated responsibilities 152–153
commons 49–50, 237–238, 254; tragedy of the commons 85, 238
community participatory monitoring 84–85
connection with nature 228–230
conservation 31–32, 96–97, 141–142, 239
conservation covenants 109–111
conservation law *see* environmental law

Convention concerning the Protection of World Cultural and Natural Heritage *see* World Heritage Convention
Convention for the Protection of New Plant Varieties *see* UPOV Convention
Convention on Biological Diversity 29–30, 52, 85, 96–97, 114, 117, 123, 194–195, 253–254; Aichi Targets *see* Convention on Biological Diversity, Strategic Plan for Biodiversity; and aquaculture 147–148; Biosafety Protocol 27, 71–74, 255; and climate change 153; economic incentive measures 107–108; ecosystem approach 23–26, 83; Global Biodiversity Framework 26–29, 111, 254, 261; Guiding Principles for the Prevention, Introduction and Mitigation of Impacts of Alien Species 37–38, 74; International Initiative for the Conservation and Sustainable Use of Soil Biodiversity 116–117; Plan of Action for soil 117, 129, 256–257, 261; Programme of Work on Agricultural Biodiversity 17–19, 33; Programme of Work on dry and sub-humid lands 125–127; Protocol on Access and Benefit Sharing 27, 53–55, 254; protocol on sustainable agriculture 27–29, 203; Strategic Plan for Biodiversity 14–15, 107, 233–234; Supplementary Protocol on Liability and Redress 73–74; and water 131–132, 135, 149
Convention on Environmental Impact Assessment in a Transboundary Context 142, 178–181
Convention on International Trade in Endangered Species of Fauna and Flora 120–121, 223
Convention on Long-Range Transboundary Air Pollution 191, 207; obligations 192–193; protocols 193–195, 198–199, 259
Convention on Persistent Organic Pollutants 191, 199–203, 207, 259–260
Convention on the Control of the Transboundary Movements of Hazardous Waste and Their Disposal 203, 207
Convention on the Prior Informed Consent Procedure for Certain Hazardous Chemicals and Pesticides in International Trade 203, 207
Convention on Wetlands of International Importance 185–186
Convention to Combat Desertification 122–125, 127–130
COVID-19 182, 210–211, 222–223, 227–230, 236, 245, 251, 260–261
crops 133, 246, 250, 254; crop genetic diversity 34, 45, 55, 69, 236–237, 254

deep ecology: the land-ethic 82–83
desertification *see* land degradation
disease 38–39
diversity 7, 36

ecofeminism 76
ecological rationality 170–171, 188, 258
ecological sustainability 12, 21, 214, 221, 228, 230, 233, 244, 250, 261; and ecosystem services 102–105, 111, 256; and environmental assessment 170, 186–188, 258
ecology 8, 168, 184–185, 188
ecosystem approach 20–26, 94, 136, 138, 141, 146
ecosystem services 18–19, 97, 103, 110–112, 134–135, 148, 256, 261; definition 94–95, 99–101; Intergovernmental Science-Policy Platform on Biodiversity and Ecosystem Services 94, 97–99, 256; Millennium Ecosystem Assessment 96, 98–99; payments for ecosystem services 105–111
environmental assessment 9, 120, 130, 167–168, 184, 188, 258–259; culture theories 169–171; ecological impact assessment 184–187, 258; environmental impact assessment 167–169, 171–175, 184, 186–187, 189; information theories 168–169; post-project analysis 174–175, 180, 185, 258; and public participation 169, 173–174, 176, 179–180, 249; strategic environmental assessment 175–176; sustainability impact assessment 176–177; and transboundary impacts 178–181
environmental justice 28, 123–124, 248–250
environmental law 61–62, 96–97, 137, 139, 153, 175, 177, 180–181, 188, 191, 202
environmental migration *see* climate migration
equitable and reasonable use 136–139, 149, 257
EU 121, 196, 216, 243; Common Agricultural Policy 15; European Food Safety Authority 66–68, 75; and GMOs 65–71, 77, 255; internal market 68, 70, 220
European Convention on Human Rights 81
European Landscape Convention 89–90, 256

farmers 35, 58, 115, 140, 190, 219, 236, 238–239, 247, 250; farmers' rights 32, 42–46, 50, 55, 254
food justice 33, 235, 246–252, 261–262
food security 112, 133, 140, 147, 235–240, 242–243, 251–252, 258, 261; definition 235–236; and GMOs 60; and international trade 215–216, 218
food sovereignty 235, 242–246, 251–252, 261
future generations *see* intergenerational equity

Gaia theory 76, 227–228
General Agreement on Tariffs and Trade 214–215, 217, 223–224
genetically modified crops (GM crops) 68, 74, 172, 246; *see also* genetically modified organisms (GMOs)
genetically modified organisms (GMOs) 3, 56–57, 62, 77, 255; authorisation 65–68; co-existence 68–71; living modified organisms 71, 73; types of 59–61; *see also* genetically modified crops (GM crops)
Global Environment Facility 28, 201
'global target, national action' 26
globalisation 56, 155, 233, 244, 247
Green Revolution 35, 236–237

herbicides *see* pesticides
human rights 146, 196–197, 220–221, 240–242, 261; *see also* right to food

ILO Convention 169; concerning Indigenous and Tribal Peoples 87–88
indigenous communities 19, 50, 55, 174, 220–221, 234, 241, 255; and agricultural practices 4; indigenous knowledge 18, 54; indigenous rights 80–81, 87–88, 110; as stewards 115, 254; *see also* traditional knowledge
indigenous farmers *see* indigenous communities
intellectual property rights 35, 39, 236–237, 244, 246, 251, 254, 261; and developing states 43; and indigenous communities 51–52
intergenerational equity 25, 137, 139–141, 143, 244–245
Intergovernmental Panel on Climate Change 98
International Court of Justice 88, 137, 178, 191
International Covenant on Economic, Social and Cultural Rights 239–241
International Plant Protection Convention 29, 36–37, 225
international trade 221–222, 233, 243, 260; and the environment 211–214, 230; *see also* World Trade Organisation (WTO)
International Treaty on Plant Genetic Resources for Food and Agriculture 29–33, 44–46, 227, 237, 253–254; Multilateral System 30, 46–50, 55, 237–238, 254
invasive/alien species 7, 35–38, 202, 250, 261–262

Johannesburg Plan of Implementation 203

Kiribati 151–152, 163–164, 257–258; agricultural industry 154–155; impacts of climate change 155–156; migration with dignity 161–162; Temaiku Development Project 161–162, 257
*Kishenganga Arbitration* 138, 149, 178

land degradation 122, 133; land-degradation neutral world 127–130
landscape 78, 83–84, 173; definition 78–80; rights to landscape 80–83
livestock 151, 189
local knowledge *see* traditional knowledge
localism 58, 247–248, 252

Mercury Convention 204–205
monocultures 35, 36, 74, 236, 255

neoliberalism 209–211, 215, 221–222, 235–237, 239, 241, 243–244, 249–251, 260–261
'no harm' rule 136–139, 149, 191, 257

One Health 210, 226–227, 229–230, 261
organic agriculture *see* organic farming
organic farming 7, 56–59, 61, 74–76, 172; International Federation of Organic Agriculture Movement 57–58, 75–77

Pachamama 98–99
persistent organic pollutants 199–200; *see also* pesticides
pesticides 8, 15, 59, 172, 189, 191, 202–203, 207, 241, 259; *see also* persistent organic pollutants
plastics 205–208, 260
pollinators 101
polluter pays principle 139–140, 143, 196; 'user pays' principle 140

pollution 139–140, 142, 145, 196, 207, 227, 233, 259–260; and cultures 197–198; international regulation 203–208; *see also* transboundary air pollution
precautionary principle 62–64, 139, 143, 145, 180, 201
prevention 24
public participation 28, 80, 110, 151, 169, 176, 179–181, 212, 249
public trust doctrine 109
*Pulp Mills on the River Uruguay Case* 178

resilience thinking 6
Revised African Convention on the Conservation of Nature and Natural Resources 118–119
right to food 235, 239–243, 246, 251–252, 261
Rio Declaration on Environment and Development 62–63, 125, 139, 211
Rio+20 127
risk 61–65; risk assessment 64, 71–73, 75, 139, 145, 224–225, 255; risk management 64–65, 72, 75, 224–225

Satoyama Initiative 84–85, 108, 255–256
socioecological networks 5, 50, 58, 149, 188, 201, 220, 238, 246; and agrobiodiversity 32; and agroecology 12–13, 94, 99, 105, 215–216, 243, 249, 253; consideration of 18, 22, 72, 133, 146; in decision-making 168, 173–174, 176, 196, 258; and ecosystem services 108–109, 111; impacts on 37, 144, 150–152, 164, 178, 183, 197, 205; integrity of 32, 175, 184, 205, 233; members of 140, 210, 212, 230, 241, 244, 247, 250–251, 254, 260–261; relationships in 25–26, 117, 132, 200, 207, 230; social and cultural elements 33, 50–51, 60, 161, 162, 235, 254, 259; as temporal constructs 190, 259
soil 112–113, 256–257; Amman Resolution on Soils 118; soil conservation 113–117, 122; soil treaty 117–122, 129; World Soil Charter 114–116, 129, 256–257
stakeholder engagement *see* public participation
stewardship 115–116
Strategic Approach to International Chemicals Management 203, 207
sustainability 103, 134, 147, 181–182, 246–247, 251, 261
sustainable development 55, 124, 137, 140, 146, 149, 193, 228, 257, 261; and climate change 162–163; and ecological rationality 170–171; and ecosystem approach 21–22, 24–25; and ecosystem services 102–105, 111; and food sovereignty 244–245; and neoliberalism 209–211; three pillars 10, 168–169, 181–182, 185, 244–245; unsustainable development 186–188, 258; World Commission on Environment and Development 10, 185, 209, 245; and the WTO 214, 230
Sustainable Development Goals 10–11, 135, 177, 190, 211, 221, 236, 253, 258, 260; and climate change 163; and justice 248–250; SDG-2 10–11, 112–113, 185, 233–234, 240, 251, 253, 261; SDG-5 112; SDG-10 112; SDG-12 11, 140, 212; SDG-13 112; SDG-15 11, 112–113, 127; SDG-16 112; and soil 112–113, 127–129
sustainable use 32–33, 49
systems-level analysis 59–60, 111, 133, 145, 184, 207, 255, 259, 260; and agroecology 6, 12, 72, 101, 104, 200, 205, 233; in the law 18, 108, 143, 183

town or village greens 81–82
trade *see* international trade
traditional knowledge 50–55, 60, 143, 146, 238, 254; *see also* indigenous communities, indigenous knowledge
*Trail Smelter* case 191
transboundary air pollution 191–192, 207, 259; in Asia 197–199, 207, 259; impacts 192; and litigation 191–192
transboundary impacts 136, 142–143, 178–181, 233

UN Conference on Sustainable Development *see* Rio+20
UN Convention on the Law of Non-Navigational Uses of International Watercourses 20–21, 136–139, 149
UN Convention on the Law of the Sea 21; Agreement on the Conservation and Sustainable Use of Marine Biological Diversity of Areas Beyond National Jurisdiction 21; Implementation Agreement on Fish Stocks 21, 144
UN Declaration on Human Rights 163
UN Food and Agriculture Organisation (FAO) 29, 34, 36, 226–227, 235; and aquaculture 145–147, 257; aspects of

agroecology 5; Codex Alimentarius 225–226; Globally Important Agricultural Heritage Systems Initiative 86–89, 256; and soil 114–116; Sustainability Assessment of Food and Agriculture 29, 181–184, 187, 188
UN Framework Convention on Climate Change 152–154, 163; adaptation 153–154; Kyoto Protocol 121, 152–153; Paris Agreement 152–153
UNECE Convention on the Protection and Use of Transboundary Watercourses and International Lakes 139–143, 149; Protocol on Water and Health 143
UPOV Convention 39–45, 55, 254

values 22, 29, 86, 101–102, 111, 228, 256

water 131, 148, 248, 257, 258; natural water infrastructure 133–135, 148
Well-being of Future Generations Act 141, 245
World Health Organisation 222–223
World Heritage Convention 88–90, 142–143
World Intellectual Property Organisation 43, 51–53, 254
World Organisation for Animal Health 223, 225
World Summit on Sustainable Development 53
World Trade Organisation (WTO) 212–214, 223, 260; Agreement on Sanitary and Phytosanitary Measures 223–226; Agreement on Trade-Related Aspects of Intellectual Property Rights 43–45, 55, 209–210, 254; Appellate Body 214, 216–218, 230, 260; Committee on Trade and Environment 213–214; *see also* Agreement on Agriculture

zoonotic disease 221–222, 229–230, 245; international regulation 222–226; *see also* COVID-19